Praise for H. Bruce Franklin's *Crash Course*

"Two threads are skillfully interwoven in this absorbing memoir: the record of a remarkable life, with rich and varied experience; and astute analysis of the background of critical historical events. The outcome is a fascinating picture of post–World War II America, all under the grim shadow of 'forever war.'"
—Noam Chomsky, Institute Professor Emeritus, MIT, and author of *Requiem for the American Dream*

"A scorching overview of the militarization of America that is simultaneously the engrossing autobiography of an historian who came of age in World War II and the early Cold War years. *Crash Course* is a vivid and sobering eye-opener for readers at every level from students to fellow seniors to everyone in between."
—John W. Dower, MIT Ford International Professor of History, Emeritus, and author of *The Violent American Century: War and Terror Since World War II*

"A passionate activist scholar, Franklin skillfully harnesses his lively and scrupulously candid autobiography to a deeply researched history of the emergence in the U.S. since World War II of what he calls the Forever War, which he places in compelling counterpoint to the growth of the widespread antiwar movement and allied progressive causes to which he himself was an important contributor. A terrific read."
—Michael Cowan, Professor Emeritus, American Studies, University of California Santa Cruz, and author of *City of the West*

"*Crash Course* is a fabulous blend of exceptional memoir and astute political analysis. A quintessential American story of political coming-of-age. Highly recommended."
—Richard Falk, Professor Emeritus, International Law, Princeton University, and author of *Palestine's Horizon: Toward a Just Peace*

"Brooklyn boy, New York longshoreman, U.S. Air Force navigator, English professor, and human rights and antiwar activist, H. Bruce Franklin is one of our most important and enduring public intellectuals. Part memoir and part historical analysis, Franklin's newest book explains how our 'glorious atomic victory in World War II' carried us relentlessly into the disastrous Vietnam War and our present campaigns in the Middle East and Afghanistan. Will we ever learn? *Crash Course* should be required reading by every American."
—John Carlos Rowe, University of Southern California, author of *The Cultural Politics of the New American Studies*

"Only the late great Howard Zinn comes close to H. Bruce Franklin as truth-telling historian whose 'the personal is political' oeuvre should be read by every American, left or right, who aspires to be informed beyond headlines and rumor. Franklin's *Crash Course: From the Good War to the Forever War*, meticulously researched, factually inarguable, is also a fascinating memoir in which the past is always prologue to the nearly out-of-body experience in which we find ourselves today. From 1939 through WWII to Korea to Vietnam to Iraq to Afghanistan to Syria to whatever is next: isn't it time we figure out how we got here? May H. Bruce Franklin's incendiary *Crash Course* crash into discussion on every street corner, in every boardroom, classroom, and bedroom in these our United States, and in the world beyond." —Jayne Anne Phillips, National Book Award finalist and author of *Machine Dreams* and *Lark and Termite*

"This is a deeply personal and compelling account of Franklin's lifelong entanglement with America's perpetual war state, from his youthful enthusiasms, to his years of flight in the Strategic Air Command, to his sustained resistance to the Vietnam War, which changed his life in so many ways. Franklin has been one of the major scholars of America's post-WWII commitment to war as policy, and here we learn how that happened. It's a rousing and inspirational life story!" —Kim Stanley Robinson, Hugo Award winner and author of *New York 2140*

"A required course for everyone concerned about how militarization has shaped American society and national identity from World War II through interventions in Korea and Vietnam to the current endless War on Terror. Especially engaging is the interweaving of personal memoir and political analysis, of social life and foreign policy, by one of our greatest myth busters." —Amy Kaplan, University of Pennsylvania, author of *Our American Israel: The Story of an Entangled Alliance*

"It's especially stunning for me personally, to read Franklin's gripping account of the era we both lived through—three years apart in age—and to realize that we followed the same unusual trajectory in beliefs and attitudes: both committed Cold Warriors at the outset—my service in the Marine Corps and working on nuclear war plans in the Pentagon overlapping his active service in the Strategic Air Command rehearsing the catastrophic enactment of such plans—his disillusion with the Vietnam War and his turn to active resistance shortly preceding my own. Readers of any age will find this an exciting and startlingly self-aware memoir of a life transformed in our dangerous epoch, and most will find in it radically new perspectives on these perilous times, up to the present mind-boggling moment. A terrific book!" —Daniel Ellsberg, author of *The Doomsday Machine: Confessions of a Nuclear War Planner*

CRASH COURSE

WAR CULTURE

Edited by Daniel Leonard Bernardi

Books in this series address the myriad ways in which warfare informs diverse cultural practices, as well as the way cultural practices—from cinema to social media—inform the practice of warfare. They illuminate the insights and limitations of critical theories that describe, explain, and politicize the phenomena of war culture. Traversing both national and intellectual borders, authors from a wide range of fields and disciplines collectively examine the articulation of war, its everyday practices, and its impact on individuals and societies throughout modern history.

OTHER BOOKS BY H. BRUCE FRANKLIN

The Wake of the Gods: Melville's Mythology
Future Perfect: American Science Fiction of the 19th Century
Who Should Run the Universities (with John A. Howard)
From the Movement: Toward Revolution
Herman Melville's Mardi (edition)
Herman Melville's The Confidence-Man (edition)
Back Where You Came From
The Scarlet Letter and Hawthorne's Critical Writings (edition)
Prison Literature in America: The Victim as Criminal and Artist
Countdown to Midnight
American Prisoners and Ex-Prisoners: An Annotated Bibliography
Robert A. Heinlein: America as Science Fiction
Vietnam and America: A Documented History (with Marvin Gettleman,
   Jane Franklin, and Marilyn Young)
War Stars: The Superweapon and the American Imagination
M.I.A. or Mythmaking in America
The Vietnam War in American Stories, Songs, and Poems
Prison Writing in 20th-Century America
Vietnam and Other American Fantasies
The Most Important Fish in the Sea: Menhaden and America

CRASH COURSE

From the Good War to the
Forever War

H. BRUCE FRANKLIN

Nov. 1, 2018

*To Miss Brydon, from
Hawthorne Melville to Marx
& Engels, and to a great
student.*

[signature]

RUTGERS UNIVERSITY PRESS

New Brunswick, Camden, and Newark, New Jersey, and London

Library of Congress Cataloging in Publication Number: 2018015317

A British Cataloging-in-Publication record for this book is available from the
British Library.

♾ The paper used in this publication meets the requirements of the American
National Standard for Information Sciences—Permanence of Paper for Printed
Library Materials, ANSI Z39.48-1992.

www.rutgersuniversitypress.org

Manufactured in the United States of America

For JANE

Of all the enemies to public liberty war is, perhaps, the most to be dreaded because it comprises and develops the germ of every other. War is the parent of armies; from these proceed debts and taxes. And armies, and debts, and taxes are the known instruments for bringing the many under the domination of the few. . . . No nation could preserve its freedom in the midst of continual warfare.

—James Madison, April 20, 1795

This is an endless war without boundaries, no limitation on time and geography.

—Lindsey Graham, U.S. senator and leading war hawk,
"Lawmakers to Revisit 9/11 Law Authorizing
Ever-Expanding War," *New York Times*,
October 29, 2017

CONTENTS

CRASH COURSE

1 ▸ THE LAST VICTORY?

W\ARS AND PRESIDENTS. For those of us Americans who relate our lives to history, those are the big markers. When I awoke one day back in 2014 to discover with amazement that I was eighty years old, I remembered that since early childhood America's wars had been defining the historical periods of my life. World War II. The Korean War. The Vietnam War. Even the Cold War had beginning and ending dates. But living in the Forever War, it was getting harder and harder to tell one war from another, or even to count the number of ongoing wars, much less figure out when they began. And Washington now has us perpetually pondering the where and whether of our next conflicts.

Syria and Russia were both on the 2014 menu, and a chorus of hawks was shrieking against America's "war weariness" and croaking that Americans have no right to be weary because our unending wars have "posed no burdens, required no sacrifices, and involved no disruptions" for us civilians. The Pied Pipers who had marched off hundreds of thousands of our young folks a decade earlier were at it again. *Weekly Standard* founder William Kristol, who had promised us in 2003 that the invasion of Iraq would be a "two month war, not an eight year war," was raving that the "war-weary public" must again be "awakened and rallied." Sounding her familiar smoke alarm, former secretary of state Condoleezza Rice was urging us to "heed the wake-up call of Ukraine" before it's too late. Offering a bizarre view of the previous six decades, the *Wall Street Journal*'s Daniel Henninger warned us that if we don't get over weariness malaise, "fatigue will allow global disorder to displace 60 years of democratic order." "Of what exactly are you weary," snarled an irate *Wall Street Journal* correspondent, arguing that those with an authentic right to weariness are only "those who have suffered severe physical and mental wounds or lost a loved one." The millions of Americans opposed to conflict with Russia or Syria were pictured as selfish, spoiled brats, betrayers of the heroes fighting wars for the freedom and security of America and the world.[1]

The anti-Russian media campaign reminded me of the abrupt switch from the nonstop media images of a heroic Soviet Union throughout almost four years of my childhood to the bloody red ogre that was used to terrify us for the next half century. The battle cries for intensifying the war to overthrow the government of Syria reminded me of my own tiny role as a Strategic Air Command navigator during the invasion of Lebanon in 1958, ostensibly in response to the threat of a Communist takeover of Syria and Iraq, but actually part of a campaign against nationalist and neutralist forces throughout the Arab world—especially in Syria, Egypt, Lebanon, and Iraq—as well as Iran.

I myself had long since become weary of our young servicepeople getting maimed and killed, weary of the slaughter and devastation we have been inflicting on the peoples of dozens of nations, and such selfishly weary of having trillions of dollars sucked out of health care, education, infrastructure, and the environment to pay for these wars. I was hardly alone. The American people seemed fed up with our nonstop wars, even the proxy ones. Polls were showing 61 percent of Americans opposed to U.S. intervention of any kind in Ukraine. During the run-up to Washington's planned military intervention in Syria in the fall of 2013, polls revealed 63 percent of Americans opposed to any form of military action, even to risk-free missile strikes on Syrian air bases.[2]

The hawks called on the troops to applaud their war whoops and tirades against war weariness. But for obvious reasons, the soldiers were even sicker of this endless combat than we civilians were. When the *Military Times* polled active-duty servicepeople during Washington's threat to intervene in Syria, the troops opposed any form of intervention by a three-to-one margin. Eighty percent said that intervention was not in the U.S. national interest.[3]

Teaching students in the twenty-first century—including the combat veterans, National Guard soldiers, and reservists in my classes at Rutgers University in Newark—I had to keep reminding myself that they had lived their entire conscious life during America's endless warfare. For them, that must seem not just normal, but how it has always been and always will be. Is that also true for the rest of us?

At eighty, I had to rethink this question. It was hard to believe that for more than half a century I had been involved in struggles to stop the wars being waged by our nation or to keep it from starting new ones. Before that I had spent three years in the U.S. Air Force in the late 1950s, flying in Strategic Air Command operations of espionage and provocation against the Soviet Union as well as launches of full-scale thermonuclear attacks. Some of these launches were just practice, but a few were actual war launches that were recalled while we were in flight just minutes before it would have been too late. (I recall with embarrassment that I never had a flicker of doubt about whether I should be participating in the start of a thermonuclear Armageddon.) And before that were four years of Air Force ROTC, which I joined during the Korean War, a war that had started when I was sixteen. From age eleven to sixteen, I had bounced from the Victory Culture at the end of World War II right into the repression and militarization of the early Cold War years.

So it dawned on me that living one's life during America's Forever War is hardly unique to those students I was teaching. How many people alive today have ever lived any part of their conscious lives in a United States of America at peace with the rest of the world? Would someone even older than I am have any meaningful memory of what such a state of peace was like? How many Americans are even capable of imagining such a state? I can clearly remember only two periods, bracketing World War II, when I believed I lived in a nation at peace. And even these were arguably mere childish illusions.

My first memory of America at peace with the world is also my first memory of a future America. I was five. On a hot summer day in 1939, my mother took me by subway from Brooklyn to Queens to visit the World of Tomorrow. As soon as we stepped out of the subway car, I saw it: the soaring white tower with its huge white ball at the center of tomorrow's world. The day we spent in that future land transformed my imagination and my thinking, then and for decades. Of course I don't remember the Court of Peace or the Lagoon of Nations or the pavilions of various nations or the big statue of

Mussolini in Italy's Salon of Honor in the Hall of Nations or the replica of the Liberty Bell in Japan's pavilion. I do remember Electro, the giant talking robot, and like my mother I was amazed by the cabinets called "television sets" that looked just like our radio, which was bigger than me, but these also let you see the people talking. I remember some images from our travel through Democracity, the wonder city of the future inside that huge white ball. But my most vivid and transformative memory of the 1939 World's Fair was GM's Futurama, where we rode around in big plush easy chairs as a soundtrack told us what we were viewing. What we saw was an animated scale model larger than any that had ever been constructed. And what we experienced was the thrill of multilane interstate superhighways with streamlined, brightly colored, driverless cars racing smoothly and with precision at spectacular speeds, slicing right through cities on steel and concrete pylons, with access to magical paths on intricately woven cloverleafs. The excitement of the cars and roads was overwhelming. When I was old enough to read the guidebook to the fair, I learned that the Futurama was GM's vehicle for promising that "the motor car" by 1960 would bring "prosperity and a better standard of living for all," part of America's glorious and wonderful World of Tomorrow. Decades later, in "America as Science Fiction: 1939," I would write that the Futurama was a brilliant invention that helped "to turn America away from the democratic future articulated as an ideal of the Fair and toward a society built around the automobile and petroleum, a society dominated by the gigantic corporations controlling these industries."[4]

Of course the fair's vision of a prosperous and peaceful World of Tomorrow was an attempt to transcend—or deny—its present world of a global depression and a developing global war. A few weeks after my wide-eyed visit to the fair came the date conventionally used as the beginning of World War II: September 1, the day Nazi Germany invaded Poland. But already Japan had invaded Manchuria in 1931 and begun to invade the rest of China in 1937; Italy had invaded Ethiopia in 1935; Japan had been intermittently attacking Mongolia and the Soviet Union ever since 1931; and beginning in 1936 the armed forces of Nazi Germany and Fascist Italy had been helping to overthrow the democratically elected government of Spain and establish Generalissimo Franco's fascist dictatorship, which had declared victory one month before the fair opened in May. And in May the intermittent fighting between Japan and the Soviet Union—despite their pavilions at the fair—turned into open warfare that raged throughout most of the fair's first season and ended with the destruction of Japan's 6th Army in the fateful Battle of Khalkhin Gol, cited by some historians as the outbreak of World War II as well as the battle that convinced Japan to go to war against the United States rather than the Soviet Union.[5]

By the end of 1939, my first memory of peace was becoming more and more darkened by the encroaching shadow of war. Every night just before getting into bed I would kneel on the floor and say my prayers, which ended, "Dear God, please keep us out of the war." That was in 1940 and 1941, when I was six and seven. Of course war was already pulsing through the veins of American culture, including the veins of us little boys. Every week I looked forward to Friday, my father's payday, the day he came home with two metal toy soldiers for me. While I was kneeling in my pajamas praying for peace, the first contingents of Boeing B-17 Flying Fortresses were being deployed to the U.S. colonies of Hawaii and the Philippines and loaded with incendiary bombs designed to carry out Air Corps General Claire Chennault's plan to "burn out the industrial heart of the Empire with fire-bomb attacks on the teeming bamboo ant heaps" of Japanese cities.[6]

But on September 1, 1939, that day when the Nazi invasion of Poland brought World War II to Europe, President Franklin D. Roosevelt denounced the bombing of cities as "inhuman barbarism" and sent an "urgent appeal to every Government which may be engaged in hostilities publicly to affirm its determination that its armed forces shall in no event, and under no circumstances, undertake the bombardment from the air of civilian populations." Alluding to the air raids by Italy, Japan, and Germany in Ethiopia, China, and Spain, he declared, "The ruthless bombing from the air of civilians in unfortified centers of population during the course of hostilities which have raged in several quarters of the earth during the past few years, which has resulted in the maiming and in the death of thousands of defenseless men, women and children, has sickened the hearts of every civilized man and woman, and has profoundly shocked the conscience of humanity."[7]

A month later he established a committee to begin research on the development of atomic bombs. While preliminary work on the atomic weapons was proceeding in secret, American newspapers and magazines—including *Popular Mechanics, Time, Newsweek,* the *Saturday Evening Post, Harpers,* and *Colliers*—in 1940 bubbled with enthusiasm about how atomic energy could bring about the futuristic wonderland projected by the New York World's Fair. Meanwhile *Liberty,* a magazine with millions of readers, serialized in 1940 *Lightning in the Night,* a novel that aimed at stampeding the nation into a crash program to build atomic bombs.

Although the United States was not yet quite at war, it was already trans-forming into the warfare state that today seems so normal and eternal. In mid-1941, months before Pearl Harbor, the government secretly prohib-ited Americans from hearing or reading anything at all relating to atomic energy, even though atomic energy and atomic weapons had been a com-mon theme of science fiction ever since the first decade of the twentieth century.[8] Even the secrecy was a secret. Discussions of atomic research van-ished even from scientific journals, where nearly a hundred articles on nuclear fission had appeared in 1939 alone. Newspapers, magazines, news services, and radio broadcasters were soon ordered not to mention atomic power, cyclotrons, betatrons, fission, uranium, deuterium, protactinium, and thorium. Army Intelligence later even attempted to block access to back issues containing popular articles on atomic energy, such as "The Atom Gives Up" in the *Saturday Evening Post* of September 7, 1940. After the war, the *Post*'s editors revealed that this vast effort "to wipe the whole subject from memory" went so far as to ask magazines and "public libraries all over the land" to turn over to Army Intelligence the names of people asking to look at those back issues.[9] In August 1941, John J. O'Neill—science editor of the *New York Herald Tribune* and president of the National Association of Science Writers—charged that censorship on atomic research amounted to "a totalitarian revolution against the American people." Pointing to the devastating potential of an atomic bomb utilizing uranium 235, O'Neill offered a fateful prophecy: "Can we trust our politicians and war makers with a weapon like that? The answer is no."[10]

When war did come, it turned out to be surprisingly glamorous and thrilling, especially for young boys. On Sunday, December 7, 1941, my par-ents and I were visiting relatives in a big Manhattan apartment building. A bulletin came over the radio: the Japanese, without warning, had attacked the American base of Pearl Harbor in Hawaii. While the adults were sol-emnly buzzing about it, I sneaked over to a window facing west from the apartment's high floor and gazed into the night, staring with a little dread and lots more excited anticipation as I scanned the sky for the first sight of approaching Japanese warplanes.

The childish emotional stew I felt that night came back up like acid reflux when I witnessed another young boy having a similar but far more dis-turbing experience in Steven Spielberg's 1987 adaptation of J. G. Ballard's semiautobiographical *The Empire of the Sun*. It's that scene when young Jamie Graham, toward dawn, spies through the bedroom window of his Shanghai apartment an approaching Japanese warship flashing its lights to signal forces on land. A bit scared but mainly thrilled, Jamie signals back with his flashlight. Then he's hurled from the window by a huge explosion, which he thinks he has caused. Unlike Ballard, I spent the war not in a war zone but in Brooklyn.

But life in Brooklyn was also life during wartime. Soon we were all participating in the war effort. Although there were everyday reminders of the war's horrors—like the growing profusion of gold stars on the windows of families whose loved ones had been killed—there were no great hardships in everyday life. Sure, there were shortages and we needed ration stamps to buy meat and sugar and shoes and to get enough gas for our family's 1936 Packard. But even we grade school kids got to share in the unity and patriotism as we participated in the war effort.

One day a week at P.S. 99, a massive four-story brick edifice for teaching obedience, we were required to bring in a bundle of newspapers to be recycled. We bought "War Stamps" that we pasted into paper stamp albums until they added up to $18.75, when we turned them in for U.S. War Bonds that would be worth $25 when they matured in ten years. As part of my patriotic duties I bought from P.S. 99 packets of vegetable seeds that I planted in my "victory garden" in the tiny backyard of our old brick row house on East 13th Street. On weekends I roamed the neighborhood with a red wagon left over from earlier childhood, collecting scrap metal that I turned in at the storefront recycling collection center a couple of blocks away on Avenue J. Also on Avenue J—right across from the gigantic movie palace where we watched the latest war newsreels in between the Saturday matinee double features—was the butcher shop where my mother and I carried the animal fat she had collected from cooking. The white-aproned butchers weighed the fat, which would be used in munitions, and issued us in return extra red ration stamps that entitled us to buy more meat.

Above the bed where I had once said my prayers for peace, there now hung a huge map of the northern hemisphere on which I marked the advance of the Allied forces and the retreat of the Axis powers with dozens of ordinary pins, each bearing a small paper flag of one of the various warring nations. Most of us boys built models of the latest warplanes and warships while imagining flying and fighting in the real things, especially the fighter planes and bombers. My most vivid war fantasies had little to do with my toy soldiers. They were visions of vast formations of multiengine bombers, B-17 Flying Fortresses and later B-29 Superfortresses, escorted high above by lines of fighters, P-51 Mustangs or P-38 Lightnings, all culminating in an apocalyptic airborne triumph just like the 1943 Disney movie *Victory through Air Power*.

The reality of war got as close as the Nazi U-boats that were sinking "Victory Ships"—the freighters and tankers sailing to Europe in vast convoys—so near to Brooklyn that oil and wreckage from the torpedoed vessels blotted the beaches of Coney Island. We had to have blackouts to keep Brooklyn's lights from silhouetting the ships, but even these were fun, especially when I got to go with my father, an air raid warden precinct captain, as he patrolled the neighborhood.

Yes, we did yearn for peace, but it was victory that we really craved. We were jubilant when President Harry S. Truman announced on August 6, 1945, that an American airplane had just dropped an "atomic bomb," a weapon that harnessed "the basic power of the universe," on Hiroshima, "an important Japanese Army base."[11] Eight days later came the electrifying news that Japan had surrendered.

August 14, 1945. I was now eleven, and I was crammed in the back of a pickup packed with other boys and girls, all yelling our hearts out as loud as we could to be heard over the cacophony of honking horns and howling air raid sirens. (My own heart was probably beating wilder than most because right next to me was my classmate Edith Kopperman, on whom I had a crush as flaming as her red hair.) We were part of an impromptu motorcade weaving through the evening streets of our Flatbush neighborhood in Brooklyn. Everywhere we went—past the sidewalk fruit and vegetable stands, the storefront A&P exuding the smell of freshly ground coffee, the fish market and the kosher delicatessen along Avenue J, the small row houses and big apartment houses on the side streets, along Coney Island Avenue, with its rows of small stores dotted with small restaurants and soda fountains, where the electric trolley cars were clanging their bells nonstop—more and more cheering people poured onto the sidewalks, waving American flags and homemade signs, hugging, dancing. We kids in the truck were all screaming, "Peace! Peace! The war is over!" We believed this was the end of not just this war but of war itself, that we were all going to live the rest of our lives in a prosperous and victorious nation, the World of Tomorrow on a peaceful planet.

Little did we know that our government was already preparing new wars. Nor did we know that this would be the last victory celebration of our lifetime.

On the same day as our celebration of V-J Day, eight thousand miles away another people were celebrating the surrender of Japan quite differently. August 14 was the first day of the August Revolution, when the Vietnamese people rose up and in less than three weeks swept away Japanese and French control and established the Democratic Republic of Vietnam.

On September 2, Ho Chi Minh read Vietnam's Declaration of Independence to half a million Vietnamese people jam-packed before him in Hanoi, the old capital of a new nation that had been fighting for its independence for more than two thousand years. "'All men are created equal,'" he began. "'They are endowed by the Creator with certain inalienable Rights; among them are Life, Liberty, and the pursuit of Happiness.' This immortal statement was made in the Declaration of Independence of the United States of America in 1776. In a broader sense, this means: All the peoples on the earth are equal from birth, all the peoples have a right to live, to be happy and free."[12] Suddenly two warplanes appeared overhead. The crowd gazed up. They saw two of those weird-looking P-38 Lightning fighter-bombers. When they recognized the U.S. insignia on the planes, those half million people, acting like a single being, let out an earthshaking cheer. Just as we kids in the truck believed in America's peaceful future, the Vietnamese believed that we Americans were their friends and allies, that we would be the champions of their freedom and independence from colonialism.

Little did they know that ten days earlier, on August 22, French president Charles de Gaulle had flown to Washington, where the Truman administration had agreed to finance, arm, transport, and sponsor a French invasion designed to overthrow the Democratic Republic of Vietnam and restore French colonial rule. This would be a joint French-American project. The United States would not only supply the weapons and the financing. It would also turn over to the French tens of thousands of Nazi troops, including Waffen-SS units, many of whom would be forced into the French Foreign Legion to be shock troops for invasion. A dozen U.S. troopships would be diverted from bringing GIs home from Europe to carrying the French invasion army—equipped with American weapons, tanks, warplanes, and jeeps—to Vietnam.[13] This was arguably the beginning of America's Vietnam War. It was also, as it turns out, the beginning of the American people's movement against that war.

As the movement against the Vietnam War surged in the mid-1960s and early 1970s, it discovered some of that early history. Yet the movement thought that it had begun in the 1960s and was unaware of its own birth within the first few months of the life of the Democratic Republic of Vietnam (DRV). The American people's struggle against our nation's war against Vietnam began, in fact, just a few months after our celebration of victory and peace in August 1945.

British troops that had been sent to Saigon to disarm the remaining Japanese forces had instead rearmed the Japanese, who had already been disarmed by the Vietnamese. Soon the Japanese joined the British and remnants of the French colonial forces to wage war against the newly declared independent nation of Vietnam. What was left of the Japanese air force, together with the British RAF, bombed and strafed any concentrations of armed Vietnamese they could find.[14] Japanese troops were deployed to control the Saigon waterfront and port facilities.

So when the U.S. troopships carrying the French invasion army arrived in Saigon in the late fall of 1945, they were met by uniformed and armed Japanese soldiers, who saluted them on the docks and commanded machine guns on towers overlooking the U.S. ships. The sailors manning the American flotilla were profoundly shocked and outraged. Every single enlisted crewman on these ships signed petitions to Congress and the president condemning the U.S. government for participating in "imperialist policies" designed "to subjugate the native population of Vietnam."[15]

The antiwar movement at home began as soon as Americans discovered that Washington was supporting the war by France against the DRV. At a large 1947 meeting of the Viet Nam American Friendship Association, six-time presidential candidate Norman Thomas explained, "It is only by direct and indirect aid . . . from the United States that colonial imperialism can be maintained in the modern world." The chairman of the Friendship Association prophetically proclaimed that "the founding of the newest Republic in the world—the Democratic Republic of Viet Nam" is "an event which history may well record as sounding the death knell of the colonial system."[16] He was right.

Vietnam's war for independence was in the vanguard of a global revolution that destroyed the old colonial form of imperialism. It helped spread the virus of revolution directly into the French empire, as Algerian, Senegalese, and other African veterans of the French Foreign Legion sent to fight against the Vietnamese returned to France's African colonies with military skills and anti-colonial fervor. Between 1945 and 1949, independence from colonial rule was won by one-fourth of the world's population, as outright colonialism crumbled throughout much of Asia, including Indonesia, India, Pakistan, Burma, Ceylon, and the Philippines. In 1949, with the victory of the Communist revolution in China, another quarter of the world's population escaped from the "Open Door" version of colonialism decreed for China by Washington in 1899. Belgium, France, England, and Portugal were determined to keep their African colonies, a fight that was decided when Belgium lost their Congo (1960), France lost Algeria (1962), Britain lost Kenya (1963), and Portugal lost Angola, Guinea-Bissau, and Mozambique (1974–1975). Just as in Vietnam, the colonial powers could count on the support of the United States throughout their losing wars. As Martin Luther King Jr. so succinctly put it in 1967, the United States was fighting "on the wrong side of world revolution."[17] Vietnam's three decades of war against European and U.S. imperialism from 1945 to 1975 exactly matched the period of the destruction of European global colonialism.

France fought desperately to keep possession of "Indochine"—Vietnam, Cambodia, and Laos. As the French war against Vietnam went on, with increasing U.S. covert involvement—such as military advisers on the ground and 250 U.S. pilots flying combat missions in U.S. warplanes with French insignia—opposition to this Franco-American war grew and intensified. In the spring of 1954, as the French were on the verge of total defeat, the administration of Dwight D. Eisenhower prepared for open U.S. military intervention.

President Eisenhower, who had run as a peace candidate in 1952, had just signed in July 1953 the armistice that ended fighting in the bloody and avoidable tragedy known as the Korean War (by accepting the terms originally proposed by North Korea back in July 1951). Before plunging the nation into a new war, the president evidently thought it prudent to test the possible reactions of the American people.

Thus on April 16, Vice President Richard Nixon floated a trial balloon, declaring that the United States may soon have to "face up to the situation and dispatch forces" because "the Vietnamese lack the ability to conduct a war or govern themselves."[18] What a strange and revealing statement, considering that the Vietnamese had just defeated France, armed with enormous support from the United States. Swift, impassioned reaction came from across the entire political spectrum.[19]

Thousands of letters and telegrams opposing U.S. intervention deluged the White House. An American Legion division with 78,000 members demanded that "the United States should refrain from dispatching any of its Armed Forces to participate as combatants in the fighting in Indochina or in Southeast Asia."[20] There were public outcries against "colonialism" and "imperialism." Senators from both parties rose to denounce any thought of U.S. military intervention in Indochina. The Monday after Nixon's Saturday speech, for example, Senator Ed Johnson of Colorado declared on the Senate floor: "I am against sending American GI's into the mud and muck of Indochina on a blood-letting spree to perpetuate colonialism and white man's exploitation in Asia."[21]

By mid-May, a Gallup poll revealed that 68 percent of those surveyed were against sending troops to Indochina.[22] Nevertheless, the Eisenhower administration was already actively shifting from supporting the French to replacing them. On May 7, the French bastion at Dien Bien Phu fell. The Geneva Conference opened on May 8. Washington had already selected Ngo Dinh Diem to be its puppet ruler of Vietnam. The Geneva Conference ended in July with unanimous recognition of Vietnam as a single, independent nation. All French forces were to withdraw to south of the 17th parallel and then leave the country, which would then have national elections, supervised by Canada, India, and Poland. But instead Washington recognized Ngo Dinh Diem's "State of Vietnam," a government seated in Saigon, as the legitimate ruler of all of Vietnam; blocked the national election; and resumed the war.[23]

One widespread cultural fantasy about the Vietnam War blames the antiwar movement for forcing the military to "fight with one arm tied behind its back." But this belief stands reality on its head. The American people, disgusted and angry about the Korean War, were in no mood to support a war in Vietnam. Staunch domestic opposition kept Washington from going in overtly. So it went covertly. It thereby committed itself to a policy based on deception, sneaking around, and hiding its actions from the American people. The U.S. government thus created the internal nemesis of its own war: the antiwar movement. That movement was inspired and empowered not just by our outrage against the war by also by the lies about the war, lies necessitated by the war, coming from our government and propagated by the media. Although it was the Vietnamese who defeated the United States, ultimately it was the antiwar movement, especially within the armed forces, that finally in 1973 forced Washington to accept, at long last, the terms of the 1954 Geneva Accords, and to sign a peace treaty that included, word for word, every major demand made by the National Liberation Front (the so-called Viet Cong) back in 1969.

Any pretense that the Vietnamese people supported U.S. intervention was of course finally blown away in the spring of 1975 when the Saigon puppet government and its superbly equipped armed forces fled in panic rather than face the advancing revolutionary army. The truth was that for three decades our nation had sponsored and then waged a genocidal war against a people and a nation that had never done anything to us except ask for our friendship and support.

The story of that war became an ahistorical narrative of a "mistake" that had led us into a "quagmire." As a nation, we did our best to forget the actual history.

Did we learn anything from what we did in Vietnam? For a while, it seemed so. Through the rest of the 1970s, there was general agreement, across the political spectrum, on one thing: no more Vietnams (a slogan so popular that Richard Nixon chose it as the title of his 1985 history of the Vietnam War). Although this pledge had different meanings to different people, there was evident consensus on two points: No more war without the support of the American people. And no more war without a clear exit strategy.

But then how would imperial war be possible?

To reopen the pathways to imperial war, it was necessary to rewrite and reimage the history of both the war and the antiwar movement. What was needed was a narrative, a cultural story that would transform the protracted nightmare into a "Noble Cause." The story of the Vietnam War was first labeled "a Noble Cause" by Ronald Reagan as he ran for president in August 1980. It was in this speech that Reagan also first equated Vietnam with the term "syndrome."[24] The Noble Cause story runs like this: there was once a small democratic nation named South Vietnam that was being invaded by the evil Communist dictatorship of North Vietnam. The United States went to help South Vietnam defend its democracy and freedom, and we were succeeding in our heroic efforts. But our Noble Cause was betrayed by privileged college students, long-haired drugged-up hippies, the liberal media, pinko college professors, and Jane Fonda. This is the narrative of the Vietnam War now dominant in American politics and culture.

Soon "Vietnam" became not a people or a nation, and not even a war. "Vietnam" became something that happened to us. America became the victim of "Vietnam," which was some kind of crippling addiction or disease or, to use Reagan's term, a "syndrome."

The Noble Cause narrative fed and was fed by tremendously powerful myths that became vital organs of a national body in a permanent state of imperial war. As the narrative reshaped our memory of the war, all the American veterans became both the real heroes of the story as well as the true victims of "Vietnam." Erased with barely a trace from the chalkboard of our memory were the two to three million Vietnamese killed by our invasion, poisoning, and bombardment of their land. In their place were multiplying images of hundreds, then thousands, of veterans still imprisoned in Vietnam, and thousands, then hundreds of thousands, of veterans being spat upon by those same antiwar protesters who kept us from winning the war. These two myths—the POW/MIA myth and the myth of the spat-upon veteran—thus turned "Vietnam" into the cultural foundation of the Forever War.

I use "myth" in the fullest sense of the word, as anthropologists and archaeologists do; a society's myths are key clues for understanding how it perceives itself and its relation to the world around it. Myths can also dramatize deep psychosocial content. But often the content and meaning of a myth are not obvious. These two powerful myths about "Vietnam" are, in part, responses to a perceived emasculation of American manhood. It's not just a coincidence that the most common form of the spitting myth has a returning vet being spat upon by a "hippie chick," usually in the San Francisco Airport. And in the Hollywood productions that burned the POW/MIA myth into the nation's memory and imagination, the POWs are betrayed by women or unmanly men such as bureaucrats and other "suits." In the first of these movies, *Uncommon Valor* (1983), Gene Hackman must begin by liberating his team of heroic POW rescuers from their imprisonment by castrating women. The climax of *Rambo* comes when bare-chested Sylvester Stallone, after rescuing the POWs, mounts the prostrate arch-bureaucrat Murdock and forces this fake man to whimper and moan in terror of our hero's gigantic phallic knife.[25]

While these cancerous myths were colonizing American culture in the 1980s, Washington was busy waging covert and proxy wars, as in Nicaragua and El Salvador, and quick in-and-out wars, as in Grenada and Panama.

The crucial year for the current form of our Forever War was 1991. From the end of World War II until 1991, our nation's number one priority, to which all social goods were subservient, was the Cold War: defending freedom and democracy from the tentacles of the red octopus of Communism. But in 1991, the Soviet Union ceased to exist. This was the moment for our long-awaited peace and our anticipated Peace Dividend, which could now fund our health care, education, infrastructure, and other social goods. But in a remarkable coincidence, it was also the moment when the Iraq War began. Mysteriously, the Cold War morphed into the Forever War.

In August 1990, eight months after the U.S. invasion of Panama, the Bush administration launched Operation Desert Shield, which poured hundreds of thousands of American soldiers into Saudi Arabia, ostensibly to protect that desert kingdom and to convince Iraq to withdraw troops from Kuwait. To avoid violating the mantra of "no more Vietnams," the administration simultaneously launched a massive propaganda campaign to generate fervor for war against Iraq. The campaign tried one line after another: Saddam Hussein is today's Hitler. We need Iraq's oil. Iraq's invasion of Kuwait is brutal aggression. Iraqi soldiers are throwing babies out of incubators in Kuwait, a fiction dreamed up and pumped into the media by Hill & Knowlton, the world's largest PR firm, which was paid millions of dollars to mastermind the campaign for war.[26] But none of these was working to get the emotional juices of war flowing through the veins of the American public. In fact, opposition to war was rapidly building. What worked was the myth of the spat-upon vet, which had been mushrooming throughout the 1980s despite the fact that there has never been a shred of contemporaneous evidence of even one antiwar protester spitting on even one Vietnam veteran.

The administration launched Operation Yellow Ribbon, the theme of which was "Support Our Soldiers." The media enthusiastically joined the campaign. America was not about to scream "baby killers" and spit on our brave fighters this time. Newspapers, radio, and TV started campaigns to write letters of support to the soldiers in Saudi Arabia. Full-page pro-war ads said nothing about Iraq and Kuwait, but showed the American people voicing support for "all the men and women participating in Operation Desert Shield." Yellow ribbons sprouted everywhere, even as magnetic emblems attached to cars throughout the land. Now we had something to fight for. As Vietnam veteran and sociology professor Jerry Lembcke put it in his groundbreaking book, *The Spitting Image: Myth, Memory, and the Legacy of Vietnam*, "The war was about the American soldiers who had been sent to fight it." And the main enemy was all those people who had spat on the Vietnam vets and who were now voicing opposition to a new war.

The campaign hampered the antiwar movement, forcing it to defend itself against the myth by insisting that it was not against the soldiers, just the war. Nevertheless, it was still a close call for the Bush administration. When the administration went to Congress in January 1991 to get authorization for possible military action, it squeaked through the Senate on a 52-47 vote. The nation that went to war a few days later was a nation festooned in yellow ribbons. It was also a nation flying omnipresent black and white flags.

The United States of America in the twenty-first century has two national flags. One is the colorful red, white, and blue banner created during the American Revolution, with stars that represent, in the words of the 1777 Continental Congress, "a new constellation." The other is the black and white POW/MIA flag, America's emblem of the Vietnam War.

The POW/MIA flag has fluttered over the White House each year since 1982. A 1987 law permanently enshrined a giant POW/MIA flag in the

Rotunda of the U.S. Capitol. The POW/MIA flag flies over every U.S. post office, thanks to a law signed by President Clinton in 1997. Each of the fifty states mandates the display of this flag over public facilities such as state offices, municipal buildings, toll plazas, and police headquarters. The POW/MIA flag hangs over the trading floor of the New York Stock Exchange. It is sewn onto the right sleeve of the official Ku Klux Klan white robe and adorns millions of bumper stickers, buttons, home windows, motorcycle jackets, watches, post cards, coffee mugs, T-shirts, and Christmas-tree ornaments. Much of my speaking in the last few years has been at the local headquarters of the VFW, Elks, American Legion, and Knights of Columbus, and over each of these buildings flies the POW/MIA flag.

The flag displays our nation's veneration of its central image, a handsome American prisoner of war, his silhouetted head slightly bowed to reveal behind him the ominous shape of a looming guard tower. A strand of barbed wire cuts across just below his firm chin. Underneath runs the motto: YOU ARE NOT FORGOTTEN.

This flag still flies as America's symbol of the Vietnam War. In 1991, its meaning shifted dramatically, as it came to symbolize America as a heroic warrior, victimized by "Vietnam," but reemerging as Rambo unbound. The yellow ribbons and the black and white flags had been transformed into symbols of American pride, not shame. This is what President George H. W. Bush meant on March 1, 1991, when he proclaimed "a proud day for America" because, "by God, we've kicked the Vietnam syndrome once and for all!"[27]

Who back then could guess that the Iraq War had not ended but had just begun? Or that twelve years later his son President George W. Bush would also announce victory in Iraq, under a huge "MISSION ACCOMPLISHED" banner? And who knew that our president in 1991 was celebrating the beginning of our epoch of endless wars?

A month after Bush's proclamation, Jane Franklin and I were on our way to Japan, where I was to teach American Studies for a few weeks as a visiting professor at Tokyo's Meiji University. I had just finished the manuscript for my book *M.I.A., or Mythmaking in America*, a history of how Richard Nixon created the "POW/MIA" category and used it to prolong the war, and how and why the preposterous belief in POWs in postwar Vietnam came to possess our nation. I thought I understood everything about the history and meaning of the POW/MIA myth. I sure was wrong. And I was about to learn something crucial about American culture and culture in general.

Where does a society's culture exist? Obviously in the artifacts, cultural productions, and discourse of the society and of course inside the heads of the people who constitute that society. That's why sometimes it can be hard to understand or even see what is most peculiar or even bizarre about one's own culture, since it's inside your own mind. It took an embarrassing event to teach me how that fact can distort one's perception of reality.

One night several Japanese scholars of American Studies, from Meiji and other universities, expressed their keen interest in the POW/MIA myth. They said that on some levels they thought they understood it, that from their study of POW movies and other cultural artifacts they saw that the prisoner of war was functioning in American society as an icon of militarism. "But," one said, "that's what we find so puzzling. When militarism was dominant in Japan, the last person who would have been used as an icon of militarism was the POW. What did he do that was heroic? He didn't fight to the death. He surrendered." I was totally flummoxed. Here I had been studying the POW/MIA myth for years, and I had missed its most essential and revealing aspect.

After we got home, I had to look once again at all those sickening but alarmingly effective POW/MIA movies. Only then did I realize that this is a myth of imprisonment, a myth that draws deep emotional power by displacing onto Vietnam the imprisonment, helplessness, and alienation felt by many Americans in an epoch when alien economic, technological, and bureaucratic forces control much of their lives. And the man on the flag is American manhood itself, beset by all those bureaucratic and feminine forces seeking to emasculate him. He incarnates America as victim, a victim who must regain his manhood in victorious war, who might be able to truthfully boast, "Mission Accomplished," and thus offer the nation its first joyous victory celebration since August 1945.

Before we left Japan, I was asked to give a lecture about the Gulf War and American culture at Hiroshima University. After the talk, Professor Hiroyuki Miyagawa offered to take Jane and me on a guided tour of Hiroshima the next day. Just three years earlier, I had demonstrated, in *War Stars: The Superweapon and the American Imagination*, that there was no military need to explode atomic bombs on Hiroshima and Nagasaki and that Truman had decided to use these bombs to intimidate the Soviet Union and to be the president who would end all war by showing that America possessed and would use the ultimate superweapon. Miyagawa was sixteen years old on the day the atomic bomb was airburst at 8:15 A.M., a time that would inflict maximum casualties on the workers going to work and the children going to school.[28] Miyagawa was home sick that day. He showed us on the diorama at the Hiroshima Peace Memorial Museum the small hill between ground zero and his home, a feature that provided enough protection so that he was able to live despite severe burns. The tour was one of the most profoundly disturbing experiences of my life, especially as I recalled my own joy on hearing the news of the atomic bomb later that day in Brooklyn.

Miyagawa's testimony got me to see how key parts of my own experience fit together. I got an astonishing view of that week in August when a sixteen-year-old Japanese boy was burned by the blast while an eleven-year-old boy celebrated the atomic bomb along with the great victory that ended the so-called good war, just as the fifty-five-year-old Ho Chi Minh was launching the Vietnamese and global revolution against the great colonial empires. Stretching forward were all those American wars designed first to support those old empires and then to replace them with a more up-to-date model.

Although cultural memory is the sum of individual memories, a society's collective cultural memory can reshape or overwhelm individual memory. Perhaps this is what convinced President Barack Obama in 2012 to issue his "Presidential Proclamation—Commemoration of the 50th Anniversary of the Vietnam War," calling for a thirteen-year campaign of thousands of events throughout the nation to honor the three million "proud Americans" who "upheld the highest traditions of our Armed Forces . . . fighting heroically to protect the ideals we hold dear as Americans." The proclamation began by defining 2012 as the fiftieth anniversary, but how did he calculate this? On Memorial Day that year, speaking at the Vietnam Veterans Memorial, the president explained that although "historians cannot agree precisely when the war began," 1962 marked the beginning of "major operations." Choosing this date conveniently consigned to a black hole of historical and cultural memory the previous seventeen years of proxy operations, the installation of a puppet regime in Saigon, covert operations, and active combat by thousands of U.S. "advisers."

"Because of the hard lessons of Vietnam," Obama declared, "America is even stronger than before." What were these lessons? The two main lessons cited by the president were actually the two main myths I have described: not to dishonor our soldiers and not to forsake our POW/MIAs. Vietnam was "one of the most painful chapters in our history," he said, "most particularly, how we treated our troops who served there." Not the war, but the treatment of its veterans "was a national shame, a disgrace." "And when an American does not come back—including the 1,666 Americans still missing from the Vietnam War—let us resolve to do everything in our power to bring them home."[29]

Recognizing the divisiveness of the Vietnam War, the president chose a neutral, disinterested, objective organization to organize and run the commemoration: the Department of Defense. The Pentagon has already organized, in collaboration with state and local governments, hundreds of events designed to carry out the mission proclaimed in the presidential proclamation.

Continuing the Forever War seems to require erasing the true history of the Vietnam War. This makes sense, because the real reasons for the Vietnam War are the same reasons for the Forever War.

2 ▸ THE BOMBS BURSTING IN AIR, OR HOW WE LOST WORLD WAR II

THE EXPERIENCE OF the students I taught for more than half a century, living their entire lives in a nation always at war, may not after all be so fundamentally different from my own. But there is one thing about our life during wartime that distinguishes my experience, and the experience of my generation, from theirs.

"I was born on a different planet from everyone else in this room," I would announce at a crucial point in my course Science Fiction, Technology, and Society. Even people buried in their smartphones would emerge with curious or puzzled expressions. "I was born on a planet where there was no known threat to the existence of our species," I explained. "None of you has ever lived on that planet."

We *Homo sapiens* are so sapient, so intelligent, indeed so brilliant that we are the only species that has ever figured out a means to destroy our own species. And we are so clever, so ingenious, so inventive that we actually designed, built, and deployed that means of self-destruction. So like my students, most of you reading these words have lived your entire life under the threat of annihilation by our own weapons. This is normal for you. It seems that life has always been that way. And, I suppose, it must seem that life will always be like that because there's nothing that you or anyone can do to put the genie back in the bottle, according to that clichéd adage. To live your lives normally, I guess you have to avoid thinking very much about our nuclear weapons and how they came to be *The Doomsday Machine*, the accurate title of Daniel Ellsberg's terrifying 2017 book. Denial thus becomes normal, maybe even necessary. But since I can remember when these weapons didn't exist, I've never quite gotten reconciled to their eternal presence in the future. Indeed, it's hard for me to imagine our coexisting with these doomsday weapons—today possessed by the United States, Russia, China, India, Pakistan, France, the United Kingdom, Israel, and North Korea—for many more decades or centuries. It's always seemed to me that since we were brilliant enough to derive ultimate weapons from the subatomic basis of matter, we are intelligent enough to figure out how to get rid of them. And having participated myself in actions that brought our planet to the brink of Armageddon, I believe that not getting rid of them is not a viable option.

When President Harry Truman announced that the United States had just dropped an atomic bomb "with more power than 20,000 tons of T.N.T." on Hiroshima, he called this "the greatest achievement of organized science in history." American "science and industry" had harnessed "the basic power of the universe," he told the world, and he went on to threaten all the cities of Japan with a "rain of ruin from the air, the like of which has never been seen on this earth."[1] I and all the kids I knew were jubilant. We got the intended messages loud and clear. The Japanese were getting what they deserve. This would end the war. America had the ultimate weapon, and no other nation could now threaten us. Maybe we could impose peace on the world. Of course we didn't know the terms "manifest destiny" and "American exceptionalism," but growing up in the victory culture of World War II America we had already internalized their meaning.

The death tolls in Hiroshima and Nagasaki that began seeping into the news did not dampen our joy because our comic books and the barrage of wartime propaganda had taught us to regard the Japanese as subhuman.[2] Most of us had already seen and cheered the complete extermination of the Japanese in that 1943 Disney animated movie *Victory through Air Power*, where gigantic American bombers blacken the sky and then magically transmute into an American eagle that claws the Japanese octopus to death. As we watched Japan being bombed and burned into smoldering rubble, we heard the swelling strains of "America the Beautiful" and then saw "VICTORY THROUGH AIR POWER" emblazoned across the screen.

Probably most adult Americans shared our childish feelings. The prevailing attitude was celebration of America's atomic victory and an anticipated Pax Americana, although right away some public voices were calling the bomb a Frankenstein's monster that would eventually threaten America. Some were even saying that it threatened the foundations of our being.[3] Nobody knew that sixty-eight of the leading scientists working on the atomic bomb had signed a petition on July 17 warning that if the United States actually used this weapon, eventually "the cities of the United States as well as the cities of other nations will be in continuous danger of sudden annihilation."[4]

In a nation intoxicated by the delicious brew of victory, who would dare spoil the party by asking the crucial question of why? Why did President Truman order the atomic bombing of two Japanese cities, causing hideous deaths for almost two hundred thousand people? The answers seemed obvious: To force the Japanese to surrender. To avoid the need for an invasion of Japan that might take even more lives. To avenge Pearl Harbor and all the atrocities carried out by the Japanese. The story that the atomic bombs victoriously ended the war seemed obvious. It soon became the orthodox, even sacrosanct narrative.

By mid-July of 1945, Japan had lost all its bases in the Pacific, and fleets of B-29 Superfortresses had reduced all but four Japanese cities to desolate ruins and smoking ashes while carrier-based Navy bombers were systematically destroying its military facilities. By late spring, Japan had no viable defenses against these devastating aerial assaults. This is why the *Enola Gay*, destined to drop the bomb on Hiroshima, had been designed and built in May without the B-29's normal protective armor and gun turrets. Japan's only remaining army of any significance was isolated in Manchuria and Korea, and could not be brought home to defend the homeland because U.S. ships were blockading Japan and shelling its coastal regions with impunity.

The leaders of the United States, Soviet Union, and United Kingdom met in Potsdam, a few miles from Berlin, from July 17 to August 2. At the Yalta conference back in February, the Soviet Union had promised to launch a war on Japan no later than three months after the surrender of Germany. Germany surrendered on May 8, so the USSR attack was expected to commence by early August. At Potsdam, Marshal Stalin reaffirmed that they would enter the war by August 15. President Truman had no doubt that this alone would end the war. In his diary for July 17, after noting that the Soviet Union would "be in Jap War on August 15," he wrote: "Fini Japs when that comes about."[5]

Truman knew that as early as April the Soviets had begun the physical process of moving their forces from the European front to launch full-scale war against Japan. Between May and early August, they transported, across 6,000 miles, more than 1.5 million men, 20,000 tanks, 100,000 trucks and other vehicles, hundreds of bombers and fighters, and the munitions and supplies necessary to service this giant battle-tested armada. They had even delivered temporary bridges to allow troops and armor to cross the great Amur River.

Up until the time he received the full report on July 21 of the spectacularly successful testing of the atomic bomb in Alamogordo, Truman and his advisers kept urging the USSR to enter the war as soon as possible. After that date, they tried instead to delay the Soviet entrance into the war. Once Truman told Stalin about the bomb, the two countries were in a frantic race, with Truman trying to drop the bomb before the USSR entered the war and Stalin trying to launch full-scale war on the main Japanese army before the United States could drop the bomb.[6]

On July 26, the United States and United Kingdom issued the Potsdam Proclamation, an ultimatum demanding that Japan accept "unconditional surrender" or face "prompt and utter destruction." Chiang Kai-shek's government of China, which was not part of the Potsdam conference, also signed the proclamation, but the USSR was pointedly not asked to sign. Truman and his advisers knew there could be no surrender unless the emperor agreed to it. They were also fully aware that the one condition essential to the Japanese cabinet, and of course to the emperor, was allowing the emperor to remain. In drafting the proclamation, the War Department stated flatly: "The primary intention in issuing the proclamation is to induce Japan's surrender and thus avoid the heavy casualties implied in a fight to the finish. It is almost universally accepted that the basic point on which acceptance of surrender terms will hinge lies in the question of the disposition of the Emperor and his dynasty."

Thus the original draft allowed Japan to retain "a constitutional monarchy under the present dynasty" as long as "such a government will never again aspire to aggression." The War Department, finding this too ambiguous, proposed an amended version that included this simple sentence: "The Japanese people will be free to choose whether they shall retain their Emperor as a constitutional monarchy."[7]

But Truman and Secretary of State Jimmy Byrnes, the policymaker most eager to drop the atomic bomb, decided to remove from the proclamation any indication whatsoever that the emperor would be allowed to remain. Thus they guaranteed that Japan would not, and indeed could not, accept the proclamation and agree to surrender before atomic bombs exploded on its cities. Historian Tsuyoshi Hasegawa, who has done the deepest research into the relevant Japanese, Soviet, and American archives, draws the logical conclusion: "Truman wrote that he issued the order to drop the bomb *after* Japan rejected the Potsdam Proclamation. The truth is quite the opposite, however: the rejection of the Potsdam Proclamation was required to justify the dropping of the bomb."[8]

The demand for "unconditional surrender" effectively rebuffed the numerous Japanese attempts to negotiate a surrender, which had been going on for months. President Truman was well aware of these, for example discussing in his diary of July 18 "a telegram from Jap emperor asking for peace." On July 25, Tokyo Radio beamed directly to the United States an explicit offer to surrender, on condition that the emperor be allowed to keep his throne. "Radio Tokyo in a startlingly frank broadcast beamed to the US" declared that "Japan is ready to call off the war if the U.S. will modify its peace terms," reported *Stars and Stripes*, the GI newspaper published under the auspices of the War Department.[9] This was major news in America the next day. "Tokyo Radio Appeals to U.S. for a More Lenient Peace" blared the July 26 front-page headline in the *New York Times.*

Thus the Potsdam Proclamation, which was never submitted directly to the Japanese government but was just broadcast by the Office of War Information radio and dropped by leaflet, can be seen as a dismissive response to the Japanese attempts to negotiate a surrender.[10] Its demand for "unconditional surrender" was a blunt statement that no negotiations were possible.

But in fact the surrender was negotiated—after the bomb. And in those negotiations the Japanese got what they demanded: keeping the emperor.

The argument with the most powerful emotional appeal and the only semblance of a moral justification for the Hiroshima bombing is that it saved hundreds of thousands of American lives, as well as the lives of countless Japanese, that would have been lost in the planned invasion of Japan. Practically all the American soldiers and sailors then in the Pacific theater, as well as most other Americans, held and still hold this belief like a religious faith. Why not? That's what our government told us, and in those days we believed our government. Even John A. Williams, author of such great subversive novels as *The Man Who Cried I Am* and *Captain Blackman*, unshakably believed during his last seventy years what he and the other sailors on his ship had been told on August 1945: They were on their way to invade Japan and so the atomic bomb had probably just saved their lives. (In our many years as colleagues and friends, this was the only issue that John and I ever disagreed about.) It is certainly true that an American invasion of Japan would have been one of the most bloody and horrific battles in the hideous history of human warfare. That is why it was never going to happen, even if the atomic bomb never existed.

When was the planned invasion, dubbed Operation Downfall, supposed to take place? The first stage of the invasion, Operation Olympic, was to be an amphibious assault commanded by General Douglas MacArthur on Kyushu, the southernmost of the main Japanese islands, tentatively scheduled for November at the earliest. The main invasion, Operation Coronet, would not follow until March 1946. Kyushu was chosen because it was the most accessible to U.S. forces and far less formidable than the principal and much larger island of Honshu, home of Tokyo and most of Japan's industry. But in early July, the U.S. code-breaking system revealed that the Japanese, anticipating the attack on Kyushu, had prepared defenses likely to inflict hundreds of thousands of U.S. casualties. This fact induced Truman and the War Department to shelve the invasion even before the successful test of the bomb. The only dissenting voice was that of MacArthur, who refused to accept the intelligence and remained eager to lead the invasion.[11]

By late July, it was clear to Truman and his advisers that there would be no need for an American invasion. They knew that a massive Soviet assault on the Japanese main forces in Manchuria and Korea was coming in a few weeks. The president was not about to order an invasion that would cause the deaths of hundreds of thousands of young Americans against a regime that was already defeated and, as the American public knew, was trying to negotiate a surrender. He would be committing "political suicide," as historian Paul Ham puts it, so "the bomb was not a substitute for an invasion for the simple reason that Truman had no intention of approving one."[12]

Truman was probably right that the advent of the Soviet forces would finish the war even if the atomic bomb was not used, which explains why he raced to use it. The Soviet juggernaut that destroyed Japan's last great land army and terrified that nation's leaders disproved the myth that the Japanese would fight to the death and never surrender. At midnight on August 8, the Red Army launched the largest land engagement of the entire Pacific war. Within a few days, almost six hundred thousand Japanese soldiers and hundreds of Japanese generals had surrendered. Eighty thousand had been killed, along with thirty thousand Soviet soldiers, almost three times the number of Americans killed in our bloody invasion of Okinawa. *August Storm*, Colonel David Glantz's fine two-volume history, marvels at the Soviet campaign, which captured from the Japanese in a week of colossal combat an area almost the size of Europe.

Of course that's not what we heard at the time, much less during the burgeoning Cold War of the late 1940s, 1950s, and early 1960s. All I heard from the adult world, and of course believed, was that the Russians had waited until we had won the war, thanks finally to our atom bombs, and then had opportunistically declared war on Japan so that they could participate in the spoils without taking any risks or losses.

The Japanese interpreted the absence of Stalin's signature on the Potsdam Proclamation to mean that the USSR would stay neutral and therefore could continue as an intermediary in their back-channel peace feelers. So they were thunderstruck by the Soviet declaration of war and full-scale offensive on the night of August 8. This was the worst nightmare of the Japanese leaders. On hearing the news, Prime Minister Kantarō Suzuki's first words were, "What we have feared has finally come." As soon as Emperor Hirohito heard the grim news on the morning of August 9, he summoned his most trusted confidant, Koichi Kido. "The Soviet Union declared war against us, and entered into a state of war today," Hirohito told Kido. "Because of this it is necessary to study and decide on the termination of the war." This and other overwhelming evidence from the Japanese archives show that it was the Soviet threat, not the Hiroshima bomb, that convinced the emperor and the political members of his cabinet to capitulate.[13]

Later that same morning, the war and peace factions of the cabinet, meeting in a bomb shelter under the Imperial Palace, were waging a furious debate about the terms of surrender they should offer in light of the Soviet invasion of Manchuria. They all agreed on one thing: the emperor must remain. But the arch militarists, who scorned the Hiroshima bomb as a cowardly attack on defenseless civilians and of little military significance, wanted to attach three other conditions to the response to the Potsdam Proclamation. A messenger arrived, bearing the news that Nagasaki had just been destroyed by another "special bomb." The news hardly entered their discussion, showing how little the atomic bomb weighed on their scales of relative threats compared to the Soviet menace. The messenger, bowing apologetically, was sent on his way. "There is no other record in other materials that treated the effect [of the Nagasaki bomb] seriously," noted the official history of the Imperial General Headquarters.[14]

It is difficult to see any military or political usefulness of the Nagasaki bomb, exploded after Hiroshima had demonstrated the power of nuclear weapons and with the Soviet assault imminent. So it is even more difficult to imagine any moral defense for either the American men who chose to murder the people of another Japanese city on the eve of the Soviet intervention or the Japanese war faction who shrugged off this genocide of their own fellow citizens as insignificant.

After the emperor himself intervened, the peace faction finally won their long struggle to make the emperor's preservation the sole precondition for surrender. But the war faction managed to word the surrender to include not just the emperor but also all his powers. So on August 10, the Japanese government, "[i]n obedience to the gracious command of His Majesty the Emperor," submitted its formal surrender proposal: "The Japanese Government are ready to accept the terms enumerated in the joint declaration which was issued at Potsdam on July 26th, 1945, by the heads of the Governments of the United States, Great Britain, and China, and later subscribed to by the Soviet Government, with the understanding that the said declaration does not comprise any demand which prejudices the prerogatives of His Majesty as a Sovereign Ruler."

The U.S. response, drafted by Secretary of State Byrnes, who before Hiroshima had been adamant in insisting on "unconditional surrender," craftily conceded that the emperor would remain the emperor and commander of Japan's armed forces, but his authority and that of the Japanese government would be "subject to the Supreme Commander of the Allied powers." Truman and his advisers, in fact, wanted the emperor to remain—despite the uncomfortable fact that he was a major war criminal—to serve as a bulwark against communism, to maintain the infrastructure of the state, and to prevent continuing warfare by diehard military commanders of the remaining Japanese forces in Japan and on the Asian mainland. They were well aware that the emperor was the only person in the world who could command the military to stop fighting and the populace to submit to the occupation. Hence this wording in what is now known as the Byrnes Note, delivered to Japan on August 11: "The Emperor will be required to authorize and ensure the signature by the Government of Japan and the Japanese Imperial General Headquarters of the surrender terms necessary to carry out the provisions of the Potsdam Declaration, and shall issue his commands to all the Japanese military, naval and air authorities and to all the forces under their control wherever located to cease active operations and to surrender their arms, and to issue such other orders as the Supreme Commander may require to give effect to the surrender terms."

While these negotiations were going on, more than a thousand Air Force and Navy bombers continued a rain of terror on Japanese cities, killing more than fifteen thousand Japanese between August 10 and 14.[15] The arch militarists of the war faction, as usual, cared nothing about the civilian deaths and continued their fight to preserve the emperor's divine power. So their struggle with the peace factions continued until August 13. The only way to break the stalemate, Prime Minister Suzuki realized, was to go for a second time to the emperor. Asked why this could not wait a few more days, as War Minister Korechika Anami demanded, Suzuki replied, "I can't do that. If we miss today, the Soviet Union will take not only Manchuria, Korea, Karafuto, but also Hokkaido. This would destroy the foundation of Japan. We must end the war while we can deal with the United States."[16] It was this meeting with the emperor on August 13 that led to the acceptance of the conditions in the Byrnes Note, something that would not have been possible if the United States had continued to insist on unconditional surrender and had not recognized the legitimacy, however limited, of the emperor's rule.

Perhaps the most grotesque and tragic irony is that it was the United States, not Japan, that conceded on this one crucial issue—*after* the atomic bombs *and* the Soviet defeat of the main Japanese army on the Asian continent. What if the atomic bomb had never been used and the Potsdam Proclamation had included the wording of the Byrnes Note? Of course we can never answer that question—which is really the question of whether the atomic bombing of Japanese cities was necessary and therefore morally defensible—because Truman chose to use the bomb both *before* the Soviet entrance into the war and *before* restoring to the Potsdam Proclamation its original provision for allowing Japan to keep its emperor.

So the big question of growing importance through the Cold War and its aftermath into our present era is not "if" but "why." As early as 1948, British Nobel laureate in physics and leading wartime military expert P. M. S. Blackett concluded that "the dropping of the atomic bombs was not so much the last military act of the second World War as the first major operation of the cold diplomatic war with Russia."[17] In the ensuing decades, a growing mass of evidence and fine scholarship has shown that President Truman, Secretary of State Byrnes, and Secretary of War Henry Stimson passionately embraced the bomb as the winning weapon in their struggle with the Soviet Union over the shape of the postwar world.[18] When Leo Szilard, the scientist who had initiated the Manhattan Project, attempted to warn Byrnes of the terrifying implications of atomic weapons, the secretary of state "did not argue that it was necessary to use the bomb against the cities of Japan in order to win the war" but rather that "our possessing and demonstrating the bomb would make Russia more manageable in Europe."[19] Stimson looked upon the atomic bomb as "a badly needed 'equalizer'" of Soviet power. He and Truman both considered the bomb their "master card" filling in "a royal straight flush" in the poker game they were playing against the Russians.[20] So one answer to "why" is now obvious to anyone familiar with the historical record.

But there are other possible answers, none of which exclude Truman's desire to "make Russia more manageable" and give the United States more power in shaping the postwar world. All the available evidence shows that Truman and his advisers "expected, indeed hoped" to use their nuclear weapons and that atomic attacks were an "active choice, a desirable outcome, not a regrettable or painful last resort."[21] But why the hope and desire? Psychologists must have some answers. But my own experience—as a child during World War II, an as eleven-year-old celebrant of victory looking forward to a peaceful future, as a college student in 1953 given the assignment in Air Force ROTC class of planning a nuclear attack on Vladivostok, as a Strategic Air Command navigator in the late 1950s, as an antiwar activist during the Vietnam War, and as a historian of American culture—has led me deep into the history of America's cultural imagination to find the answer most relevant to our situation today.

Hiroshima and Nagasaki are part of a fateful continuum in American culture dating back to the eighteenth century. That was when Robert Fulton invented and built superweapons designed to bring about perpetual peace and prosperity. It continued until we created the weapons capable of annihilating our species and plunged ourselves into a perpetual state of increasingly ominous war. Along the way, Harry Truman came to imagine himself in a role dramatized in future-war fiction that he read as a young man, the role of an American president who uses the ultimate weapon to create a perpetual and prosperous Pax Americana. Truman believed what I and the other eleven-year-olds in the back of that pickup believed. But he was even more childish than we were. And like us boys building our model bombers and basking in the glow of America's fleets of Flying Fortresses and Superfortresses, the president was unaware of how the American belief in the ultimate superweapon had somehow morphed into the fascist doctrine of "strategic bombing."[22]

Dozens of books and hundreds of articles have argued that the Hiroshima and Nagasaki bombings mark the definitive beginning of the Cold War and led to our losing the peace. A more difficult and troubling question is whether they made us lose the war. After all, if this was a war against fascism and militarism, who won?

The atomic bombings grew directly out of the matrix of the fascist doctrine, codified by Italian general Giulio Douhet, British air marshal Arthur Harris, and American general Billy Mitchell, of "strategic bombing," a euphemism for the terror bombing of civilian populations, and the applications of this doctrine in World War II. The aerial terror bombing of civilian populations began as a means of colonial control, first by Italy in Libya in 1911, and later by France and, most extensively, by Britain in Iraq. The British firebombing of German cities, including Hamburg and Dresden, was a blatant example of the fascist theory of warfare. But the United States has long pretended that the massive bombing of German (and many other European as well as Asian) cities by vast fleets of heavy U.S. bombers was actually "precision bombing." During the war, we were told that it was a marvelous American invention that made this precision bombing possible: the Norden bombsight. Being in those years an ardent fan of the bombers, I believed in the miraculous powers of the Norden bombsight, including its advertised ability to drop a bomb "into a pickle barrel from 20,000 feet." But how could a fleet of hundreds of bombers, unloading long strings of high-explosive bombs through winds they could not compute (and often under attack by antiaircraft fire and Nazi fighter planes), possibly "precision bomb" a particular target in the middle of a city? They couldn't, and they didn't. Ironically, the Norden bombsight was used in the two least "precision" bombings of the war: Hiroshima and Nagasaki.[23]

To maximize casualties, both bombs were detonated in the air over the cities (Hiroshima at 1,900 feet, Nagasaki at 1,650 feet), so accuracy was not a major concern. Nevertheless, each bomb was supposed to be aimed at a specific target, not to minimize but to maximize casualties. The Hiroshima bomb missed its target by about three football fields. The Nagasaki bomb missed by almost two miles, greatly reducing casualties because it exploded over a valley, leaving many people somewhat protected by intervening hills.

Controversies about World War II bombing swirled through a series of panels and symposiums on the history of strategic bombing, hosted in the nation's capital by the Smithsonian's National Air and Space Museum in October 1989. The series was arranged by the museum's new Director, distinguished astrophysicist Martin Harwit, who was hired in 1987 to help shift the institution away from catering to mere gawkers at military and space hardware to a more intellectually challenging site. As a participant in the series, I remember presentations by World War II bombardiers and pilots about the unmasking of "precision bombing." Early in the bombing campaign a preflight briefing officer would post a large city map and point out to the assembled crews the raid's target, such as a tank factory or a railway yard. One panelist described how puzzled the assembled crews were the first time a briefing officer merely rolled down the map of a city. "Where's our target?" some bombardiers called out. "There," he responded, leveling his pointer at the city.

The incendiary bombing of the cities of Japan made it blatantly clear that "strategic bombing" was really the terror bombing of civilian populations, exactly what Douhet, Harris, and Mitchell advocated. Some historians lay all the blame on Air Force general Curtis LeMay. Having served as a Strategic Air Command navigator and intelligence officer under LeMay, and also knowing of his alarming role in the Cuban Missile Crisis, I consider him to have been a dangerous madman, indistinguishable from General Jack Ripper in *Dr. Strangelove*. But LeMay did not originate the strategy of cremating Japanese cities and the people who lived there. He merely carried it out—with extraordinary zeal and frightening efficiency.

The strategy came from far higher levels. Napalm was developed by American scientists specifically with the goal of creating unquenchable, self-sustaining firestorms in the cities of Japan, especially in the working-class districts, with their dense concentrations of wooden homes. The civilian population was the main target, as can be seen in replicas of typical Japanese homes constructed in 1944 at Maryland's Edgewood Arsenal, complete with shoji screens, Tatami mats, and bedding, constructed for testing napalm bombs.[24] A city's "crowded districts of highly inflammable houses offered"—as the official history of the Army Air Forces explains—an "ideal incendiary target."[25] Even First Lieutenant Ronald Reagan had a role in what he called one of the major "secrets of the war, ranking up with the atom bomb": building in Hollywood a complete miniature of Tokyo, so authentic in detail that even top Air Corps generals could not distinguish films (with Reagan's thrilling voice-over narrative) of the burned-out toy city from the burned-out real city, evidently obliterating, along with Tokyo, boundaries between illusion and reality.[26]

When Brigadier General Haywood S. Hansell Jr., commander of XXI Bomber Command, was ordered to switch from "precision" bombing of industrial targets to saturation firebombing of entire cities, he protested. He was promptly removed and replaced, on January 20, 1945, by LeMay.

LeMay got right to work. His firebomb raid on Tokyo on February 25 left one square mile of the city burned out. Encouraged by these results and the total lack of any Japanese air defense, LeMay ordered all defensive armaments removed from the B-29s so that they could carry even more incendiary bombs. Dropping any pretense of precision bombing, he swiftly began his full campaign to incinerate the cities of Japan. Within a few months, this strategy would produce more casualties among Japanese civilians than their armed forces suffered throughout the war and also kill far more people than were killed by the Hiroshima and Nagasaki atomic bombs.

On the night of March 9, the target was a twelve-square-mile rectangle in Tokyo that housed one and a quarter million people. For three hours, hundreds of B-29s unloaded their firebombs. Instead of mere firestorms, the blazes produced a new and even deadlier phenomenon—the sweep conflagration, a tidal wave of fire igniting every combustible object in its path by radiant heat, melting asphalt streets and metal, leaping over canals, and searing the lungs of anyone within reach of its superheated vapors. The heat was so intense that it generated towering thunderheads with bolts of lightning. The last waves of bombers had difficulty finding anything left to bomb, and they were tossed around like leaves by the thermal blasts from the fires below. Sixteen square miles of the city were burned out. More than 267,000 buildings were destroyed, and over a million people were rendered homeless. More than 100,000 people died that night in the Tokyo inferno. No wonder LeMay had contempt for the atomic bomb.

The success of the Tokyo raid ratified the genocidal strategy of cremating the population of Japan. By the end of June, every major city—except a few reserved for a new secret weapon—had been destroyed. By early August, all that were left were the four reserved cities, any of which could easily be destroyed by a routine incendiary raid. Two of these were Hiroshima and Nagasaki.

Forgotten was President Roosevelt's 1939 "urgent appeal" to every warring government "that its armed forces shall in no event, and under no circumstances, undertake the bombardment from the air of civilian populations." By 1945, would anyone still, like FDR, call the "ruthless bombing from the air of civilians" a "form of inhuman barbarism" or say, as he did, that it "has sickened the hearts of every civilized man and woman, and has profoundly shocked the conscience of humanity"? Imagine any secretary of state in 1945, claiming as FDR's Secretary of State Cordell Hull did in 1939, to be "speaking for the whole American people" when he asserted, "No theory of war can justify such conduct."[27]

Thus we need to confront a profoundly troubling question—not whether the bomb helped win the war, a question we should now put to bed, but a question about the Good War itself. If what we were fighting against in World War II were not just enemy nations but fascism and militarism, then did the atomic bombs that massacred the defenseless populations of Hiroshima and Nagasaki—coming as a grand climax to our "strategic bombing" of European and Asian cities—help bring us victory? Or defeat?

Enthusiastic audiences packed the Air and Space Museum's series on strategic bombing, thus encouraging Harwit's continuing development of provocative exhibits and programs. In 1991, I was commissioned to evaluate for the museum a proposed exhibit on the original *Star Trek* TV series. I suggested turning it into a deeply historicized exhibit, exploring *Star Trek* within its context of the Vietnam War, the antiwar movement, the "long, hot summer" urban revolts, changing concepts about gender roles, and other features of the sixties. The result was *Star Trek and the Sixties*, an exhibit for which I was the advisory curator.

Meanwhile, tens of millions of miles away the robot spacecraft *Magellan*, peering with its radar devices through the boiling acid clouds that shroud Venus, was in the process of transmitting a complete topographic map of the surface of Earth's sister planet, as sharp and as clear as photographs. "We now have a better global map of Venus than of Earth," exclaimed one Jet Propulsion Laboratory scientist, explaining that no map of our own planet had so completely traced the topography beneath the oceans.[28] An amazing achievement of space exploration, this topographic picture of Venus was acutely relevant to our own destiny, showing what a catastrophic greenhouse effect could do to a geologically similar planet.

As the advisory curator of *Star Trek and the Sixties*, I was working in the museum on the exhibit's script and design during the late summer of 1991. Each day as I entered the museum I passed two large video monitors flanking the entrance lobby. The one on the left was playing a spectacular computer-enhanced color video of *Magellan*'s grand tour of Venus. The one on the right was playing *Weapons of the Gulf War*, familiar footage of missiles and warplanes, still streaming on TV into American households months after President George H. W. Bush had declared a swift and decisive victory in what has since turned into our endless war in Iraq. The largest group I ever saw watching the Venus video was three people; sometimes nobody at all was at that monitor. But every day a mob of people jostled for viewing space in front of *Weapons of the Gulf War*. Many, especially boys and young men, beamed with pleasure and excitement.

I remembered my own boyish excitement about the American wonder weapons of World War II. But these monitors and the museum as a whole reminded me more keenly of the thrills I felt during my many visits, from boyhood through my teens, to the old Hayden Planetarium in Manhattan, where there were no weapons and where space travel was just an exciting exercise of the imagination. The Smithsonian's Air and Space Museum of the 1990s, on the contrary, brimmed not only with artifacts and videos from our actual space travel but also with the superweapons that can annihilate our species, including the intercontinental missiles.

The contrasting reactions to the videos projected on the two monitors were not an auspicious omen for the serious side of our *Star Trek and the Sixties* exhibit, which attempted to highlight such things as *Star Trek*'s evolving didactic messages about the Vietnam War, racial conflict, and gender roles. Anticipating a large audience, Mary Henderson, who was the museum's art curator and the main curator of the show, and I arranged for the endless lines that would be feeding slowly into the show to pass between two long walls containing giant iconic pictures that would give visitors the experience of simultaneously entering the world of *Star Trek* and the world of 1960s America.

Star Trek and the Sixties turned out to be the most popular exhibition in the history of the Air and Space Museum. After more than a million people attended the exhibit in Washington from February 1992 to January 1993, it traveled to that old Hayden Planetarium of my youth (before that venerable institution was demolished and replaced by the high-tech high-concept new Hayden Planetarium).

The success of *Star Trek and the Sixties*, including extremely favorable visitor reviews, even for some of the most potentially controversial parts of the script including my Vietnam War and urban rebellion texts, encouraged Martin Harwit to move forward with a long-planned 1994 exhibit titled *The Crossroads: The End of World War II, the Atomic Bomb and the Cold War*. The central artifact of the exhibit, set to open on the fiftieth anniversary of the atomic bombing of Hiroshima and Nagasaki, was the cockpit and nose section of the *Enola Gay*. Advised by a distinguished panel of academic and military service historians, the museum's curators carefully crafted a script that explored the historical context from different perspectives, including controversies about the atomic bombings.

On its way to Hiroshima, the *Enola Gay* flew unmolested without any fighter escort over a devastated nation with few remaining antiaircraft defenses. The giant plane would not encounter its first combat until forty-nine years later, in Washington, D.C. The Air and Space Museum's *The Crossroads: The End of World War II, the Atomic Bomb and the Cold War* exhibit was intercepted by barrages of flak from the Air Force Association (an aerospace industry lobbying group), the American Legion, and platoons of right-wing radio hosts and politicians who wanted the *Enola Gay* to be an icon of victory and who denounced the museum and the script writers as anti-American puppets of all those liberal professors who had hijacked the universities and American history itself. Adding to the furor, many World War II vets proclaimed that they owed their lives to the atomic bombs. On September 23, 1994, the U.S. Senate passed a resolution, by a vote of 99-1, declaring that "the role of the Enola Gay during World War II was momentous in helping to bring World War II to a merciful end, which resulted in saving the lives of Americans and Japanese." The Senate had come a long way since 1939, when it condemned the "inhuman bombing of civilian populations."

The Senate resolution reviled "the current script for the National Air and Space Museum's exhibit on the Enola Gay" as "revisionist and offensive to many World War II veterans."[29] By this time, "revisionist" had become the standard term used to brand all historians who deviated from what was supposed to be the triumphal orthodoxy of all loyal and patriotic Americans: The sacred gospel that the atomic bomb ended World War II in a glorious American victory over fascism and saved the lives of hundreds of thousands of American soldiers who otherwise would have died in the invasion of Japan.

The Smithsonian was forced to deep-six its script and leave the *Enola Gay* to speak for itself to those throngs of tourists who pour through the Air and Space Museum, mainly to ogle its hardware. Martin Harwit, who had presided over some of the museum's most popular and intellectually challenging events, was forced to resign in May 1995. In his letter of resignation, he wrote: "I believe that nothing less than my stepping down from the directorship will satisfy the museum's critics." As for the *Enola Gay*, the iconic plane was later fully restored and remains on display at the Air and Space Museum's annex at Dulles International Airport.

Although political and cultural orthodoxy won the public battle over the *Enola Gay* and the atomic bombings, it had already lost the war among historians. More uncertain is the outcome of the cultural war waged against "intellectual elites," as Republican Senate majority leader Bob Dole labeled historians in a 1995 speech to the American Legion, in which he blasted the Smithsonian and its scriptwriters with these words: "Where we see a proud past, they see a legacy of shame."[30]

The war over the atomic bombing of Hiroshima and Nagasaki is not, however, a battle between the emotions of pride and shame. It is about how we understand the past and its effects on the present and the future. Six years after our glorious atomic victory, our government was presenting Bert the Turtle as a great role model for American citizens and youngsters. So soon all over America, children were not cheering about peace but practicing "duck and cover," as they cowered under their desks at school.[31] And today we are spending tens of billions of dollars annually "modernizing" our thermonuclear weapons and perfecting the means of delivering them while abandoning all hope of getting rid of them.

3 ▸ NEW CONNECTIONS

THE FIRST TIME I went to Bedford-Stuyvesant was when my mother brought me home to 1437 Dean Street. It was 1934, and I was just a few days old. My mother had been born twenty-nine years earlier in another old Bedford-Stuyvesant house, 1608 Fulton Street, just five blocks away.

Saying "Bedford-Stuyvesant" to most New Yorkers, especially those from Brooklyn, is like saying "Harlem" to most other Americans. Right away people start thinking race. For many decades the Bedford-Stuyvesant section of Brooklyn has been a kind of second Harlem, an African American center of black experience and culture, viewed by many white New Yorkers as hostile alien territory. Even today, when the skyrocketing price of New York City real estate is driving affluent white home seekers into rapidly "gentrifying" black and brown neighborhoods, whites remain a small minority in "Bed-Stuy."

But until the mid-1930s, Bedford-Stuyvesant was a cluster of tree-lined neighborhoods where white middle-income families basked in the American dream of permanent homeownership, especially of their old brownstone row houses, like 1437 Dean Street. Then the Great Depression struck like a plague. When many of the homeowners lost their jobs and small businesses, they could no longer afford to pay off their mortgages or maintain their spacious dwellings. As the Depression drove these homeowners out, it drove in a much larger population of renters, black families swept out of the economically devastated rural South and into the overflowing rentals of Harlem. Bedford-Stuyvesant's new identity was welded by steel in 1936, when the IND Fulton Street subway line was completed, providing, not by coincidence, a direct rapid transit connection from and to Harlem.

My father and mother were neither white homeowners being driven out nor black renters being railroaded in. They were a young Jewish couple seeking shelter from the hurricane of the Depression.

Though born in Jersey City, my father lived in Brooklyn from the time he was a few weeks old in 1903 until he died in 1963. He attended high school for five months before dropping out at the age of fifteen to support his mother. His first job was as a runner on Wall Street, where he worked in various white-collar jobs the rest of his life, except for several years after the stock market crash in 1929. During the forty-five years from 1918 to 1963, he never missed a day's work except when unemployed, when his mother died, and when he himself was dying.

He met my mother, a commercial artist, in the mid-1920s. At the age of fifteen, her portfolio had gotten her into Cooper Union, where she studied for four years. During later hard times she used her art background to get jobs like clerking in the art supply section of an Abraham & Straus department store and selling wallpaper in a decorating store.

My parents' choice reminiscences were about speakeasies and other naughty fun in the Jazz Age. My favorite works by my mother are stunning pen-and-ink drawings of flappers, which ran in newspaper ads for hip feminine garb of the 1920s.

After they married in 1928, Mother and Dad rented and furnished an apartment at 115 Lenox Road. They had some help from my mother's parents, Isaac and Sadie Cohen, the homeowners of 1437 Dean Street. Grandfather Isaac was doing well with a small shoe store he owned in a Brooklyn working-class neighborhood. He was even able to lend my father money to set up a one-man stock-trading operation on Wall Street.

Then came the crash. My father's business venture was wiped out. Unable to pay the rent on their home, my parents had to sell their furniture and move into 1437 Dean Street. In 1930, my grandfather was forced to sell his shoe store. My dad was able to scrounge up jobs: sanding floors, clerking in a furniture store, and two stints of assembly work in a radio factory. The two families were able for a while to keep their heads above the economic tsunami. For the only time in their married life, my parents in 1933 thought they were doing well enough to have a child. Hence the arrival of

Howard Bruce in 1934. Calamity came the next year, when Grandfather Isaac died. Grandma and my parents were shocked to discover they were broke and in debt. Grandfather had borrowed $1,200 from his brother, which my father now had to pay back at $5 a week, each payment duly acknowledged by the lender's signature on a tattered piece of notepaper I discovered in my mother's desk after her death. Mortgages and taxes had eaten away all the equity in 1437 Dean Street, which had to be sold in 1935 to pay off back taxes. My family never owned another home.

Forced out of this home, my parents rented the bottom floor of a large old wood-frame two-family house at 1731 East 51st Street right around the corner from the old trolley barn in Flatlands, then a low-income, mainly Irish and Italian working-class neighborhood. Grandma Sadie lived with us there. This is the first house I remember. According to my parents, we were the only Jewish family in this all-white neighborhood.

My lifetime ambition on East 51st Street was to be a garbage man like the three uncles of Gene McPartland, my best friend and next-door neighbor. Gene and I stood in awe of the macho guys—all white—who rode the garbage trucks, yelling and swearing and banging the big metal cans they effortlessly hurled.

In 1940 the four of us moved to Flatbush, into 935 East 13th Street, a narrow red brick row house in a neighborhood of middle-income workers, shopkeepers, and professionals. Behind our row houses ran a dirt delivery alley used by the coal trucks, whose men rolled barrels of coal down their metal ramp over our cellar steps with a deafening roar that drove our cat, Blackie, into a terrified frenzy while our cellar filled with coal dust that had to settle before my father could shovel the excess piles into the coal bin (with some help from me in a few years). The alley was also used by the ice truck, whose driver deftly carried big blocks of ice with his tongs right into the top of our icebox, which was scrapped in the industrial boom after World War II when we got our first refrigerator. Behind the alley were two tall apartment buildings that faced onto East 14th Street. On the north corner of our block was an Orthodox shul. On the south corner was the Midwood Theatre, one of the grand movie palaces of the 1930s, where I spent most of my Saturday afternoons, watching double features, matinee serials, and the latest RKO newsreels of the war. Waves of Jewish refugees retreating from the Nazi advances in Europe were pouring into the neighborhood, displacing many of the professional and working-class homeowners. The Italian American family that shared the wall on one side of our house stayed, and I can still taste the figs from their backyard trees, originally brought over from Sicily and wrapped every winter in multiple layers of colorful thick quilts. The genteel Protestant family that shared the wall on the other side was replaced after the war by a young couple of Zionist gunrunners who tried to be as unobtrusive as possible about their nighttime deliveries and shipments of wood crates.

In 1952 our landlord decided to sell our house and gave us first dibs. But we couldn't afford to buy, and rents were rapidly rising around us in those boom times. A couple of Mother's cousins agreed to let us rent the top floor of their two-story frame house at 246 Westminster Road, in the third exclusively white neighborhood I was to call home. So from 1936 until I left to join the Air Force in 1956, I never had a home that was, as far as I know, within several miles of the home of any black family.

Until 1956, when I married Jane Morgan, who had grown up on a tobacco farm in North Carolina, I had always thought that racial segregation was what they did in the South. Jane had thought that racial integration was what they did in the North. But she grew up playing with the black children of the tenant farmers on her parents' land, and she stayed in touch with one of these childhood friends for several decades. I never really knew a black person until I was fifteen. True, Jane went to all-white public schools from first grade through high school, schools legally mandated to exclude the black kids who walked past her grade school to their one-room "Colored" school and were later bused many miles to Nash County's only "Colored" high school, legally "separate but equal" to the county's thirteen all-white high schools. But I too went to all-white public schools. Unlike Jane, I knew nothing about the schools attended by the black children of my hometown. Jane and I have been learning about America from each other for more than six decades now.

I think that one reason my parents moved from Flatlands to Flatbush was to get me into a better public school. So from first grade to eighth grade I went to P.S. 99, a huge old brick four-story building that looked like a prison and was run like one. Because there were three other boys named Howard in my first grade class, I got to be Bruce but had to keep the H., bestowed on me in honor of Hannah, my dad's mother who died shortly before I was born. I started out being a good boy, for which I was rewarded by being skipped one semester three times, thus getting me bullied and socially ostracized by my classmates, who were all almost two years older. My only friends were two kids who also were skipped, Robert Factor and Edith Kopperman, my red-headed heartthrob. Then I discovered that being a bad boy could make me more or less socially acceptable. By the seventh grade I had even gained admittance to a small gang or, as we called it, a club, named the Rockets.

Some of my new friends prided themselves on minor shoplifting. One easy target was a candy store and soda fountain we passed on the way home. My first loot was just two pieces of candy, which evoked howls of ridicule from my pals. So the next time I grabbed a bunch of candy with both hands. Before I could stuff my swag into a pocket, a large shape appeared behind me, big hands seized my neck and arms, and I was hurled into the street with curses and threats bombarding my ears and ego. My humiliation became excruciating when I noticed Edith watching from a few feet away.

The experience convinced me that I should get better at being a bad boy. I was soon getting into minor scrapes in the streets and piling up demerits in school. By the eighth grade I was getting suspended so often that sometimes my mother was in P.S. 99 more days than I was.

My parents rescued me by getting me admitted in 1946 to Brooklyn Friends, a small Quaker school in downtown Brooklyn. To me, now twelve, it was like heaven. Teachers were friends to the students, not their dictators. We were encouraged to lead an active intellectual life, something I had never experienced in school. Here I encountered the first progressive ideas I had ever heard coherently expressed: mild pacifism, idealistic internationalism, militant anti-racism, and a philosophy of community and mutual respect. Our education was liberal in content and democratic in form.

But even at Brooklyn Friends, racial integration was just beginning. The first two black students—children of the school janitor—were now in the first two grades. So the preschool and upper ten grades in this pre-K-to-12 school were still all white.

It was a bit awkward for the totally segregated America that emerged from World War II to proclaim itself as the leader of the "Free World" and the champion of universal democracy. So in the early postwar years, the liberal wing of the rampaging anti-Communist legions launched an offensive against segregation on multiple fronts. In 1948 President Truman issued Executive Order 9981, ordering desegregation of the armed forces. Hollywood contributed such timidly anti-racist films as *Home of the Brave* (1949), *Pinky* (1949), and *No Way Out* (1950). Sports, though, were destined to lead the way.

In the spring and summer of 1947, just after my first year at Brooklyn Friends, racial issues were the talk of the town in Brooklyn as Jackie Robinson joined the Dodgers, becoming the first black player in baseball's "major" leagues (which of course didn't include any of the "Negro" leagues). Dad and I sometimes went to a neighborhood bar on the corner of Coney Island Avenue and Avenue I on a Saturday to cheer with the other local guys as we listened to Red Barber's exciting play-by-play radio broadcast of a Dodgers game. There was no regular TV broadcast of baseball games yet, since there were only about 44,000 TV sets in America, including about 30,000 in New York City. Before the game started, many of the guys were ranting about the "uppity nigger" who was ruining baseball. They opined that colored people didn't have the same ambitions as white people, were generally contented with their lot and probably were happier than white people because they weren't caught up in the rat race, and that one college-educated smart aleck like Robinson (none of these commentators had been to college) could create a lot of trouble for innocent colored people, mainly by stirring up a lot of racism. When my newfound social consciousness prompted me to question some of this, I was told that I was just a typical thirteen-year-old kid who didn't know what I was talking about, especially since I obviously had never known any colored people.

That was true enough. Although I had grown up in a city containing almost two million black people, that city was so thoroughly segregated that I had never personally known a single black individual. The closest I had come was when my father hired a middle-aged African American man who owned a pickup to help us move. Then the three of us had sat around in the kitchen, the two men drinking beer, joking, and telling stories. Dad used to tell people about this as an event, and as an example of Negro and white people treating each other as equals.

The subway I took home from Brooklyn Friends, usually at rush hour, was the Brighton Line of the BMT. When I got on at Lawrence Street, near Borough Hall, about one third of the passengers were black. A few more would get on at the DeKalb Avenue, Atlantic Avenue, and Seventh Avenue stations. Then the train, which had been underground all this time, would go through its final long tunnel and emerge into the open air at the Prospect Street station.

By this time, the subway car would be close to half black. Here we were, riding along, all mixed up, black and white, standing and sitting, dozing and reading newspapers, paperbacks, and ads. Wasn't *this* integration? This wasn't like the segregated South, where blacks had to sit in the back of the bus and even give up their seats to white people. Years later, when I went to the South for the first time, riding a bus from New York to New Orleans, I was still shocked when we crossed the Mason-Dixon Line and all the black

people, as though acting on some silent command from an invisible dictator, got up and moved to the back of the bus.

But there also seemed to be a silent command from an invisible dictator
as we approached the Prospect Park station. Every black face would point
toward the doors on the right side of the car, every black body would begin
to move toward a door, and the white bodies that had been standing would
move back away from the doors, many of them heading for warm seats just
vacated by black passengers.

As soon as the doors opened, every black person, with rare exceptions,
would leave the car. Where were they going? They were transferring to the
Franklin Avenue Shuttle, which would take them to Bedford-Stuyvesant, my
birthplace. Many would probably get off at the Dean Street station. Maybe
someone would even walk to 1437 Dean Street. Others would get off at the
other stations in Bedford-Stuyvesant. Maybe some were on the way to
Harlem. Having started at one end of the shuttle, they would get off at the
other end, the Franklin Avenue station; there they would transfer from the
BMT to the IND and board the Fulton Street Line, that mass-transit fast-
track link to Harlem completed in 1936, the year my family moved from
Bedford-Stuyvesant.

I didn't know this history then, nor did I have any concrete images of the
destinations or lives of these black people. I had no sense of Bedford-
Stuyvesant as my first home. To me, like most of my fellow white Brook-
lynites, it was just a dangerous foreign land inhabited by dark aliens.

One of the life-changing pleasures of a tiny school like Brooklyn Friends
was the opportunity for anybody to compete in interscholastic team sports.
I had never played any sports except street stickball where East 13th Street
dead-ended on a train culvert, and our games were usually cut short when a
neighbor called the cops on us. Short and slim, I was usually one of the last
guys picked for a team. But at Friends I got to play on the varsity soccer,
basketball, and baseball teams for two or three years. Yet in all the games
we played, I can remember only two when our all-white team encountered
a black player, just one, on an opposing team.

Of course most of us boys at Friends were also crazed sports fans. I was a
bit more obsessive than most. At age thirteen I was subscribing to the weekly
Sporting News. So being a bit nerdish, I could quote Duke Snider's batting
averages as I followed him through the Brooklyn Dodgers' minor league
farm teams at Fort Worth and St. Paul, promising classmates that he would
make them forget our hero Dixie Walker. On non-school days, some of us
would lurk around the Sullivan Place entrance to Ebbets Field before 11 A.M.

to get autographs from the Dodgers as they straggled in before lunch and batting practice. I tried to model myself on Eddie Stanky, the second base-man known as "The Brat," who made the most of his limited natural talent, or, as his manager Leo Durocher put it, "He can't hit, can't run, can't field. He's no nice guy. . . . All the little SOB can do is win." I was elated when Stanky led the way in supporting Jackie Robinson against the hostility of other players, led by the outspokenly racist Dixie Walker, now our fallen idol. We were part of a new generation of Brooklyn boys cheering for Rob-inson and two other black stars that the Dodgers brought in from the Negro Leagues, Roy Campanella (1948) and Don Newcombe (1949). I sometimes wonder how the men in that local bar and elsewhere around America responded to one sign of the changing times: the TV ad of Campanella shav-ing with a Gillette razor.

On winter weekend nights, we went to Madison Square Garden to copy the shooting styles of our favorite New York Knicks, and sometimes we even managed to get their autographs after the game. Here my idols were Bud Palmer, whose jump shot I tried to copy, and Carl Braun, the skinny shooting guard whose two-handed overhead shot helped me compensate for being just five foot eight inches, especially when shooting from the cor-ner against a zone defense. In all the many NBA games we watched, we never saw a black player because there weren't any—until the winter of 1950, when Sweetwater Clifton, a superstar from the fabulous Harlem Globetrot-ters, took the court in a Knicks uniform.

A major presence for us boys was Wally Longley, our fine soccer and baseball coach and virtuoso basketball coach. A former professional basket-ball player in that sport's early rough-and-tumble years, Wally magically transformed our limited talent into a fairly formidable team. On defense, he had us switch back and forth, on signal in the middle of play, from man-to-man to a variety of zones, bamboozling most of our opponents. If anyone bungled a pass in practice we had to go through all of our offensive plays with a medicine ball. He taught me how to study every mannerism of oppos-ing players so that when I played out front in our 1-3-1 zone I could steal passes and lead fast breaks. For many of us, this burly Irishman was a father figure and lifelong influence. I'm still guided by his two favorite watchwords: "hustle" and "improvise." Wally also linked some of us to another life he led, as the director of Camp Pratt, a large YMCA camp on Prince's Bay, a small cove of Raritan Bay, on the south shore of Staten Island. Each sum-mer the camp took thousands of the poorest boys from the slums of New York, five hundred at a time, and gave them two weeks of all the joys of summer camp—blighted only by a rigid barracks discipline and the polluted waters of the bay.

In 1949, Wally gave me my first full-time summer job, hiring me as a dishwasher, spare laborer, and snack-bar counterman at Camp Pratt. He also expected me to work on getting my basketball and soccer skills in shape for the coming year (even assigning a former professional Scottish soccer player as a kind of individual coach who trained me as a goalie).[1] One of our perks was swimming in that blighted bay, taking off from a long wooden pier and clambering onto a big float anchored about fifty yards away to sunbathe in off-hours. Camp Pratt was abandoned in 1952. I barely recognized the site the next time I entered Prince's Bay, on a small boat, fishing with three friends in 1997. All that was left were a few rotting fragments of the old pier, a stark contrast to the ostentatious new mansions now lining the south shore of the island.

Camp Pratt was another world for me. About two-thirds of the boys attending the camp and about half the camp's working staff were black. The counselors of course were all young, and so were most of the rest of us on the staff. It may have been a sign of the changing times or of the idealistic mission of the camp, or maybe it was the ambience of this interracial island inside the almost all-white Staten Island, that we young people from different races and backgrounds related casually, often as friends, without a quarrel that I can remember, or even hints of racial tension that I, in my myopic naïveté, could detect. Looking back, I am sure that our good relations masked plenty of racial tension but at the same time were sincere efforts to overcome our dreadful inheritance from America's history of slavery, segregation, and racial oppression, past and present. My ignorant belief that this terrible legacy was mainly a southern problem was probably shared by many of the other white workers, but it could hardly have been a delusion shared by the black workers.

This is not to dismiss all our good intentions. Our generation would soon provide much of the passion and courage, and many of the black and white ground troops, of the civil rights movement.

And something else was happening, though I didn't know was it was at the time. For decades, streams of African American culture, notably in dance and other music, had been flowing in the dominant culture, forming a subversive undercurrent. Blues, jazz, and the Lindy hop, Black Bottom, and Charleston dances appealed so powerfully to sections of young white Americans that a whole era of American history was named the Jazz Age.[1] In the 1930s, African American literature was a prominent feature of the most popular anthologies. Reaction came in many cultural forms. The New Critics, who announced their aims in *I'll Stand My Stand* (1930) and *Reactionary Essays* (1936), succeeded in valorizing the "Old South" and restoring an all-white literary canon. *Gone with the Wind* (1936 novel and 1939 film) brilliantly updated the benign vision of slavery dramatized in Woodrow Wilson's film favorite *Birth of a Nation* (1915).[2] But there seemed no antidote to the fatal attraction of millions of young white people to African American music and dance. When we black and white workers danced at Camp Pratt, our favorite was the Hucklebuck, that wildly provocative dance craze that burst out of Harlem and swept the nation in 1949.

I found my own world rapidly expanding as for the first time in my life I was relating to black people, from the slum kids to my fellow workers—and to my boss. We two dishwashers worked without machines in a kitchen that was feeding about six hundred people each meal. Our boss was Boisy, the African American chef. Like a couple of other cooks in charge of large kitchens in which I've worked, Boisy was eccentric, tyrannical, and quick-tempered. He ran his kitchen with an iron hand, one that sometimes menacingly brandished a meat cleaver, and I did what I was told, including eating second and third and fourth helpings whenever he or his wife, Carrie, thought we kitchen workers were not showing the proper appreciation for their cooking.

In between cleaning with my fellow dishwasher the thousands of plastic cups and dishes, trays, and utensils from the lunch meal and helping to get the kitchen ready for supper, my main job was working behind a counter in the late afternoon when the boys who had any spare change could stand in long lines to buy hot dogs, ice cream, and soft drinks. The other person who usually worked behind the counter was Joan, a nineteen-year-old African American woman who spent most of the day typing and keeping books in the front office. Joan was working her way through CCNY, the city's great historic college, America's first free institution of higher learning. She was the most sophisticated woman I had ever known. We quickly got to be friends. Then I fell madly in love with her.

I was a fifteen-year-old with no previous sexual experience, except a few clumsy childhood encounters. So I had no clue how to bridge the chasm between the passionate visions that kept me awake at night and the presence of the real Joan during the day. Joan and I slept in the same building, at opposite ends of the cavernous gymnasium-theater, which had the sleeping quarters for the men workers upstairs in the front and for the women workers upstairs in the back.

The main office was also in this building, and at night a bunch of us would hang around drinking beer, smoking, and socializing. One night every seat in the office was filled when Joan walked in, looked around, and, to my paralyzing astonishment, sat on my lap. As the evening went on, I hardly dared to move a muscle. People started drifting away and other chairs became vacant, but Joan, amazingly, stayed sitting on my lap, sharing a can or two of beer with me. Eventually everybody else left, and we were still sitting there. I had no idea what to do next and was still worried that she might be offended by anything I might do. We must have sat there in silence for close to a quarter of an hour, while I agonized in timidity and dread that she would say goodnight and leave. Finally, I thought of what seemed to me a cool, sophisticated thing to say.

"You know something, Joan," I whispered in her ear.

"What?" she asked softly.

"I've never kissed you," I replied cavalierly, omitting the fact that about the only people I *had* ever kissed were relatives, friends of my parents, and girls in spin-the-bottle and post-office games.

"That's true," she said patiently. We spent most of the rest of the night in the office.

After that, we sometimes would go to our respective sleeping quarters, wait until everyone else seemed asleep, then tiptoe downstairs to meet in the big gym-theater room, and walk down to the beach, where we would stay until near dawn.

I loved Joan deeply and believed, in my innocence and romanticism, she felt the same way about me. It was more likely that she felt free to relate to me because I posed no threat of a serious relationship that might derail the planned course of her life. I was clueless then and still have few clues about Joan's inner thoughts and feelings, but they must have been more reality based than mine. Whatever she felt, I'm still grateful for our time together.

In what seemed to me the very relaxed relations among all of us black and white workers, we made no effort to hide our relationship, but we also never displayed any physical signs of it, not even holding hands while in public. I never told anyone about it, but there were hints that it was no secret to Joan's best friend. Sometimes it seemed that Joan was less guarded about our relationship among white people—even when that might pose physical danger—than she was among black people. That puzzled me.

One night Joan and I were out watching the moon at the end of the wooden pier along with James, an African American fellow worker older than me and younger than her, whom I considered a close friend. We were sitting there, our backs to a railing, smoking and drinking beer, with Joan in the middle. After a while I put my arm around her. She took it away quickly and tried to tell me something. James stood up angrily and strode off down the pier without looking back. I thought he was just jealous. Joan patiently explained to me that James disapproved of any black woman relating to a white man. "How could that be?" I insisted. "He just wants you to relate to him." James never spoke to me again.

Staten Island was an incongruous place for new connections in 1949. Although it is one of New York City's five boroughs, its only physical connections with land back then were three ancient bridges linking it to New Jersey across the narrow waterways of Arthur Kill and Kill Van Kull. To get to Staten Island from Brooklyn, Queens, or the Bronx, one had to first get to the southern tip of Manhattan and then take the Staten Island Ferry across New York Bay. Disconnected from the city, Staten Island was bypassed by those great waves of African Americans pushed from the South in the Depression and subsequent decades. Many of New York City's white cops joined the resulting white flight to Staten Island to abide by the letter of the regulation that all New York Police must reside within the city. In 1949, fifteen years before the Verrazano Bridge connected it to Brooklyn, Staten Island was a white island. Even today it is the only one of New York's boroughs where non-Hispanic whites are the majority.

I think Joan and I both enjoyed defying the glaring white racist world surrounding the interracial Shangri-la of Camp Pratt, and being with each other during the day on Staten Island outside the camp probably added to the excitement of our relationship. But generally we had company in our forays into hostile territory. On our days off, Joan and I were sometimes part of a group of black and white workers from the camp who took a bus about seven miles to spend an afternoon at a miniature golf course in the town of New Dorp. We got lots of hostile stares, especially at a local diner, but we were young and confident in our strength and unity. And Staten Island was not in Mississippi.

Only once were Joan and I brazen and crazy enough to go on an expedition as a lone couple. We took a bus all the way to the main Staten Island city of Saint George to see a movie she was especially interested in. She was the only black person in the huge old ornate theater, which seemed to bulge with a menacing white audience. We were prudent enough to sit in the last row of the balcony. The movie was *The Fountainhead*, starring Gary Cooper and Patricia Neal in Ayn Rand's first cinematic dramatization of her individualist philosophy. Joan's choice was not as incongruous as it might appear. Although Rand was a prominent figure in the postwar anti-Communist repression and remains a leading ideologue of the twenty-first-century far right, her glorification of defiant individualism might also be taken as a counter to conformism then and even now.

The anti-Communist and racist frenzy of the period was hardly an expression of any kind of individualism, including Rand's. During our last week of August, near Peekskill, New York, white mobs armed with baseball bats and rocks attacked the interracial audience of concertgoers awaiting the arrival of the world's most famous singer and black civil rights leader, Paul Robeson, who had previously given three successful concerts at the same venue. The attack, facilitated and encouraged by the police, left more than a dozen victims in the hospital. The attack turned out to be just a dress rehearsal for the violence—this time with enthusiastic police and Ku Klux Klan participation—inflicted on the people leaving the rescheduled concert on September 4, which left hundreds seriously injured.

At the end of the summer, Joan and I were more in love than ever, or so I thought. We each went back home to Brooklyn, she to Bedford-Stuyvesant and me to Flatbush. I told her that I'd call her and we'd go out the first weekend. When my parents learned that I had been going out with a "Negro girl," their agony knew no bounds. We had a terrible quarrel. They forbade me to see her. I said I might marry her.

I called Joan, and we arranged to meet at a movie theater near the Atlantic Avenue BMT stop. When I saw her on the street in front of the ticket booth, she looked nervous and uncomfortable. We held hands in the movie, but we both knew the summer was over and we were back in Brooklyn. I don't know what movie we saw that day. We never saw each other again. Not even on the subway.

In September I went back to my all-white Quaker high school. Two years later I would begin four years of 1950s-style higher education at Amherst College, which had admitted its first two black students the year before I got there. As the leader of the Free World, America was striving to look a bit less apartheid than South Africa. It had to. During that summer of 1949 at Camp Pratt, the Soviet Union had tested its first atomic bomb. And in October came the birth of the People's Republic of China, a nation whose people were not of European descent and who made up a quarter of the world's population.

4 ▸ WORKING FOR COMMUNISTS DURING THE KOREAN WAR

AT 7 A.M. on Monday, June 4, 1951, I eagerly but nervously walked the half block up East 13th Street, turned onto Avenue J, and passed the two blocks of small stores on the way to Coney Island Avenue. The vacant storefront where I had turned in my collected scrap metal for the war effort from 1942 to 1945 was now a thriving kosher delicatessen. A trolley car was sliding along the street rails in the middle of Coney Island Avenue, clanging away, its tilted electric mast sparking against the overhead lines. I raced to catch it and climbed aboard. It took me to Mayfair Photofinishing Company, where I would begin working for leading members of the Communist Party of Brooklyn.

I had just graduated from high school on Friday and had had a boozy wild time at our prom that night amid the faded elegance of the grand ballroom of the old Hotel St. George in Brooklyn Heights. The Korean War had been raging for just a year. Or so I thought.

On the night of August 10–11, 1945, as Soviet forces were destroying the Japanese army in Manchuria and Korea, Army Colonels Dean Rusk and

Charles Bonesteel were ordered by the War Department to draw a line across Korea, a nation with a two-thousand-year history. They were given thirty minutes to complete the task. Neither of the two young men, each born a year before Japan annexed Korea in 1910, was familiar with Korea's history or even its geography, other than what they could glean from a small outdated National Geographic map.[1]

Japan's occupation of Korea, facilitated by President Theodore Roosevelt in 1905, had been brutal and grotesquely exploitative. During World War II, hundreds of thousands of Koreans were forced to work in Japanese mines and factories, and countless numbers perished under the U.S. bombing, including ten thousand or more who died in the atomic bombing of Hiroshima. Tens of thousands of Korean girls and young woman had been forced to become "comfort women," sex slaves for the Japanese army. But the occupation was about to end. Advance Soviet forces had already landed by sea, and large numbers were pouring across Korea's northern border with the USSR. The nearest U.S. forces, however, were six hundred miles away in Okinawa and would be unable to get there for about a month. The fate of Korea had not previously been discussed by Washington and Moscow. Hence the War Department's frantic decision to draw a line across Korea without a minute to spare. The idea, as Dean Rusk remembered, was to "keep at least some U.S. forces on the Asian mainland, a sort of toehold on the Korean peninsula for symbolic purposes."[2] Thus Japanese forces south of the line would be instructed to surrender to U.S. forces; those to the north were to surrender to the Soviets. Once Colonels Rusk and Bonesteel drew their line, it would be forwarded up the military chain of command all the way to President Truman, who would then submit the proposal to Premier Stalin. The two colonels chose the 38th parallel north latitude, simply because that put the capital city of Seoul under U.S. control. President Truman of course approved. Premier Stalin, to the surprise of the line drawers, made no objection, although Soviet forces could easily have occupied all of Korea weeks before American forces could arrive.[3] Neither Washington nor Moscow consulted the Korean people about this decision.

Except for Seoul, most of southern Korea was agricultural, and most of the people were peasants working for a small class of large landowners. When the American military finally did arrive on September 8, they discovered two competing infrastructures in their occupation zone. One was a police state created by the Japanese occupiers, designed to protect the wealth and power of the large landowners and the mercantile elite in the cities and towns. The other consisted of hundreds of "People's Committees" throughout the land, all part of the "Korean People's Republic" proclaimed in Seoul just prior to the U.S. arrival. Guess which side the United States chose. Thus very quickly the Japanese military occupation was replaced by a strikingly similar American one.

All that was missing was a puppet government. This gap was filled a month after the U.S. Army began its occupation. The Office of Strategic Services (OSS, the predecessor of the CIA) anointed Syngman Rhee, who had been living in the United States for thirty-five years, as the head of government. A military plane flew Rhee from Washington to a secret meeting with General Douglas MacArthur in Tokyo, and MacArthur's private plane, *The Bataan*, then whisked Rhee to his new capital of Seoul. In the ensuing three years of overt U.S. military occupation, Rhee's Japanese- and now American-trained police waged a remorseless campaign to eradicate all dissidents suspected of being Communists or having communist leanings, including land reformers and those seeking independence from the United States.[4]

In March 1948, during the third year of the occupation, the year-old Central Intelligence Agency, along with the intelligence divisions of the Departments of State, Navy, Air Force, and Army, prepared an eye-opening secret report: "The Current Situation in Korea." This document recognized a fundamental class conflict between the overwhelming majority of poor people in the south and a "numerically small class which virtually monopolizes the native wealth and education of the country," a "class that could not have acquired and maintained its favored position under Japanese rule" without "collaboration" with the occupiers. Seeking a ruler untainted by this collaboration left only such "imported expatriate politicians" as Syngman Rhee, "demagogues bent on autocratic rule." The report recognized a "reservoir of popular resentment against the police," who are "ruthlessly brutal in suppressing disorder." It predicted that "Extreme Rightist Rhee" would sweep forthcoming elections held under the auspices of the U.N. because of "the demagogic appeal of the Extreme Right" and because "the Left will boycott the elections." Then "Soviet propaganda would be provided with a substantial basis in fact for charging the regime with being 'corrupt, reactionary, and oppressive.'" As for northern Korea, the CIA analysis acknowledged that "there is no reliable evidence of any serious disaffection" because of "the characteristically shrewd Soviet recognition of the basic needs of the native population (land reform, political participation, education, etc.)."

The report concluded that it is "unlikely that any government erected in South Korea under UN auspices could long survive the withdrawal of US forces unless it were to receive continuing and extensive US economic, technical, and military aid."[5] The CIA was quite right. From the election of Rhee until the outbreak of the full-scale Korean War in June 1950, civil war raged in South Korea. Major rebellions were put down only with the assistance of the U.S. military, and over a hundred thousand South Korean civilians were killed, many tortured to death.[6]

Soviet forces withdrew from North Korea in 1948, leaving behind a government led by Kim Il Sung, a Communist who had spent much of his life as an anti-Japanese guerrilla leader in Manchuria. The southern government in Seoul and the northern government in Pyongyang have always agreed, then and now, on one thing: Korea is one nation, not two. Each has always claimed, then and now, that it is the legitimate government of Korea. Leading up to the events of June 1950, Seoul and Pyongyang each initiated attempts to reunify the nation—on its own terms, of course. The southern government's attempts were crippled by several problems. As the CIA report made clear, it lacked a viable economy independent of massive U.S. aid. Historically, it had been dependent on the north for coal, industrial products, and, crucially, electric power generated by power plants on the Yalu River. In February 1950, the U.S. Congress enacted the Korean Aid Bill, mandating that all U.S. aid would cease "in the event of the formation in the Republic of Korea of a coalition government which includes one or more members of the Communist Party or of the party now in control of the government of North Korea." The United States thus nullified any possibility of near-term peaceful unification. Then in May, South Korea's first somewhat free election was a disastrous defeat for Rhee's government, leaving him with only forty-five seats in the 210-seat Assembly, but not stopping his threats to invade North Korea.[7]

Armed conflict across the 38th parallel between the equal-size armies of the two governments had been going on intermittently since 1949. There is still conflicting evidence about which one started the fighting before dawn on June 25, but the issue is unimportant. The North Korean army was in a position to drive across the foreign-imposed and arbitrary dividing line of the 38th parallel, taking advantage of the illegitimacy and unpopularity of the Rhee government, which helps explain the immediate collapse of the South Korean army.

But this was not the narrative we Americans heard. For us, the "beginning" of the war was framed as a repeat of the beginning of our World War II narrative: an unprovoked surprise attack by treacherous Asians.

It sure was a surprise to me. So was my response. Earlier in 1950, Wally Longley had resigned the directorship of Camp Pratt and bought a run-down camp on a lake in rural New Hampshire. He hired several of us from the school basketball team to help rehabilitate the camp and then stay on as camp workers while sharpening our basketball skills during that summer. Once again, because I was still too young to be a counselor, my bosses would be Boisy and Carrie, whom Wally had lured from Camp Pratt to run the kitchen. They may have been the only black people for many miles around. Even when I hitchhiked to Concord, the state capital, every Wednesday to do my laundry and watch a movie, about the only dark-skinned people I saw were construction workers who must have spent many hours in the northern sun.

Getting the camp fixed up before the kids' arrival was frenetic work. Along with some of the counselors, we recruits from Friends cut trenches and laid tile lines for sewage, cleared brush and trees, sprayed under-eave wasp nests, and repaired buildings. We were all amateurs in these jobs.

On one hot Sunday June afternoon, we cut about halfway through a towering pine, only to realize that it was going to fall on a building it overhung. Since we couldn't un-saw it, the only solution seemed to be to get a stout rope fastened near the top and then have everyone pull on the rope to guide it away from the building while the chainsaw finished the cut. To execute this madcap scheme, someone, with rope attached, would have to climb the tree. Being the lightest guy, I was chosen by unanimous vote (except for mine). Vainly I pleaded my acrophobia and youth. My terror was almost paralyzing. The pine swayed more and more ominously the higher I climbed, while the rope gained weight from each new yard added to the length dangling from my waist. Then I had to use both hands to untie the rope, loop it around the tree trunk, and tie a secure knot.

We didn't get finished felling the pine and cutting it up until early evening. After a hurried dinner, some of us retired to the barracks-style building where we were housed. One of the counselors turned on a portable radio to get some music. Instead we heard the grim voice of a newsman denouncing the North Korean Communists for launching an invasion of South Korea without warning or provocation. It was June 25 in America, June 26 in Korea.

Two days later President Truman in a brief radio message to the nation announced that he was sending "air and sea forces to give the Korean Government troops cover and support" as well as "military assistance to the forces of France" in "Indochine." This all sounded to me like moderate, maybe timid responses to the Communist invasion. But Truman also announced that he was sending the 7th Fleet into the waters between China and Formosa to keep the Communists from attacking Formosa and to force "the Chinese Government on Formosa to cease all air and sea operations against the mainland." Why, I wondered, was the president not backing up General MacArthur, one of my wartime heroes, who wanted to unleash Chiang Kai-shek's anti-Communist forces to take back China? Was he under the influence of all those dozens of Communists in the State Department, who had been exposed a few months earlier by the intrepid Senator Joseph McCarthy?

On June 29, Truman told a press conference, "We are not at war." He heartily agreed when a reporter asked if this was just a "police action," a term that stuck, something like a pie on the president's nose. It wasn't until July 8, after the South Korean capital of Seoul had fallen and the North Koreans were still racing south after defeating the first U.S. forces, that the Pentagon acknowledged that large numbers of American troops would soon be fighting on the ground and that the draft might have to be greatly expanded. That night the conversation in our quarters was all about the war. Two of the counselors were eighteen. They were worried about getting drafted. I announced that I'd like to be two years older so I could go fight the Communists.

Really? I had just been terrified of dying from a fall out of a tree. So now I was some movie hero ready to die fighting to save my country and the Free World? Was I still as blind to the reality of war as that kid looking out the Manhattan apartment window on December 7, 1941, eagerly awaiting the Japanese warplanes? Maybe my bravado could be excused because of my age and because I had grown up in the intensely militarized culture of World War II. But how could a nice, liberal Jewish Brooklyn boy attending a Quaker school also be such a rabid anti-Communist?

During World War II, patriotic Americans were supposed to see the Russians as our heroic allies. And we did, maybe especially us kids. When I was eight, General Douglas MacArthur told the nation that "the hopes of civilization rest upon the worthy banners of the courageous Russian Army" and that their heroic "resistance to the heaviest blows of a hitherto unde-feated enemy, followed by a smashing counterattack which is driving that enemy back into his own land" is "the greatest military achievement of all time."[8] At age nine, I was thrilled when I saw Frank Capra's 1943 government-sponsored documentary *The Battle of Russia*, with its gloriously inspiring vision of the Soviet Union's epic struggle against the Nazi invasion, in the gigantic Midwood movie theater on the corner of East 13th Street and

Avenue J, half a block from my brick row house. Many years later, Jane told me how thrilled she was when she saw the film at the same time in the small segregated theater in Bailey, population two thousand, the nearest town to her North Carolina farm. Our government also encouraged the production, sometimes with help from the Office of War Information, of lots of other pro-Soviet movies such as *Mission to Moscow* (1943), based on the book by U.S. ambassador to Moscow Joseph Davies; films with special appeal to youngsters like *Three Russian Girls* (1943) and *The Boy from Stalingrad* (1943); *The North Star* (1943); the romantic *Song of Russia* (1944); and *Counter-Attack* (1945). In 1944, I was proud of my Dad when he gave an electrifying speech in support of Russian War Relief to an overflow crowd that packed another of those giant 1930s movie palaces in our neighborhood, especially when the audience responded with an ovation and many buckets of their hard-earned dollars.

The process of transforming me into a true believer in a Soviet empire on a mad quest to conquer the world and in a vast underground conspiracy of American Communist traitors eager to do its bidding was swift. It was well on its way by 1946, when I was twelve. By then the inspiring images of Russian soldiers in their dazzling white uniforms staunchly advancing across vast frozen snow-covered steppes were replaced in my mind by thick red paint spreading over the globe from the North Pole and a giant red octopus squatting on top of the planet, each of its thick red tentacles clutching a helpless nation (replacing the giant yellow octopus representing Japan until mid-August 1945).

From 1946 until the summer of 1951, the only narrative I ever heard—or likely could have heard—about the Soviet Union and Communism was the Red Menace. Like just about everyone of my age as well as most adult Americans, I had no idea that America had been intermittently participating in anti-Communist and anti-Soviet campaigns ever since the Russian Revolution, with World War II as just a brief intermission. President Woodrow Wilson dispatched thousands of American troops to Russia to join military forces from fourteen nations in the war against the "Bolsheviks" from 1918 to 1920. The United States did not recognize the Soviet government until 1933, ten months after FDR took office, and then the FBI and Congress redoubled their anti-Communist witch hunts.[9]

If President Truman in the months after the end of war were looking for the one person in the world with the longest and most fanatical anti-Communist career, what better candidate could he have found than Winston Churchill? Churchill, who said frequently that "Bolshevism should have been strangled at birth," had been a central figure in organizing that fifteen-nation military intervention in Russia. In May of 1945, just after Germany's surrender but while World War II was still raging in Asia, Churchill had the British chiefs of staff draw up a plan, code-named Operation Unthinkable, for a surprise attack by forty-seven British and American divisions plus ten German divisions to take place on July 1 against Soviet forces in Europe. On March 5, 1946, Truman took Churchill by train to Fulton, Missouri, where the president introduced the speech by the former prime minister that is often cited as the official declaration of the Cold War. The speech was to guide America on a path that Churchill promised would lead to a world of universal freedom, democracy, and prosperity. We have indeed followed that path—to the present state of the world.

The speech provided two metaphors that proved essential to the Cold War outside and inside the United States: the "Iron Curtain" (a term coined in 1943 by Nazi Minister of Propaganda Joseph Goebbels) and "Communist fifth columns." With the magic wand of his oratory, Churchill transformed all Communist parties, including those heroic leaders of European Resistance against Nazism and Fascism, into "Communist parties or fifth columns [that] constitute a growing challenge and peril to Christian civilization," while he transformed the "British Empire," then overlord of about a quarter of the earth's surface, including enslaved colonies in Africa, Asia, and the Middle East, into the guiding light of global freedom and democracy. "Soviet Russia" and its "fifth columns," he explained, desire "the indefinite expansion of their power and doctrines." Since "there is nothing" the Russians "admire as much as strength, and there is nothing for which they have less respect than weakness, especially military weakness," we must abandon "the old doctrine of a balance of power." "A quivering, precarious balance of power" would merely offer "temptation to ambition or adventure." On the contrary, the Anglo-American alliance for the free and prosperous future must be based on total military supremacy, "an overwhelming assurance of security."[10] Though I didn't hear the speech, I soon soaked up its message from my culture and my government.

In 1947, the Central Intelligence Agency (CIA) was created, the Department of War was reorganized and renamed the Department of Defense, and on March 12 President Harry Truman convened a joint session of Congress to proclaim that "the gravity of the situation which confronts the world today" forces the United States to lead a global struggle against the "totalitarian regimes" that "endanger the peace of the world" and "the welfare of our own Nation."

In his statement, which came to be known as the Truman Doctrine, the president defined Greece and Turkey as the two fronts where America must immediately act because both nations were in danger of being taken over by the international Communist conspiracy. There was no specific event, much less a Pearl Harbor or a 9/11. Anyone today familiar with the actual historical situation might have trouble understanding how two such flimsy pretexts could have stampeded the nation to plunge into the frenzy of militarization and repression that would follow.[11]

Nine days after his call for a global anti-Communist crusade, President Truman issued Executive Order 9835. Claiming that "the presence within the Government service of any disloyal or subversive person constitutes a threat to our democratic process," Order 9835 required loyalty oaths from almost three million government employees and an investigation into their beliefs and associations. Subsequent executive orders soon extended the loyalty oaths and investigations to three million members of the armed forces and three million workers in war production, now renamed the "defense industry." Within two years, twenty million U.S. citizens would have secret dossiers in the files of federal police agencies.

The Red Menace now became the horror story of a nation so obsessed with hunting down every American Communist, every "sympathizer," "dupe," and "fellow traveler" that it succeeded in establishing a quasi-police state and a state of permanent war. The savage repression particularly targeted anyone with access to a public audience, especially filmmakers, writers, journalists, librarians, and teachers at every level from grade school to graduate school. The House Un-American Activities Committee (HUAC), which had begun ferreting out Communists in 1938, led the charge, publishing a list of 608 "un-American" organizations. In December, ten distinguished Hollywood writers and directors were indicted, and later sentenced to prison and blacklisted, for refusing to discuss their political beliefs and affiliations under interrogation by the HUAC, which thus forced total anti-Communist subservience on the entire filmmaking industry. Loyalty oaths proliferated throughout colleges, universities, newspapers, and radio and TV networks. Employees who refused to take oaths or who cited the Fifth or First Amendments to the U.S. Constitution in refusing to answer Senate or House committee questions about their beliefs or associations, or the beliefs and associations of other people, were summarily fired. Since the Soviet Union was holding international conferences and sponsoring organizations (such as the World Peace Council) calling for peaceful coexistence and the outlawing of nuclear weapons, all "peaceniks," especially those in the Ban the Bomb movement, were generally regarded as Communist sympathizers or dupes, if not worse.[12]

By 1948 and 1949, anti-Communism was as pervasive in America as the air we breathed (which was loaded with radioactive contaminants from our land and sea nuclear bomb tests). I was exposed to it whenever I picked up a copy of *Readers Digest*, the *Saturday Evening Post, Life, Look*, and the *New York Times*. Even when I bought a copy of the *Brooklyn Daily Eagle* just to read its brief account of one of our high school basketball games and to find in its box score how many points I had scored, I couldn't quite escape a dose of anti-Communism. Now when I walked up the block to enjoy a Saturday afternoon double feature at the Midwood theater, instead of pro-Soviet and anti-Nazi newsreels and features I saw anti-Soviet anti-Communist newsreels and features like *The Iron Curtain* (1948), *Walk a Crooked Mile* (1948), *The Red Menace* (1949), *The Red Danube* (1949), *Conspirator* (1949), and *I Married a Communist* (1949), later given the sexier title *The Woman on Pier 13*.

The U.S. attorney general published a list of 160 "subversive" organizations and declared that Communists were "everywhere" in America, "in factories, offices, butcher stores, on street corners, in private business. And each carries in himself the germ of death for our society."[13] Liberals agreed that Communism was a disease. Senator Hubert Humphrey called it a "political cancer in our society." Illinois governor Adlai Stevenson said it was worse than "cancer, tuberculosis, and heart disease combined."[14] The problem now was the great difficulty in telling ordinary wholesome Americans from those who had become aliens after being infected with the insidious Communist disease, like the alien body snatcher in one of my favorite science fiction stories, John W. Campbell Jr.'s 1938 novella *Who Goes There?* So like other good Americans I was now wary of people with symptoms of Communist infection, especially teachers and politicians.

Then in 1949 the Russians tested an A-bomb, and "we" "lost" China to the Communists. How, asked our political leaders and our media, could all that have happened without the connivance of the Communist fifth column of traitors burrowing deep into our defenses and government and dedicating themselves to destroying America? So my response in June 1950 to the Korean War was not as demented as it seems to me today. In fact, it was quite typical and representative of loyal patriotic Americans. Maybe we were all demented. Or just tragically gullible.

Like 81 percent of Americans, at first I enthusiastically supported Truman's decision to send U.S. forces into action in Korea. Congress greeted the news with actual applause, and no newspaper opposed the move except the *Daily Worker* on the left and the *Chicago Tribune* on the right.[15] Flush with the rush of victory culture from World War II, we had no doubt that our indomitable soldiers, backed up by the air force that had crushed Germany and Japan, the navy that had won the Pacific, and American industry and technology, would have little difficulty defeating some primitive troublemakers like the North Korean Communists. And if China or Russia wanted to pick a fight with us, that would just give us a chance to unleash our invincible forces, which had been held back while the Reds were grabbing China.

Meanwhile, back at the camp, I was having a fun summer, playing basketball and swimming every day. Across the lake was a girls' camp. The favorite hangout for workers from the two camps was at the north end of the lake, at a hotdog and soft drink stand run by vaudeville star Pat Rooney Jr., who taught us tap-dance routines. A counselor from the girls' camp I'd met at Pat's sometimes would pick me up in a canoe, which was sort of romantic but turned out to be not the optimal venue for lovemaking.

During July, disturbing news intermittently broke through this summer idyll. The U.S. and South Korean forces (now referred to as "the U.N. forces") were suffering humiliating defeats and were steadily being driven south. In early August, they finally halted the North Korean advance, but by then the only U.S. toehold was inside the Pusan Perimeter, a mere 140-mile line defending the southeast tip of the Korean peninsula. The news during the rest of the summer was less demoralizing, since the line was holding against repeated North Korean attacks.

When I arrived back at Brooklyn Friends in September for the start of my senior year, the military situation seemed stalemated, with the "U.N. forces" still holding Pusan against "fanatic" attacks by "hordes" of North Korean Communists. Unlike World War II, the war in Korea flitted only fitfully through daily life. There were no victory gardens, scrap metal drives, or ration stamps, and of course no air raid wardens, blackouts, or remnants of torpedoed ships washing up on the beaches of Coney Island. There was puzzled frustration about why we weren't winning the war and a growing, angry sense of disbelief as we became aware that we might be defeated.

Every day I pored over the *New York Times* for the latest news from Korea. Like most Americans, I was thrilled on September 15 by the electrifying news that General MacArthur, in a brilliant maneuver, had struck back with a surprise major amphibious landing at Seoul's port of Inchon on Korea's west coast, just a hundred miles south of the 38th parallel. The U.S. and South Korean forces swiftly recaptured Seoul and drove north against relatively light resistance. When MacArthur reached the 38th parallel, it seemed the United States had successfully achieved the objective of the intervention, and many people believed the war would now end.

On September 30 and October 1, China repeatedly warned the United States that it would intervene if U.S. forces crossed the 38th parallel and continued toward the north. Most of us were delirious with the intoxicating taste of victory as MacArthur ignored this warning and audaciously split his troops, sending one prong northwest toward the North Korean capital of Pyongyang while a major force raced northeast along the coast toward the Yalu River, Korea's border with China. Pyongyang was captured on October 19, and in the east the mad dash toward China was meeting little resistance. A truly victorious end of the war now seemed near.

But suddenly on October 25 the Chinese struck, bloodying major South Korean and U.S. units and forcing a chaotic retreat from the race to Yalu. Then the Chinese forces mysteriously disappeared. MacArthur's forces on the west and the east resumed their push to the north. They encountered virtually no resistance. On November 20, an advance U.S. unit reached the Yalu River. The U.S. troops in the field could now pause on November 23 for a full Thanksgiving turkey dinner with all the trimmings.

The next day General MacArthur flew from his Tokyo headquarters to visit the soldiers and to launch an all-out final offensive to capture the rest of North Korea right up to its borders with China and the Soviet Union. "This should for all practical purposes end the war," declared MacArthur's official announcement, and "enable the prompt withdrawal of United Nations military forces."[16] "I hope to keep my promise to the G.I.'s to have them home by Christmas," he informally announced to the press.[17] On his flight back to his Tokyo headquarters later that day, he ordered his personal plane, an unarmed Lockheed Constellation, to fly along the Chinese border, defiantly wagging its wings.[18]

During the weekend of November 25–26, we heard the inspiring news that the Home by Christmas Offensive was rolling north on all fronts, encountering nothing but token resistance. But on Monday, as we returned to school from the Thanksgiving vacation, the *New York Times* reported that "strong enemy counter-attacks led by soldiers of the Chinese Communist armies stalled yesterday the United Nations general offensive," "some small units" had been "cut off in the enemy advance," one large unit had "pulled back as much as twelve miles," the enemy had "reoccupied the key town of Tokchon," one U.N. line was "crumbling," and one U.N. division was "reorganizing."[19] Like everyone I knew, I accepted the vision conjured up by the radio and newspapers of "hordes" of Chinese overwhelming badly outnumbered U.S. troops (a quantitative falsehood now set in the stone of American culture). The Chinese soldiers in my mind had the same faces and showed the same Oriental disregard for individual human life as those Japanese screaming "Aiiieeee!" in my World War II comic books.[20]

In history class that day, Mr. Harold Vaughan recapitulated the disturbing news and asked us to discuss the intervention of the Chinese forces. My own thinking was radically challenged by what happened next, which is why I remember the scene so vividly. Mr. Vaughan was the conservative of our faculty. He was also the most debonairly dressed man I have even known. Each day he appeared, his sandy hair neatly parted and combed flat, in a freshly pressed dapper suit, tailored to fit his trim body, which he carried with an almost military posture. Nothing so unusual about that. But unlike Albert Einstein, who was rumored to have seven identical suits so that he never had to waste time figuring out which one to wear, Mr. Vaughan never wore the same suit, not ever, at least as far as we could remember. We had various theories to explain this remarkable phenomenon. Maybe he was fabulously rich and just discarded or donated each suit. Maybe he was a model for a suit manufacturer. Well, whatever the inconsistent consistency of his dress, Mr. Vaughan predictably and consistently taught history from a purely conservative perspective. This was a bit odd for a Quaker school, but Mr. Vaughan never forced us to accept his views. Quite the contrary. He invited controversy.

Well, he got it that day, after he explained MacArthur's strategy. From Eddie Siegel. Tall, lanky, brilliant and knowledgeable, perpetually bursting with nervous energy, Eddie didn't fit any of the roles most of us were playing. He never tried to act macho like the would-be bad boys or super sophisticated like the would-be intellectuals (while I was trying to act both). He was sort of the class pinko. I was a conservative disciple of Mr. Vaughan, who fostered my lifelong interest in history. Eddie was a dear friend, who had managed my campaign for student body president. When he raised his hand, I sensed an impending confrontation. Eddie silently untangled his long legs from his cramped student desk, ambled up to the blackboard, snatched a piece of chalk, rapidly sketched a pretty good outline map of Korea, and then firmly drew a long line, running diagonally northeast up from the 38th parallel along the North Korean coast to the Chinese border.

"Why do you think," Eddie asked, glancing sideways toward Mr. Vaughan while twisting his head to face the class, "that MacArthur got all these troops stretched out into this long vulnerable line? Does it make any sense?"

"Here's China," he indicated, as he labeled the northernmost chalk line "Yalu R." Then he drew a bold fat arrow from the middle of the Yalu River border right through that thin line marking the advancing U.S. troops.

"This line was an invitation," Eddie announced. "MacArthur was inviting a Chinese attack. Because he wants a war with China."

Wow. I fancied myself a student of military history (having just done a term paper on the Franco-Prussian War of 1870), and I had been following the war in detail ever since the school year had begun. I was shocked. Even the normally imperturbable Mr. Vaughan looked stunned. After about a minute of silence, hands were waving all over, and soon the room was abuzz with opinions about the war and MacArthur.

I still think about this scene and wonder whether Eddie was right. His argument was at least as plausible as the explanations offered by historians ever since to account for one of the greatest blunders in military history: failure of military intelligence to detect two hundred thousand or so Chinese troops hidden in the mountains between the two prongs of MacArthur's offensive; the general's psychology, prone to hubris, arrogance, recklessness; overconfidence; an old man losing his mojo; a lengthy record of abysmal military judgment, evinced in his deplorable and disastrous conduct of the defense of the Philippines. After all, in October, after the earlier warning, the Chinese had displayed both their willingness to fight and their potent abilities. Why then were the U.N. forces encountering practically no resistance as they raced toward the Chinese border and the precious hydroelectric plants on the Yalu River, vital to both China and North Korea? It was like someone who had never heard of tsunamis blithely walking out onto the wet sand left as the ocean mysteriously retreated.

Eddie's high-school classroom intervention was the first truly dissident voice I can remember hearing in all those five years following World War II. Sure, there were ordinary people as well as politicians saying that we should never have gotten into a war in Korea or saying that we should stop fighting with one hand tied behind our back or saying both (all arguments that would soon become familiar about Vietnam). But I am embarrassed to say—in this epoch of the Vietnam War, the Afghanistan War, the Iraq War, and the dozens of other U.S. invasions and military interventions since 1945—that this was the first time I considered the possibility that American officials might concoct pretexts for our wars. Maybe I had never even wondered why the battleship *Maine* happened to be in Havana harbor, thus inviting a pretext for the Spanish-American War. Anyhow, Eddie succeeded in activating dangerous trains of thought in my sixteen-year-old brain.

By the end of the week, even the *New York Times* was letting us know that disaster had struck. Those Chinese forces hidden in the central mountains had split the U.N. forces, broken all their lines, shattered unit after unit, and forced even some of the best trained U.S. units into headlong flight, leaving behind most of their equipment and many wounded comrades.

In the next ten days, the news kept getting grimmer. Like a careless campfire, the offensive had ignited a forest fire. As I read and heard about the catastrophe, my mind kept picturing Eddie Siegel's chalk diagram. MacArthur's entire army was disintegrating amid the rout, with dreadful consequences for the soldiers—bleeding, wounded, and dying in temperatures 25 to 30 degrees below zero, often surrounded and sometimes abandoned, their units being chopped to pieces, retreating or fleeing in panic, some having to fight through enemy lines to reach ports where U.S. ships were evacuating survivors. By the middle of December, the U.N. forces, which had been on the verge of occupying the whole country, had been driven completely out of North Korea and were back once again below the 38th parallel. In January, the North Koreans once again captured the South Korean capital of Seoul. The Home by Christmas Offensive had turned into what was arguably the most humiliating defeat in the history of the U.S. Army and Marines.

A Gallup poll in January showed that two-thirds of Americans simply wanted to "pull out" of Korea altogether.[21] Meanwhile, however, renowned World War II general Matthew Ridgway was put in charge of the battered U.N. forces, which he soon led to a successful defensive line and then into a powerful offensive. By March his troops had once again recaptured Seoul and were moving steadily north.

On April 11, President Truman announced to a stunned nation that he had just removed General MacArthur from his command and replaced him with General Ridgway as supreme commander of the U.N. forces in Korea. A political firestorm exploded.

Having closely followed the news of MacArthur's calamitous defeat in North Korea, did I applaud Truman's decision? Hardly. I still revered the general, whom I now saw as a sacrificial victim of a contemptible president. How was this possible?

Growing up during World War II, I was acculturated even more than older Americans into a profound admiration of MacArthur as a military and then political leader. Like most Americans, I knew nothing about his woefully botched defense of the Philippines, eventually dooming seventy-three thousand of the men under his command to the horrors of the Bataan

Death March. Though he was informed of the attack on Pearl Harbor and then had almost nine hours to prepare for the expected attack on the Philippines, Japanese planes were able to annihilate on the ground most of his air force, including a fleet of potent B-17 Flying Fortresses and almost a hundred formidable P-40 Warhawks (the fighter plane with its grinning shark mouth already made famous by the Flying Tigers). Throughout the rest of the war, the administration and the media outdid each other in glorifying MacArthur and his egotistical promise, "I shall return."

So I had contempt for Truman for getting us into this "police action" and then denying MacArthur a free hand to fight the war. I was in the majority. A mere 28 percent of the American people supported the president.[22]

When MacArthur returned to the United States, a joint session of Congress gave him a standing ovation. Millions cheered him in ticker-tape parades in San Francisco, Chicago, and New York. Sitting in her class in Bailey High School, sixteen-year-old Jane Morgan was surprised to hear her mother delivering a long speech denouncing the president and lionizing MacArthur, piped from the principal's office through loudspeakers into every classroom.

While the nation was being possessed by MacArthur and listening to his Pied Piper tune, Ridgway's forces were crossing the 38th parallel and then holding partly just above and partly just below that line with no intention of continuing north. Negotiations to end the fighting would soon begin. Washington then would concoct a bizarre POW issue, successfully designed to deadlock negotiations for two years while U.S. bombers burned down every city and almost every village in North Korea, turning the entire land into a hellish desert. In those two years, American casualties from the war doubled. The exploitation of this issue succeeded in creating a destructive reimaging of POWs in American culture.[23] Both sides would then finally accept the 38th parallel, or more accurately the two opposing military lines straddling it, as a military armistice line, not a national boundary. Which is exactly where things still stand today, with the governments in Seoul and Pyongyang each claiming to be the legitimate government of Korea, which both recognize as a single nation.

So when I boarded that trolley car on June 4, 1951, and headed for my new job at Mayfair Photofinishing Company, the Korean War was almost back where it started a year earlier. And I was minutes away from meeting my bosses but weeks away from realizing they were Communists. And decades away from any understanding of them and from any knowledge of the true history of the Korean War.

The outside of Mayfair Photofinishing at 2817 Coney Island Avenue between Avenues Y and Z was just a storefront business that offered to develop, print, enlarge, or restore photographs. Behind the rear door of the store was a little office where Molly the bookkeeper worked and a four-room photofinishing factory that by 8 o'clock on this Monday was getting the first trickles of a flood of undeveloped snapshots taken over the weekend.

Ever since George Eastman in 1900 introduced his one-dollar Brownie box camera, mass-produced fifteen-cent film roll for it, and set up in Rochester commercial processing for its photographs, we have taken for granted the ability of anybody to make pictures of everyday life and record memorable moments and events. After the tough times of the Depression and World War II, increased leisure time and affluence helped the snapshot explode into a major industry and feature of American culture. It was also somewhat seasonal, which is how I was able to get my photofinishing job in the summers of 1951 and 1952.

Mayfair at that time was one of the largest photofinishing operations in New York City, where multiple neighborhood drugstores and camera stores competed to develop and print everyone's precious photos. Most people with undeveloped rolls of film as well as negatives for which they wanted multiple prints took them to the nearest drugstores. Choosier people took them to camera stores that promised expert photofinishing. But throughout Flatbush, Coney Island, and the Rockaways it made no difference; except for the rare pictures that were actually custom finished, almost all ended up at Mayfair. There Molly's husband, Phil, the developing man, working at a frantic pace in the cavernous darkroom where the only light was red and the temperature never dropped below 85 degrees, would load each metal film spool onto a rack holding thirty spools, pull the negative down from the spool, and attach a heavy clip to the bottom end of the negative. Each rack was slotted into a chain-driven machine, activated by Phil, that slowly moved the racked negatives through giant tanks of developing and fixing fluids. All the spools from the drugstores and the camera stores, and an even larger number of spools from Mayfair's robust mail order business, moved at the same pace through the same fluids, utterly disregarding all the carefully handwritten how-to-process notes on the envelopes attached above the rolls.

As soon as the negatives dried, we batch workers unclipped them, reunited them with their envelopes specifying print size and number of copies, and carried stacks to the four or five men working the printing machines. Then the prints, each now stamped with the number of its envelope, went through another developing process, emerging on a huge cylindrical rotating drier, to be picked off and sorted, mainly by eighteen-year-old Maria, who had recently arrived from Puerto Rico and was the only person of color at Mayfair. When the flow of prints accelerated, Maria got reinforcements from any of us batch workers not working the film racks, which gave us opportunities to flirt with her, while she seemed to enjoy using us to sharpen her English.

The printers included the three big muscular brothers who owned Mayfair: Joe Winston, the oldest at maybe mid-fifties and the calmest even on the most frenzied days; Murray Weinstein, gruff, tough talking, usually grim-faced, and the real boss of the shop; and Ben Weinstein, youngest of the three brothers and the most gregarious. I had a smidgeon of contempt for Joe, who had evidently changed his name to conceal his Jewishness, and respect for Murray and Ben for not following suit. The fourth printer was Dave Sherman, the union shop steward, who often made clumsy passes at Maria. At times when we were getting overwhelmed with volume, the aged father of the three brothers would work part of the day as the fifth printer. All told, about a dozen of us did all the work of the company.

We batch workers also worked the pickup and delivery shifts and routes, and Monday was the frantic pickup day that then deluged Mayfair with piles of envelopes filled with film rolls demanding to be developed and printed before promised deadlines. So I got home late and tired and hungry that night of my first day on the job. As I sat down to eat a hastily made sandwich, I picked up the afternoon's *New York Sun*, which was lying on the kitchen table. I was happy to read that the U.S. Supreme Court, by a 6-2 vote, had upheld the convictions of some top Communist Party members for "conspiring to teach and advocate the violent overthrow of the United States government." I did feel, though, that the five-year prison sentence for each man was too harsh considering that none of them had done anything but talk.

When the Court thus decided *Dennis v. United States*, one of the most important legal cases of the postwar period, it cemented the foundation of the repression essential to the Cold War and the militarization of American society. I was blithely unaware of how its outcome overhung every day of my two summers working at Mayfair.

The case originated on July 7, 1945, when J. Edgar Hoover ordered all the field offices of his FBI to gather material for a legal case to convict the Communist Party of being an illegal organization. After three frustrating years of searching for evidence of illegal activities, Hoover acknowledged in a secret memo to Assistant Director D. M. Ladd, "It is going to be a tough case at best." Ladd recognized the high stakes, noting that it would "result in a judicial precedent being set that the Communist Party as an organization is illegal," thus making it easy to prosecute "individual members and close adherents or sympathizers."[24] The government opted for the favorite charge of prosecutors without much of a criminal case: conspiracy. In this case, the eleven defendants, all on the national board of the Communist Party, were charged with conspiracy "to teach and advocate." To teach and advocate what? The overthrow of "any government in the United States by force or violence." The FBI and prosecutors indeed had a tough job because, as historian Ellen Schrecker puts it, "They were particularly troubled by the fact that the prospective defendants not only did not call for the overthrow of the American government by force and violence, but explicitly denied that they wanted to do so. Even worse were the inconvenient passages in the party's constitution that specifically abjured revolutionary violence and provided for the expulsion of people who advocated it."[25]

What could the prosecutors do? The main evidence they submitted were classic texts of Marxism-Leninism, such as *The Communist Manifesto*, published in 1848, and Lenin's 1917 treatise *The State and Revolution*, and testimony from informers and defectors, cherry-picked to exclude any who disbelieved the flimsy case. Judge Harold Medina, a rabid anti-Communist who believed that Communists were trying to hypnotize or possibly even assassinate him, presided over the trial, which went on for a full year from November 1948 to October 1949, establishing a record for the longest federal trial in history. Medina even cited all five defense attorneys for contempt and sentenced them to prison.[26] The conduct of the trial, its outcome, and media hostility to the defendants were all influenced by two events that occurred during the proceedings: the first Soviet test of an atomic bomb and the Communist victory in China.

The Communist defendants, underestimating the virulence of the political and cultural surround, openly proclaimed their true beliefs as a crucial part of their defense. They also naively believed that their convictions would surely be overturned by the Supreme Court. By June 4, 1951, when I learned of the decision, any member of the Communist Party or anyone deemed to be a "Communist sympathizer" had to expect to be fired from employment and criminally prosecuted, as well as shunned and scorned by people considering themselves loyal patriots. The more open they were about their beliefs and associations, the more obviously they were in jeopardy. But the less open they were, the more conspiratorial they seemed, thus confirming the cultural and political stereotype and now legal definition of "Communists."

I didn't think of any of this as I went back to work at 7 A.M. the next day at Mayfair. Weekends, unless they were rainy, made our usual summer workweek look something like this: Monday, 8 A.M. to midnight; Tuesday, 7 A.M. to 1 A.M.; Wednesday, 8 A.M. to midnight; Thursday, 8 A.M. to 7 P.M.; Friday 9 A.M. to 5 P.M.; Saturday, 9 A.M. to 1 P.M. There was no time for small talk during the very first days, but the relatively relaxed hours toward the end of the week encouraged conversation, the usual male ribbing, and even horseplay (especially arm wrestling because working the heavy clips on the drying racks gave us all pumped-up forearms). My 1951 patriotic political antennas soon detected in some of Murray's remarks, and to a lesser extent in Ben's, something suspiciously left of normal liberal, maybe not so much in content as in didactic style. And I wondered why Murray was often engaged in earnest, but rather one-sided conversation with Maria, which seemed to have a loftier motivation than Dave's flat-footed come-ons.

At lunchtime I sometimes went to the little candy store and soda fountain at the corner of Avenue Z to get a malted milk. One day during my second week at Mayfair, Ben came through the door and beckoned to Mike, the owner, who as usual was working the counter. He didn't seem to notice me, sitting at the far end of the counter noisily slurping the last dregs of chocolate through a straw. Mike reached under the counter, pulled out what looked like a rolled-up newspaper, and quickly handed it to Ben, who turned and left without a word to anyone. The next day, the scene repeated itself, this time with Murray getting the mystery package. My curiosity overcame my prudence.

"Was that a newspaper?" I asked Mike as he came for my empty glass.

"Yes, the *Daily Worker*," he almost whispered, though nobody else was at the counter. "They get me to order a daily copy for them. I'm not too crazy about doing it, frankly. But they're good customers, so I do it as a favor." After a pause, he added reassuringly, "Besides, it's just part of the business anyhow." Mike convinced me that he was merely a reluctant part of this menacing conspiracy.

Well, Murray and Ben must be Communists. Although the U.S. attorney general had warned us that Communists were "everywhere" in America, "in factories, offices, butcher stores, on street corners, in private business," most of us had never known for sure when or even if we had been exposed to a real live Communist and the deadly disease they were spreading.[27] So I would now have a fascinating opportunity to observe two of these alien beings in action, perhaps even as they tried to subvert me.

In those late-week slack hours, the conversation tended to drift, or more likely get steered by Murray, toward current events. Murray would look up from his printer, peer over his rimless glasses, and give a little speech, backed up by Ben's somewhat choral comments. When they talked about the desirability of peace and the need for the world to get rid of nuclear weapons, what I heard was Communist propaganda, no doubt designed to make America defenseless. Even when I completely agreed with them, as when they inveighed against racism and racist oppression in America, what they said still sounded to me like Communist propaganda. Why? Part of the problem was vocabulary. Whenever words such as "capitalist" or "imperialism" came out of their mouths, automatic responses were triggered in my highly acculturated brain.

Decades later, I took advantage of the lesson learned. Addressing a rally or political meeting or even a university class in the sixties and seventies, I would use one of these trigger words, such as "imperialism," and then pause, watching the responses, which were, at least back then, visible. Then I would ask, "What happened inside your head when you heard the word 'imperialism' come out of my mouth?" The resulting discussion was often quite educational.

There was another reason why the word "capitalist" garbled the message my two Communist bosses were trying to send to me, and other Mayfair workers may have had the same problem. After all, the plant was literally a sweatshop. The marathon hours combined with the frantic speedups under the watchful eyes of three bosses were enough to jeopardize health. The sauna temperature in the developing room was more or less endurable, while we could only work in the drying room, where any exposed metal was too hot to touch, for twenty- or at most thirty-minute stretches. Four of us were paid seventy-five cents an hour, plus time and a half for hours over the first forty in a week. So Murray and Ben's fulminations against the capitalist system mainly taught me that even capitalists, at least very small ones, can consider themselves "Communists." That later helped me understand how "Communist" leaders of the Soviet Union and China could preside over a system of crony capitalism that enabled their own self-enrichment.

Maybe I was being unfair to my two Communist bosses. Although they were making their living by exploiting their workers' labor, what other choices were available to them amid the anti-Communist fanaticism of the fifties? Besides, Murray and Ben, though co-owners of a small capitalist enterprise, were hardly well tailored and manicured parasites. Physically and mentally tough, adept in all the material aspects of the business, they worked as long and hard as any of us (though they did stay out of the developing and drying rooms). They never acted as our social superiors. Though hostile to most of their politics and resentful of my piddling pay for being what they might have called their "wage slave," I liked them personally and had a grudging respect for their steadfastness. If they were bona fide Communists during our anti-Communist fervor at home and war in Korea, I could regard them as traitors but certainly not as cowards.

Murray and Ben, as I gradually surmised, were not just members but also fairly high officers of the Communist Party in Brooklyn. Although their membership was an open secret, the subject itself was taboo. Sometimes they even made some faint pretense of not being affiliated. This of course made them seem furtive, reinforcing the stereotype and making me feel like a spy. They sure would have made more headway with me if they had been very open about their membership, but the *Dennis* case had turned them both into criminals the day I began working for them. And maybe Murray and Ben had more important tasks than trying to educate an opinionated and argumentative seventeen-year-old who admired Douglas MacArthur and supported Republican senator Robert Taft and Joseph McCarthy.

One of their most counterproductive arguments was praising the Soviet Union in comparison with the United States, such as telling me that I wouldn't have to work summers to pay for my college education because there all higher education was free and students were even paid a stipend. I kept to myself the fact that my public school was so bad that my parents had to get me into a private school. Since I knew that I really knew nothing about life in the Soviet Union, I sidestepped these arguments while becoming more convinced that American Communists really did serve as agents of our enemy.

To me their most preposterous argument was that our so-called democracy was a charade designed to make us believe that the government was truly our government when actually it was the government of the "capitalist ruling class." In the fifties, most Americans would, like me, have considered this Communist argument literally outlandish. Tweak Murray and Ben's wording just a bit—maybe by substituting "the one percent" for "the capitalist ruling class"—and most Americans today would likely nod or respond, "Everyone knows that."

And how many people today, especially in comparison with the 1950s, believe that the government is our government, a democratic government, a government of the people, by the people, and for the people? Since 1958 the University of Michigan has been conducting a scientific study every two years in which a broad range of Americans are asked this question: "Would you say that the government is pretty much run by a few big interests looking out for themselves or that it is run for the benefit of all the people?" In 1958, 17.6 percent believed a "few big interests" while 76.3 percent believed "for the benefit of all." During the Vietnam War, the percentages rapidly and steadily shifted. By 1974, 66 percent believed "a few big interests" and only 25 percent believed "for the benefit of all." By 2012, the 1958 ratios had completely reversed, with 79 percent believing "a few big interests" and a mere 19 percent believing "for the benefit of all."[28]

My second Mayfair summer came after my first year at Amherst College, so I was now an Air Force ROTC cadet, a fact I kept to myself. Too bad. Murray and Ben might have had some interesting things to say if I had told them about my ROTC experience.

Air Force ROTC training had a curious but revealing fit in the education offered at this pretentious little liberal arts school for men. The four-year program of required ROTC courses meant that I had to take more academic units under Air Force officers than I was able to take in any discipline outside my English major, more than history, more than science, more than social science, more than language. We learned how to march in formation, salute properly, stand at attention and parade rest, and put a glossy spit shine on our black dress shoes. We also trained more appropriately for our role as Air Force officers. In one assignment, for example, each of us was given a Soviet city to destroy using nuclear bombs. My city was Vladivostok. Planning its annihilation was, admittedly, more fun than studying the traditions and organization of the United States Air Force.

Curiously, though, it was in a ROTC course that I encountered the only deviation from Cold War orthodoxy that I can recall throughout my four years of college from 1951 to 1955. One of our instructors was an affable major, paunchy and balding, who had been a fighter pilot during World War II. He was an anachronism, a living fossil of wartime ardent anti-fascist culture. One day he shocked and angered us Amherst men by opposing the unification of East and West Germany, touching off a discussion, an anomaly for a ROTC class. In response to our spouted anti-Soviet rhetoric, he said he was more worried about a resurgent Germany dominating Europe.

Nothing I learned at Amherst helped in my political duels with Murray and Ben, which had actually gotten rather casual. I tried countering their moves by citing facts I had gleaned from the media. They counterattacked by telling me, and the other workers, that all my facts and opinions came from radio and TV networks and newspapers owned by the capitalist "ruling class."

The media in this summer of 1952 were reporting three shootdowns of innocent, unarmed U.S. aircraft that were on "routine survey" missions, "weather reconnaissance," and "training" flights, citing these attacks as proof of Soviet aggressiveness and barbarous disregard of international norms and human life. The *New York Times* also publicized new witnesses to the Soviet shootdown of "an unarmed Navy Privateer" way back in April 1950. So I brought to work clippings from the *Times*, the paragon of our free press, to prove that all our planes were in international airspace when subjected to these wanton attacks. This must have gotten to Ben, who opened a drawer and, much to my astonishment, actually whipped out a copy of the *Daily Worker*, which claimed that all three incidents were part of continual U.S. espionage flights into Soviet airspace, that Soviet fighters used internationally recognized signals to order the planes to land, and in each case the U.S. bomber fired first at the Soviet planes. This of course succeeded only in confirming all I had ever heard about preposterous Communist propaganda and their use of the Big Lie.

Here was one of our very rare arguments that might be decided by verifiable facts. So who wins for accurate and honest reporting, the *New York Times* or the *Daily Worker*? Although I was then planning to be a fighter pilot, I ended up involved as a navigator in similar allegedly innocent missions. More on that later. The best published research on the shootdowns would have to wait until the present century: Larry Tart and Robert Keefe's 2001 volume *The Price of Vigilance: Attacks on American Surveillance Flights*, a glowing homage to the U.S. airmen who conducted military aerial surveillance of Communist countries. Despite their unconcealed partisanship, the authors' deep research in American and Russian archives and interviews is meticulous and honest. They acknowledge one key fact: "As late as 1949, U.S. aircraft were violating Soviet airspace at will, not only over the sea but well inland as well, and there was little that Soviet authorities could do about it." Their exploration of these three shootdowns, including declassified contemporaneous handwritten reports by the Soviet pilots, discredits the *New York Times* and validates the *Daily Worker*'s account, though leaving some uncertainty about who fired first and the precise location of the initial aerial contact. Far more important, the basic facts about these three shootdowns have crucial significance in the history of the so-called Cold War.

In World War II, U.S. Air Force theory prioritized the development of strategic bombers capable of self-defense, even when fighter escort was unavailable. Hence the B-17 Flying Fortress and the B-29 Superfortress, with their iconic names. Thus the ring of postwar U.S. strategic bomber bases encircling the USSR provided both an ongoing threat of a first-strike nuclear attack and also invulnerable reconnaissance of the Soviet defenses against such attack. These facts help explain Soviet attempts to create geographic buffer zones, actions viewed by Washington as aggressive and by Moscow as defensive.

The shootdown of the Navy Privateer on April 8, 1950, just months before the U.S. entrance into the Korean civil war, was a potential game changer. The Consolidated PB4Y-2 Privateer was a heavily modified version of the World War II Consolidated B-24 strategic bomber. Contrary to the persistent claims by Washington and the media that the plane was unarmed, it had the very latest in defensive armament, including twelve high-caliber machine guns in six turrets operated electrically by five gunners, all aboard on that fatal day. It was shot down by four La-11s, developed after World War II as the most advanced Russian piston-driven fighter plane ever produced. So no longer could American bombers penetrate Soviet airspace with impunity.

The next two shootdowns occurred during the Korean War and not far from the conflict. The first, a P2V Neptune two-engine bomber, was shot down on November 6, also downed by La-11s. Neither the Privateer nor the Neptune was capable of high-altitude high-speed flight, unlike the B-29 Superfortress, the mainstay of America's strategic air power. The B-29 could fly almost two miles higher than the effective combat ceiling of the La-11, was almost as fast, and had far more firepower, so had little to fear from the Soviet fighter. The B-29 lost on June 13, 1952, encountered a more far formidable foe, the MiG-15 jet fighter, an aircraft the USSR was essentially forced to create to meet the constant threat of U.S. nuclear attack.[29] This shootdown meant that the United States no longer had any reconnaissance aircraft that could safely penetrate Soviet airspace.

More ominous handwriting was already on the wall, spelling out the message that the MiG-15 made the entire fleet of U.S. strategic bombers, all piston-driven subsonic prop planes, essentially obsolete as an attack force against the USSR. Hanson Baldwin, the military reporter for the *New York Times*, had already issued that warning in "Challenge of the MIG—And the Answer," an article I had read on December 9, 1951. The Air Force had discovered the obsolescence of the B-29, even as a tactical bomber, when it sent eight of them, protected by a hundred fighters, to bomb an airfield under construction in North Korea in October 1951. As Baldwin noted, the MiGs' score was "eight out of eight," all lost or severely damaged. If the B-29s, even updated as B-50s, or the giant six-engine but slow B-36s were to attack the USSR, they would have limited or no fighter escort. Few, if any, would be likely to make it to their targets. Baldwin's "answer" to this problem was the insane but tragically prescient logic of the Cold War arms race: develop jet bombers "like the swept B-47 and B-52" and "long-range guided missiles."[30]

Even more prescient was I. F. Stone's analysis of the catastrophic October raid, which unfortunately was kept from publication until 1952: "The Air Force suddenly faced the prospect of losing control of the air over Korea. It found that the long-distance subsonic bomber, on which the Americans had relied for delivery of the atom bomb, was obsolete. It woke up to discover that the despised and technologically backward Soviet Union was producing better jet planes than the United States." Unlike Baldwin, whom he cites, and various Air Force spokesmen whom he quotes, Stone saw the grave "implications for world peace" if the U.S. responded, as usual, to the USSR by upping the ante in the arms race game.[31]

Although "peace" had become a dirty word associated with Communists and their sympathizers, I was, like most Americans, fed up with the stalemated Korean War and with its ever-mounting casualties and interminable negotiations about whether POWs on both sides would be allowed to choose not to be repatriated. Although the Republican platform adopted at their convention in July promised to end the war promptly, nobody called them "peaceniks." So there were no rallies, marches, other forms of protest, or any antiwar movement at all—that I had heard of. There was one, but it took the advent of the internet for me to find it. It took place a year before my first summer at Mayfair. If I had known about it, it would have changed my attitude toward my Communist bosses.

The single quotation marks in a front-page headline in the *New York Times* of August 3, 1950, reveal levels of meaning: "Red 'Peace' Rally Defies Court; Routed by Police; 14 Held, 3 Hurt." "Paul Robeson, the singer, and others who have taken the Soviet position on 'peace,' were to have spoken," the *Times* reported, but a judge had denied a permit for the rally, to be held in Lower Manhattan's Union Square Park, because it would "seriously inconvenience many thousands of homegoers." So to block it, "more than a thousand police," including "seventy-five detectives, forty mounted men, and some motorcycle men and radio-car patrolmen," cordoned off the park in the afternoon. Before the resulting demonstration was over, about fifteen thousand people participated according to its sponsors, two thousand according to the police. "Except for the arrest at 4:30 P.M. of a woman who refused to move on and insisted on making a speech about the First Amendment, nothing happened until 5:40." She was "charged with disorderly conduct for using loud and boisterous language." Then a contingent of about five hundred people, "displaying hitherto concealed banners that read 'Hands off Korea!' 'We Want Peace,' and similar sentiments," rushed across the street and tried to get through the police line to enter the park, but "mounted and motorcycle police made frequent sorties to drive the intruders back." Although "some of the demonstrators who refused to obey orders to disperse were badly beaten by the police," the police showed "restraint" and restored "order" by 7 P.M. However, at about 9 P.M. "persons known to be Communist sympathizers began to appear in Times Square," but seven hundred police were there to meet them, and their "small groups" were "quickly and easily broken up."

I imagine that Murray and Ben were on the front lines of this confrontation. If so, they were, like all these demonstrators, brave and admirable. Two years after this abortive attempt to hold a rally for peace and against the Korean War, I was, unknowingly, about to participate in another one.

In mid-August, Murray and Ben told us that Paul Robeson was going to sing at a concert in New York on Wednesday, August 20, and the plant would shut down early so we could all attend. A living legend as an athlete, singer, stage and screen actor, anti-fascist, and crusader for peace, civil rights, economic equality, and independence for colonized nations, Robeson had recently become targeted by the U.S. government and the media as domestic public enemy number one.

By 1915 Robeson had done more to integrate higher education and college sports than any other single individual in American history. As one of two black students at Rutgers College, he overcame physical abuse by the football team to become its superstar and was chosen twice as a national All-American while also starring on the college's basketball and baseball teams, not to mention being the valedictorian of his class. From the 1920s until the mid-1940s he had wowed movie and live audiences on at least three continents with his groundbreaking acting roles and his inspiring singing of Negro spirituals and folk songs. In 1943, he was the first black actor ever to play the title role of Othello in America, thus making love to a beautiful white woman and then murdering her on stage, all in front of overwhelmingly white audiences and critics. Amazingly, audiences responded with passionate ovations and most critics enthused.

But defying and undermining America's oldest and deadliest sexual and racial taboo proved far less hazardous than violating the most sacred political taboo of postwar America. Although not a member of the Communist Party, Robeson spoke enthusiastically about the achievements of the Soviet Union, contrasted his experience there with the racism he had experienced throughout his life in the United States, and opposed the Cold War. As a gigantic presence in American and international culture, he could not be safely ignored. He had to be destroyed. And destroyed he was.

Eighty-five of his concerts that had been eagerly booked in the fall of 1948 were swiftly canceled by wintertime. As a substitute, he easily booked a four-month concert tour in Britain and Europe, where he was enthusiastically received and where he spoke out against colonialism in Asia and Africa as well as apartheid in South Africa. On April 20, 1949, Robeson sang several songs to the two thousand delegates from fifty nations meeting in Paris at the World Peace Congress. He then made some brief extemporaneous remarks, including this: "We do not want these hysterical imbecilities to make us go to war against anyone. We have a strong will to fight for peace. We do not want to go to war for anyone and against anyone. We do not want to go to war against the Soviet Union."[32]

On April 21, newspapers across America blared front-page headlines such as this: "Negroes Loyal to Russia, Says Robeson." Below the headlines was an AP story claiming that Robeson had said, "It is unthinkable that American Negroes would go to war on behalf of those who have oppressed us for generations against a country which in one generation has raised our people to the full dignity of mankind."[33] A media war against Robeson swept across the nation, with African American leaders such as Bayard Rustin and Roy Wilkins providing ammunition. In July, HUAC held hearings featuring prominent African American personages, including Jackie Robinson, condemning Robeson's alleged words, as reported in the AP dispatch. On August 27 and September 4 came those savage physical attacks by racist mobs, local police, and New York State troopers on concertgoers near Peekskill, with Robeson barely escaping unharmed from both ugly events.

America's blacklist left fewer and fewer domestic venues available to Robeson, forcing him to seek speaking and signing engagements in Britain and Europe. Then in the summer of 1950, the State Department revoked his passport on the ground that his international travel would be "contrary to the best interests of the United States." When he booked a 1952 concert in Canada, a destination not requiring a U.S. passport, the State Department ruled that he could not leave the country. This led to his triumphal concert in May 1952 at the Peace Arch, halfway across the bridge from Washington to Vancouver, where thirty thousand Canadians cheered his presence and performance. But this was the only successful concert in a fifteen-city early summer tour because many venues were blocked by local, state, and federal authorities.[34]

Thus the concert scheduled for August 20 could be a momentous event. For several days Ben was bustling about, looking very busy and very worried. Someone told me that he was in charge of Robeson's personal security during his stay in New York. At Mayfair, the concert was sort of a command performance, all of us being expected to attend. With our bosses providing transportation for some of us, we all made it.

The concert took place at night in a stadium on Randall's Island, right off East Harlem at the confluence of the Harlem River and the East River under the Triborough Bridge. The 22,000-seat stadium was packed, and there was a large standing-room crowd. Never having heard Robeson sing, my senses were overwhelmed by that rich, deep bass voice that made the stadium itself pulsate like a beating heart. When he sang "Ol' Man River," with background from the shrill whistles of tugboats on the rivers surrounding us, it sounded like the voice of an entire people.

Thrilled as I was by Robeson's songs, I found the rest of the long evening disappointing. I was eager to be fascinated and angered by authentic Communist propaganda. But the speeches just seemed to spout platitudes standard at the Republican and Democratic conventions. Curiously, the audience kept responding with passionate enthusiasm. I heard nothing remotely controversial. with one startling exception.

The final speaker declared something like this: "I have the greatest personal respect for Vincent Hallinan. But he has no chance of winning this election. We must stop Eisenhower, and the only man who can do that is Adlai Stevenson." Stevenson of course was the Democratic candidate for president. But, I wondered, who is Vincent Hallinan? Before I could ask, thousands of people were on their feet booing and angrily yelling. Thousands of others were on their feet clapping and cheering. A fistfight broke out right behind us. Scattered fights erupted in other parts of the stadium. For the first time that night, I felt like a clueless alien from some other land.

On the drive back to Brooklyn I asked Murray, "Who is Vincent Hallinan?" He told me that Hallinan was a lawyer running as the Progressive Party candidate for president. He added, with an air of impatience hinting he didn't see much hope for my future political development, that Hallinan was recently imprisoned "for political reasons." He looked like he didn't want any more of my questions.

In 1952, I was a teenager who thought of the Communist Party as part of the international Communist conspiracy to conquer America and the world. Two decades later, I was part of the New Left that dismissed the CP and the rest of the Old Left as namby-pamby "revisionists." As a self-declared Marxist revolutionary in 1972, I wanted to learn more about that puzzling 1952 Randall's Island evening. Since there was no internet, I searched the massive bound index volumes to the complete microfilm collection of the *New York Times* in a Palo Alto library. I could find no mention of the event.[35]

Where could I turn? To the *Daily Worker,* naturally. But where could I find back issues of the *Worker*? Of course, in that great citadel of anti-Communism: Stanford University's Hoover Institution. But I had been banished by court injunction from Stanford, even before the hearing that decreed my firing in January. Oh well, I decided to commit my first crime on Stanford's thirteen-square-mile campus since arriving there in 1959. After slightly altering my appearance, I passed through Hoover security by waving my faculty ID card and descended into the basement, where the *Daily Worker* was stored.

Sure enough, a rally had taken place on Randall's Island on the night of August 20, a standing-room-only crowd had jammed the stadium, Paul Robeson had sung "Ol' Man River," and the last speaker had stirred up some controversy when he announced that "he expected to vote for Governor Stevenson." I was surprised to learn that the entire event had been an antiwar rally. For years I had been telling young people in the movement against the Vietnam War that there had been no organized movement or rallies against the Korean War. How could I have sat for hours through this large antiwar rally without realizing what it was?

That *Daily Worker* of August 22, 1952, solved the mystery. Its account had no more radical content than my memory of the rally, named "Peace under the Stars." The *Worker* hailed it as "New York's biggest outdoor rally for peace." But by then everybody claimed to be for peace and ending the Korean War. I remembered Eisenhower was running his campaign on "my pledge to the American people" "to bring the Korean war to an early and honorable end" and to serve "the cause of peace."[36]

In addition to Robeson, the rally featured Pearl Primus and her dance group, actors Morris Carnovsky, Howard Da Silva, and Karen Morley, "noted pianist and her trio" Mary Lou Williams, ministers, rabbis, union officials, and even some officials of the American Legion and the Veterans of Foreign Wars. After "prayers for peace," a clergyman spoke and "the audience broke into applause at his first mention of 'peace,' and the applause grew louder as he urged an end to the fighting in Korea." Then came various skits showing "the fight for liberty, democracy, and peace in America throughout the generations," punctuated by quotations from Thomas Jefferson, Abraham Lincoln, and Franklin Delano Roosevelt. Amid all the patriotic fervor, evidently nothing was said about the U.S. role in Korean history, the causes of the war, U.S. imperialism, or any connection between the war and the repression at home. The *Worker*'s most radical sentence was a mention of one speaker's claim that "Wall Street" was profiting from the war.

So, I arrogantly thought, the rally was just as innocuous and vapid as I had remembered, and so was the *Daily Worker*. But then I thought of the effects of repression, which I had supported in 1952 and which I was beginning to experience. I had no right to judge those who opposed the Korean War during the ferocious unrestrained repression of the fifties by the standards of the sixties and seventies, when even COINTELPRO, the FBI's campaign of extralegal and illegal acts designed to destroy individuals and organizations, was forced to operate clandestinely. (It was not until 1974 that I learned of J. Edgar Hoover's personal campaign to "neutralize" me, as a secret 1969 FBI document put it.) As part of a mass movement in which many millions of Americans battled against the Vietnam War, I now appreciated the courage of that tiny minority of Americans who bravely stood as Communists or with Communists against the monster right-wing tides of 1950s Cold War America. In 1972, when many hundreds of revolutionary newspapers were being published everywhere from army base coffeehouses to high schools to aircraft carriers launching fighter-bombers against Vietnam, I looked back with admiration at the lonely figures of Ben and Murray having to sneak into a candy store to buy their daily copy of the newspaper I was now studying to understand myself and my country's history in the 1950s. With these thoughts, I sneaked out of the Hoover Institution and off the Stanford campus without being noticed and cited for contempt.

The next three years were my years of being blacklisted. Rejected for employment by hundreds of colleges and a few publishers, I figured my only hope for a livelihood that could support my family was self-employment in some nonpolitical, uncontroversial business. Maybe that was the path that had led Murray and Ben to Mayfair Photofinishing. So I used my GI Bill benefits to complete a one-year program at the College of San Mateo that led to my certificate in environmental horticulture. But when I sought my first job in horticulture, the FBI went around to greenhouses and land-scaping companies, effectively preventing me from subverting the bushes and trees.

Eventually in 1975, after a couple of temporary academic jobs, I found the only college or university that would hire me: Rutgers—not the New Brunswick campus where Paul Robeson was the superstar athlete and scholar, but the Newark campus, developed in response to the urban rebellions of the sixties and later designated by *US News and World Report* fifteen years in a row as America's most multiethnic research university. When I went there for my interview, I was invited to eat lunch with some faculty at the student center. As we passed through the front entrance on Martin Luther King Jr. Boulevard, I found myself facing a wall plaque emblazoned with the name of the building and giving some facts about the man it honored. I thought, with wonder, that destiny had steered me to the right place. For the next forty years, every time I passed through that entrance into the Paul Robeson Center—to go to the cafeteria or the faculty dining room or the art gallery or the theater or even the convenience store and the ATM— I heard Robeson's voice, lamented his fate at the hands of our society, and felt grateful for all those who had changed that society enough for me to avoid his fate and the fate of all the other people whose lives were destroyed by the plague of anti-Communism.

5 ▸ ON THE WATER FRONT

RED HOOK

Because the Statue of Liberty was built to face France, the only New York neighborhood from which one can see its broad face is Red Hook, a section of Brooklyn that juts out into New York Harbor. With water on three sides, its two great artificial harbors of Erie Basin and Atlantic Basin constructed in the nineteenth century, and direct access to the Gowanus Canal, Red Hook was for more than a century one of America's busiest ports. By the late nineteenth century, Red Hook had become notorious for its gangs, giving it a reputation as the most dangerous neighborhood in the nation, a reputation it maintained at least through 1990, when *Life* magazine named it "the crack capital of America" and one of its worst places to live.

In the first decades of the twentieth century, factories clustered close to Red Hook's chains of wharves and piers, and throngs of longshoremen and their families, mainly Italian and Irish Americans, packed its tenements and, later, Red Hook Houses, a thirty-eight-acre 1938 public housing project of 2,800 apartments. They were followed after World War II by immigrants from Puerto Rico, who established in Red Hook one of their first mainland communities.

Prohibition had allowed some of the area's gangs to graduate from street crime to lucrative businesses, including rackets and systematic large-scale theft that siphoned wealth from the thriving waterfront. In the longshoremen's neighborhood communities and on the docks, the highest authority was probably the mob known as the Anastasio family.

No subway was ever extended into Red Hook, so in the summers of 1953 and 1954 I had to transfer from the Coney Island trolley to a bus to get from Flatbush to my job at Carb Manufacturing Company on Carroll Street, a block from the warehouses adjacent to the Atlantic Basin docks. Walking down a deserted Carroll Street on the first day, I searched in vain for the factory. The address I had been given led to a single ancient dingy brick four-story building that spanned almost a whole block and seemed to be filled with nothing but tenement apartments. Even after finding a small "CARB MFG. CO." sign over three concrete steps leading to a narrow entrance in the middle of the building, I still couldn't tell from the outside where the factory ended and the tenements began. I soon found out that there was no way to tell from inside either. And why.

Mr. Nathan Carb was the sole owner of the factory and the tenements. Carb Manufacturing did almost exclusively government contracts. Mr. Carb would occasionally withdraw a large amount of cash and bustle off to Washington to pave the path to a new contract or to calm the pressure from failing to meet the terms of an old one. While I worked there, we were mainly making furniture for the Navy and Air Force, principally couches and chairs made of aluminum, leatherette, and foam. Production in no way seemed to be affected by the end of the Korean War in midsummer 1953, hardly a surprise considering the full-speed military buildup of the mid-1950s. I learned that the plant had recently completed a contract to make parachutes, a thought that haunted me throughout my flying career in the Air Force. Whenever I checked out a chute before a flight, I always made sure it wasn't labeled "CARB MFG. CO."

My first job was webbing springs and stuffing cushions in the upholstery department on the fourth floor. This was the only floor in the plant where English was spoken—except of course in the front office. On every other floor all the workers were Puerto Rican, except for a few Cubans. Up here, the main production was done by two lines of women, about half Puerto Rican and half African American. They sewed cushion covers together on sewing machines that looked like they had been hijacked from a museum. There were only two other men, both African American. One was my twenty-three-year-old foreman, Sylvester, who had grown up in Bedford-Stuyvesant.

I never asked if he knew Joan, who was about a year older. The other was Jasper, who had just arrived from Georgia, where he had been working in the cotton fields for five years. He was about my age, nineteen. Sylvester, Jasper, and I spent time boxing, arm wrestling, weight lifting with rolls of leatherette, bragging, and doing anything else we could think of to impress the women, who all were working too hard to pay any attention to us and our antics.

After I had been there a few weeks, one day Mr. Carb called me into his office. He told me that production was being held up by a bottleneck in the sewing lines, making us fall behind on an important contract. What he was going to do, he told me, was to put all the "girls" up there on piecework until we got caught up. "You're a bright young fellow, and about the only person around here I can trust," he said in a semi-whisper. "So what I want you to do is keep track of each girl's production."

So I did, scrupulously. The rate of production more than tripled. The women on the lines now had a chance to make close to half of a living wage. All small talk ceased, and so did my horseplay with the men. Each woman worked at top speed, and the cushion covers were literally sprinkled with sweat. The ancient machines started breaking down. Mr. Carb refused to replace any of them or even pay to have them serviced. So I had to repair them, always with an operator anxiously watching, begging me to hurry. The small piles of finished cushion covers grew into a wall of towering stacks, completely cutting off the sewing lines from the area where I used to cavort with Jasper and Sylvester.

Mr. Carb had given me our production targets. When we reached this goal, I dutifully reported that to him. "Well, let's just keep going and get ourselves a margin of safety," he replied, with a smile and a pat on my back. So the frenetic pace continued, until we had run out of storage room and were weeks ahead of the rest of the production process. Then Mr. Carb fired three-fourths of the women in the sewing department. I was ashamed of my role using the women's own labor to destroy their livelihood. Years later, when I encountered the concept of "alienated labor," I saw those stacks of cushions as a material manifestation of how the products of workers' labor can confront the workers as their enemy, indeed their Frankenstein's monster.

Whenever I think of Carb manufacturing, I think of rats. Since the plant was located just over a block from the waterfront, hordes of huge wharf rats made their homes in the walls and debris of the building. To us they seemed the real owners, and none of us would have trespassed into their domain after nightfall. When we reported for work each morning, we first threw bolts and yelled into each room, and then didn't enter until we could no longer hear any scurrying. Sometimes rats would come out onto the middle of the floor, even right next to us while we operated noisy machines. Occasionally one would sit up on its haunches staring at us until one of us succeeded in hitting it with a bolt.

Part of the ground floor was a large warehouse area whose floor was covered with piles and layers of materials, mostly from past contracts and some for current production, all scattered about helter-skelter and in various states of decay. When we had to venture into this industrial wilderness, we walked on bridges of wood planks, hoping that our work shoes would protect our ankles from the rats that infested the morass underneath. One day I went to Mr. Carb's office and proposed that he have us collect all the old materials scattered around the warehouse, inventory them, determine what might be used, sell the rest, and then utilize the cleared space for production. His face contorted and became livid with rage. "All those materials are mine, do you understand that? They are mine! I am the only one who can decide what to do with them. Do you understand that?"

When I first arrived at Carb, there was one other worker who was neither Hispanic nor African American. This was Angelo, a barrel-chested, muscular Sicilian, maybe in his late forties or early fifties, whose face always looked unshaven and scowling. Angelo was the foreman of the shipping department. He ran that department by thundering curses in a kind of pidgin Spanish, shoving anybody he suspected of "loafing" up against a wall, and severely beating any worker who "didn't know his place" as an "example." Three of his workers one day stopped the ancient rattletrap freight elevator between floors and beat Angelo into a three-day coma. After he was shipped to the hospital, I was recruited to take his place as foreman of the shipping department, where all the workers were Puerto Rican.

The Puerto Rican people who worked at Carb had come from the island nation as part of the great waves of immigration that had begun in the late 1940s. In 1952, Puerto Rico had been magically and officially transformed from being an American colony into a "Commonwealth" of the United States, thus pushing wave after wave of cheap workers into the U.S. economy. Working with the men in the shipping department turned my high school and college Spanish into something serviceable though not fluent. It also cured a lingering racism I'd been harboring ever since a painful event in 1949. Before working at Carb, the only Puerto Rican I had known personally was Maria, my co-worker and friend at Mayfair Photofinishing. My only other contact was back in 1949, when two friends and I had gotten into a very one-sided fight with a Puerto Rican gang in a Puerto Rican neighborhood a couple of blocks from the Brooklyn Navy Yard. We should have known better than to intrude on someone else's turf and got badly beaten up. After I got all stitched back together, my father called over to our home a friend from his air raid warden days, now a police sergeant in the precinct of our little brawl. He and my dad mulled over various schemes for revenge, which all soon dissolved in their beer. At one point this beefy cop held up both hands, knuckles out, to show me that almost every finger had been broken "beating the shit out of these little punks, for all the good that it does." No wonder, I thought to myself, that those guys jumped us.

The shipping department was also where I first discovered the most lucrative operating procedures of Carb Manufacturing. Only about half the production was done in the main factory. The rest took place in small shops secretly scattered throughout the adjoining tenements. There, large Puerto Rican families lived among the rats in squalid two-room apartments. "¿Qué hacen con las ratas?" I asked two of the men. They told me that people took shifts at night to keep the rats at bay, especially away from the babies and young children. The rooms where we worked were permeated by the reek of garlic, used by the tenants to overpower the stench of stale urine in the halls. Safely tucked away from the government inspectors who periodically visited the main plant, we assembled frames made of aluminum two or three grades below government specifications, added foam remnants, and covered the final product with paper-thin leatherette. We carried the finished products on our heads through narrow subterranean tunnels into a secret passageway opening into the shipping department at the back of the main factory. There we crated them up and shipped them out.

The crated couches each weighed 275 pounds. The workers were so poorly nourished that it would often, especially toward the end of the workday, take six men to carry one crate. Whenever we had to load onto trucks that lacked hydraulic tailgates, the only people with enough energy and strength to handle the two-man job of lifting them to the inside of the truck were myself and a man nicknamed "El Grande" because of his great size, which was about the same as mine—five feet eight, 148 pounds.

In the main shipping room, where we crated the junk assembled in the tenements, we kept on hand a supply of good furniture, one or two samples partially crated, all covered by tarpaulins. When a Navy or Air Force inspector arrived in the office at the front of the plant, someone was dispatched to come running back yelling, "El inspector! El inspector!" We quickly yanked the tarps off the good stuff and threw them over the junk. By the time the inspector got back there, we were busily crating a fine specimen. One day the head Navy inspector approached me.

"Hey, Bruce, you know old man Carb takes care of me, but I still got to be sure the stuff he's sending out of here isn't too crappy. Hope you're keeping an eye on it."

"You know me, Mel. It just wouldn't pay for us to lose this contract. Look right here, for instance. I'm sending this one right back up to have those scratches on the legs ground off."

I showed him a perfectly good couch, pointing out a couple of minor scratches on the back legs. He half smiled at what he took as my overzealousness.

"Oh, that's okay, Bruce. You don't have to worry about minor stuff like that. I just want to make sure that no real crappy stuff is going out. I'll tell you what I'm going to do, because I trust you and I know you'll be careful. I'll let you have the stamp so you can stamp the crates yourself. That way you guys won't get jammed up down here and I won't have to make so many trips over. You scratch my back, Bruce, and I'll scratch yours. But you got to promise to keep being careful."

So Mel gave me the official U.S. Navy stamp of inspection and approval, which I cheerfully smacked onto every crateful of junk we shipped, sometimes even before we stenciled the destination and CARB MFG CO on the crate.

Practically all the workers were making seventy-five cents an hour, and some were trying to support families, often large. The most skilled production workers at Carb were welders, who made eighty-five cents an hour. In that filthy, foreign, treeless jungle of Red Hook, Gowanus, and the Navy Yard district, Puerto Rican people were daily being hunted down by rats, cops, unemployment, hunger, dope pushers, the draft, and disease. Was working for Mr. Carb their best opportunity in life? For teenagers, maybe the best unit of security was the street gang, which was beginning to take the place of the family as the center of loyalty. For adults, a livable income was available for those who worked for the mobs who ran these neighborhoods, and the mobs needed Puerto Ricans for some of their most lucrative rackets. The most pervasive was the numbers.

Every Carb worker's daydream was hitting a number and hitting it big. Some people actually dreamed numbers at night. Each day's number at that time was the last three digits of a racetrack's total pari-mutuel figure as published in the *Daily News*. When you picked a number, the odds were therefore 999 to 1 against your winning. If your number hit, the Syndicate paid you 500 to 1. This meant that they kept half of each day's money bet in the entire city. Every floor of our factory had a numbers runner, who was just one of the workers. Each floor runner recorded every person's bet and passed all the money to the runner for the factory, who passed the money to the head runner for the immediate area, and so on up the line. The Syndicate was absolutely scrupulous in its payments. The exciting topic of conversation each morning was numbers—who had missed by one digit, what numbers people had dreamed, what to bet today, tales of famous hits, and of course who, if anyone, had actually won and how much. Hits were not rare. With about a hundred workers, the odds for a winner were one every ten days. Numbers were the only chance most Carb workers had to ever find a way out. A dollar hit equaled a third of a year's pay. If you worked at Carb for a year and half and never spent a dime you earned, you would not have as much as a five-dollar hit.

The Syndicate also ran Red Hook itself. It was the most lawless, dangerous area I have ever experienced. The city didn't even try to police Red Hook. In my two summers working there, only twice did I ever see any cops, and they were in squad cars driving through fast.

My parents of course thought that Harlem and Bedford-Stuyvesant were the most dangerous areas in the city. Sylvester's nineteen-year-old sister, Cassandra, got hired in the upholstery department shortly after me. He and his wife and Cassandra and I went out on some Saturday nights, usually starting out at the clubs in Harlem. There were a few white women in those clubs, but I never saw another white man. These were peaceful, fun places, unlike the all-white bars in my suburban Flatbush neighborhood, which were all quite dangerous for any strangers on Saturday nights and where of course no sane black person would ever venture. Our foursome's most memorable event in Harlem was when Sugar Ray Robinson dropped in at a club, evoking a loud round of applause. We would end those nights riding the Brighton Line to Coney Island, where we bought gin and ginger to drink while eating hotdogs at Nathan's. A couple of times I dated Cassandra at her home in Bedford-Stuyvesant. My parents decreed that I couldn't drive the car there because "it was just too dangerous." So I took the Brighton Line to Prospect Park, then integrated the Franklin Avenue shuttle, and walked to her place, which was just a few blocks from my first home.

The streets and bars of Red Hook, even during daytime, were truly scary. A lot of the young Italian American guys who lived around the neighborhood of Carb Manufacturing had graduated from the teenage street gangs into a fairly systematic livelihood based on stealing cars, mugging, numbers running, and occasionally providing extra muscle for the Syndicate. Directly across the street from the front steps of the factory was a pool hall and bar where an Italian American gang hung out during the day. Being the only white worker in the plant, I was elected to go over there whenever we wanted some beer to wash down the lunch that we ate on those steps. As I approached the front door, I could hear loud conversation and the clicking of pool balls inside. As soon as I opened the door and stepped inside, the place became as quiet as an empty tomb. It was like everyone was a player in that game where someone yells "Freeze!"—except that everyone had turned to stare at me. I knew that all I had to do to get myself in trouble was to return any of those challenging stares. So I would alternatively look at my shoes and the ceiling while walking to the bar, getting the bottles of beer, paying, and walking directly to the door.

Since the plant was in Red Hook, Mr. Carb had a special economy plan for bringing the weekly payroll, which had to be in cash because most of the workers had no way to cash checks. Rather than hiring an armored car security service, which would have offered a prime holdup target, he would send me, dressed in my regular work clothes, to pick up the entire payroll. Of course no bank was reckless enough to have a branch in this neighborhood. I would walk a long block and a half to catch a bus, transfer to another bus, walk a couple of short blocks, go into the bank, hand a certain teller a sealed envelope, and be given the payroll in small bills. The way back to the plant was terrifying, especially that last block and a half, which seemed three miles long. I was ready to surrender the payroll on the first request.

Mr. Carb made Ebenezer Scrooge look like Santa Claus. He would hire new workers to work four ten-hour days at the federal minimum wage of seventy-five cents an hour (thirty dollars for forty hours) and then fire them so he wouldn't have to pay overtime. When he had overseas shipments to make from a nearby pier, he would avoid having the loading done by longshoremen by sending me down with two truckloads of sealed crates, workers from the plant (all of course at seventy-five cents an hour), and a pocketful of five-dollar bills to pay off the pier's loading boss. We loaded under fiery stares from the longshoremen and the sightless eyes on the broad face of the towering Statue of Liberty.

Needless to say, there was no union at Carb. One morning, two men and two women greeted us all at the entrance to the factory and handed us leaflets headlined on one side, "ONLY ONE WAY! JOIN THE UNION TODAY!" and on the other, "¡SOLAMENTE UN MEDIO! ¡INGRESAR

EN LA UNION HOY!" The copy I still have explains in Spanish and English:

> Remember the laws of this Country protect you. Should your department head or any other supervisor discuss the Union with you or should they antagonize you in any way—report this to one of the organizers immediately—steps will be taken before the National Labor Relations Board to put a stop to this. The laws of this Country give you the right to join a Union without discrimination for doing so by your Employer.
>
> The Miscellaneous Industrial Employees Union, Local 138, D.R. & W.W.I.U. of A.—A.F.L. consists of intelligent members and responsible leadership. The policy of this union is to exercise utmost responsibility toward strife and quarrels.

Mr. Carb's office looked out over the area. Only three people stopped to talk to the leafleters. At noon, Mr. Carb called these three in, informed them they were fired for inefficiency, and gave them their pay in cash. The next day, two of the workers in the plant tried to encourage people to send in applications to join the union. On their way home both were jumped and savagely beaten by a gang of thugs. Mr. Carb fired them for not reporting to work the next day. Other workers called the telephone number at the bottom of the union leaflet to report the situation. They were told that the union had decided that "the workers in Carb were not ready for a union," and they could therefore do nothing further to help.

No doubt those union organizers were fine, dedicated, honest people. The New York waterfront, and Red Hook in particular, was not the place for organizers like that. What the Carb workers needed was a union that knew how to deal with employers like Mr. Carb, a union like the Teamsters or the one with the largest and most loyal base in Red Hook, the International Longshoremen's Association. If you had an automatic response to those last three words, remember it as you read the rest of this chapter.

The last month I worked there in 1954, Mr. Carb gave me the grand title of supervisor of production for the whole plant and raised my hourly wage to eighty-five cents. Then in my final week he proposed that I quit college and stay there, promising me that I would eventually have a really fine future working for him. I made the difficult decision to decline his kind offer and return to Amherst, where I learned in four years less than I learned in two summers at Carb Manufacturing Company in Red Hook.

THE EMPIRE'S HARBOR

It was toward the end of July 1955. Behind us, the setting sun was close to sinking below the giant Colgate factory on the Jersey City waterfront, a couple of blocks from where we had sailed. The hands on its fifty-foot roof-top clock, visible from Manhattan, showed everyone in the harbor that it was 7:30 P.M. Ahead of us, the skyscrapers of Wall Street were gleaming copper towers, with windows of burnished gold. New York, the Empire City, seemed a magical metropolis soaring above the harbor, creating its own dazzling, perfect horizon. The water of the river, wrinkled by a light breeze, was azure flecked with more gold, shimmering with rainbows reflected from pools of floating oil. Even the shoals of floating condoms might be mistaken for masses of gently undulating lily pads.

I was the mate on a Pennsylvania Railroad tugboat, a job I landed while awaiting my orders into active duty in the Air Force. We were heading for a pier just north of the financial district, where we were to pick up three barges. None of us was prepared for what we were to find when we got there. I didn't know that we were already in a war zone.

The captain deftly eased the tug toward the barges. I climbed over the rail, out onto the bow, and stood on the tug's bumper, a mass of knotted-up half-rotten old towing lines fastened to the front of the bow. My right hand was holding a partially opened two-foot "eye," or loop, of heavy towing line, thicker than my wrist, feeding through my left hand to the coil piled on the tug's deck.

For each of us who worked on the deck, that eye was as essential to our craft as a drill is to a dentist. The first thing an apprentice deckhand learned was how to form that two-foot loop by unraveling the three strands of rope from one end of a towing line and weaving them back into the line in an invulnerable splice. Being double, the eye is as heavy as the next four feet of line; this extra weight makes it possible to throw the line accurately at a distant target, such as a bitt (a metal pillar, fat at the top and narrowing toward the base, strong enough to hold a freighter or a fleet of barges) or a cleat (a thick metal stanchion with a horizontal horn at each end). Throwing the eye is not like throwing a lasso. You hold the loop open, lift it just enough to clear the surface you are standing on, build momentum by giving it a pendulum motion, and heave, smoothly using your whole body timed to coincide with the swing of the loop to give it the needed acceleration. Then comes the hard part.

To catch a bitt, the eye must land right on top and fully open. But with a cleat, you aim at one horn with the line going sideways toward the center of the stanchion. When the line lands on the horn, you use one of the niftiest tricks of the trade, the trick that makes it possible to manipulate the far end of these extremely heavy lines at considerable distances. Holding your end of the line with both hands, you smoothly, almost gently, flick one wrist and move your arm as though throwing something through the center of the line. What you "throw" is the desired twist, curve, lateral, vertical, or backward motion in the form of a wave that travels down the length of line. With the eye now hanging on one horn and the line stretched between vessels shifting in a fluid medium, you watch your wave undulate along the line until it reaches the eye. The loop opens, flops over the opposite horn, and encloses the entire cleat.

Retrieving the line is also tricky. With dozens of feet of churning, filthy harbor water in between, and vessels moving around you, you can't just step out and fetch it. So you throw a different wave, the line snakes, the eye opens and pops straight up. If the line now falls into the water, its weight will double and the salt water will rot it until it turns into a potential death trap. So just as the eye rises, you snap your wrist and arm to direct it straight toward you. Most of us could drop the eye back at our own feet like magic.

As the gap between us and the nearest barge gradually narrowed, I picked out a cleat for a target and began to calculate my heave. But as I glanced down at the water, now in shadow and filling up with clumps of garbage pushed by our hull, I noticed a dark blue patch of cloth billowing up above the surface as though attached to a large object underneath. Peering closer, I could see that it was the back of a man's shirt on a body, floating, head down, under the water.

The stern-line man and the deckhand, who were both also ready to cast their lines, as well as the captain up in the pilothouse, were all watching me for signals. Realizing that we were about to drift over the body, I signaled to the captain to back off. As our propellers reversed, their swirls washed over the body and spun it slowly around.

Joe Barnes, reputed to be the best railroad tugboat captain in the harbor, maneuvered us to within a couple of yards of the body and held even with it, while keeping the stern pointed out to open water. I conferred with Sonny, the tall, blond Irish American deckhand, who had now lost his customary jovial, fun-loving, boisterous manner. About my age, Sonny was the real leader of the deck. When years later I read Melville's description of Billy Budd, his archetypal fair Handsome Sailor, Sonny was the man I saw. We decided to drop an old towing line under the body and pull it up, trying to hook one leg in the eye of the line. Each leg was swollen to double its normal girth, making it push through the rotting blue work pants. I swung the line out, dropped it down, and caught a leg on the third try. Sonny began reeling in our catch hand over hand, carefully coiling the line on the deck. Pieces of the pants and of the flesh on the leg stripped off in jellyish clumps. As a heavy, sweet, putrid smell wafted over the deck, I found myself fighting to control the nauseous heaving in my stomach. Sonny looked like I felt. As the line tore loose from the rotting leg, both legs came up, then dropped down, rocking the head into full view for the first time. Through the back of the neck was stuck a bag hook, the standard hand tool of the longshoremen. Tony, our wiry, tough, grizzled Italian American stern-line man, grimly muttered, "It's another ILA execution."

In two months, our fleet of Pennsylvania Railroad tugs working out of Pier H, Jersey City, had picked up five bodies—of either longshoremen or foot soldiers of rival gangs or both—floating in the harbor, all executed in the same manner. The docks and the dock workers were up for grabs that year, and a brutal war for control over them was being fought by the International Longshoremen's Association, the American Federation of Labor, the 170 stevedore and shipping companies represented by the New York Shipping Association, clashing gangs of mobsters that would in two years consolidate into the Gambino and Genovese families, and the governments of New York, New Jersey, and the United States.

Tugboat men felt sorry for "those poor guys" working on the docks and were glad we had our own superior position. Most thought that we were just spectators to the struggles raging around us. I myself had not yet encountered the phrase "aristocracy of labor" as used by Jack London and, a bit later, by Vladimir Lenin to describe that section of the working class that is bought off with some of the superprofits of a capitalist empire. If someone had dropped in on us while we were having one of our pleasant, relaxed philosophical discussions on deck during a long tow, while keeping an eye on the barges all safely secured to the sides of the tug, and said, "You men are a real aristocracy of labor," everyone would have enthusiastically agreed. We were all male, white, skilled, able-bodied, and highly paid, and we belonged to a democratic union—the Associated Maritime Workers, International Organization of Masters, Mates, and Pilots (AFL)—that represented our interests.

The union fought for good working conditions and our safety. Younger members were as well represented as older ones. Even the greenest spare deckhands, called in to stand by on Pier H to fill in for any absentees, were paid full hourly wages from the time they reported, whether or not they got assigned to a crew. If they were given crew assignments after waiting some hours, these hours were added at time and a half to the hours they worked. The egalitarian pay structure went so far that the wage differential between the lowest and highest ranks on the deck—the deckhand and the mate— was merely seventy-three cents a day. So as soon as a young deckhand learned the ropes, if he was any good at all the deck crew usually asked him to be mate, because nobody wanted the responsibility of making decisions. That's how I got to be mate just a few weeks after getting on a regular crew. Of course the office was mostly a formality; when in any doubt, I asked Sonny and Tony what "orders" I should give them.

This little floating island of democracy was surrounded by docks where the longshoremen labored in the yoke of shipping lines, stevedore compa- nies, federal and state agencies, and mobsters fighting over shares of the wealth pouring through New York Harbor in the postwar boom. Beyond the docks were impoverished masses of people, mostly black and Puerto Rican, desperately seeking any paid work, even in the sweatshops of the garment district and Chinatown or the myriad clones of Carb Manufactur- ing in Brooklyn, Queens, and the Bronx, and living in rat-infested tenement apartments like the ones owned by Mr. Carb. For the men, a longshore job would have been like an ascent into heaven. For the women of course it was unimaginable.

Since there were no black men on any of the crews in our fleet, no one seemed to think there was anything offensive in using the traditional name of the large black iron bitts on piers: "niggerheads." Even Jews were a rarity. Once when Tony was sick, the scowling, beer-bellied stern-line man who took his place made some reference to "dirty Jews" while eating lunch. I jumped up all excited and asked if he wanted his teeth for dessert or some such smart remark. Sonny tried to smooth things over by saying that the stern-line man hadn't "meant any harm" and wouldn't have said it if he had known I was Jewish. The stern-line man said, "That's right," and sullenly "took it back."

It was also a male world where we didn't even see many women. We would steer out of our way to run alongside a harbor cruise boat so we could ogle the women on board, show off, and call out hopeless invitations, which sometimes elicited playful responses. When we were working middle trick, about the same hours as a factory swing shift, we sometimes rushed to fin- ish early. After the last tow, we washed up and changed out of our work clothes. When we got back to Pier H and were securing the final lines, we single guys had to prance around daintily in our fancy stepping-out clothes, me with my bright blue wide-shouldered jacket, light gray pegged pants, Windsor-knotted tie, and Wildroot Cream–trained pompadour.

Besides the captain and the deck crew, each tug had an engine crew, consisting of an engineer and either two stokers on a steam tug or one oiler on a diesel tug. Each tugboat had its regular crew, which knew all its capabilities, problems, and dangers. After my apprenticeship, somewhat shortened because of my previous work on a fishing boat, I was assigned to one of the six "roustabout" crews, which rotated through all the tugs in the Pennsy fleet, taking each tug for two-day stints while its regular crew was off. We were supposed to be the most skilled crews because we had to handle both steam and diesel tugs as well as cope with the idiosyncrasies of each individual vessel. In my half year, I think I worked on all thirty Pennsylvania Railroad tugs.

Those of us who worked on the deck considered ourselves beings on a higher social level than the men in the engine room. Years later, Melville's *White-Jacket* and *Israel Potter* made me see connections with the hierarchy on sailing ships, where social status was proportional to the altitude of sailors' jobs. We never acknowledged the fact that the engine room was strictly taboo to us (most of us had never been inside one), while of course the engine-room crew were free to join us on the deck. And the superiority of the deck environment on nice sunny days was blown and washed away by any cold wind or rain.

About half of that fleet were steam tugs. Working on them it was hard to avoid sensing the impending end of an era. They had been built in the early years of the twentieth century with the great industrial craftsmanship of the era, and were the last steam tugs, maybe the last steam craft of any kind, in the harbor except for the transatlantic steamships. We preferred them to the newer diesels, mostly built after World War II. They were heavier than the diesels and were therefore a more stable platform to work barges around. Although the diesels could get up to top speed faster, that was no real advantage in our kind of work. When we got up a full head of steam, we easily outran the latest diesel tugs, and this kind of speed was useful for long hauls. The piercing steam whistle, which could be heard for miles, was a wondrous power in clearing a path through the harbor, which in those days was crowded day and night with freighters, tankers, transatlantic luxury liners, warships, ferries, self-propelled barges, tourist cruise boats, police patrol boats, and scores of tugs shuttling back and forth with barges, lighters, and floats holding as many as twenty railroad cars apiece. The steam tugs also shortened our workday, for we were allowed an hour and a half to sail to one of the approved disposal areas and then pull the ashes out of the hold with a bucket hung from a pulley. It only took us about half an hour because we just posted a lookout for the harbor patrol and in daytime dumped our ashes in any convenient hiding place and at night anyplace in the river.

One of our tasks was ferrying railroad car floats back and forth between railroad yards along the New Jersey shore and the fruit and vegetable markets in Lower Manhattan. Each float had railroad tracks and a track switch secured to its concrete surface. The smaller floats held ten railroad cars; the larger ones held twenty. When loaded, the mass of the floats was immense. We towed empty floats to a wide floating platform called a "bridge," which was controlled by a bridge operator in a high structure straddling the scene. Working together, he and the deck crew got the tracks of each float aligned with the tracks on the bridge, which led to the tracks in the rail yard. There, long parallel lines of loaded railcars awaited their turn to visit New York City and disgorge their cargo. Switchyard locomotives at the other end of the trains shunted them up onto "humps." Brakemen, working one of the most dangerous jobs even on the treacherous waterfront, would disconnect some of the cars, which then slid, gravity driven, toward the various bridges. Because these loose cars with their tremendous mass move almost soundlessly, they are stealthy killing machines. With the bridge operator working his track switches and us working the floats' track switches, we filled two floats with the loose cars and then secured them, one on each side of the tug, for their brief voyage. Although the river was teeming with commerce, no vessel dared get in our way as we hauled the massive floats, each as long as a football field, with more than half their length sticking out in front of our bow.

During the peak hours—between 5 P.M. and 1 A.M.—dozens of railroad tugs scurried back and forth across what we called the North River (the lower Hudson), each towing twenty or forty railcars laden with fruits and vegetables. As soon as the front of the floats touched the dock in Manhattan, even while we were still securing them, dockside crews would trot on board stringing lights and opening up the cars. Between the river and the streets jammed with trucks was the market: row after row of vast warehouses, a hive frenetically buzzing with forklifts, truck drivers, wholesalers, inspectors, and merchants, all selling, buying, handling, loading, and carting off fruits and vegetables as fast as we could tow them over.

New York seemed some unimaginably gigantic animal gobbling down hundreds of freight-car loads of produce every hour. Seeing this awe-inspiring dependence of the city on the countryside, I sometimes wondered what the city did for its living and whether it was worth it. After all, its main products did not come from its light industry like Carb Manufacturing or Mayfair Photofinishing or even the garment center, but from the labyrinth of Wall Street, where people like my father expended their lives buying and selling, or just pushing pieces of paper representing the nation's and the world's property relations: stocks, bonds, title deeds, promissory notes, insurance policies, options, mortgages, contracts. What, I wondered, did New York produce or do for the migrant workers who picked the canta-loupes that roared north on the Atlantic Coast Line trains two hundred cars long?

Sometimes we towed cattle floats to the slaughterhouses on Manhattan's west side. These vessels were tall double-decked stockyards, several times the size of the tug. My father, whose older brother was a butcher in a slaughter-house, used to tell me about an animal called a Judas goat. But before I towed my first cattle float, I had always assumed that this was a mythical beast, one of the creations of Dad's whimsical fantasy. We secured the cattle floats to special docks fenced with a labyrinth of animal walkways. If a float contained sheep, a goat would saunter up to its exit gate. When the gate opened, the goat would lead the sheep, obediently following, through the maze of walkways to the top of a ramp. At the last moment, the goat stepped through a small swinging door to one side. The sheep kept walking until they each tumbled head first over a ledge. As they fell, their hind legs were roped together and jerked straight up. A butcher slit their throats, kosher style, under the supervision of a rabbi. Years later, this often struck me as a great image of the relationship between our leaders, political and military, and those of us who mindlessly follow, unaware of the interests those leaders serve.

In mid-August, just as Hurricane Connie was hitting the harbor, the work-ing tugs received emergency orders to tow all vulnerable vessels to safer berths. We had almost finished our day's work, so this would be a double trick (nautical lingo for "double shift"). The sky was blackening, and wind-driven rain was sweeping across the water. Bad luck dealt us a cattle float, where we deck men had to work on the narrow catwalks surrounding the lower deck. Slippery manure from the upper deck normally accumulated on these catwalks, and now the storm was making it cascade down like water-falls on both us and the catwalks, where some of the mounds were getting two feet deep. The towing lines, drenched with water and shit, were slippery and more than twice as heavy as usual. It was precarious to stand, even trickier to walk, and seemingly almost impossible to toss a line.

Throwing and securing a tow line is always a dangerous procedure. The two vessels (or the vessel and pier) have to be either stationary in relation to each other or slowly closing. If the space between the two is widening as the line is thrown and connected to a bitt or cleat, the line is likely to snap, whipping back with enough speed and force to kill. If the space is rapidly closing as you throw, any impact involving your platform can hurl you overboard to be crushed. The deck crew thus always depended on one another and the captain to maintain the vital stability of the moving parts. But the hurricane kept us from hearing one another, and the double-decked superstructure of the cattle float kept us from seeing the other deck men, the captain, and often even the tug itself. The great part of living through that night is getting to tell about it.

On most days we worked with barges. This took us throughout the entire waterway system of New York Harbor, with its seven hundred miles of shoreline, giving free lessons in geography, history, and sociology. We worked up and down the Hudson River between Jersey and Manhattan, down past the Statue of Liberty on Ellis Island, through Kill Van Kull into Newark Bay, into the narrow Arthur Kill between Staten Island and New Jersey, out across Raritan Bay and the Upper Bay to "Tough Tony" Anastasio's Brooklyn piers in Red Hook (a block from Carb Manufacturing), up under the iconic Brooklyn Bridge, the Manhattan Bridge, the Williamsburg Bridge, the Queensboro Bridge, the Triborough Bridge—those beautiful marvels of earlier American technology and industry spanning the so-called East "River," which is really a saltwater sluiceway between Long Island Sound and New York Bay. The deadliest spot on all these waters is the aptly named Hell Gate, where the tidal rip of this sluiceway is so fierce and steep that the lines mooring the barges had to be replaced every twenty-four hours. From the East River we occasionally towed up the Harlem River, which makes Manhattan an island, all the way to Spuyten Duyvil, Dutch for "Spouting Devil" or "The Devil's Whirlpool," the tidal sluiceway connecting to the Hudson River.[1]

Barge work demanded intricate maneuvers and complex calculations, some involving dozens of barges. On a typical day, we received a list of barges to be picked up from widely scattered piers, docks, and ship sides and the destination to which each barge was to be towed. We had to know the type of load on each barge and then solve a set of problems involving tide, wind, current, weight, point of origin, destination, and relations among the barges. We might have to tow at one time fourteen barges, with cargoes whose weight varied as much as cotton and concrete. Barges were often moored four or more abreast, with five or six of such groups end to end along the length of a pier. The particular barge we were after might be the third in a group of four, four groups in from the end of the pier. This would be hard enough to disentangle if it were the first barge of the day. But we might already have eight or ten barges secured along our sides and bow. If this particular barge were loaded with steel, it would have to go right alongside the tug, balanced against another heavy barge on the other side. In this case we would have to let the barges already in tow go partly free, swinging in the tide, wind, and current, while at the same time also letting several groups of barges alongside the pier swing partly free. Then we would have to maneuver the barge into its proper towing position, while simultaneously maneuvering and resecuring them. The three men on the deck crew had to climb and scramble around on all the moving vessels, throwing and repeatedly untying and tying lines. We had to work in precision with one another and with the captain, who had to be just as precise in relation to the engine room crew. Each operation had to be planned and timed to take into account all the natural and mechanical forces in a fluid environment.

Danger lurked in the lines themselves, especially those kept on the barges, whose "captains" were mostly former tugboat men, mostly old, some alcoholic, and some who had been crippled on the job. We didn't have time to inspect these lines. On top, where the sun kept them dry, they would appear sound. But underneath, salt water residue might be rotting them, especially at the core. In the midst of the trickiest barge operations, our key lines were often these barge lines. Under the tremendous masses and forces in motion, even sound lines could snap.

After throwing a line, you belay or make fast your end, usually by throwing a figure-eight knot or some other quick-release knot as fast you can onto the bitt or cleat from which you are working. Your hands are working close to the metal. The most common accident is to have several fingers crushed or even sliced off by a sudden tightening of the line, which is why deck men all wore oversized, loose-fitting work gloves. But if you concentrate too much on this danger, you can miss the only warning you will get of a line about to snap, the unraveling of a tiny strand a second before the explosion. We all had close calls. Once Sonny had time just to yell "Duck!" I did. And a thick towing line whipped just over my head with enough speed and mass to kill.

With luck and skill, a man could avoid all the dangers of his job, but not the dangers to all these jobs, which were menaced by forces that no individual could evade. By December, I'd be heading for the Air Force. But the livelihoods of the other men, and the fate of the whole floating railroad industry—tugs, barges, lighters, and railroad car floats—were inextricably interwoven with the fate of the Port of New York longshoremen and workers on the railroads themselves. And soon all would be gone from the harbor. Scant memory remains of the old industrial port and the warfare over its control. Almost entirely gone is any knowledge of the railroad tugboats and their role in the economy of the city.

The tugboat men had a vague sense of solidarity embracing all railroad workers, but certainly not enough to consider any kind of collective action as the railroads stripped away jobs. In April 1954, the New York, New Haven and Hartford Railroad—whose acquisition of fifty railroads arranged by J. P. Morgan made it the dominant line throughout New England during the first half of the twentieth century—was taken over by new management, which began getting rid of "excess" workers who were just "featherbedding." Among the first to go were half the track-inspection crews, which led to a flurry of minor derailings. On July 14, 1955, that line's crack express derailed at Bridgeport, plunging seven cars over an embankment. Management blamed the engineer, who could hardly argue the case since he was killed in the wreck.[2]

The next target was the deck crews of the New York, New Haven, and Hartford tugboats, which management cut from three men to two. We read the railroad's comments about the surplus workers on the deck, three men who just threw a few lines around from time to time. Tony, ordinarily a man of few words and knowing looks, suggested that we ask the managers of the railroad and the smart boys who wrote their stories to come down here and show us how two men could do barge work. But when these first cuts on the line's tugs were made, leading to a brief strike by its tug crews, all we did about it was sympathize. In 1968, our own Pennsylvania Railroad would merge with the New York Central to form the Penn Central, which then took over the New York, New Haven and Hartford. By 1970, the combined fleets of all these railroads consisted of twelve tugs.[3]

The nineteenth-century railroad robber barons—Jay Gould, J. P. Morgan, Leland Stanford, Andrew Carnegie, Cornelius Vanderbilt, Collis Huntington, Mark Hopkins, Edward Harriman, Charles Crocker—got the national and state governments to legalize their plunder of land and labor. Indeed, their main acts were mostly committed with pieces of paper. They used legal documents to steal the land from the native peoples, used legal contracts to bind hordes of Chinese and European immigrants to their will, and bought with checks the labor of an unending supply of convicts who laid thousands of miles of tracks. Everything was legal, even forcing convicts to live jammed into iron cages that rolled on the track they just laid, even selling their daily urine to tanneries, even selling their bodies—at the end of their two-year average life span—to the nearest medical college for dissection.[4] Sure, faced with strikes or other resistance the railroad barons sometimes had to deploy armies of hired gunmen, some in uniform, and gangs of thugs and goons, some acting in the name of law and order. Although they were all swindlers and cheats, they were not outlaws. Because they made the laws.

The same cannot be said for the gangsters who were making minor fortunes from a variety of waterfront rackets. The criminal syndicates that had amassed wealth and power from Prohibition remained outlaws, strictly speaking, even after the U.S. Navy handed them the waterfront during World War II. In 1942, the Navy, seeking order, discipline, and efficiency, recruited Lucky Luciano (New York City's top mobster, then doing time in a maximum-security prison), Albert Anastasia (head of Murder, Inc.), "Cockeye" Dunn (notorious hit man later executed for murder), Joe Adonis (killer of a rival gang boss), Meyer Lansky, Frank Costello, and other leaders of the major Mafia families to serve as the rulers and police of all the piers and docks on the New York and New Jersey waterfront.[5] Gang rule was thus sanctioned and institutionalized by the government of the United States.

We tugboat men could see no difference between "organized crime" and the employers of us and the other workers all over the waterfront. New York City's 283 piers were handling about one-third of America's seaborne trade in manufactured goods.[6] Crime was everywhere. Most, but not all, of every cargo we saw being loaded or unloaded went in the marked trucks and vessels of legal businesses. Part went into unmarked trucks. The rest went to anyone who could grab it.

All kinds of commodities were siphoned off in broad daylight, not just radios, cases of aspirin, canned goods, clothing, .45 automatics, and bags of coffee beans but even bulk copper and cotton, machinery, great lengths of structural steel, and jeeps. The collusion was on such a vast scale that "organized crime" just seemed to be the junior partner of big business, their even better-organized senior partner. Historically, it made perfect sense. American industry and banking, after all, rest on land gained by swindles and massacres of its original inhabitants and used to raise cotton and tobacco produced by slaves kidnapped by the millions from Africa.

Crime was no more dominant on the docks than in the surrounding neighborhoods. I remembered how dangerous it was to buy our lunchtime beer in the pool hall across from Carb Manufacturing and to walk the Carb payroll down that last block to the factory. In fact, the criminal culture was just as blatant in my favorite bar on a corner of Coney Island Avenue six blocks from my home on peaceful 13th Street. One neighborhood gang more or less ruled the bar, making it relatively safe for regular patrons like my father and me, but three people had been murdered there in separate incidents. Everyone in the bar got a free drink whenever any gang member passed the exam to become a cop.

I briefly knew only one actual waterfront mobster, Johnny DiGilio, and he was then just a likable tugboat deckhand a year older than me on his way up. Unlike Terry Malloy (Marlon Brando's character in *On the Waterfront*), Johnny was already a welterweight contender who had won his first fifteen professional fights. Since he and I were exactly the same height and weight, and since I fancied myself a pretty good boxer, we once sparred for fun on a Hoboken dock. Though he was taking it easy, he taught me quickly enough that I was a sucker for a right cross. Thanks to his later success in running various rackets for the Genovese family along the New Jersey waterfront, *Fortune* magazine in 1986 listed him as number thirty-nine of the fifty most powerful Cosa Nostra bosses in America. In 1988, he was tried in Newark on federal racketeering charges involving his position in the International Longshoremen's Association (ILA), along with two other Genovese mobsters, including Donald Carson, executive vice president of the union. All three men were to be represented by lawyers selected by the Genovese family. Evidently figuring that he was being set up to be the fall guy to protect Carson so that the family wouldn't lose Carson's powerful position in the ILA, Johnny decided to defend himself. He put on a great show, climaxed by throwing cassette tapes of his phone conversations, which he dismissed as "locker room talk," into a wastebasket. He was the only one acquitted. Three days later, Johnny's wife reported him missing. Three weeks later, his decomposed body, with two bullet holes behind the ear, turned up in a mortician's bag floating in the Hackensack River. Carson's position was taken over by a member of the rival Gambino family. Years later, Louis Auricchio, a member of the Genovese family, confessed to shooting Johnny in a car driven by George Weingartner, a high-ranking member of the family.[7]

Working in the culture of the waterfront, we ourselves indulged in the anarchy of petty crime. Unlike our bosses, we knew that we would be jailed if we got caught. While we were tying up floats at the fruit and vegetable markets, a couple of men from the engine room would grab from the open freight cars enough special delicacies, such as grapes and melons, for the whole crew to enjoy. We laughed one night as we watched another crew that seemed to have suddenly grown obese, but with bright colors peeking out from under their work clothes, sneaking past the railroad detectives back at Pier H; they were swaddled in big bundles of ladies' fancy silk pajamas they had purloined for their wives and girlfriends from a barge they had towed.

One time late at night, we were ordered to tow a single barge from midtown Manhattan all the way to the Army terminal across the bay in Brooklyn. The barge was riding low in the water, indicating a heavy cargo, and it was most unusual to tow a lone barge on such a long haul. We speculated it must contain something like hand grenades or .45 automatics. We waited until we were alone in the middle of the bay. Then Tony and I climbed onto the barge, and, without any lights to give us away, broke in. Sure enough, the barge was filled with heavy cartons. We took a couple of dozen and passed them back to the tug, where the engine room crew stashed them in the hold. After delivering the barge, we waited until we were back in the middle of the bay to inspect our loot. All twenty-four cartons were filled with Campbell's bean and bacon soup. Unwilling to admit defeat, we slurped the soup for three nights. On the third night, we capitulated and threw the rest overboard. I have never again eaten any bean and bacon soup.

We would not have thought about stealing from one another or from any other person. Our personal property was always safe. What we considered criminal was the behavior of the railroads, stevedore companies, shipping lines, and ILA and American Federation of Labor (AFL) leaders who were stealing the labor and lives of working people. We thought of our petty pilfering as a tiny bit of payback.

We saw the war raging around us as class war, with powerful and wealthy interests feuding among themselves over their shares of the profits to be squeezed from people whose only resource was their labor. We knew that unions were the only means working people had of obtaining living wages and endurable livable working conditions. And we were aware that unions were under attack, ferociously and by different forces, on the waterfront. We had no concept of how spectacularly successful the attack would be.

The labor militancy of the Depression was put on hold during World War II, a hold enforced on the waterfront by that compact between the

Navy and the Mafia. It returned, as strong as ever, even before the postwar boom. On October 1, 1945, just six weeks after the end of the war, wildcat strikes swept across the harbor. Thirty-five thousand longshoremen walked off the docks, completely shutting down the port. When Joe Ryan, the ILA president for life, tried to speak to a mass meeting of the strikers in Brooklyn, they booed, hissed, and shouted him off the stage. Ryan declared, "This so-called rank-and-file committee is a tool of the Communists," a charge echoed and amplified in the media, and he turned his gangsters loose on the men, who fought back until they won major concessions, including a 23 percent increase in hourly pay.[8]

Over the next two years, workers throughout the industrialized regions of the country, energized by returning veterans and led by the militant Congress of Industrial Organizations (CIO) unions that had fought for labor rights in the New Deal era, demanded their share of the postwar American Dream. In response came the anti-Communist crusade that turned the "radicals" and "reds" leading these struggles into enemies of the state.

The weapon that crippled America's unions was the Taft-Hartley Act of 1947, which outlawed many of their crucial activities and rights. At the time of its passage, about one in three American workers was a union member. Today only about one in ten belongs to a union, and almost half of these are government workers who have no legal right to strike. And the Taft-Hartley is still used by state after state to destroy unions, typically by passing so-called right-to-work laws. The most crippling section of the act affecting the war in New York Harbor was Section 9(h), which required all union officials to sign a federal oath swearing that they didn't "believe in" or "support" Communism. Many who did sign were later convicted of perjury and sent to prison. In 1950, the CIO expelled eleven of its most militant, honest, and best-run unions for "following the Communist line," and then destroyed ten of them by setting up and financing rivals that raided their membership.[9]

The only survivor was the International Longshoremen's and Warehousemen's Union (ILWU), which had organized the waterfront workers of the Pacific coast into a model of integrity and militancy after winning an epic victory in 1934. The ILWU developed a fair hiring hall system to replace the exploitative shape-up system at the corrupt core of the ILA. It has continued to prove that a large industrial union can be a formidable representative of its members while fighting for progressive causes in American society. In the 1960s, while ILA goon squads were physically attacking anti–Vietnam War protesters, the ILWU was in the vanguard of antiwar activities. I recall with gratitude the help of ILWU Local 6 in helping to build our 1966 campaign in Redwood City against the use of napalm, which initiated the great national and international campaigns. My strongest feelings about the ILWU, however, come from an incident during a 1969 strike by the Oil, Chemical and Atomic Workers at the Chevron refinery in Richmond, California, after Richmond police had badly beaten the secretary-treasurer of the striking local. I was among dozens of students and workers from the Palo Alto area who joined the picket line, which was soon attacked by the Richmond police, who succeeded in driving us all back into a remote corner of the giant refinery. Looking furious, the cops pulled their visors down from the blue helmets, pointed the three-foot-long batons at us, and got set to charge us in lines that left no room for escape. Suddenly, in a Hollywood-like sequence, two speeding buses abruptly braked to a stop right behind the police lines. Out of the buses poured two columns of ILWU longshoremen singing "Solidarity Forever" and bearing small American flags on long, stout poles. We cheered and joined the singing. The cops moved aside, put up their visors, and broke into small casual groups, some now lighting cigarettes and chatting.

Although the ILWU recognized that "Joe Ryan and his mob of assorted gangsters were always nothing else but hoodlums posing as union leaders," nevertheless in the 1950s it saw the ILA as a brother union fighting for its life against governments run by and for the capitalist class.[10] The ILWU's view of the war on the New York waterfront was far more complex and insightful than that projected in *On the Waterfront*, the 1954 movie that has enshrined in American culture a perversely falsified history and reality. *On the Waterfront*—whose scriptwriter Budd Schulberg and director Elia Kazan had both betrayed friends by naming names to HUAC—presents the Waterfront Commission as the force of virtue dedicated to defending the interests of the longshoremen, the longshoremen as a flock of helpless sheep, the ILA as just a pack of wolfish criminals devouring the workers, and an informer as a heroic figure leading the workers to earthly and spiritual salvation. In reality, the longshoremen were fierce fighters for their own rights who saw the Waterfront Commission—which was primarily an agent of their employers and the anti-union governments of New York, New Jersey, and the United States—as their main and deadliest enemy; the ILA, though gangster-ridden and corrupt, was the only force capable of protecting the economic interests of longshoremen; and all the media at the time, with the exception of a few remaining radical journals, were engaged in an unrelenting and remorseless campaign to destroy the ILA. *On the Waterfront* was a slick and effective part of that campaign.

To understand the 1950s war on the waterfront, a little chronology is necessary. In 1951, ILA president Joe Ryan signed a weak contract with the New
York Shipping Association (NYSA), the longshoremen's main employer—
which had been paying him for years. New York longshoremen launched a
wildcat strike that spread up and down the East Coast. Ryan again cried
"Communists!" and unleashed his goons and gangsters. The strikers fought
back with fists and cobblestones. The strike lasted twenty-five days, paralyzed the Atlantic coast, cost the shippers hundreds of millions of dollars,
and ended in victory for the longshoremen—despite all the efforts of the
shippers, state and federal governments, media, gangsters, and their own
union leaders to force them back to work.[11]

In the midst of the strike, the New York Chamber of Commerce asked
Republican governor Thomas Dewey to have the New York Crime Commission investigate the ILA. The investigation took place during 1952 and
1953. In 1953, President Eisenhower signed legislation creating the New
York and New Jersey Waterfront Commission, the AFL expelled the ILA
and created the International Brotherhood of Longshoremen (IBL) as a rival
union to take over the docks, and Elia Kazan began filming *On the Waterfront*. The Waterfront Commission replaced the shape-up with an "open
register," allowing anyone, not just union members, to sign up for longshore
work, thus filling the docks with excess workers and undermining any
union's bargaining power.[12] When the ILA, refusing to work without a contract, called a strike in October, Eisenhower forced the men back to work by
invoking the Taft-Hartley Act.[13] In the December National Labor Relations Board (NLRB) election to determine whether the ILA or IBL
would represent the longshoremen, the majority of the men voted for the
ILA, even though every newspaper in New York except the *Daily Worker*
rigorously campaigned for the IBL and the NLRB threw out hundreds of
ballots cast for the ILA. The AFL asked Governor Dewey to overturn the
election, which he promptly did. But the ILA again defeated the ILB in the
May 1954 election and was declared by the NLRB to be the official representative of the longshoremen.[14]

In 1955, riding on the Brighton Line subway from Flatbush and on the
old Hudson-Manhattan "tubes" (now known as PATH, the Port Authority
Trans Hudson line) on my way to Jersey City, almost every day I was reading stories about the waterfront struggles in the *New York Times*. After reading a story about how the workers were now happy because the Waterfront
Commission had gotten rid of the shape-up, I walked on my way to Pier H
past the giant Pier F, owned by United Fruit (whose directors Allen Dulles

and John Foster Dulles had just arranged the overthrow of the democratically elected government of Guatemala) where the usual glum semi-
circle of longshoremen were grudgingly dropping five-dollar bills into a can
labeled "To buy flowers for Johnnie Jones' widow Annie Jones." For months
there were stories about murders committed by rival gangs fighting for
waterfront territory, especially in Brooklyn, where the "Irish locals" in Bay
Ridge, aligned with the ILA's top leaders, were in border wars with Tony
Anastasio, who was expanding from his base in Red Hook. The ILA was
resisting the increasing control by the Waterfront Commission, which was
now requiring registration and fingerprinting of every longshoreman and
attempting to fire any with a criminal record, as if these men had any other
way of making a living wage. The American Civil Liberties Union (ACLU)
was denouncing these rules as "a frightening step toward statism" that was
putting longshoremen with criminal records in "moral double jeopardy."[15]
By July, the commission had already revoked work permits of over six hundred working longshoremen with criminal records.

Then on August 22 the Waterfront Commission decreed that Mickey
McLoughlin, for years a longshoreman, would no longer be allowed to work
on the waterfront, because of a previous criminal record dating back to 1924.
When McLoughlin was turned away by the Grace Line on its Pier 57 in
Manhattan, the 192 other longshoremen on the pier all refused to work. The
scene *looked* almost identical to the climactic scene in *On the Waterfront*,
but the reality was exactly the opposite of Hollywood's projection. Unlike
Terry Malloy, McLoughlin was not an informer to the Waterfront Commission, but a man stripped of his job by the commission, perhaps because
of an informer. The longshoremen were rebelling not against the ILA or
gangsters but against the commission itself.[16]

"A wildcat strike involving one man on one pier spread like an epidemic
yesterday and threatened port-wide paralysis today," read the front page of
the *New York Times* I was reading on my way to work on the 24th. The leaders of the ILA opposed the walkout, but the "president of the union was
hooted down when he tried to get the men back to work," and "there is no
indication they will go back, there is so much bitterness against the Waterfront Commission."[17] Our tug shuttled all around the harbor that day, securing barges that were not getting unloaded, while Tony, Sonny, and I gawked
at the chaotic scenes of spirited and sometimes clashing groups of longshoremen and cops, as well as the laughable scenes of passengers from the
Queen Mary and another luxury liner struggling in their elegant clothes to
unload their trunks and other cumbersome baggage after docking from

their transatlantic voyage, a fashionable vacation in those days before jet travel.

After a two-week hiatus, the ILA, now following the rank and file, officially supported their strike and demanded the Commission adopt a more "understanding and humane approach toward men with police records," stop flooding the piers with new men, and cease its efforts to have the AFL union recognized as the men's official representative. On September 7, the strike shut down the entire port and spread to Baltimore, Philadelphia, and Boston. Temporary unity even reigned among the rival gangs, pasting over the conflict between Tony Anastasio and ILA top officials. Close to two thousand longshoremen came to a Brooklyn meeting called by Anastasio and, to the surprise of a New York Times reporter, "wildly cheered" when the head of the ILA "said that all the union wanted was for its men to be 'treated like human beings.'"[18] Similar throngs of longshoremen the next day cheered their leaders at meetings throughout the port, prompting the Times to admit grudgingly that "the attitude of the rank and file union men" "appeared to refute the conviction of the Waterfront Commission that the average longshoreman was opposed to the strike."[19]

As the strike rolled on during the week, we had to cram barges loaded with rail freight alongside holding piers, and we saw perishables rotting on eerily vacant piers. The internal truce among the rival factions fighting for control of the ILA broke down when Tony Anastasio ordered his Brooklyn locals back to work on September 12 and roving gangs from Manhattan "persuaded" his men to disobey.[20]

The only vision of the waterfront wars available to the general public was the one skillfully projected by On the Waterfront and reinforced almost daily by the media, especially the New York Times, which not only reported the news from the same perspective but also wrote enthusiastically about both the movie and Budd Schulberg's novel Waterfront.[21] So I too tended to see the longshoremen as dupes and victims of mobsters in control of the ILA, and the Waterfront Commission as an instrument designed to protect the men from the gangsters. Neither I nor Sonny, Tony, or the rest of our crew—not to mention all those people who got their news from the media—was aware that the Waterfront Commission was actually a government organization financed entirely by the longshoremen's employers, the New York Shipping Association.[22]

So we were all supposed to believe that an organization created by a Republican governor, a Republican congress, and a Republican president, and financed by an employer, was serving the interests of the employees. Too bad we didn't have access to the ILWU's newspaper, *The Dispatcher*, which was explaining how the commission "gives absolute job control to the ship-owners," thus flooding the docks with newcomers, tripling the work force, and driving down wages: "The over-supply in the labor force . . . explains why New York longshoremen last year had an average annual wage which was less than half that of our own West Coast longshoremen." Although the ILWU was hardly naive about the presence of mobsters in ILA officialdom, it exposed how that fact was being used to mask the real issues:

> Newspaper reports about the recent strike in New York gave and were calculated to give the impression that our brother longshoremen in the ILA were fighting the Bi-State Waterfront Commission in order to keep racketeers on the waterfront.
>
> Another also carefully nurtured impression is that the commission, itself, was created for the purpose of eliminating criminals from the waterfront.
>
> Both notions are so much hogwash.[23]

In "Why They Stick to the ILA," investigative reporter Richard Sasuly, writing just after the strike ended with the longshoremen successfully defending their union shop contract and with New York governor W. Averell Harriman firing the Army general who headed the Waterfront Commission, ridiculed the notion "that the longshoremen needed to be redeemed by a stool pigeon under a priest's direction." After being "the butt of endless investigations," undergoing "a steady barrage" from "the New York newspapers," facing hostile machinations on every level of government, and being run by mobsters, why, he asked, has the ILA retained the loyalty of the long-shoremen? Because, he answered, most of them, on all levels of the union, lived in tightly knit communities: "Mobsters in books and pictures emerge as sinister and shadowy silhouettes. Mobsters in the flesh live in particular houses on particular streets, very often the same streets where longshore-men live. If there are arrangements between them, they are arrangements within a community."[24]

True, "Tough Tony" Anastasio was a mobster and the brother of Albert Anastasia, head of Murder, Inc., but he was also considered by the rank and file in his Brooklyn locals to be a tough battler on their behalf. (Every article in the *New York Times*—except for its 1963 obituary—erroneously spelled Anthony's last name like his infamous brother's, an "error" repeated in many books and articles about the New York waterfront.) Anastasio worked for years to ditch the shape-up and switch to the rotational hiring system of the ILWU; during the 1955 strike he reached out to the ILWU, which responded with financial aid for the ILA. The ILA then complained to the commission that it was being lax on the Communists.[25]

The denouement of the overlapping gang wars for control of the waterfront rackets would come in 1957 when Albert Anastasia was gunned down in a spectacular barbershop assassination, leaving the Brooklyn and Manhattan waterfront in the hands of the Gambino family. Anastasio later said, "I ate from the same table as Albert and came from the same womb but I know he killed many men and he deserved to die."

During my half year on the tugs amid the raging waterfront wars, an aging tanker moored on a dock in Newark was being converted into the vanguard of the juggernaut that would sweep away the longshoremen with their bag hooks, the railroad tugboats, the barges and floats they towed, the waterfront markets, and the steamships being loaded and unloaded at the piers, consigning them all to memory. Most of the piers would become rotting hulks disappearing into the water. The factories and warehouses clustered near the waterfront would also disappear or be resurrected as fashionable condominiums. On April 26, 1956, that ship would head for Houston on a fateful voyage that would do as much to change the world as Columbus's first voyage. Stacked on its deck were fifty-eight boxlike aluminum truck bodies that would be lifted by crane onto fifty-eight trucks waiting in Houston to take them to their fifty-eight destinations. Thus began the containerization revolution that, linked to computer technology, would create our globalized planet.[26]

In the closing scene of the original version of *Invasion of the Body Snatchers*, which also appeared in 1956, the protagonist is left screaming on a highway as trucks filled with pods pass him by while no ordinary person realizes how the pods are changing the world. Only after reading Marc Levinson's *The Box* did I think about the significance of all those containers on all those trucks I encounter on the highway. The container, that forty-foot box that can be lifted to and from ship and train and truck, has reshaped the global economy and its geography of manufacturing and consumption. Nowhere are the changes more blatant than in New York Harbor.

Today the longshoreman sits in a room, usually windowless, facing a screen and operating a computer that has been preprogrammed to assign each container to or from its designated place on a ship or railcar or truck.[27] He controls a gigantic crane in Port Newark's labyrinth of trolleys and cranes resembling a horde of imperial walkers.

In today's harbor, the shipping and commerce industry of the past has been replaced by the recreation and sports industry of the twenty-first century. Sailboats, kayaks, speedboats, and even a few water skiers skim the waters of the Hudson River. A few of the surviving piers are still berths for multilevel cruise ships. Others have been replaced or converted into fancy entertainment sites, such as the Chelsea Piers Sports & Entertainment Complex, which spans a range of piers on Manhattan's west side. In 2016, on what will probably be my last voyage in the harbor, I caught a three-foot-long striped bass from a charter boat drifting around the southern tip of Manhattan.

6 ▸ THIRTEEN CONFESSIONS OF A COLD WARRIOR

1. HOW I GOT TO BE A PROFESSIONAL HIRED KILLER

Thousands of us streamed through Lackland Air Force Base in San Antonio, Texas, in the 1950s. We were Air Force ROTC second lieutenants, future flyboys destined for the front line of America's global strategy and eager for our mighty big jobs: Making the world safe for democracy by stopping the Communists from conquering the planet. Keeping the Russians from obliterating the United States with their armada of nuclear-armed bombers. Preparing to obliterate them first if ordered.

I got there in January 1956, a few months after Paramount Pictures released *Strategic Air Command*. Fresh in my mind were those thrilling images of Jimmy Stewart defending the Free World by flying the giant ten-engine B-36 and the brand-new first all-jet B-47 superbomber, so sleek and dazzlingly gorgeous, with its slim body and swept-back wings, that it makes him forget all about his wife (June Allyson) as he exclaims, "She's the most beautiful thing I've ever seen in my life."

The first day was like college orientation, and that night we got to cruise the bars along San Antonio's River Walk. The next day we got our first

indoctrination lectures. The best show was put on by the base's flight surgeon, a beefy lieutenant colonel who chomped his cigar pugnaciously just
like General Curtis LeMay, the fearsome commander of the Strategic Air
Command (and of course like square-jawed tough guy Frank Lovejoy as
Hollywood's larger-than-life image of LeMay in *Strategic Air Command*).

"You men," he roared into the microphone, "are now nothing but Uncle
Sam's professional hired killers."

Our hearts thumped with patriotic pride and manly excitement. This
was what most of us had always wanted to be when we grew up, swaggering
out of Saturday afternoon gangster, western, and war movies and shooting
it out in the back alleys or country roads on the way home from school.

"So don't think," he went on, "that you're going to walk into my base hospital and get your skinny ass grounded just because your li'l ol' nosey
caught the sniffles. Uncle pays you top dollar to do your job, and he's going
to spend one quarter of a million little green ones to train each motherlo-
vin' son here how to do it right. Anybody here now who thinks he can't hack
it in this man's world?"

"Don't be bashful," he thundered at the five hundred of us sitting in the
auditorium. "Just raise your hand."

2. A PATRIOTIC WEDDING IN 1956 AMERICA

But my heart sank the next day when I learned that I wasn't destined to be
what I long yearned to be: a fighter pilot. My physical exam revealed that
everything was fine except for my right eye, which was not quite 20/20,
something no other eye exam had ever disclosed. So I was assigned not to
flight school but to navigator training. Later I discovered that many of my
classmates were also rudely awakened from their pilot dreams by hitherto
unknown minor physical effects. Could that have something to do with the
Air Force's needs in 1956? Fighter pilots would be in high demand if fleets of
Soviet bombers were threatening the United States. Navigators, bombardiers, and electronic countermeasures officers—all graduates of navigation
training—would be in high demand if fleets of bombers were being manned
to threaten the Soviet Union.

Before going off to navigator flight training at Ellington AFB outside
Houston I got a ten-day leave. Time enough to pursue a different dream.
So I flew back to Brooklyn to get together with a woman I'd met a few
months earlier through a benign quirk of fate while she was working in the

Information Department of the United Nations and I was working as a tug-boat deckhand in New York Harbor.

Back in September, I was driving through Central Park with my friend Randy Van Sant, who in 1954 had become something of a celebrity at Smith College and Amherst. The fifties were the era of the "panty raids," when hordes of men from all-male colleges would descend on the dormitories of all-female colleges to steal panties as trophies. One night hundreds of Smith College women, organized and led by Randy, had conducted a retaliatory underpants raid of Amherst dorms. Randy had now just moved into a residential nursing school on Manhattan's West Side. We were headed for a nightclub in Yorkville, but I made a wrong turn in the park and came out instead a block from the East Side apartment Randy had just moved from. We decided to skip the club, grab some beer and sandwiches, and go up to her old apartment.

We arrived to find Randy's two former roommates interviewing some-one to take her place, a strawberry blonde named Jane, newly arrived from the South. Jane, I learned from the conversation, was a farm girl from North Carolina, an all-county high-school basketball star, and also a star English-major graduate from Duke.

I managed to find out that Jane's last name was Morgan and that she was temporarily living in the Barbizon Hotel for Women. Two nights later, after our tugboat had dropped off some barges at a Manhattan pier, I spied a pay phone on the pier, dialed the Barbizon, and asked for Jane Morgan. The woman who was called to the phone sure had a southern accent, but it seemed even thicker than what I remembered. After a couple of minutes, she announced, "Ah believe you have the wrong Jane Morgan. Ah'll get the raight one." And she did.

On our first date, the right Jane Morgan and I had a heated argument—about T. S. Eliot. Then the relationship with this sexy intellectual from an alien land got a lot hotter. Neither one of us had been looking to get married, but after about six weeks that's all we were talking about when we weren't talking about literature, politics, world affairs, music, basketball, and sex. We even set the month: June of 1956. In January I left for the Air Force.

At the end of that month, when I found out about that ten-day leave before going to Houston I immediately called Jane at the West Side apartment she was now sharing. One of her four housemates told me how to reach her at a nightclub where she had gone to listen to jazz pianist Johnny Mehe-gan. So pay phone to pay phone, I tried to talk about marriage. Then a fire broke out in the club's kitchen, and firemen dragging their big fire hoses stormed by Jane's phone booth while Johnny Mehegan kept playing above the din.

So our next argument had to wait until we got together. I tried to persuade her to marry me in early February because this was the last leave I would get before reporting for my regular Air Force assignment, and who knows where that might be.

But she was having a ball in New York and wanted to wait until summer. The last place in the world she wanted to go was Texas. She loved her job at the U.N. She did not want to be an Air Force wife. But we were madly in love. And this was 1956.

So we borrowed my parents' 1951 Ford and drove to Jane's parents' tobacco farm between Wilson and Zebulon, North Carolina. Jane's mother, who had told me on the phone that I might not know Jane well enough to marry her, was now frantically preparing for the wedding.

This was the first time I had been in the South since that shocking bus ride when all the black passengers had to get up and move to the back. Very conscious of being a Jewish boy from Brooklyn, I was now an alien in a strange land. All the gracious southern hospitality and politeness made me feel even more like a barbarian with no proper manners. Some strict, formal protocol seemed to govern all social interactions. Jane's father called me "sir," some kind of man-to-man code, even though I was only twenty-one. Each "sir" sounded to me like a nineteenth-century patriarch addressing his daughter's raffish young suitor or maybe a southern gentleman addressing his opponent in a duel. It was relaxing and wildly interesting to stroll around the farm with Jane. The only other time I had been on a farm was around 1943: a New Jersey chicken farm bought by a family acquaintance so he could, much to my disdain, get a long-term draft deferment. Jane introduced me to the cows, chickens, mules, guinea hens, and even a fierce beast isolated behind a sturdy fence, the lone bull kept for stud with the farm's cows and others whose owners could afford his services. Jane told me the birthing of calves was strictly men's domain, although once as a kid she had unsuccessfully tried to peep from another part of the cow barn, an area reserved for feral cats who kept down the mouse population.

We married in a small Methodist church, one of a handful of buildings in a crossroads called Mount Pleasant. Our only radical action was omitting "obey" from Jane's vows. I had planned to wear my only dark suit, but at the last hour decided to wear my Air Force uniform as a more all-American outfit. And besides, I was really quite proud of my uniform and my shiny new gold lieutenant's bars.

At the reception, the uniform seemed a good choice. Jane's two brothers-in-law were at the party. One was a major in the Marines and the son of a Marine general. He would later command a combat unit in Vietnam. The other was a Navy commander who cut our wedding cake with his ceremonial naval dress sword. In 1962, the destroyer he commanded would come close to starting World War III. And there was Jane's younger brother, who had recently gotten out of the Air Force. Jane's older brother couldn't make it to the reception because he was an Air Force fighter pilot stationed in Japan.

3. A 1950S AMERICAN FAMILY

It took the government a quarter of a million 1956 dollars, forty-two weeks, and hundreds of hours of flight time at Ellington AFB to train me to be a navigator. It was like the training part of those World War II movies about the Army Air Corps. Ellington Field was one of the main bases where World War II navigators and bombardiers had indeed trained. It was closed after the war but reopened as the primary base for most navigation training in 1948, that fateful year when America committed itself heart and soul to the Cold War.

In 1947 President Truman had announced the Truman Doctrine and instituted the Federal Employee Loyalty Program, requiring loyalty oaths of all federal employees and empowering the FBI to investigate two million Americans for possible Communist influence. That year was when the Department of War morphed into the Department of Defense, and when the CIA, the National Security Council, and the U.S. Air Force were all born. In 1948 the president inaugurated the peacetime draft.

One minor product of the frenzied militarization was Convair's T-29, which appeared in 1950 and went into mass production in 1955, just in time to be our flying classroom. It was a nifty plane for our purposes, with each student having a table for maps, LORAN scope, altimeter, and radio compass as well as access to a drift meter and an astrodome for shooting stars with our bubble sextants. Knowing that my life and the lives of others would depend on my doing my job well, I studied hard for the first time in my life.

I studied even harder after Jane became pregnant a month after we set up house in Pickwick Apartments, a Houston complex of one-story duplexes. Pickwick Apartments housed many other married navigators in training, making it easy for us to form carpools. Soon Jane was in her own carpool with three other officers' pregnant wives doing their periodic visits to the obstetrics department of the Ellington AFB hospital.

Houston in 1956 was a boom city. Drilling rigs and pump jacks were popping up like crocuses and bamboo shoots all around town. The city itself hit pay dirt when oil was struck in the main municipal garbage dump. Nothing could stand in the way of the black gold rush. Almost overnight, a giant drilling rig sprouted up through a gas station we had been using just four blocks from our apartment. To drive the seventeen miles from Pickwick Apartments to Ellington AFB, you had to shield your nose and eyes from the acrid fumes and haze spewing from the gas flares of the Pasadena oil fields.

Pasadena, along with six other incorporated areas, had been annexed by Houston in 1948, more than doubling the size of the city, though most of those areas were still only thinly inhabited. The shrewdest guy in our squadron and his wife, both Texans, made a lot of money by buying a newly built house in Pasadena and selling it ten months later. At the house party they threw for the rest of us, we admired both their financial savvy and their nasal fortitude.

Jane and I made the best of life in Houston. We saw the latest movies, played miniature golf, gawked at the wild alligators, and went to avant-garde plays at Rice University. We played one-on-one basketball, with me vainly trying to block Jane's deadly hook shot, until her pregnancy blew the whistle on that game. The Houston summer was a bummer, but we enjoyed watching the sudden boiling up of the gigantic afternoon thunderheads, often soaring to 40,000 feet, especially when their anvil top pointed our way, a sure sign that we would soon get a black sky, one of the greatest fireworks shows on earth, and cooling rain. Once we drove out after dark and parked in an oil field, awed by the towering automaton jacks dutifully swinging their cumbersome metal arms up and down, pumping up the gooey remains of ancient rain forests to power our postwar cars and trucks and airplanes.

Karen was born in December. Like Gretchen, who was born almost two years later in Maine, her health care was paid for by the Air Force. Karen was a healthy baby, but two of her tear ducts were plugged. We were advised by one of Jane's relatives to take her for treatment to a prominent pediatric doctor, who operated on her tear ducts at Houston's esteemed Texas Children's Hospital (a completely needless operation, we later discovered). This was also covered by the Air Force. But when we handed the Air Force payment forms to the doctor, he was outraged.

"That's socialism!" he exclaimed, his face reddening with anger as he went on. "I will not accept payment from the government for my medical services."

When we said we weren't going to pay, he responded, "All right, I'll just write you off as a charity case."

Of course the doctor was right. Everyone in the military, as well as all those good folks who make our laws, receive socialized medicine.

We left Houston a few days later in our 1950 Chevy coupe, with Karen sleeping in a flimsy car bed that hung from the back of the front bench seat, on our way to my new assignment in the Strategic Air Command (SAC).

4. WELCOME TO THE STRATEGIC AIR COMMAND

Choice of assignment upon graduating was according to class rank. But as we flocked around the board where the available assignments were posted, we discovered that the whole class, except for three slots, was going to have to do months of more schooling at Mather AFB to be trained as navigators, bombardiers, and electronic counter measures officers for SAC's B-47 and brand-new B-52 bombers. Government and Air Force priorities could not have been clearer. There was one posting for the Military Air Transport Service, which would involve long overseas flights to the dozens of U.S. bases strewn around the globe, an exciting life for a single man, and two postings to aerial refueling squadrons operating out of the continental United States. I chose SAC's 341st Air Refueling Squadron, an Arctic squadron whose home base was Dow AFB in Bangor, Maine.

Jane and I rented a house on an eight-acre abandoned farm overlooking the Penobscot River. It was the only brick structure along the eight miles of country road leading to the base. Later we discovered in a hidden attic room documents belonging to the builder, a ship captain who had hauled those bricks up the river in 1839. Then we found a large secret underground room that turned out to be part of the Underground Railroad. In the forest behind the farm was an abandoned apple orchard, where on days off duty I hunted the grouse (known locally as partridges) that came to fatten their plump white breasts but sometimes ended up as our dinner.

But we had no time to enjoy country life before we finished unpacking because I had to report for duty at Dow AFB. As I drove up to the gate, proudly wearing my new navigator wings, my first sight of a SAC base was this sign:

STRATEGIC AIR COMMAND
"PEACE IS OUR PROFESSION"
HOME OF THE 4060TH AIR REFUELING WING

When I found my squadron, the grizzled master sergeant who issued my equipment said, with a sly smile, "Well, you're just in time."

"For what?" I asked.

"To go with the rest of the squadron to Newfoundland."

So for the next two months, Jane would have been left alone with baby Karen in the Maine countryside if my mother had not come up from Brooklyn to be their companion. Meanwhile, I was navigating KC-97 tankers flying out of Harmon AFB, Newfoundland, doing midair refueling of B-47 and B-52 bombers over the North Atlantic, the Canadian Arctic, and points north. How far north I was soon to discover.

As I walked up to a KC-97 for my first flight, it sure looked big, bigger than any plane I had seen close up, bigger even than the Lockheed Constellation or the Douglas DC-6, then the four-engine giants of civilian airliners. Most civilian air travel, including my own, was still by two-engine versions of military transports. U.S. jet airliners wouldn't be around until late 1958, and I had never been close to any multiengine jet. But from any angle, the KC-97 sure wasn't "the most beautiful thing I've ever seen in my life." It looked more like a pregnant whale. But any disappointment was nudged aside by a little rush when I realized what a KC-97 actually was: a converted B-29 Superfortress. I was going to fly a version of the most advanced bomber of World War II, that iconic plane whose vast fleets had thrilled me in the Saturday afternoon movie newsreels of 1945. This was the marvel of American technology that finally won the war for freedom and democracy by burning down the cities of Japan and A-bombing Hiroshima and Nagasaki.

Boeing had added a lower fuselage to the B-29, giving it that pregnant whale look and making it able to serve as a large cargo plane (the C-97), a jumbo airliner seating a hundred passengers on the upper deck with a luxury lounge on the lower (the Stratocruiser), or a flying tanker (the KC-97).[1] As the official Air Force history of post–World War II bombers states, the KC-97 "transformed the B-47 into an intercontinental bomber."[2]

The body of the KC-97 was jammed with double-stacked fuel tanks that held jet fuel to be pumped into SAC's bombers to extend their range. Trailing behind the tail was a long rigid flying boom for off-loading the fuel. The tanker was indeed an engineering wonder, with intricate plumbing and electrical systems to control the refueling, as well as an ever-modernizing array of electronic equipment for navigating and rendezvousing. But despite all the latest radar, LORAN, transponders, and other electronic equipment, navigating over water or in the Arctic in the 1950s was a formidable challenge.

The flight crews were all male and all white, and you couldn't see many differences among us in our baggy flight suits and combat boots that made us look like scruffy oil field workers. But when we junior officers wore our dress khakis, an informed observer could easily tell us ROTC guys, who might have passed for tourists in casual blousy shirts, from the Officer Candidate School (OCS) guys, with their glistening spit-shined shoes and shirts all sharply trim from their painstakingly sewn waist tucks. Most of the flight engineers were senior noncommissioned officers (NCOs) who had been on bomber crews during the Korean War or even World War II, like the senior officers who ran the squadron and flew just enough hours to get their flight pay. The radio operators were mostly young working-class enlistees, but a few of the boom operators had been tail gunners in Korean War B-29s.

I think we all took pride in our skills and our job. I don't know how many of us believed in that SAC motto: "Peace Is Our Profession." I sure did.

5. NAVIGATING THE COLD WAR ON THE TOP OF THE GLOBE

Few people in the 1950s were aware that their fate depended on what was and what was not happening in the air over the frozen wastelands at the northern reaches of planet Earth. The icy polar air was not just a hot front of the Cold War but also the most perilous for civilization. The mixture of nuclear-armed U.S. bombers and Soviet jet fighters was explosive enough without being compounded by the perils of Arctic navigation in that primitive era.

As one flies toward the magnetic pole, the magnetic compass becomes increasingly useless. After all, over the magnetic pole, the magnetic compass would tell you that "north" is straight down. Besides, the magnetic pole wanders around dozens of miles each year in different directions. The Earth's true pole, which is hundreds of miles away from the magnetic pole, isn't much help either. At the true North Pole, the four conventional directions become meaningless, because any direction and every place on Earth is south. This might not be a big problem if you were flying over identifiable geographic features that could be tracked by radar. But over most of the subarctic and Arctic, there are no more consistent features than in the middle of the ocean. Even mountains and lakes unpredictably change their configurations depending on snowfall, freezing, thawing, and shifting ice sheets. So on our northbound missions, we didn't use maps. We plotted our track and position on special blank grid paper that we labeled with lines of latitude and longitude.

Our most precise method of navigation was celestial. Nowadays, the GPS on your cell phone instantly, continually, and within a few feet monitors your position by using a type of celestial navigation. We got our information from observing the position of stars, planets, the moon, and sun combined with specific times. Your GPS uses a different kind of celestial body: thirty or so Global Positioning System satellites orbiting about 12,400 miles above Earth. Like us primitive navigators, your GPS does "trilateration": it determines the angle of three of these heavenly bodies together with the time. Each GPS satellite "knows" when and where it is and is constantly transmitting, at the speed of light, its precise position and time. Your cell phone calculates its distance from each of the three satellites by measuring how long it took for the messages to arrive and thus instantly pinpoints your position.

But the stars, planets, moon, and sun probably do not know where they are, nor do they know the time of our day, and even if they had that information they have no way or motivation to send it to us. So in pure celestial navigation, we had to identify and then "shoot" three celestial bodies using a bubble-leveling sextant stuck through a receptacle in the roof of the control cabin of a bouncing airplane, timing each shot for at least one minute. Since those heavenly bodies didn't tell us the time, we had to get it from our watch, which we kept as accurate as possible. Since they didn't tell us their position, we had to consult the Air Almanac, a thick volume that told us the relative angle of the moon, sun, Venus, Mars, Jupiter, and about sixty named stars from any specific position and time on Earth. The Air Almanac assumes that all the stars (including those that are actually galaxies) are just points of light on a sphere whose surface is equidistant from Earth. All that matters is the angle or "altitude" recorded by the sextant. For each body we shot, we compared the angle from where we guessed we were to the angle in the Air Almanac. This corrected our guess. The result was three "lines of position" intersecting to form a triangle, the smaller the better. Then we put a dot in the center of the triangle. This dot was a "fix"—that is, our position. But of course since all of this took time and the plane was traveling at close to 300 mph, the fix wasn't where we were then but where we had been.

Your GPS device can "see" at least four of the orbiting satellites at any time from any position on Earth. Our celestial navigation depended on three bodies being visible to the human eye, which rarely happens except at night. Ideally we needed three bodies about 120 degrees away from one another. A cloudy sky was a problem, and so was the aurora borealis, those gloriously beautiful northern lights that at far northern latitudes often obliterate the stars in half the night sky. Even worse was the wide band of twilight in the polar region; we used a circular cardboard "Twilight Computer" to help plan the shortest path through the dreaded Twilight Zone. In the daytime, we were forced to shoot the sun, which was too big to get a precise reading, or the moon, also too big as well as too rapidly moving.[3]

If everything went well, we could get a "fix" that was within a mile or two of our actual position. Or, rather, our actual position back when we shot those heavenly bodies several minutes earlier. The top speed of our KC-97s was about 300 mph. Because SAC's B-47s and B-52s were going at about twice that speed, they had an even more difficult job of navigating. As I was about to discover.

6. MISSION IMPROBABLE

My first refueling mission was to navigate the lead ship of a four-plane "cell," SAC-speak for formation, on a nighttime flight. My performance was to be monitored by Dave, an instructor navigator about my age. Our plane and the second ship were KC-97Gs; the other two planes were the older KC-97F model. In mixed cells like ours, the Gs always took off before the Fs because—according to the Boeing manuals and the Boeing tech rep on the base—they climbed and flew faster than the Fs, making it dangerous to have the slower planes up front. I did wonder how the G, with an additional seven-hundred-gallon tank under each wing, could climb faster than the F, since both models had the same four Pratt & Whitney supercharged piston engines. As we taxied out, Dave told me, "These G models are all heavier and slower than the Fs. Boeing just keeps selling the Air Force more shit to put on these planes to make money. So I want you to watch out for numbers three and four after takeoff."

As we made our turn into takeoff position, I noticed that the Newfoundland ice fog—water crystals frozen in the frigid air—was so thick you couldn't see more than halfway down the runway. As we lifted off, we could barely see our own wingtips. Five minutes after takeoff, I noticed two blips on radar, each less than a hundred yards off either wing.

"What are these blips, Dave?" I asked.

"Jesus Christ! That's three and four climbing right through us. They don't even know we're here. Jesus Christ!"

We called the other planes and spent the next ten minutes vainly trying to reestablish our formation. Finally, we gave that up and decided that all four would meet at the orbit area, where we were to await four B-47s. The center of the orbit was a set of coordinates in the North Atlantic three hundred miles northeast of Newfoundland. All four of us arrived in the area and began orbiting. But the orbit pattern was an oval, so nobody knew which plane was which, and we needed to get ourselves in order before the bombers arrived. We decided to fire colored flares to find out who was who. It was fun, sticking the flare gun through a receptacle in the control cabin and shooting off green double stars and red-green double stars. But none of this so far was anything like Hollywood's *Strategic Air Command*.

We finally got ourselves straightened out. The B-47s still hadn't showed up. Then, thirty minutes after the scheduled rendezvous, I saw a squiggly green line on the scope of my transponder. This meant that my transponder unit had triggered the sister unit on the lead B-47. I established radio communications with its A/C (aircraft commander, SAC-speak for "pilot"), and began giving him corrections to steer into the rendezvous. He informed me that they had gotten lost en route, were low on fuel, and would need all we could give them.

Lost? That had scary implications that I thought more deeply about in the next two years every time I tried to contact lost bombers, some wandering around with thermonuclear bombs on board.

The B-47s were still at 39,000 feet, while we were circling at 15,000. This was normal procedure. At the proper range, I told the B-47 lead plane to begin the descent of their four-plane flight. Simultaneously, I gave the signal to our A/C to break out of our orbit and proceed down the refueling track. The other three ships in our cell followed us out on a diagonal line to our right at quarter-mile spacing. If everything went as programmed, the four B-47s would hit this diagonal line at the same spacing, and we would refuel them in formation.

I watched with satisfaction as the green squiggles on my transponder scope followed my instructions perfectly and lined up directly behind us. I was a bit disturbed, though, when the B-47 crew couldn't see us as they crossed the half-mile range indicator. According to regulations, refueling was to be completed only if the bomber could see the tanker at one-half mile. I watched the signal approach, and radioed, "You are now at one-quarter-mile range. Do you have visual contact?" "Negative," came the reply. At this point, Dave, seemingly unperturbed, said, "Hey, Bruce, you may not get to see a refueling when you're on your own. So let me take over while you go on back and take a look." I still wonder whether he was really as tranquil as he seemed or whether he didn't want a newbie in charge of the developing danger.

I grabbed my chest-pack chute and jogged back through the aisle between the double-stacked rows of fuel tanks that lined both sides of the plane's body from floor to roof. I stopped just short of the pod in the tail, and squatted so I could look out through the pod window. The boom operator—who had been a B-29 tail gunner in the Korean War—lay on his stomach inside the pod, peering out back through the inky soup. Although the B-47 had been only a quarter mile back when I left the control cabin, it still wasn't in sight. Suddenly, a large vertical line materialized about three feet behind the pod window. What in the world could that be? Hmm. It must be the top of the vertical stabilizer of the tail of the B-47. How puzzling, I mused.

"Oh my God! Oh my God! Oh my God!" the boom operator screamed, partly into the intercom and mostly to heaven. "He's right underneath us and he hasn't seen us! Oh my God! Please save us!" Only then did I comprehend that the big jet was so close that we were nearly touching. And that its crew had no idea that we were a few feet above them.

In a tone you might use to someone standing an inch from a coiled rattlesnake, our A/C told the B-47's A/C where he was. The vertical stabilizer dropped back and down from the pod window. The rest of the tail then slid into view, followed by the tapered narrow fuselage. In the murky midwinter subarctic black night, the full bomber, with its six jet engines slung under its swept-back wings, now appeared as a shadowy but thrilling engine of death.

Meanwhile we got a radio message. The other three B-47s had all homed in on our number two KC-97. Eventually, the four bombers got hooked up to the right tankers. And I got to see a refueling. The boom operator grasped the stick that controlled the rigid refueling boom that he actually flew, like a big model plane, below and behind our tail. When the bomber was in position, he flew the boom toward the refueling receptacle, then extended its tip into the hole, and finally activated an electromagnetic connection that completed the hookup. A few times during the refueling, the boom popped out, spraying the bomber's windshield with fuel, and had to be reinserted. It was like a surreal mechanical caricature of a human hookup.

I jogged back to my navigation position for the last of my duties during a refueling. The B-47 (like the B-52) could burn our aviation gas, but one pint of their JP-4 jet fuel (a mixture of kerosene and gasoline) backflowing through our valves would cause fuel contamination and quickly knock out our engines. (A few months later, such backflow caused a KC-97 to lose all four engines and go down in the Atlantic.) After giving a bomber all the JP-4 we had on board, we were supposed to let it have all the aviation gas we could spare. So I calculated how long it would take us to get back to Harmon, and prepared to give the time en route to the flight engineer so he could compute how much aviation gas we should withhold for an adequate reserve. But Dave stopped me.

"You've computed a thirty-knot headwind component," Dave said. "It should be ninety knots."

"You can check my figures. I'm sure it's thirty knots at the most."

"Oh, nobody told you about the navigator's life-insurance policy. Add ten knots headwind for each man aboard. Then the engineer will add the engineer's life-insurance policy to that."

As we headed home, I asked Dave about something I found puzzling.

"How come we completed this mission when we were below minimum visibility for takeoff and refueling?" I asked, trying not to sound too chicken. "Wasn't it just a routine practice mission? Couldn't it have been rescheduled?"

"Didn't you realize that these babies are going all the way?"

"All the way?"

"Sure, to Russia."

I had already been informed that many of our missions were refueling spy planes penetrating Soviet airspace for electronic surveillance. But I had understood that these were radio-silence missions, conducted with high security so that the bombers wouldn't be detected and shot down. So what was going on?

The B-47 we had just refueled was not a reconnaissance plane. The B-47 fitted out for reconnaissance, designated the RB-47, had a distinctive feature familiar to the air refueling crews: the refueling receptacle was not in the center of the nose but had been offset to the right side to make room for the extra electronic equipment. I flew on many subsequent missions on which B-47s and B-52s were heading for the Soviet Union. Some of these were reconnaissance planes, and in each case we refueled them on a radio-silence mission. And our briefing, takeoff, and flight plans for these missions all carried a high security classification. But I also participated in many missions on which we refueled B-47s and B-52s not fitted up for reconnaissance and heading toward the Soviet Union. Most of these were like the one I just described, filled with radio chatter, and often well within range of Soviet radio receivers. What was the purpose of those missions?[4]

7. BEARBAITING IN THE DARK

The answer to that question was beyond the limits of my consciousness for several more years. Like most Americans back then, I trusted our government and believed we were in a life-and-death struggle with a slimy Communist octopus determined to wrap its tentacles around the planet.

By the time I left active duty in December 1958, I had done my job as navigator of aerial tankers in four kinds of flights by SAC bombers toward or over the Soviet Union: reconnaissance, provocation, practice, and false alarms. Only the first of these fit comfortably into my 1956 consciousness. It would take the Vietnam War to force me to comprehend the true purposes and consequences of most of these missions and to repent my minor role in them. Only after the Cold War morphed into America's perpetual war did I finally realize the relevance of my experience to life in the twenty-first century.

Aerial reconnaissance of the USSR began at least as early as 1949 and was hugely escalated under direct orders from Dwight Eisenhower as soon as he became president in 1953. Some spy flights led to aerial combat, and at least eleven U.S. planes were shot down, with the loss of over a hundred American crewmen.[5] But our government consistently denied all of this. Overflights of Soviet territory were attributed to navigation errors, and shootdowns were denounced as evidence of Communist inhumanity. The lies of course were intended to deceive not the Soviet Union but the American people.

By late 1958, SAC's reconnaissance flights over the Soviet Union were being phased out. Through my experience both flying and as an intelligence officer, I gradually learned why.

When I joined the squadron I was assigned, whenever not flying, to Squadron Intelligence, and I eventually became the squadron intelligence officer. I worked in a vault where we stored all our confidential, secret, and top-secret documents. The thick steel vault door had explosive hinges. In the event of an enemy attack, presumably by the extensive Communist underground in Maine, I or another intelligence officer was to push a button setting off the charges, thus sealing ourselves in the vault, which we were then to defend with our .45 pistols. If the Communists were about to breach the vault, we were to hurl incendiary thermite grenades into the steel cabinets where all the classified documents were stored. These were, indeed, dangerous documents. For SAC, anyhow.

Another young navigator who had a desk in the vault was Joseph "Frosty" Frobisher, whose flaming red hair and walrus mustache framed a permanently bemused expression that always suggested that he had some secret worth discovering. His official designation was, appropriately enough, the squadron's "Top Secret Control Officer." One day in early 1958 Frosty handed me a stack of aviation magazines, those cheerleading weeklies and monthlies for all fans (especially male) of flying machines, and said, in a conspiratorial tone, "Take a look at these mags, and tell me what you think is going on with the U-2." Well, this snooping into possible government secrets was not something we were supposed to be doing, but then again it was not something we had been told not to do. In a couple of hours of connecting dots scattered through the magazines, we figured out—or, rather, confirmed—what Frosty probably had already figured out. The official story presented the U-2 as a high-altitude weather-research aircraft being used to get precise data on the jet stream, wind shear, and extreme air turbulence. The obvious first clue was that curious "U," a designation that supposedly stood for "utility," a category that meant nothing at all. The mechanical specifications gleaned from the aviation magazines proved that the U-2 was an extraordinarily fragile craft with very limited maneuverability, totally unfit for flying in conditions of heavy wind shear and air turbulence. A plane designed for investigating these conditions should have stable wings, not the exceptionally long U-2 wings, so flexible that they flapped and needed external wheels for takeoff and wingtip skids for landing. So Frosty and I agreed that it must be being used for something else. What could that be if not high reconnaissance? How high? We noted an order for an altimeter calibrated to the unheard of altitude of eighty-five thousand feet. That wasn't just high; it was about ten miles above the maximum operating altitude of Soviet (or U.S.) fighters and miles beyond the reach of any known antiaircraft missile. Other details suggested its range. We surmised that the U-2 was flying with impunity over the Soviet Union, probably from bases in

Norway, Germany, and Pakistan. Because we had never heard of a U-2 tak-ing off or landing at an Air Force base, we figured it was a CIA operation.

If two junior Air Force officers could deduce all this from readily avail-able public magazines, certainly Soviet intelligence was quite aware of the U-2 missions, even more brazen than the missions of some of the bombers we were refueling. And how could the Soviets not know, since the U-2 flights would be visible on their radar? So here was another major activity of our government classified as higher than top secret to keep the American people, not the Soviets, living in blissful ignorance. Frosty and I also sur-mised that the Soviets were no doubt feverishly working on means to shoot down a U-2.

Before long, Frosty was proven right on all counts. President Eisenhower and a handful of insiders were actually relying on the invulnerability of the CIA's U-2s, flying at seventy thousand feet, six miles higher than the B-47 or B-52, and, unlike SAC's bombers, supposed to be far above any possible Soviet air defenses. The result was a disastrous event that blew holes in the cover of the reconnaissance missions of both the CIA and SAC—and big-ger holes in the credibility of our government.

On May 1, 1960, a CIA U-2 flown from a secret base in Pakistan headed across the USSR heartland toward a destination in Norway, photographing Soviet defense installations along the way. On May 5, the Soviet Union claimed to have shot down a U-2 spy plane over its territory. Washington responded with a concoction of elaborate lies released as a statement from the National Aeronautics and Space Administration. The alleged NASA press release claimed that one of its U-2s had disappeared while research-ing weather over Turkey, that its civilian pilot had evidently passed out after reporting a problem with his oxygen system, and that the plane might have then flown on autopilot into Soviet territory. A spokesman emphasized that the plane was clearly marked "with the letters N.A.S.A. in black on a gold-yellow band and with an N.A.S.A. seal, a globe inside calipers."[6] Another CIA U-2 was hastily repainted to match this description and shown to reporters, who were then informed that NASA's entire fleet of U-2s had been grounded to repair possible defects in the oxygen system. The *New York Times* obediently published a map showing the plane's planned route inside Turkey, with a cross indicating where the plane presumably crashed inside the USSR, barely across the Turkish border.[7]

The Soviets responded by producing pictures of the wreckage of the unmarked U-2 more than twelve hundred miles into its territory, rolls of films that the plane had taken of top-secret Soviet installations, and the pilot, Francis Gary Powers, a former U.S. Air Force captain and presently a GS-12 CIA operative. Soviet premier Nikita Khrushchev initially interpreted the intrusion as an attempt by out-of-control U.S. agencies to wreck the summit scheduled to convene in two weeks, an interpretation bolstered by ambiguous statements from Washington officials. But soon President Eisenhower not only took responsibility for all the U-2 espionage flights but defended the necessity for them, causing the summit meeting to collapse on its first day.

Two months to the day after the U-2 shootdown, a Soviet fighter shot down a SAC RB-47 over the Barents Sea inside or along the periphery of Soviet airspace—depending on which side you choose to believe. The two surviving crew members were rescued by a Soviet trawler, imprisoned while awaiting trial, and released "in a sincere desire to lay down a basis for a new stage in relations between the Soviet Union and the United States," just in time for incoming president John F. Kennedy to announce their return in January at his first presidential news conference.[8]

Meanwhile, the era of continual U.S. spy flights over the USSR had already been brought to an end by two technologies: Soviet missiles and U.S. photography from space. Back in August, a month after the RB-47 shootdown, came the first successful mission by a U.S. spy satellite.

Ever since the 1960 U-2 shootdown, there has been debate about whether the flight was merely reconnaissance or at least partly provocation. A question with far wider implications is the one I couldn't quite confront much less resolve at the end of my first refueling mission. Were SAC bombers engaged in a policy of intentional provocation? If so, what was the purpose? To heighten the Cold War? To turn it into a hot war, maybe even provoking Soviet responses that would justify a U.S. nuclear attack? Or something else?

Several months before I joined the 341st Air Refueling Squadron, it was sent to Thule AFB in Greenland to participate in Project Home Run. For seven weeks in the spring of 1956, Project Home Run flew 156 B-47 sorties along or over the border of the Soviet Union. On a typical mission, KC-97s would refuel the bombers near the North Pole, and then one B-47 would fly across the border to activate Soviet radar and communications defenses, while another B-47 cruised along the border electronically painting the picture of these defense systems. The ostensible purpose of all 156 sorties was "reconnaissance." When the Russians protested, Washington simply denied that any such flights had occurred or blamed the proximity of the planes on the difficulties of Arctic navigation, as in this later declassified diplomatic note: "Navigational difficulties in the Arctic region may have caused unintentional violations of Soviet airspace, which, if they in fact had occurred, the U.S. State Department regretted."[9]

The grand climax of Project Home Run came on May 6. Six RB-47s launched from Thule, climbed to forty thousand feet, headed over the North Pole straight for Siberia, and then flew in formation in broad daylight for six hundred miles over Russia, outracing Soviet fighter planes that tried to intercept them.[10] During this intrusion, the Soviet military and government could have only two possible interpretations of this bomber formation: a provocation or the beginning of nuclear war.

Well, if this wasn't a provocation, what would be? The most benign explanation was offered in John Carroll's 1966 book *Secrets of Electronic Espionage*: "Soviet radar and radio men realized that when they kept their equipment turned on, U.S. ferrets could plot the locations of the stations and deduce their capabilities. Accordingly, the Soviets did not turn on their equipment unless they thought the U.S. plane was actually going to attack them. And so the restraint exercised by Soviet radar men forced U.S. ferrets to intrude on Soviet airspace and simulate an actual attack to get the Russians to turn on their radar."[11]

Besides reconnaissance and provocation, there were two other kinds of SAC missions in which I participated that were at least as threatening to the Soviets and as perilous for the world as the flight of those six massed bombers. One was practice attacks, known as EWP (emergency war plan) exercises. Some involved single planes, others giant formations of bombers refueled by formations of tankers.

Were these truly just practice, another form of provocation, or intimidation? How would we have responded if the Soviets had conducted such practice missions within striking range of the United States? Of course they never did. They couldn't, because the giant Soviet nuclear-armed bomber fleet was a mythical beast.

And then there were the real deals, when SAC's awe-inspiring bomber armadas streamed toward the Soviet Union with the full intent of launching an all-out nuclear holocaust. None of these, as far as I know, ever went beyond the Fail Safe Line because they did not receive the required coded order to keep going. These all turned out to be false alarms.

Unlike the other three kinds of bomber missions aimed at the USSR, these Washington acknowledged. On April 7, 1958, the United Press issued a government-authorized dispatch, proclaiming that such aborted full-scale attacks had happened "many times": "The great counter-offensive striking force of the Strategic Air Command has been sped on its way by alerts created by meteoric flights registering on the DEW one radar-scopes, by interference from high-frequency transmitters or by the appearance of foreign objects, flying in seeming formation, that simply never have been explained."[12]

Looking back on my own participation in these missions has had a profound effect on my later life, including my writings and teaching. The most painful and embarrassing realization is that I never had the slightest twinge of conscience or even any recognition that I was making a moral choice. It never occurred to me to ask, "Should I be doing this?" Although I was not on a bomber crew, I was aiding and abetting what could be the greatest mass slaughter of our species and the most fateful act in human history.

There were at least two fundamental moral questions, each with profound implications for individuals and for nations. Each came from a different possible reality. What if the Soviets had not in fact already initiated a nuclear attack on the United States and our attack proceeded because of mistakes or a willful decision to launch a nuclear first strike? In that event, I was participating in what would have been an atrocious, unforgivable act of mass murder. My only defense might be, "I was just following orders," a defense that the Nuremburg and Tokyo war crimes trials had decided was not even legal, much less moral.

"Oh," you might say in my defense, "come on, you didn't know a Soviet attack was not in progress." Oh, but I did. At least by mid-1958 I had more or less deduced from classified documents that the Soviets did not have the means to deliver a nuclear attack. All I can say in self-defense is that, unlike our military and political leaders, I did not have overwhelming evidence of the impossibility of a Soviet attack.

But what if the Soviets *were* already striking first, and we were merely retaliating? Even though that was impossible then, it wouldn't be impossible for long. The moral issue in that "what if" would become even more crucial and probably far more relevant to the closing decades of the twentieth century and at least the first decades of the twenty-first century. Why? Because of the advent of the intercontinental ballistic missile, those ICBMs that today still pose an imminent threat of a global war of nuclear extermination, unleashed by human or electronic error.

A decade earlier, in the early stages of the Cold War, while I was still in grade school, science fiction writer Theodore Sturgeon had looked beyond the nuclear bombers of the 1950s to the age of mutual assured destruction, aptly known as MAD, posed by ICBMs. In his 1947 story "Thunder and

Roses"—published two years before the Soviets tested an atomic bomb and a decade before the advent of intercontinental missiles—America is annihilated by a sneak nuclear missile attack launched by two unnamed nations. Every person in America is dead or about to die from the radiation. There remains one bank of controls programmed to launch an equally annihilating holocaust on the two murdering nations. At the end only the protagonist, a lowly sergeant, has the choice of either pulling the fatal switch or destroying the only means of retaliation. If he chooses the nuclear option, it may mean the end of our species and possibly the extinction of all other terrestrial animals. What should he do?

This is the moral question that those of us flying a presumed nuclear retaliation, and especially those who issued our orders, chose to ignore. Maybe that question poses a fundamental dilemma underlying any theory of the just war. It was shoved in our face by Hiroshima, Nagasaki, and the firebombing of Dresden. Ignoring that question is fundamental to the strategy of mutual assured destruction and its twenty-first-century variants. The justification for MAD is that it deters nuclear war. But what if it doesn't, and a nuclear first strike is launched intentionally or by a computer glitch or human error or a breakdown in command and control? Should the destroyed nation then destroy the attacker? Even if this dooms global civilization and perhaps our species?

8. THE BOMBERS THAT WEREN'T

Like almost everyone else, I had believed that America was under constant menace from a vast armada of Soviet long-range nuclear bombers—more or less like our fleet—capable at any moment of turning the cities of the United States into Hiroshimas and Nagasakis. These were the days of the frantic building of public and private fallout shelters, the time when children all over America were diving under their desks and covering their heads to protect themselves from the Communists' atomic bombs, as instructed by Bert the Turtle in the 1951 civil defense film *Duck and Cover*. I had already had some doubts about the "bomber gap," for it was hard to believe that the Russians actually had more bombers than we had, much less bombers superior to our B-47 and B-52.

One of our main jobs in SAC intelligence was to prevent anyone in the United States, and particularly our own flight crews, from knowing that the

Soviet Union lacked any ability to deliver a nuclear attack. Their main bomber fleet consisted of a few hundred propeller-driven TU-4s, copied from the B-29, with a maximum loaded range of twenty-two hundred miles. Their only operational long-range bomber was what NATO designated the Bear, a turbo-prop with a maximum range of four thousand miles and a maximum speed of 450 miles per hour. No Bears were stationed at forward bases, and it is unlikely that any could have penetrated the U.S. air defense. The myth of the fleet of operational bombers capable of attacking the United States was a joint creation of Soviet and U.S. intelligence, each functioning with a contrary purpose.

At the 1955 Soviet Air Day Show in Moscow, flight after flight of Soviet-engineered swept-wing jet-powered bombers similar to B-52s soared by. Dubbed the Bison by the Pentagon, this new bomber became the basis of the "bomber gap" (precursor of the bogus "missile gap"). The Air Force submitted to the Senate Committee on Armed Services a 1956 report, "Study of Airpower," claiming that America's strategic air power had fallen dangerously behind that of the Soviet Union. The entire United States, America was told, lay almost naked before a vast Soviet bomber armada.

In reality, both Air Force intelligence and the CIA knew that the Bison was not even operational. The swarms of Bisons flying over Moscow actually consisted of at most eighteen planes, all prototypes, flying over and over in a large circle. CIA Director Allen Dulles later admitted this in 1963.[13] The maximum loaded range of the Bison was only three thousand miles, and the Soviet Union had no bomber base within three thousand miles of the continental United States. The Bison was also an insatiable fuel guzzler, and even as late as 1958 the Soviet Air Force had no operational midair refueling units.

In mid-1958, I received a top-secret report about a Soviet attempt at midair refueling. The Russians were trying to use a flexible-hose system, similar to that used by the U.S. Navy and unlike our rigid-boom method. In their desperate attempts to convince us of their aerial refueling capability, they staged this operation right over Moscow. Unfortunately, the entire refueling system broke loose from the tanker and crashed into one of the city's apartment complexes, killing a family and starting a major fire. The story made news in the European press, and these press reports were included in this top-secret document. Then why the top-secret classification? The Russians knew the story all too well. And since it happened over Moscow and was reported in the European press, they knew that we knew. And we knew that they knew that we knew, the third-level intelligence shibboleth. Air Force intelligence was keeping this a top secret from only one group: the American people.

The Soviet motive for trying to convince us that they had a strategic nuclear capability was simple: they wanted to deter us from launching a nuclear attack. But what was our motive?

The Air Force of course wanted to keep getting huge appropriations to augment the SAC force of 1,400 B-47s, 350 B-36s, and 400 B-52s armed with nuclear bombs in a ring of bases around the USSR and manned by a force of almost two hundred thousand military personnel. And at the other end of the pipeline were many young but retired Air Force officers with lucrative jobs in the mushrooming aerospace industry. But was the Air Force fooling the president and all our other political and military leaders?

What a naive and embarrassing question! I had to learn the history of the Vietnam War, I'm ashamed to admit, to get the picture.

9. FUN AND GAMES

On those occasions when we did actually launch right up to the Fail Safe Line, no explanation was given, even after the recall, not even to squadron intelligence officers. But on two occasions I did find out specific causes.

Once a flight of four multiengine jets heading south was picked up on the Distant Early Warning (DEW) Line in the Canadian Arctic and then again on the second radar fence, the Mid-Canada Line. The planes failed to identify themselves, despite repeated warnings. It turned out that it was a flight of B-52s. I still wonder why they failed to identify themselves. Was it to simulate a Soviet first strike?

Besides launching in response to that attack by presumed Soviet intercontinental bombers, we once launched in response to an attack by presumed Communist saboteurs. Someone shot and killed a guard at a "Special Weapons" (i.e., nuclear bombs) storage area on a SAC base. Who was the shooter? A fellow guard with a grievance? A jealous husband? A hunter challenged by the guard? Evidently none of these far-fetched possibilities was taken seriously by SAC. It seemed far more likely that this was the leading edge of a sabotage campaign by the Communist underground to cripple SAC, possibly as a prelude to air assault by Soviet bombers. I never learned who the shooter was, though it was commonplace for SAC headquarters in Omaha to send teams of armed intruders to test the defenses of a base.

It is difficult to determine how much of SAC's paranoia about internal security was actual fear of a Communist attack, how much was self-serving scare tactics, and how much was just fun and games. One night in late 1957, a six-man SAC infiltration team drove up in a civilian sedan to the main gate at Dow at 2 A.M. They flashed phony IDs at the Air Police officers (the ID photo on one card was Mickey Mouse), who saluted and waved them on through. They drove directly to Air Police headquarters, kicked open the door, and walked in with leveled assault rifles. "Bang, bang," they said. "You're all dead."

One of the intruders picked up the phone and called the wing commander: "Sir, this is Sergeant Smith, desk sergeant at Air Police headquarters," he said. "Something very serious has happened, sir. I don't think I should discuss it on the phone. Could you come on down here, sir?"

"Right, sergeant, I'll be right down."

The same routine was pulled on the base commander. So the two top-ranking officers on base were quickly taken prisoner. Next, the team called all the numbers on the Air Police alert list, informing each that this was a "Siegfried 7 Level Alert." "Report immediately to your Siegfried 7 Alert post," they concluded, and hung up. Within fifteen minutes the base switchboard was jammed and every key person on the base was trying to call some other key person to ask what to do in a "Siegfried 7 Alert." Then three men from the infiltration team piled into an Air Police armored half-track parked out front. They nonchalantly drove up and down the flight line, aiming the half-track's recoilless rifle at some planes and pasting big stickers marked "BOMB" on the fuselage of others.

After this, an armed guard was posted at each of our planes. One night, a truck drove up to a KC-97 and unloaded a large wooden box. "This is a new latrine for the plane," the guard was told. "Guys will be by in the morning to install it." I was given the distressing duty of being the investigating officer in the court-martial of the guard, a young airman second class who had been found at dawn sitting on the box, on which was stenciled "BOMB."

A few months later, I found myself being part of a crew suspected of being either SAC infiltrators or Communist invaders.

In January 1958, the wing instituted a new competitive program designed to boost our SAC "war readiness" scores. Each month the outstanding flight crew was named "Crew of the Month" and given their choice of a semi-vacation flight to any part of the country. Our crew was the first winner, and we decided to go to California, where most of us had never been. In March, we flew to Castle AFB, and then had a couple of days off in San Francisco. The official purpose of the flight was to bring a group of NCO mechanics who had received special training at Castle back to their home base, Westover AFB, Massachusetts, headquarters of our own parent, SAC's famous Eighth Air Force.

After landing at Westover on the way back, we were ordered to hold our taxi at a runway intersection. As I finished my log, I glanced out the little window facing my position. Two machine guns manned by four men, plus a recoilless rifle mounted on an Air Police armored half-track, were pointed at me. Well, okay, it wasn't just me. Everyone else in the control cabin was also staring into gun muzzles. We were surrounded by a wall of machine guns and recoilless rifles manned by dozens of Air Police. Major Schoppe, our pugnacious squadron operations officer and a Korean War veteran, who had bootlegged himself along on the ride, grabbed the mike and started yelling at the tower. We were told to "stand by for boarding by the Airdrome Officer." Out of the jeep that sped to our plane boldly stepped a first lieutenant sporting a white silk scarf and a leveled .45. He climbed into the cabin, .45 still leveled.

"What the hell is going on?" bellowed Major Schoppe.

"That's just what we'd like to know," answered Lieutenant White Scarf. "You will have exactly five minutes after I disembark to get this craft off our base."

They must have figured we were a SAC infiltration team pretending to be a Communist assault unit, and they were going to treat us like the real thing. The problem was that our SAC clearance had not reached the base. "Listen, Lieutenant," said Major Schoppe, "we have your own men on board here. Besides, we just flew all the way from California, and we don't have fuel for another takeoff."

"That's your problem, Major," said Lieutenant White Scarf, his .45 now pointed at Major Schoppe's belly. The lieutenant looked crestfallen when the tower called to say they had just found our SAC clearance.

To stop SAC infiltrators at our base, a new policy was adopted just in time for the winter of 1958. Any person who lacked appropriate identification was to be ordered to strip naked and lie on the ground. For two weeks that winter, the temperature at our base never got above 20 degrees below zero and occasionally dropped to 40 below. We had no infiltrators that winter.

The games were not all fun. A pilot stationed at Loring AFB, Maine, drove through the gate without getting a wave-through from the Air

Policeman and failed to heed the order to stop. The AP shot and killed him. Unlike the airman sitting on the BOMB box, this guard was not court-martialed.

10. THE GAME CHANGER

No, America was not menaced by Soviet bombers or secret cells of Communist saboteurs. So we were not really risking a global nuclear apocalypse by flying bombers over the Soviet Union or sending swarms of bombers toward that nation for practice or on false alarms. But the days of SAC's games were about to end, because the game was about to change.

In August 1957, the Soviet government announced that it had just tested an intercontinental ballistic missile. Any doubts that they had such technology were erased in October, when the Soviets launched Sputnik I, the first human-made satellite. SAC's bombers, with their espionage and provocation missions against a USSR unable to retaliate against a nuclear attack, had succeeded in forcing the Russians—and thus the world—into the epoch of the ICBM. This was a new game, the missile game, a game infinitely more dangerous than the bomber game. And it's a game we are still playing.

One ominous difference between these games is that bombers can be recalled and missiles cannot. This alone fills every day with opportunities for apocalypse by accident or by a breakdown of command and control. The relative speed of missiles wildly multiplies the risks by eliminating practically all time for decision-making once what may or may not be an incoming missile is detected. There is no longer time to launch bombers, to determine whether an actual attack is occurring, and to decide whether or not to proceed with retaliation. The maximum speed of the B-52 or even the twenty-first-century B-2 bomber is just over six hundred mph. Ballistic missiles fly at fifteen thousand mph. A missile fired from Russia could strike any part of the United States in less than thirty minutes after launch. A submarine-launched ballistic missile (SLBM) could strike the United States within fifteen minutes after its undersea launch.

Thus the logic of MAD. Any nation committing a first strike must be "assured" that it will be entirely destroyed. Since a thermonuclear first strike on Washington would likely kill the president, the vice president, most of Congress, and everyone in the Pentagon, the authority and ability to launch nuclear retaliation must extend far and wide. Hence the logic and policy of placing that ultimate power in the hands of (among others) the top three officers of nuclear-armed submarines, each of which can launch 124 independently targeted thermonuclear warheads, enough to destroy any nation.

There is no practical defense against ICBMs or SLBMs, despite all the billions of dollars spent trying to develop one. Most of the proposed defenses would force us to let computers make the most important decision in human history.[14] I have never believed that either Washington or Moscow would ever order a nuclear first strike, but human error, equipment malfunctions, and software bugs have brought us perilously close to nuclear holocaust not just a few times, not dozens of times, but at least hundreds of times decade after decade since 1959. Back in 1980, when a few of these blood-chilling close calls leaked into the media, the Senate got Senators Gary Hart and Barry Goldwater to investigate. They reported that just between January 1979 and June 1980 there had been 147 "serious" false alarms (more than one every four days) and 3,703 "routine" alarms (an average of almost seven a day).[15]

By 1958, I was beginning to realize that placing even such relatively benign toys as nuclear bombers in the hands of our political and military leaders is like letting your six-year-old run around the house playing war with a loaded handgun. In 1959, my last contact with someone from my squadron left me so permanently terrified of ballistic missiles that I could almost regret that strategic bombers have gone the way of carnivorous dinosaurs.

11. THE DEMISE OF THE STRATEGIC BOMBERS

Although neither the USA nor the USSR deployed operational ICBMs until mid-1959, SAC intelligence went on an intensive campaign throughout 1958 to convince every flight crew that a Russian nuclear missile strike could already be just fifteen minutes away. Since, as we explained, the first target would be our SAC bases, every base from now had to run as though it were fifteen minutes away from annihilation.

A quarter of the crews were placed on fifteen-minute alert at all times, meaning they had to be able to be airborne within fifteen minutes. Each alert crew had to stay together twenty-four hours a day. Often we would fly a mission, which might last as long as fourteen hours, preceded by four hours of preflight and followed by two hours of debriefing, then go home, only to be woken up a few hours later on an alert call, from which we might not return for a week. Minor accidents were happening frequently, and there were growing rumors about B-47s crashing because of pilot error or mechanical problems or even blowing up in midair.

On April 10, 1958, our crew was on a one-plane refueling sortie. We were holding in orbit at fifteen thousand feet near Erie, Pennsylvania, on the southern shore of Lake Erie. The B-47 we were waiting for was now half an hour late, so we had to request a new flight clearance. Air Traffic Control responded, "Tomcat 89, you are cleared for refueling on airways to Buffalo and then on over Rochester and Syracuse."

Chuck, our A/C, asked the copilot and me what we thought of that. Refueling on airways over cities, we said, risked the lives of everyone flying through and everyone living underneath. So Chuck asked for and got a clearance to refuel on a track parallel to the airways and twelve miles south. Since the weather was clear, we got clearance to fly the mission VFR (Visual Flight Rules), which meant that we would take responsibility for our own separation from traffic.

Just then, the first signal from the B-47 showed up on my transponder scope. I established radio contact and began talking him into rendezvous. As we broke out of orbit and down the refueling track, I instructed the bomber to begin its descent. Everything was going routinely.

At one mile range and closing fast, the B-47 was just slightly off dead center on my scope. I gave him a final correction, "Queen 76, five degree right turn . . . now." Their A/C came back: "Roger, Tomcat 89, I am now in visual con—"

His transmission broke off sharply in the middle of the last word. At exactly the same instant, the green squiggle that represented the bomber on my scope disappeared.

"Queen 76," I called, "this is Tomcat 89. Do you read me?" No answer.

Chuck called back on our interphone to the boom operator, "Rector, do you see him back there?"

No answer from Rector.

"Rector, what the hell is going on? Are you alright back there?" Another silence. Then Rector stammered, "Y-yes s-s-sir. He just blew up. Right behind us. I'm okay."

Chuck quickly put us into a steep bank. A big fireball and a smaller fireball, each about two hundred yards away, were arcing forward following the path we had just left and slowly dropping toward the ground. We circled above the two fireballs, which seemed to be just slowly drifting down. We desperately but futilely scanned the sky for parachutes. Before the two fireballs hit the ground, two small planes were circling below us. We watched as the two fireballs hit and exploded about half a mile from a highway, where traffic was stopping. The two explosions bracketed a farmhouse and started fires in some fields.

I got a quick fix on our position. We were exactly twelve miles south of Buffalo, a city of over a half million population, where many people lived in old wood-frame houses. Even out there in the fields, we learned later, the fires burned for forty-eight hours. If we had taken that original clearance a firestorm might have swept through Buffalo.

Within fifteen minutes, twelve private planes, a small commercial airliner, and two rescue helicopters Chuck had called from the nearest airbase were circling the area. We watched as the firetrucks tried to get past the long line of stalled traffic. I checked my watch again: it was 5:30 P.M. Rush hour.

"A/C, this is the navigator," I said into the intercom. "Let's get back on that track so I can get an accurate reading on the wind for the accident report."

We followed all our checklists all the way back to the base.

Everything turned back into our normal flight routines. When we got back and reported to the wing commander, Chuck had to get on the phone with the commanding officer of the B-47's wing back at Lockbourne AFB, Ohio, and describe the event. We learned that there had been four men on board.

For some time, none of us seemed to have much of a recognizable emotional response. It was all too unreal, something like watching a movie, but with dull checklists instead of exciting background music and dramatic lines. It hit a couple of people that night. I didn't wake up screaming until the middle of the next night.

The investigation pinpointed the cause of the accident, despite the fact that many small pieces of the B-47 were gathered by souvenir hunters and despite the contradictory reports of hundreds of eyewitnesses. A number of people had observed a midair collision between two planes. Some saw one plane, trailing flames and dense clouds of black smoke for miles, heading toward another. Two or three saw a plane flying upside down before it exploded. Some saw a plane flying straight down into the ground.

The real cause was diagnosed from spectrographic tests of the parts and the pattern of their distribution on the ground: it was metal fatigue in the center wing section. The wings of big jets are not rigid but flexible. This B-47 had metal fatigue from too much movement in the very center where the wings join. It's like bending a thin beer can back and forth until it rips. When the center wing section snapped, the fuel lines running through it ruptured. The plane exploded almost instantaneously.

We had already been hearing rumors that B-47s were falling out of the sky like shot clay pigeons. Then on April 15, five days after the one behind our plane blew up, two more B-47s blew up, one out of Pease AFB, New Hampshire, and one over Tampa Bay, Florida. Ten days later a B-47 crashed at Goose Bay, Labrador.

Meanwhile, on April 19, the Soviet Union denounced, in the U.N. Security Council, the constant overflights of Soviet territory by armed B-47s and B-52s. On May 1, Soviet defense minister Rodion Malinovsky charged that SAC bombers carrying hydrogen bombs were continually hurtling to, and often over, the Soviet border, and he denounced these flights as "provocative." On May 2, Secretary of State John Foster Dulles claimed these flights never crossed the Soviet border, were merely for reconnaissance, and had to take place because of legitimate U.S. fears of surprise Soviet nuclear attack from secret air and missile bases in the northern part of the Soviet Union.

I decided to use my position in intelligence to do some private investigating. It turned out that at the end of 1957 SAC had decided that the B-47 was already obsolescent. Flying at its ceiling of about forty thousand feet and its maximum speed of six hundred miles per hour, it could not penetrate the increasingly sophisticated Soviet radar and antiaircraft defense. So the B-47s were ordered to practice LABS (Low-Altitude Bombing System maneuvers), better known as "toss-bombing." The bomber would fly at extremely low altitude, using the landscape and curvature of the earth to block defensive radar. Then it would pull up sharply and simulate the release of a nuclear bomb, which presumably would continue in a long forward arc. The B-47, with its six jet engines slung under wings almost 120 feet from tip to tip, had to pull up and back in a half loop followed by a half roll, as though it were a fighter plane.[16] Enormous stress was placed on the center wing section, which of course was not designed for acrobatics. Within a few months, B-47s were routinely disintegrating just like the one we had been about to refuel.

I also discovered that SAC had been trying out their new technique on the Soviet air defense. Some of those B-47s we had been refueling in the far north would descend to under one thousand feet, streak toward the Soviet Union, fly through their radar line, and then simulate their toss-bombing or another maneuver known as "pop-up bombing."[17] These were some of the flights that the Soviet Union denounced as "provocative," explained away by Dulles as purely defensive in nature.

Who was telling the truth? There were no civilian eyewitnesses much less a media presence in the Arctic. But those B-47s exploding over America could hardly be denied for long. Back on March 13, two bombers exploded in midair, one directly over Tulsa, generating national publicity. Then came ours on April 10 and the two others that disintegrated in flight in the next five days. The Air Force response came on April 16, as recorded by the *New York Times* in this one-sentence article: "The Air Force said today it was making a 'thorough investigation' of recent B-47 jet bomber accidents but did not consider the ratio of accidents to flying time 'excessive or alarming.'"[18]

This clumsy lie was exposed on the front page of the May 3 *New York Times* along with a glimpse of the Air Force's panicky response to the crisis. The Air Force now acknowledged the loss of fourteen B-47s along with thirty-four crewmen just since January 1 (actually an undercount of three bombers and twelve crewmen). The only loss specifically mentioned in the Air Force media briefing was the one behind us. Blaming the problem on "structural inadequacies," it declared that the remaining fourteen hundred B-47s would be "beefed up."[19] SAC combat units were informed that all B-47s would be grounded until the center wing sections could be reinforced, in a secret operation code-named Project Milk Bottle.

The Air Force admissions were designed to conceal the dimensions and implications of the B-47 story. A cloak of secrecy continued to cover the truly ugly history of the B-47, which leaked out in dribs and drabs over several later decades. Years before the toss-bombing maneuver, B-47s were disintegrating as early as 1951. The first officially acknowledged midair explosion came in 1952. In 1955, just a few months after Jimmy Stewart in *Strategic Air Command* was star struck by "the most beautiful thing I've ever seen in my life," two exploded in midair, one over Texas and another over Kansas. In 1957, twenty-seven B-47s blew up or crashed. Fourteen were lost in 1958 before our event on April 10, and 1958's losses eventually totaled thirty-one. Many dozens of crewmen died in those fifty-eight disasters in just these two years.[20]

In evaluating the Air Force claim that the ratio of B-47 accidents to flying time was not "excessive or alarming," let's make a comparison. SAC at that time had fourteen hundred B-47s, almost exactly the same number of planes operated during 2017 by United Airlines and Delta combined. Compared to these commercial airliners, which are in constant operation except when in maintenance, a relatively small percentage of the B-47 fleet was in the air at any given time. To get a glimpse of the B-47 catastrophe, imagine fifty-eight United and Delta airliners blowing up in midair or being totally destroyed in fatal crashes in a two-year period. Here's another comparison: In the three years of the Korean War, B-29s flew twenty-seven thousand sorties, often under heavy fire from radar-guided antiaircraft batteries and fierce attacks by formations of MiG-15 jet fighters; their total combat losses were thirty-four planes.

In 1980, the Air Force approved the public release of "The History of the Aircraft Structural Integrity Program," a report that revealed previously classified information about "a series of catastrophic B-47 accidents in early 1958" that "immobilized the entire B-47 fleet," thus causing a national crisis. "The immediate problem was to keep the B-47's flying" because "of an approaching summit meeting in Geneva." The authors didn't explain how flying B-47s would help lead to a successful summit.

Especially shocking to me was this revelation: "On 4 April ARDC [the Air Research and Development Command] agreed that 'continued, unrestricted operation of the B-47 fleet was hazardous.'" If SAC had acted on this recommendation, that B-47 would not have blown up behind us six days later. The day after this tragic event, the Air Force banned all B-47s from flying faster than two-thirds of its top speed. Then on April 25, ten days after still another B-47 exploded in flight, the Air Force issued new restrictions on all B-47s that had not been inspected for cracks: they were not allowed to do any low-level flying except takeoff and landing, fly faster than half their top speed, or fly in turbulence. They also had strict limitations on midair refueling, takeoff weights, and many normal maneuvers.[21]

But things could have been worse. Although the Air Force has always been reluctant to acknowledge the presence of nuclear weapons in accidents, we now know that between 1956 and 1958 thermonuclear weapons were jettisoned, destroyed, or lost in at least eight separate losses of B-47s. In some cases, the high explosive charges designed to initiate critical mass detonated, spreading radiation or causing injuries on the ground.[22] At least ten other nuclear weapons were involved in incidents involving B-52s and other SAC bombers.[23] The Soviet Union had no way of delivering nuclear bombs on the United States, but SAC did.

12. LAUNCHING THE FOREVER WAR IN THE MIDDLE EAST

Late on the night of July 14, 1958, we refueled a lone B-52 on a secret radio-silence mission near the Arctic Circle. As we approached the Gaspé Peninsula on our way home, our number three engine conked out. We got permission to make an emergency landing at Loring, the big B-52 base in northern

Maine. As soon as we touched down, we were ordered to clear the runway. Suddenly the squawking of Klaxon horns pierced the night. Jeeps flashing red lights materialized out of the darkness and sped to the row of giant B-52s on standby alert, each loaded with thermonuclear bombs. Flight crews raced from the jeeps to the planes. One after another, the B-52s started their eight engines, taxied out, and launched into the black sky.

When we finally got to the operations building, we stopped one of the men wildly scurrying around and asked, "What's going on?"

"We're going into Lebanon!" was the answer shouted over his shoulder as he darted off.

We returned with our repaired plane to Dow early the next day, July 15, where we found all crews on full-scale alert. Later that day the combat crews of both squadrons were to have a briefing on the situation from the wing intelligence officer. Meanwhile radio bulletins were excitedly updating the news. Yesterday's overthrow of the king of Iraq had been led by left-wing revolutionary officers. In response, the United States was sending a nuclear-equipped armada of seventy-four ships, including three aircraft carriers and two squadrons of destroyers, to Lebanon. American marines were landing in Lebanon to quell disorder.

For a time at Amherst, I had intended to become a historian of the Middle East. So I was aware of the enormous historic forces that were colliding in the region, and I was trying to figure out what role our SAC bombers were supposed to play in the collision.

The Arab world in the early and mid-1950s was being swept by rebellion against European colonialism and its own feudal monarchies. By 1956, Syria, Morocco, and Tunisia had all won independence from France, which was being torn apart by Algeria's long and bloody war of independence. Britain's vast global empire was rapidly disintegrating. It had lost its greatest colony, India, which it had divided into India and Pakistan in 1947. The next year it lost Burma. The empire was desperately struggling to maintain its dominance over Egypt, Jordan, and Iraq through ties to their puppet monarchies, but had suffered a huge setback in Egypt when nationalist forces, led by Gamal Abdel Nasser, overthrew King Farouk and established a secular republic. So in 1955 Britain instituted the counter-revolutionary Baghdad Pact among the United Kingdom, Pakistan, Turkey, Iraq, and Iran (where the United States two years earlier had orchestrated the overthrow of the democratically elected government and the establishment of a dictatorship by the shah). Nasser opposed the Baghdad Pact, supported the Algerian war of independence, and linked up with India in pushing a global movement of the nonaligned nations that would accept aid from either side in the Cold War while allying with neither. As punishment, the Eisenhower administration on July 19, 1956, withdrew its promised offer of aid in building the giant Aswan Dam, designed to harness the power of the Nile and expand agriculture in its floodplain.[24] Nasser responded a week later by nationalizing the Suez Canal. Israel, Britain, and France promptly invaded Egypt's Sinai Peninsula and the Suez, leading to the closure of the canal for several months. Like most Americans, Jane and I were relieved when President Eisenhower in October vowed "there will be no United States involvement in these present hostilities" and felt proud of our nation when he rebuked the invaders and led the United Nations to force their withdrawal from Egypt.[25]

But just three months later, in January 1957, the president in his "Special Message to the Congress on the Situation in the Middle East," announced a policy soon known as the Eisenhower Doctrine, which was codified into U.S. law by Congress in March. The law empowered the president to use our armed forces "to secure and protect the territorial integrity and political independence" of any Middle East nation "requesting such aid against armed aggression from any nation controlled by international communism." So was Lebanon requesting such aid? If so, what nation "controlled by international communism" was engaged in "armed aggression" against it? Was it Iraq, the home of the Baghdad Pact, whose king, a staunch ally of Britain and the United States, had been overthrown just the day before? A more likely culprit was the United Arab Republic (UAR), formed in February 1958, when Syria had merged with Egypt. But because Nasser had outlawed the Communist Party, Syria had to outlaw its own Communist Party as a condition of the merger.[26]

To find out what was really going on, I eagerly awaited the wing briefing, an assembly of all the officers and flight crews of both squadrons. The wing intelligence officer, a captain in a spiffy starched uniform, strode to the map in front of the large auditorium where we sat, now not in uniforms but in flight suits.

"Over here is Egypt," he indicated with a tap of a long wooden pointer. "It is now run by a man named Nasser. Nasser is a Communist dictator. The first thing he did when he took over was to seize the Suez Canal from its legal owners and start to run it in the interest of his bosses in Moscow. A few months ago he grabbed Syria, which is over here," he said, tapping with his pointer. "This country over here is Iraq." Tap, tap. "Yesterday, Nasser's fifth column inside Iraq overthrew the democratic government and set up another Communist state."

"Now, notice the position of Lebanon." Emphatic tap, tap, tap. "Lebanon is right in the middle. It is the next target for Nasser's Communist aggression. Last month the Communists in Lebanon began open warfare against the democratically elected government. We have landed in Lebanon to protect the legitimate government, to safeguard world peace, and to show the Communists they can't keep making incursions into the Free World. If we don't hold the line here, the entire Mideast will fall to Moscow."

Of course our lecturing captain had not written this script. Much the same briefing was no doubt being given to every SAC unit and throughout the U.S. military. In truth, it was just a slightly dumbed-down application of the Eisenhower Doctrine. In order to invoke the doctrine, the president needed to brand the UAR as a nation controlled by the international Communist conspiracy to take over the world. This was indeed central to the speech that he delivered on national radio and TV at 6:30 P.M., a few hours after the wing briefing, in which he cited "Soviet and Cairo" support of the revolution in Iraq and turmoil in "tiny Lebanon" as part of the Communist campaign of "direct and indirect aggression throughout the world." This was how, Eisenhower declared, "the Communists attempted to take over Greece in 1947," "took over the mainland of China in 1949," and "attempted to take over Korea and Indo China, beginning in 1950."[27]

"Any questions?" the captain asked, as he concluded his briefing. "Lieutenant Franklin, you have a question?"

"Well, sir," I said, standing up with an acceptable military posture, "it's more of a statement. Nasser is not a Communist, and there are no Communist governments in the Mideast. In fact, Nasser actually outlawed the Communist Party in Egypt. I think that we're driving these people into the arms of the Communists by invading their country. And I think we here in the wing should be told the truth about what's going on."

I hastily sat down. A wing briefing was not a college class, so what were they going to do with me? To make matters worse for the captain, the smart-ass guy who was arguing with him was the intelligence officer of one of the wing's two squadrons. He reddened, looked around uncertainly, and then walked over to whisper with Colonel Zethren, the wing commander.

"Lieutenant Franklin," the captain said finally, "we just want the men here to understand the basic facts of the situation. I'll be glad to discuss these more intricate details with you privately. Please report to me at wing headquarters."

This was my one and only political act in my Air Force career. If one can even call it a political act. Maybe it was more like all my talking out of turn that had kept getting me suspended from P.S. 99 in Brooklyn. I had no idea in 1958 how many times in the future my big mouth would get me in trouble.

When I went up to wing headquarters, I expected at least a reprimand and maybe the threat of a court-martial. But all I encountered was the captain, who seemed flustered and embarrassed as he asked me, as a favor, "not to confuse the men." "After all," he said, "we're not being asked to make policy, just implement it. Our responsibility in Intelligence is to explain it in such a way that the men are willing to carry it out."

What a revealing statement. Would any intelligence officer have uttered such words on December 8, 1941?

The captain's words, however, apply beautifully to all of our wars ever since, most obviously in the Middle East and southern Asia stretching from Vietnam to Afghanistan. Each requires some simple rationale that ignores history.

Life for all the intelligence officers, presidents, and other Pied Pipers leading us off to war was sure a lot easier when they had that good old Cold War narrative about the international Communist conspiracy against the Free World, even though it did take lots of red makeup to make Gamal Abdel Nasser look anything like a Soviet puppet and total ignorance of Middle East reality to justify a U.S. invasion of Lebanon. After the final dissolution of the Soviet Union in 1991 flushed that handy Cold War narrative down the garbage disposal, the hawks had to work much harder to create narratives to feed to the public.

So the 1991 invasion of Iraq relied on spurious narratives, such as one concocted by PR firm Hill & Knowlton of Saddam Hussein's army murdering babies by throwing them out of incubators in Kuwait, as well as the extremely effective myth of the spat-upon Vietnam veteran, which was used to turn the impending war into a demonstration of our loyalty to the American soldiers sent to fight it.[28] Our 2003 invasion of Iraq depended on a melodramatic fantasy about Saddam's fictitious arsenal of nuclear bombs and chemical weapons raining down on America. In 1958, President Eisenhower could safely count on Congress, the media, and the American people to back all necessary military action—even by those nuclear-loaded B-52s and Sixth Fleet aircraft carriers—to defend "tiny Lebanon" from "armed aggression" by "international Communism." In 2003, faced with a skeptical Congress and a swelling antiwar movement, President George W. Bush had to scare us into war with the specter of Iraq's alleged intercontinental drones, part of its "growing fleet of manned and unmanned aerial vehicles that could be used to disperse chemical or biological weapons" on "missions targeting the United States," as well as a "mushroom cloud" looming over America.[29]

So now we have a tangle of narratives that resembles a box of miscellaneous fishing worms, any of which we are free to bite on. Besides those weapons of mass destruction now casually known as WMDs (Iraq, Iran, North Korea, and Libya), there's the Brutal Tyrant (Saddam Hussein, Muammar Gaddafi, Bashar al-Assad, Kim Jong-un, Vladimir Putin) and the Axis of Evil (Iraq, Iran, and North Korea). Then of course there's the omnipresent and eternal War on Terror with its cast of generic "bad guys," not to be confused with the heroic Freedom Fighters (such as the jihadists we armed and organized in Afghanistan and later in Libya and Syria).

Looking backward from today's Forever War to what we now know about the events of the 1950s, we can clearly see a continuum of U.S. Middle East policy, remarkably consistent in its hidden and masked real purposes.

Since 1952, Washington had been financing Camille Chamoun, Lebanon's Christian president, who served as a reliable guardian of U.S. economic interests, particularly the Trans-Arabian Pipeline, constructed by the Bechtel Company to bring the oil from Saudi Arabia to Lebanon's port city of Sidon, from which it was shipped to Europe and the United States.[30] Owned and run by the Arab-American Oil Company (Aramco), a consortium of U.S. companies now known as Exxon, Mobil, Texaco, and Chevron, the Trans-Arabian Pipeline seemed threatened by the waves of anti-imperialism rising throughout the Arab world, especially after the 1956 invasion of Egypt by Britain, France, and Israel. Planning for Operation Blue Bat, the official title of the 1958 invasion of Lebanon, began in the fall of 1957, a few months after Congress signed off on the Eisenhower Doctrine.[31] Civil war soon broke out in Lebanon, with much of the Muslim population and even many Christian Arabs eager to link up with the UAR. On May 13, 1958, Secretary of State Dulles sent detailed instructions to Chamoun on how to word a request for U.S. military aid, explaining that since there was no "armed aggression from any country controlled by International Communism," the request would simply have to ask for help "in protecting American life and property" and preserving "the independence and integrity of Lebanon." On the same day, the Sixth Fleet was ordered to sail toward Lebanon. By May 26, the Sixth Fleet was routinely stopping merchant ships off the Lebanese coast. By late June, Chamoun's government, despite U.S. military aid, controlled at most 30 percent of Lebanese soil, according to U.S. intelligence estimates.[32]

Washington turned for help to King Faisal of Iraq, asking him to back up the regimes of both Jordan (ruled by his cousin King Hussein) and Lebanon, and thus provide an Arab component to any U.S. intervention. Faisal responded by ordering Iraq units from its frontier with Iran to move to Jordan. Since the intended route would take the troops near Baghdad, their officers decided to seize the opportunity to overthrow the hated royal regime. They met practically no resistance in Baghdad. At 6:30 A.M. on July 14, the rebels proclaimed on Baghdad radio the end of the monarchy and the establishment of the Republic of Iraq, to be governed by a democratically elected president and parliament. The army units stationed in Baghdad joined the revolution, and the population of the city jubilantly poured into the streets, shouting anti-imperialist slogans, destroying the statues of King Faisal and the British general who had seized Baghdad in 1917, and burning down the old British Chancellery.[33]

When Chamoun heard the news from Baghdad, he sent the request dictated to him by Dulles a month earlier when Washington, despite its secret funding of the monarchy, had no inkling of any impending revolution in Iraq.[34] By the afternoon of July 14, Eisenhower ordered the Sixth Fleet to commence Operation Blue Bat. According to the official chronology, the first military action came just before 1 P.M. Lebanon time (7 A.M. EDT) on July 15, as the Marines were landing. But, as I knew from our experience at Loring, those B-52s had launched on their SAC Emergency War Plan hours earlier, speeding with thermonuclear bombs toward the Soviet Union late in the night of July 14–15.[35]

Like the wing briefing, President Eisenhower's speech to the nation in the late afternoon of July 15 was also a briefing designed to explain policy in a way to get us all willing to carry it out. When he included what he called the Communist attempt to "take over" "Indo China, beginning in 1950," it meant little or nothing to me in 1958. Within a few years, trying to undo that falsification of history would become central to my life.

13. THINGS FALL APART

Although the invasion of Lebanon was brief, life in the 341st never returned to normal during the rest of 1958. The squadron was placed on continual high alert, and the normal number of crews rotated to nonstop week-long alert was doubled. Being on alert wasn't hazardous and didn't entail too much flying. Quite the opposite. With all our alert duty and with the grounding of much of the B-47 fleet, we weren't getting to fly enough for our taste. After all, flying was what we all had always wanted to do. We enjoyed the excitement, the use of our skills, and the sense of fulfillment that came with a successful refueling mission.

Crews on alert would get to fly only if an emergency war plan was activated. Practice takeoffs would be too dangerous because the KC-97s on alert were loaded with so much extra JP-4 fuel for the bombers that each tanker exceeded its safe takeoff weight by twenty thousand pounds.

So we stood by, like firemen waiting for the alarm. For meals, officers went to the officers' club while the enlisted men went to the NCO club. So each crew had two jeeps, one for the officers and the other for the enlisted men, both ready to race to their plane. Each crew's three officers had to wear a .45 at all times in order to guard a locked metal box containing our EWP orders, always chained to the wrist of one of the three (we took turns) and always in the presence of the other two.

During those last six months of 1958, only once did an alert crew take off on a solitary mission. That little adventure fueled my growing suspicion that SAC's commanders were dangerous lunatics.

That day I was on the lead crew, not my regular crew but one commanded by one of the squadron's best pilots, a tall, chiseled-featured hotshot with captain's bars who looked like he stepped right out of a Hollywood Air Force flick. Captain Hotshot, the copilot, and I were enjoying a leisurely lunch at the officers' club. Suddenly an excited out-of-breath waiter bumped into our table and blurted out that there was a phone call for the lead alert crew. A phone call? For the lead alert crew? How bizarre. Captain Hotshot nonchalantly asked me to take the call.

The waiter led me to a telephone booth (commonplace conveniences back then). I picked up the handset, which was dangling on its wire below the little shelf where you could sort your change or open the local telephone directory.

"Hello," I said, by now more and more puzzled.

"This is General mumble mumble calling from 8th Air Force headquarters at Westover." I soon wished I had gotten his name. "Are you on the lead alert crew?"

"Yes, sir. This is Lieutenant Franklin, the navigator."

"Launch immediately, Lieutenant. I repeat. Immediately. You will receive further instructions when airborne."

"Yes, sir."

There were no Klaxon horns blaring or any of the other signs of a possible war, as there had been at Loring on the night of the massive B-52 launch of July 14, so the copilot now had to trot back to the phone booth to call the NCO club to order our flight engineer, radio operator, and boom operator to scramble. With both jeeps' red lights flashing, we all careened out to the plane.

We had already done much of the plane's normal preflight, but there was still an abbreviated checklist to go through, even as we taxied onto the runway, revved all four engines, and rolled right into takeoff. About halfway down the runway, just beyond the go/no-go point (beyond which you can't safely abort the takeoff), engine number three sputtered and died. Knowing that we were already twenty thousand pounds over our safe takeoff weight, I didn't see how even Captain Hotshot could save us. I knew that he had to keep the plane on the ground as long as possible while gaining maximum speed by pushing the remaining three engines to their limit. I watched, wide-eyed and helpless, as we hurtled faster and faster toward the tall pines looming just beyond the runway. Just yards short of the end of the runway, Captain Hotshot yanked back hard on the yoke. The tops of the pines rushed toward us and then bent down from our wind as we barely grazed them.

Maintenance crewmen told us later that the guys watching the takeoff were betting money, at three to one odds, that we weren't going to make it.

With number three still spluttering but not feathered, we labored to gain altitude. The flight engineer then used his magic and got number three back into operation, and we climbed steeply to fifteen thousand feet. Then we got our orders. A B-47 out of Westover AFB was having mechanical problems and needed refueling. I received the bomber's location, got us heading toward it, and began preparing a rendezvous procedure. We established radio communication with the B-47 and asked them the nature of their problem. We had assumed that they must be having trouble with their landing gear and needed more fuel while they circled and tried to fix it while crews on the ground were putting foam on the runway and readying ambulances and fire engines. We were wrong about everything but the ground crews. The bomber had lost one of its six engines and was heading for an emergency landing at Westover. They did not need any more fuel, and in fact had already dumped some to make the landing safer. They had not asked for a refueling. They knew, as did we, that a B-47 flying on five engines would certainly stall out while attempting a refueling from a KC-97. We asked them to explain that to the generals at 8th Air Force headquarters, and wished them luck.

Well, what to do next? According to SAC's standard operating procedure (SOP), we should now dump all the jet fuel on board over the New England towns and farms and forests below us. After a brief consultation, we decided that instead of wasting taxpayer dollars and polluting the environment we would see if there was another bomber in the vicinity that would like our JP-4. We reported our proposal to Westover control, which put us in touch with a nearby B-47 that was low on fuel. We rendezvoused with it, gave them all our jet fuel, and headed for home. We were overjoyed to be alive and rather pleased with ourselves for our good deed.

As we taxied off the runway at Dow, we got a tongue-lashing and a torrent of officious abuse from wing control. It was, we were told, a violation of SAC SOP for us to take off at EWP weight except on an EWP launch. SOP mandated that we were to dump our JP-4. Wing command at our base had not authorized us to refuel any B-47.

Once again, I was glad to be flying, or now driving, with Captain Hotshot. As soon as we parked the plane, he vaulted into our jeep, waved the copilot (with the EWP metal box strapped to his wrist) and me aboard, and launched us up to wing headquarters. The three of us stormed in, enraged and trying to look menacing with our strapped-on .45 pistols. For once, I left the talking to someone else, the man who had saved our lives.

There was scuttlebutt about a new study (one I've never been able to locate) showing that SAC flight crews had the highest rate of alcoholism, divorce, and nervous breakdowns of any occupational group in the country. There was sure plenty of alcoholism and divorce-inducing behavior, but I suspect several other occupational groups would be quite competitive on both scores. Yet it would be no surprise if "nervous breakdowns," what today we might call PTSD, were indeed high among SAC crews in 1958, at least among the bomber crews, and one case in our squadron almost ended my life.

The officially sponsored paranoia about an imminent rain of Russian bombs or missiles had driven millions of American civilians into that duck-and-cover and fallout-shelter lunacy of the 1950s (as so hilariously projected in the classic 1982 documentary *The Atomic Cafe*). We lived inside SAC's version of the Red Scare nightmare, with its 24/7 fifteen-minutes-to-doomsday alert preceded by an any-minute-now infiltration by Communist saboteurs. The false alarms and official falsifications of our own actions made our connections with reality ever more tenuous. Meanwhile, the B-47 crews were taking casualties as high as in combat, but their enemies were their own disintegrating planes and crazed commanders.

Our squadron had accidents and close calls, but unlike the B-47 squadrons we had no fatalities during my time in the 341st. So we experienced none of the profound psychological damage inflicted by the loss of friends, the grief of their families, and the cover-ups and other forms of denial of the crisis. Yet contact with the loss of just one bomber along with the lives of just four total strangers infected at least one of us with severe and potentially deadly psychological consequences.

Chuck had been a fine pilot and an effective A/C before that B-47 blew up behind us in April. Throughout that event, nobody could have done better than he did. During and after his telephone conversation with the B-47's commander at Lockbourne, he seemed emotionally distraught, a normal human response. As the weeks went on, though, he began exhibiting some hallmarks of PTSD—continual anxiety, hypervigilance, and emotional instability. By midsummer, he was on the edge of panic during every mission. And with a kind of self-fulfilling prophecy, he was turning every flight into a potential disaster.

Copilot Charles "Charlie Brown" Ferry and I began expressing our concerns to each other. Then one night, when the tower ordered us to abort a landing at two hundred feet because dense fog kept us from seeing the runway, Charlie Brown, realizing that the plane was about to stall because Chuck was banking too steeply to the left at a dangerously slow speed, grabbed the wheel to correct to the right. He and Chuck were soon wrestling for control of the wheel with Chuck screaming, "The tower! The tower! We're going to hit the tower!" My duty on landings was to monitor the flight path on radar and warn of any hazards. During the entire approach, I had been observing the tower; it had stayed just where it was supposed to be, safely off to our right.

Another night we were hooked up to a B-47 at 12,500 feet. On board was Major Brynildsen, a blubbery bureaucrat who got flight pay for sitting at a desk for thirty-five hours a week and spending four hours a month as a passenger on a flight. The major was in the back watching the refueling. Suddenly he burst into the control cabin screaming, "A fuel leak! A fuel leak! We've got a fuel leak! There's fuel spurting out all over back there!"

Chuck instantly reached up and hit the emergency decompression button. Then he hit the master switch, knocking out in one instant all the electrical power on board. The plane was plunged into blackness. All our electrical equipment, including most of the instruments in the control cabin, stopped functioning. And since we had lost our electromagnetic disconnect, we were now mechanically locked to the bomber.

Chuck then pushed the nose of the plane down into a virtual power dive. We ripped loose by brute force from the B-47 and plunged down like a fighter plane. I caught a glimpse of the bomber circling overhead, apparently trying to figure out what had happened to us. Of course without electricity we had no radio communication.

Chuck leveled off at two or three thousand feet. I crawled around on the floor and found my flashlight. Then I persuaded a reluctant Major Brynildsen to go back to show me the fuel leak. It turned out to be a dripping valve. I fixed it by tightening a connection with a wrench, and mopped up the spillage with one rag. Then I went back to the control cabin and yelled at Chuck to turn on the goddamned power. It took some minutes to find my maps, which were scattered all over the floor, get the radar functioning, and figure out where in the world we were. (This all earned me a laughable commendation on my officer efficiency report for "exceptional courage and coolness faced with extreme danger.")

When things got back to more or less normal, Charlie Brown, flight engineer Master Sergeant Emard, and I demanded that Chuck explain why he had created this mess. "I hit the decompression button to clear the fumes," he said. "Then I hit the master switch so there wouldn't be any sparks to ignite the fumes." We pointed out that when you hit the master switch before shutting down most of the equipment you get the maximum possibility of serious electrical arcing, either in the electronic equipment, where the capacitors and condensers hold a charge, or as the circuit breakers all snap at once.

"But, anyhow, why the power dive?" asked Charlie Brown.

"That was because I had hit the decompression button. We had to immediately dive down to an altitude where there was enough oxygen to breathe."

I looked at Charlie Brown and Sergeant Emard, as we all sat there in silent disbelief. Finally Sergeant Emard said quietly, "But, sir, lots of people actually *live* at 12,500-foot altitude."

After the next incident, Charlie Brown and I reported our concerns to Major Schoppe. Chuck was diagnosed with ambiguous medical problems and taken off flight duty.

About this time, a SAC directive went out allowing anybody who had been accepted by a college or graduate school to get out up to thirty days before his scheduled date of release, if this were necessary to begin a new term. I was due out on February 3, 1959. I ransacked the college catalogs at the base library looking for a graduate school where a term started on January 3. I found one: Stanford University.

Jane's tour of duty as an Air Force wife was almost up, and before she agreed to marriage we had talked about my going to graduate school and becoming a professor after three years in the Air Force. But now I was getting cold feet about going back to school after grade school, high school, and four wasted years at Amherst. Jane and I had a heart-to-heart talk about choices and the future. I expounded on alternatives to graduate school. Strange as it may seem, I laid out the attractions of staying in the Air Force. With flight pay, the salary was excellent and would continue to get better as I got promoted. Jane, Karen, and Gretchen, who had just been born in October, would continue to have free complete health care. At twenty-four years, I had only seventeen years left before I could retire with great benefits at age forty-one. Or I could return to the tugboats and we could live in New York. Or I could get a position that would make lots of money. Or anything to avoid becoming a school kid again and sitting for years in classrooms. But Jane helped me come to my senses, and Stanford became our destiny.

Here comes my last confession of 1958. The options that might be open to Jane constituted a world of possibilities that never entered our conversation.

Just before I left the Air Force, dysfunctionality sometimes seemed to be approaching the norm. The personification of it all was a man who became known as Captain Overlook. Being a captain and a pilot, Captain Overlook had to qualify as an aircraft commander, not a copilot. But though he had been in the squadron almost an entire year, he had flunked checkout flight after checkout flight. Finally, through a fluke or misguided charity, he passed. He was now officially a combat-ready aircraft commander, with his own combat-ready crew.

One week later our wing was due to fly a big emergency war plan practice mission, refueling two wings of B-52s over the north Atlantic with almost no rest between flights. Our performance would be closely graded by 8th Air Force and SAC. What in the world could be done with Captain Overlook? Obviously he would be a menace if he was sent up on a refueling mission, where he would have to fly and refuel in close formation with three other tankers and four B-52s. But all crews had to participate, because our score was based on the performances of every combat-ready crew and aircraft.

Major Schoppe came up with the solution. Captain Overlook would pilot the command ship. All he had to do was orbit fifty miles from the refueling area, with the squadron commander on board. Everything went routinely on takeoff and flight. The command ship, with Captain Overlook at the controls and the squadron commander on board, then came in for Captain Overlook's very first landing as a checked-out combat-ready A/C. Touchdown was a little rough, but the plane did end up on the runway. Captain Overlook reached out to reverse the inboard engines, numbers two and three, to slow the plane down. But instead his fingers pulled engines one and two, the two engines on the left wing, into full reverse. The command ship spun around and around until it finally ended up stuck in a snowbank. As I was leaving the 341st Air Refueling Squadron, nobody had yet figured out what to do next with Captain Overlook.

Months later I was living with Jane and our two daughters in Stanford Village, World War II hospital barracks converted into housing for Stanford's graduate students (later converted into laboratories for war research conducted by Stanford Research Institute). Two doors down from us lived George Sheldon, a copilot from the 341st who had also gotten out thirty days early, to go to Stanford Business School.

On August 25, 1959, George burst through our back door laughing and whooping and waving a newspaper. On the front cover was a picture of Captain Overlook, taken at Vandenberg AFB, California. Captain Overlook now belonged to the 1st Missile Division of SAC. He had just been placed in command of our nation's first operational intercontinental ballistic missile.

Five years later, I saw another movie about the Strategic Air Command. This one replaced the B-47 with a B-52 as the film's starring superbomber. The aircraft commander was not Jimmy Stewart but Slim Pickens. The critics seemed to think that *Dr. Strangelove* was an over-the-top absurdist satire. I thought it was pretty realistic.

7 ▸ WAKE-UP TIME

The SOVIET SPUTNIK that went into orbit in October 1957 launched the space race, doomed the human species to an ongoing threat of annihilation from intercontinental missiles, threatened America's belief in its scientific and technical supremacy, and suddenly showered torrents of money down on American higher education. No school benefited more than Stanford University, which was already being transformed by its mushrooming appendage called Silicon Valley.

Jane and I arrived at Stanford with our two young daughters in January 1959. We both were now good liberals. We were enthusiastic believers in civil rights but not taking any action to promote them. Our experience with high-quality Air Force medical care, what that surgeon in Houston had called "socialism," coupled with our awful experience in the private hospital where Gretchen was born, had converted us into advocates of socialized medicine. The Air Force had also made us wish for nuclear disarmament and made us less terrified of the Soviet Union than we were of the Strategic Air Command and President Eisenhower, but we still were ardent believers in American democracy and opponents of Communism. Thanks to Herbert Matthews's 1957 *New York Times* reports of his interview with Fidel Castro amid the guerrillas in Sierra Maestra, we were admirers of the Cuban revolution against the Batista dictatorship, but we didn't think of it as Communist. We were bothered by our government's support of other dictatorships in the Americas and its enormous military budget. We were fitfully concerned about the U.S. covert war in Vietnam. In 1960, we worked hard to help elect the eloquent and inspiring youthful war hero John F. Kennedy.

Literature was important to both of us, which is one reason Jane had advocated for my going to graduate school and becoming a university professor. At Stanford I gave little thought to the fact that all my professors in the English Department were white and male, and I didn't notice until years later that during my entire education as an English major at Amherst and a doctoral candidate in English and American literature I had never been asked, much less required, to read a single work by a nonwhite author (and had been asked to read a mere handful of works by female authors).

When we ended Jane's three-year tour of duty as an Air Force wife, we agreed on a new deal: I would get a doctorate within three years. The money we had saved from my flight pay might not have financed us for the two and a half years it took. But thanks to the lingering influence of my day at the 1939 World's Fair and my binge reading of science fiction in high school and in the Air Force, as well as my Air Force technological training, I could find exciting and easy pickings in Silicon Valley's booming stocks, such as Hewlett-Packard, Fairchild Semiconductor, Ampex, and Varian Associates. So by the time I completed my doctoral work in May of 1961, we had enough money to buy a modest house in Palo Alto, and by that fall I was a Stanford assistant professor of English (thus getting to join the faculty vote that made my doctorate official).[1]

House hunting was another kind of education. Back then, you didn't have to be rich to own a house in Palo Alto, but you had better be white. Established in 1894 by robber baron Leland Stanford as an adjunct to his university, Palo Alto in 1961 had a few hundred "Negroes" in a population of 53,756. Some of the black people were confined to a small neighborhood of shacks bypassed by the city's garbage collection, forcing the residents to burn their own refuse. Most of the city's subdivisions were governed by this clause: "No person not wholly of the white Caucasian race shall use or occupy such property unless such person or persons are employed as servants of the occupants." As many thousands of black people fleeing the South after World War II poured into the vicinity, real estate agents, banks, and the Federal Housing Administration's lending rules all conspired to herd them into the segregated unincorporated area known as East Palo Alto.[2]

Struggling to subvert this apartheid was the Palo Alto Fair Play Council, formed in 1945 to help find housing for the Japanese Americans who had finally been released from California's wartime concentration camps. In 1948, members of the council concocted a brazen scheme: create an inter-racial neighborhood. They negotiated the purchase of a sizable tract of land in an undeveloped area of southern Palo Alto for $2,500, payable only in cash. Paul Lawrence (then a doctoral candidate at Stanford and later the first African American superintendent of education in California) dis-creetly took the cash to prominent Realtor and later four-term U.S. senator Alan Cranston and then arranged the permits necessary to create a new cul-de-sac, secure utilities, and pave the street and sidewalks. The twenty-three new housing lots were sold to a multiracial mixture of families includ-ing some council members, such as Franklin Williams, then the West Coast Director of the NAACP. When the new homeowners—nine African Amer-ican, seven white, and seven Asian American families—realized they were about to create a literally groundbreaking interracial community, they named it Lawrence Tract in honor of Paul Lawrence and took measures to preserve it. So they turned one of the main weapons of segregation into a boomerang for integration, ironically adopting a restrictive covenant for the new subdivision: owners had to agree to sell to members of their own race.

Jane and I, and especially our daughters, got lucky. A Realtor took us to 982 Lawrence Lane, a two-bedroom plus den, one-bathroom house being offered by a white owner for under $13,000. The first thing we saw was a pack of black and white and Asian kids, some about the ages of almost five-year-old Karen and almost three-year-old Gretchen, riding bikes and trikes and pulling wagons in the middle of the traffic-free cul-de-sac. By June we had our VHA loan and were moving in and meeting our new neighbors.

Few Americans in the early 1960s had an opportunity to live in an inter-racial community. Of course some white and black Americans were living in close proximity with one another, especially in urban areas and on south-ern farms. Typically in cities and suburbs, racial proximity was literally fleeting, as white families fled whenever black families moved into their neighborhoods. Sure, black and white tenant farmers lived near one another on Jane's family farm, but who would call that a community?

Except for being interracial, Lawrence Tract in important ways was just like any other tightly knit American neighborhood. Kids flowed freely in and out of their friends' homes. Most people's closest social relations seemed to be simply with the people who lived closest to them. Some of us young guys played pickup basketball games in the tract's large field behind

Lawrence Lane's dead end. Almost everybody pitched in for barbeques in the field, where the main dish was once a whole pig, pit-roasted with the expertise of some of the southerners. Jane and I loved to dance at the house parties thrown by Dorothy and Damon Hamill. Lulabelle Jones showed her snapshots of the area taken when she and her husband, Pat, built one of the first tract homes, right across the street from the Piers Dairy Farm and its grazing cows. When I bought a 1955 Chevy with a blown engine for $150 and a good engine for $50, Pat and I rented a winch, found a crucial part in one of the ubiquitous junkyards of East Palo Alto, hauled out the old engine, and installed the new one. After a couple of years, Cathy Jenkins's daughter got old enough to babysit for Karen and Gretchen. Geraldine Kickbusch told us how she fled Germany, leaving her German husband behind. Like the rest of America, the neighborhood, including the children, lived in terror for thirteen days during the October 1962 Cuban Missile Crisis. While I rushed Jane to Stanford Hospital on May 15, 1963, and stayed with her until she delivered Robert the following morning, Hazel Leler spent the night with our girls, and Melba Gee then got them up and took them to school. Jane and I found that our changing thoughts about America were shared with Barbara and George Lampkin, who had us dash to their house on November 24, 1963, just in time to jointly watch the rerun of Jack Ruby stepping forward with his snub-nosed .38 revolver to shoot Lee Harvey Oswald, which seemed to all four of us an event set up with the connivance of the Dallas Police.

Though Lawrence Tract was not post-racial America, it was a little piece of an America that seemed possible, one that could transcend the white supremacy and racism central to America's history and embedded in its culture. But our tiny interracial island was also part of the actual America of the early 1960s, an apartheid nation being rocked awake by an epic struggle between the civil rights movement and the implacable defenders of black segregation and white supremacy. The forces met head on in Birmingham in April and May 1963, when Bull Connor imprisoned Martin Luther King and ordered the city's police to sic vicious attack dogs on nonviolent demonstrators, and the city's firemen to blast black children with fire hoses. On August 28, we heard King articulate many of our own hopes in his "I Have a Dream" speech, delivered to the huge historic interracial civil rights march in the nation's capital. The response from Birmingham's white supremacists was a series of bombings, culminating on September 15 in the dynamiting of a three-story black church central to the civil rights campaign. Timed for a Sunday to inflict maximum casualties, the explosion injured scores of people and killed four young girls. When thousands of protesters gathered at the site, Alabama governor George Wallace sent state troopers and police to attack them, leading to citywide rioting, a harbinger of the next five years in America.

Lawrence Tract played a small and quiet but not insignificant role in the struggle. When Franklin and Shirley Williams decided they needed a bigger house for their growing family, they got turned down by Eichler Homes, whose daringly innovative mid-century modern houses (sliding glass exterior walls, open floor plans, exposed post-and-beam construction, radiant heat embedded in concrete slab foundations, skylights, merged exterior and interior) were changing the meaning of "California living" for the state and much of the nation. Williams argued heatedly with company founder and boss Joe Eichler, citing the experience of Lawrence Tract, until the two men became friends and Eichler became a widely influential partisan fighter for nondiscrimination in housing, opening all eleven thousand Eichler Homes to people of any race and religion.

Integration did spread from Lawrence Tract, first to a few homes on the other side of Greer Road, then here and there in a nearby Eichler tract. The *Palo Alto Times*, which had once campaigned in favor of a Chamber of Commerce resolution calling for a "segregated district for the Oriental and colored people of the city," by the 1950s was editorializing for nondiscrimination. Yet by the second decade of the twenty-first century, the city was even whiter than it was in the 1960s, with black people comprising less than 2 percent of the population.[3] The problem was no longer conscious racial segregation but economic class segregation. Someone had added a third bedroom and a second bath to our modest little home at 982 Lawrence Lane; in 2017 it was valued by Zillow and Trulia at $2.5 million. By then, even East Palo Alto was getting "gentrified," driving more black people, and working-class people in general, even farther away from Stanford and Silicon Valley.

In 1967, while serving as U.S. ambassador to Ghana, Franklin Williams received a package that contained nothing but a picture of a young black boy and a young white boy walking arm in arm. Its inscription read: "To Franklin, who helped make this dream possible. Joe Eichler."[4] But by then Martin Luther King's 1963 "I Have a Dream" speech sounded like an ancient fantasy. In April of that year, King delivered his sermon against the Vietnam War, in which he declared that America was on "the wrong side of a world revolution" and "I could never again raise my voice against the violence of the oppressed in the ghettos without having first spoken clearly to the greatest purveyor of violence in the world today—my own government."[5]

While King and his sermon were being denounced by the media and many civil rights leaders, millions of Americans—including me—were elated because he had finally spoken out and given the nation the history lesson it needed. I wished that every American could hear it. I still do. From 1984 until I retired in 2016, I assigned it every year to my Vietnam class and suggested that they hear and read it again to review the history needed for the final exam.

Back on January 17, 1961, outgoing president Eisenhower had warned that the "economic, political, even spiritual" influence of "the military-industrial complex" "is felt in every city, every State house, every office of the Federal government." Many of us hoped that incoming president Kennedy would free us from the clutches of this "military-industrial complex" that had grown into Godzilla during the eight years of the Eisenhower administration.

But less than ninety days into his presidency, Kennedy launched the Bay of Pigs invasion of Cuba—armed, trained, and led by CIA officers, transported in U.S. vessels, and supported by napalm and high-explosive raids by U.S. bombers. The invasion force received none of the anticipated support from the Cuban people and was swiftly captured. Revelations about the fiasco exposed a stream of lies by Kennedy and his administration. At the same time, top officials of the CIA, the Joint Chiefs of Staff, and many other hawks blamed the failure of the invasion on the president's refusal to fully support it with U.S. naval and air power.[6]

Although his inaugural address had warned of the menace of nuclear apocalypse and called for international control of nuclear weapons, the poisoning of Earth's environment continued with the testing of ever more ominous weapons. By the end of Kennedy's first year in office, America had exploded more than two hundred nuclear weapons, many in the Pacific, well on its way to its eventual heinous achievement of more than one thousand nuclear tests. On the advice of our pediatrician, Dr. Joseph Davis, Jane purchased in the summer of 1961 a year's supply of powdered milk so we could avoid filling Karen's and Gretchen's bones with the heavy doses of Strontium 90 by then contaminating the fat of whole milk. "We need the rain, but not the radioactivity," she wrote in a letter to her family.

The ensuing months were some of the bleakest—and most dangerous—of the Cold War. These were the days of the growing arsenals of Soviet and U.S. ICBMs, the deployment of U.S. MRBMs (medium-range ballistic missiles) on the border of the USSR, the crisis of Berlin and the Berlin Wall, and the emergence of exceedingly dangerous SLBMs (submarine-launched ballistic missiles).

Yet in the summer of 1962 came a historical event that let Americans experience for two days the postwar world of Soviet-U.S. friendship that might have been. Thirty years later, Payton Jordan, Stanford's track coach at the time, said, "I constantly hear people say it was the best event they've ever been to in their lifetime."[7] Many consider the U.S.-USSR match of July 21–22 the greatest track-and-field meet of all time. It is certainly the most glorious event in the history of Stanford. More important, it was a life-long inspiration for many of the 155,000 people who were there, the largest number ever to attend any track-and-field competition in the United States. Americans like Jane and me, who had grown up during World War II, were thrilled to relive our feelings of friendship and unity with the Soviet people.

The Soviet athletes arrived at Stanford on July 14 and were housed in the Stern Hall dormitory. They traveled freely and were welcomed with warm enthusiasm everywhere, from dinners hosted in private homes in the Palo Alto area to a grand tour of San Francisco. When a bunch of Stanford English Department graduate students, along with Jane and me, were getting ready to play some casual softball near their dorm on July 15, about a dozen of the Soviet athletes started chatting with us and then tried their hand at softball. Since none of them knew how to bat and judging a fly ball baffled them, we made a collective decision to switch to volleyball and to distribute Americans and Soviets equally on the opposing teams. One surprise was that many of the Soviets had good command of English (and of course not one of us literature scholars knew any Russian). Another surprise was that these world-class athletes were not volleyball superstars. I thought Jane was about as good as any of the Soviet women, but I was prejudiced, and after all she had been an all-county basketball star in North Carolina. Anyhow, the game was all about friendship and fun. It was the most enjoyable game of my lifetime. When it ended, there were eye-opening conversations and many warm embraces.

Jane and I took Karen and Gretchen to both days of the meet. Like the rest of the eighty thousand people in packed stands, we applauded the Soviet athletes and cheered wildly for the U.S. team. Our favorite American athlete was sprinter Wilma Rudolph, the holder of three world records and winner of three gold medals in the 1960 Olympics despite having grown up in poverty, segregation, and disease—crippled by polio and having to wear a leg brace until the age of eight—who would retire after this meet and become a civil rights leader. Soviet high jumper Valeriy Brumel, already the world record holder, provided the most memorable moment in the competition when the bar was raised to seven feet, five inches. A hush fell over the stadium as Brumel galloped faster and faster toward the bar, which towered sixteen inches over his head, and leaped, hurling his body over but brushing the bar. It felt like tens of thousands of us were holding our breath as we watched the bar quiver. As it settled, we leaped into a five-minute standing ovation.

The closing ceremonies were supposed to end with the two teams marching off the field in separate lines. But the flag bearers, Soviet javelin thrower Viktor Tsybulenko and American high jumper John Thomas, held a brief summit meeting and decided to lead the teams on an unplanned victory lap. The two lines of athletes embraced and then walked arm in arm around the track, as we all rhythmically clapped and cheered our hearts out, and many of us wept. Tears are running down my cheeks as I write this in 2018—as hate for Russia spews daily from our leaders and the media.

Even after the last athletes disappeared, the crowd didn't want to leave this miraculous scene. The U.S. Marine Corps Band played "The Star-Spangled Banner," "The Anthem of the Soviet Union," "Pomp and Circumstance," "God Bless America," and other songs for almost an hour. Then we all filed back to 1962 America.

Back in June of 1961, just three months after the failed Bay of Pigs invasion, the United States began the deployment of fifteen Jupiter nuclear missiles to Turkey, which shared a border with the Soviet Union. Each missile, armed with a W49 1.4 megaton thermonuclear warhead, was equivalent to 175 Hiroshima bombs. With their fifteen-hundred-mile range, the missiles were capable of annihilating Moscow, Leningrad, and every major city and base in the Russian heartland. Each missile could incinerate Moscow in just sixteen minutes from launch, thus wildly raising the possibility of thermonuclear war caused by technological accident, human error, miscommunication, or preemptive attack.

In August, the USSR and East Germany began building the Berlin Wall. We heard lots and lots about the Berlin Wall. Of course we didn't hear anything about the Jupiter missiles.

And we didn't hear anything about Operation Mongoose, the top-secret plan launched on November 1, 1961, to overthrow the government of Cuba through a systematic campaign of sabotage, coastal raids, assassinations, subversion leading to CIA-sponsored guerrilla warfare, and an eventual invasion by the U.S. military. The armed raids and sabotage succeeded in killing many Cubans and damaging the economy, which was hit much harder by the economic embargo announced in February. However, the assassination plots were foiled, and all attempts to develop an internal opposition failed. Many of the CIA agents and Cuban exiles who infiltrated the island by sea and air were captured, and quite a few of them talked, even on Cuban radio, about the plans for a new U.S. invasion, which was planned for October. Cuba requested military help from the Soviet Union, which by July was sending troops, air defense missiles, battlefield nuclear weapons, and medium-range ballistic missiles equivalent to the U.S. Jupiter missiles in Turkey.

At 7 P.M. eastern time on Monday, October 22, John F. Kennedy delivered the most terrifying presidential message of my lifetime. Declaring that the Soviet Union had created a "clear and present danger" by placing in Cuba "large, long-range, and clearly offensive weapons of sudden mass destruction" "capable of striking Washington, D.C.," he announced that U.S. ships would immediate impose a "strict quarantine," a transparent euphemism for a blockade, on the island. Knowing that the American people knew nothing about the recent and ongoing U.S. deployment of the Jupiter ballistic missiles, capable of striking all the cities of the Russian heartland, he stated, "Nuclear weapons are so destructive and ballistic missiles are so swift that any . . . change in their deployment may well be regarded as a definite threat to peace." And knowing the American people knew nothing about Operation Mongoose and its previously planned invasion of Cuba in October, the president stated over and over again that these Soviet missiles were "offensive threats" with no defensive purpose. Here was his most frightening sentence: "We will not prematurely or unnecessarily risk the costs of worldwide nuclear war in which the fruits of victory would be ashes in our mouth—but neither will we shrink from that risk at any time it must be faced."

On Friday Jane wrote a long letter to her family:

Oct. 26, 1962

Dear Family,

Marie, your letter from the east helped rouse me from a state of paralysis in which I have been suspended since Kennedy's speech on Monday. . . . Bo, I am glad your orders so far are not changed. . . . I had figured Bill must be in the blockade. . . .

I find it hard to believe that the president has risked nuclear war and therefore risked all our chances for life, liberty, and happiness. . . .

Thursday night Bruce was one of three faculty who spoke on this crisis. Dr. Leppert, a nuclear physicist (he watched the effects of nuclear blasts in Nevada), and Dr. Holman of the medical school were the two other speakers. There was a large audience. The discussion afterwards was intelligent and constructive. But part of the time there I felt like crying because all their hope and desire for reason is, in effect upon those in power, like the vaguest ripple of a breeze. When we once sent a telegram urging no resumption of nuclear testing, we received in return a very brisk, official pamphlet on how to prepare for a nuclear attack. . . .

Tuesday in the middle of the night Karen appeared at our bed and said through tears, "I've been having a nightmare about an atomic bomb." We had been being careful about our words around them, but the radio had been on constantly. . . . Tuesday I had periods of wishing I weren't pregnant, but I keep telling myself that instead of bringing one more person into the shadow of nuclear war, I'll be bringing one more person up to hate hate, respect respect, and love love.

Until I recently read her letter, I had forgotten my talk. According to the *Stanford Daily*, I had mainly explained how Kennedy's blockade of Cuba violated international law and asked the audience to judge it on "pragmatic, ideological, and ethical" grounds. That all sounds embarrassingly tame and bookish. Jane obviously would have done better.

The recipients of Jane's letter included her sister Marie and her husband, Bo Sims, a Marine lieutenant colonel stationed at the Pentagon, and her sister Bobbie and her husband, Bill Morgan, the captain of a destroyer. Bill was the man who cut our wedding cake with his ceremonial Navy sword. Although he and I rarely agreed about anything—except the Gulf of Tonkin incidents of 1964—I always figured that he was probably a good, albeit gung ho, naval officer, fair to his crew and responsible about his duty. Only in 2017 did I discover that the destroyer under Bill's command was the USS *Cony*. The day after Jane was writing her letter, Bill was indeed carrying out his orders professionally and efficiently. On October 27, the *Cony* discovered and then tracked for four hours the Soviet diesel-electric submarine B-59 out in the North Atlantic Ocean several hundred miles from Cuba.

The *Cony* was one of eight destroyers and an aircraft carrier hunting for Soviet submarines that might be heading for Cuba. They were under orders to force any such sub to surface by bombarding it with "signaling depth charges," designed to cause explosions powerful enough to rock the sub, while also pounding it with ultra-high-amplitude sound waves from the destroyer's sonar dome.

Meanwhile, the B-59's last orders from Moscow were not to cross Kennedy's "quarantine line"—500 miles from Cuba—but to hold its position in the Sargasso Sea. After that, it received no communication from the Soviet Union for several days. It had been monitoring Miami radio stations that were broadcasting the increasingly ominous news. When the sub-hunting fleet of U.S. ships and planes arrived, the submarine was forced to run deep, making it lose all communication with the outside world, and to run silent, relying on battery power. The batteries were close to depleted, the air conditioning had broken down, and water, food, and oxygen were running low when the *Cony* began its hours of bombardment with the depth charges and high-amplitude sonar blasts. Other destroyers joined in an ongoing barrage of hand grenades and depth charges.

The Soviet officers were unaware of the existence of "signaling depth charges," and international law has no provision allowing one warship to bombard another with small explosives unless they are in a state of war. Since the B-59 was hundreds of miles out in the Atlantic, not within the blockade area and not heading toward Cuba, its crew and officers logically deduced that war had started. If so, it was their duty to attack. The officers knew that with one weapon on board, they could destroy the entire sub-hunting fleet of destroyers and the aircraft carrier that had been pursuing them—along with themselves.

Neither Bill Morgan nor anyone else in the U.S. Navy or government was aware that the B-59 was armed with a T-5 nuclear torpedo, approximately equivalent in explosive force to the Hiroshima bomb. If the sub fired its T-5, it would plunge the world into nuclear holocaust.

One nuclear weapon fired from any of the American or Russian subs still prowling the oceans would do the same today, decades after the end of the Cold War. Hardly anyone in America then or now is aware of the command-and-control protocol on nuclear-armed submarines. In order to deter an opponent's "decapitating" first strike, which would wipe out all of the nation's leaders with the authority to launch a nuclear retaliation, the three top officers of a nuclear-armed sub have the authority and ability to launch a nuclear attack under certain circumstances. On October 27, 1962, the Soviet command-and-control protocol for launching nuclear torpedoes was even riskier: only the sub's captain and its political officer had to agree.

On the B-59, Captain Valentin Savitsky and his political officer realized that it was now or never. Their choice was either to surface—which was equivalent to surrender while they, perhaps alone, had the ability to launch a significant counterattack—or to fire their nuclear torpedo. They decided to attack and readied to aim for the aircraft carrier at the core of the submarine-hunting fleet.

Only one man stood in the way of a nuclear Armageddon, and he was on board the B-59 by chance. He was Vasili Arkhipov, the commander of the four-submarine Soviet flotilla, who vetoed the attack, leaving Captain Savitsky with no alternative but to surface.

"This week's events have brought home," Jane had written in her letter a day earlier, how few people have any say "about nuclear war before it may be brought down upon their heads by the handful of people who decide man's fate." Even that handful of people in the White House and Pentagon didn't know about those nuclear torpedoes. And that handful of people in the Kremlin didn't know that the U.S. Joint Chiefs of Staff had been itching for an excuse to launch a full-scale thermonuclear attack on the Soviet Union and that now, led by the "mad"—President Kennedy's word—ravings of my ex-boss Curtis LeMay, these dogs of war were demanding to be let off their leashes.[8]

The Missile Crisis ended with the USSR removing all "offensive" weapons from Cuba in return for a public U.S. commitment not to invade Cuba and a secret agreement to remove the Jupiter missiles from Turkey within several months. Years after the Jupiter missiles were withdrawn, we were told that they were "obsolete," a term still used in almost all accounts of the crisis. But if the Jupiter missiles in Turkey were obsolete, then so were the equivalent Soviet missiles in Cuba. In reality, the problem with both deployments was not obsolescence but reckless brinkmanship, initiated by the United States. Fortunately, Moscow and Washington ended up mutually recognizing that neither was willing to live with a gun that close to its head.

What may have looked to the public like a Soviet capitulation turned out to be a successful, desperate, and potentially fatal gamble by the Soviet Union. They won a tit-for-tat removal of the land-based missiles within sixteen minutes of incinerating either Moscow or Washington, with a bonus of stopping the imminent invasion of Cuba and possibly future invasions as well, all without having to commit to the future defense of Cuba.

Behind the scenes, Kennedy now had to deal with the shrieking hawks, furious at the president both for missing the golden opportunity to annihilate the Soviet Union and for an ignominious surrender of America's exceptional right to invade Cuba and to station nuclear weapons wherever it pleased.

Alarmed by how close we had come to nuclear apocalypse, Kennedy and Soviet premier Nikita Khrushchev set up a telephone hot line to enable direct communication, developed a personal relationship to ease tensions, and succeeded in August 1963 in banning nuclear testing in the atmosphere, under water, or in space. The president inspired many of us with an eloquent June 1963 American University commencement address about the world's crucial need for an enduring peace. He even urged "every thoughtful citizen" who desired peace to "begin by looking inward—by examining his own attitude toward peace, toward the Soviet Union," which he extolled for its heroic World War II sacrifices. But then of course he went on to claim: "The Communist drive to impose their political and economic system on others is the primary cause of world tension today." His final remarks began with this statement: "The United States, as the world knows, will never start a war."

So it must have been Vietnam that started a war with the United States. In 1961 President Kennedy authorized Operation Hades, later euphemistically renamed Operation Ranch Hand, the ten-year chemical warfare campaign designed to destroy the major rain forests of South Vietnam and wipe out food crops available to the people revolting against the U.S.-installed dictator. Among the sixteen to seventeen thousand acknowledged U.S. "advisers" fighting in Vietnam by mid-1963 were whole U.S. combat units. For example, a U.S. Marine helicopter squadron consisting of 550 Marines played a key role in major search-and-destroy missions as early as August 1962.[9]

America's war against the Democratic Republic of Vietnam began before most Americans had ever heard of Vietnam. When did Vietnam start becoming an important part of my life? Tens of millions of other Americans may have asked themselves the same question. The harder I try to answer it, the more the Vietnam War seems at first to have been like a mosquito whining around my head while I was asleep. When that whining got close to my ear, I would impulsively swat at it. Of course I missed. But some of the swats landed on my own head, waking me from my slumber and illusory dreams about my country.

Jane seems to have waked up a bit earlier. In early 1962, before the Cuban Missile Crisis, she was already writing letters to senators, clipping news articles, and participating in the Palo Alto chapters of both the Women's League for Peace and Freedom and the newly formed Women Strike for

Peace. By the summer of 1963, the whining mosquito had metamorphosed into an ugly thunderbird roaring daily on the nation's TVs. The streets of Saigon were filled with students, Buddhists, and ordinary citizens rebelling against the brutal dictatorship of Ngo Dinh Diem, whom Washington had installed in 1954 as the supreme ruler of a "democratic nation" called "South Vietnam." We witnessed Buddhist nuns and monks immolating themselves as ultimate acts of protest. Amid his self-ignited inferno, Quang Duc sat unmoving in the lotus position until his charred body finally toppled over into living rooms across America. Then came mass arrests of thousands and savage raids on the Buddhist pagodas by the secret police and soldiers commanded by Diem's brother, Ngo Dinh Nhu. Madame Nhu obligingly gave a TV interview in flawless English, laughingly dismissing Quang Duc's self-sacrifice as a "monk barbeque show."

On November 1, the protesters were all gone from the streets of Saigon, which were filled all day and much of the night with battles raging between ground troops, tanks, and jet fighters commanded by generals on Washington's payroll and outnumbered forces loyal to Diem and Nhu. By morning, the Ngo brothers had been secretly executed and a cabal of the generals had taken over the government. Madame Nhu bitterly accused Washington of "inciting and backing" the coup. Of course she was right, as we all learned definitively eight years later from the leaked Pentagon Papers, which included this astonishing statement in an August 1963 cablegram from U.S. ambassador Henry Cabot Lodge Jr. to Secretary of State Dean Rusk:

> We are launched on a course from which there is no respectable turning back: the overthrow of the Diem government. . . . There is no turning back because there is no possibility, in my view, that the war can be won under a Diem administration, still less that Diem or any member of the family can govern the country in a way to gain the support of the people who count, i.e., the educated class in and out of government service—not to mention the American people.[10]

Three weeks after the overthrow of the Diem government, the government of John F. Kennedy was overthrown by either a lone assassin or a sophisticated conspiracy. Well, which was it? Instead of closing the case, each of the four officially sponsored investigations opened new ones, and each new case opened cans crawling with slippery deadly worms.

The Warren Commission (1963–1964) was exposed as a band of government loyalists trying their best to conceal, expunge, or falsify all evidence embarrassing to the FBI, CIA, Dallas officials and police, President Kennedy, and Attorney General Robert Kennedy. The U.S. Senate Select Committee to Study Governmental Operations with Respect to Intelligence Activities (the Church committee, 1975–1976) revealed numerous conspiracies by U.S. administrations and agencies to assassinate foreign leaders. Although the House of Representatives Select Committee on Assassinations (1976–1979) concluded that the Kennedy assassination was probably part of a conspiracy, it sealed all its primary documents for fifty years, and later its chief council asserted that its investigation was crippled because the committee had been compromised by the CIA. The Assassination Records Review Board (1992–1998) managed to declassify five million pages of eye-popping evidence only to discover that the CIA had suckered the board into letting it withhold the potentially most damaging evidence of all.[11]

Throughout all the decades since 1963, the corporate media have sanctified the lone assassin scenario and ridiculed, when they could not ignore, the dozens of books presenting evidence and arguments pointing to possible, probable, and in most cases undeniable conspiracies relating to the murders of Kennedy and Oswald. The most notorious and influential murder case of modern times has not been closed or solved, as proved by the many deeply researched twenty-first-century volumes on all sides, such as Michael Benson, *Who's Who in the JFK Assassination* (2003); Michael Kurtz, *The JFK Assassination Debates* (2006); Vincent Bugliosi, *Reclaiming History* (2007); James Douglass, *JFK and the Unspeakable* (2008); and David Talbot, *The Devil's Chessboard* (2015).[12]

It's understandable that the CIA, FBI, corporate media, military leaders, U.S. senators, congressional representatives, judges, and other high government officials would want to pop all those worms back in their cans or simply quash them. But they couldn't, because we had learned too much about the CIA, Oswald, Ruby, the FBI, the Kennedys, and their squirming interrelations.

What were these worms we had seen? CIA Director Allen Dulles, who had masterminded the 1961 Bay of Pigs invasion of Cuba, blamed its failure on Kennedy for withholding U.S. naval and air support. The Joint Chiefs of Staff believed that Kennedy had jeopardized national security by backing down and not attacking Cuba during the 1962 Missile Crisis. They also vehemently opposed his conspiracy to overthrow the Diem government and his willingness to consider withdrawing from Vietnam. CIA Director Dulles had, with the approval of President Eisenhower, conspired with mob bosses John Roselli, Sam Giancana, Santo Trafficante, and other organized crime leaders in numerous attempts to assassinate Fidel Castro. During these conspiracies, Roselli in 1960 introduced Kennedy, then running for president, to Judith Campbell (later Exner), who became the mistress of both the president and Giancana, shuttling between them and Roselli as a link in new conspiracies to kill Castro. Giancana and Roselli were both murdered, one just before and one just after testifying to the Church committee.

Beginning a year before the assassination, Kennedy had fired Dulles and his top CIA deputies, Richard Bissell and Charles Cabell (brother of Dallas mayor Earl Cabell). Kennedy's successor, Lyndon Johnson, made Allen Dulles a key member of the Warren Commission. Whether or not the CIA was involved with Oswald in a conspiracy to assassinate President Kennedy, there is irrefutable evidence that Oswald played a significant role in one or more CIA conspiracies having to do with Cuba. Oswald also had complex relations with the FBI and was probably a paid informer for that agency. Elements of the CIA and organized crime worked as partners in creating an international heroin cartel based on opium poppies grown in the landlocked Golden Triangle (mainly in Laos), flown out on CIA airlines such as Air America, refined in Saigon, and distributed by the same Sicilian Mafia families to whom the U.S. Navy gave control of New York Harbor during World War II. When Washington installed Diem as ruler of "South Vietnam," his first battles (with the Binh Xuyen) for control of both Saigon and the opium traffic from the Golden Triangle were organized by Edward Lansdale, the CIA wheeler-dealer who later ran Operation Mongoose, the Kennedy administration conspiracy for a planned new invasion of Cuba that led directly to the Missile Crisis of October 1962. Organized crime supplied women to the FBI and CIA to serve as "honeypots" to blackmail political leaders. J. Edgar Hoover thus had records of some of Kennedy's numerous sexual affairs, including with Judith Campbell. Jack Ruby had multiple deep ties with both organized crime and the Dallas police, his strip clubs were linked to the national "honeypots" system, and at least once he smuggled guns to CIA-sponsored terrorists in Cuba. Members of the Dallas Police Department arranged for Ruby to access the basement where Oswald was going to be paraded.

Most of us old enough to experience the events of November 22 and 24, 1963, were profoundly shaken. The later revelations from these events had even deeper effects on our lives, forcing many of us to rethink fundamental questions about our country and its history, about what it means to be an American, and what to do about what we were learning. Younger people are probably not shocked by what we learned, because a secret government wallowing in conspiracies may seem as normal today as the internet, robots dutifully reporting their discoveries on Mars, and a permanent state of war.

Few of us knew in November 1963 how long the American war in Vietnam had been going on or could possibly guess how long it would continue. What would Kennedy have done? This other huge question about the assassination cannot possibly be resolved. After nine years of sponsoring and financing the French war and nine years of sponsoring, financing, and waging covert war for the Diem regime, there would seem to have been two choices: find an exit or commit to an overt U.S. war. Kennedy's plan was to gradually turn the war over to the Saigon government and complete a pullout by 1965. But Nixon tried the same strategy, called "Vietnamization," beginning in mid-1968 and ending in disaster in 1973. And from his inauguration until his murder, Kennedy had been escalating the U.S. combat role.[13]

We do know what new president Lyndon Johnson did. On November 26, he authorized top-secret National Security Action Memorandum 273. Here is Paragraph 7 of NSAM 273:

7. Planning should include different levels of possible increased activity, and in each instance there should be estimates of such factors as:
     A. Resulting damage to North Vietnam;
     B. The plausibility of denial;
     C. Possible North Vietnamese retaliation;
     D. Other international reaction.[14]

Whether a conspiracy led to Kennedy's murder is still a debatable question. But there is no room for rational debate about this question: Did a conspiracy lead to America's overt war in Vietnam? Thanks to Daniel Ellsberg's leak of the Pentagon Papers in 1971, we got to be a fly on the wall observing the machinations of our political and military leaders as they hatched and launched their secret plot to plunge our nation into a major war in Vietnam while deliberately and continually lying to us about what they were doing. The "damage to North Vietnam" would be inflicted by top-secret air, land, and sea operations planned each month under Operation Plan 34A, better known as OPLAN 34A.[15] Any "North Vietnamese retaliation" would legitimize the next steps in escalation. And "plausibility of denial" would soon become the watchword of the government of the United States.

Like our neighbors on Lawrence Lane and many of my colleagues at Stanford, Jane and I were becoming more and more apprehensive as the first of many military juntas, led mostly by North Vietnamese officers who had fought in the French forces, took over the Saigon government. But we were still leading the normal and unremarkable lives of a university professor and a professor's wife with three young children in a comfortable home in an affluent university town.

Like my English Department colleagues (all of whom were male and white), I tied one of my many striped ties in a proper narrow knot (not the Windsor knot of my pseudo-gangster youth), donned my tweed jacket, and drove off to enlighten Stanford students about great works of the literary canon. Envisioning a future in which I might spend decades teaching the same works of this canon over and over again, I committed the most radical act of my first three professorial years. Not having had a chance to read any of my favorite genre since starting graduate school, I decided to give a course in science fiction, which turned out to be one of the first of two regular science-fiction courses in an American college (the other was started simultaneously by Mark Hillegas at Colgate). This little attack on the literary canon raised some eyebrows and created a minor stir in the department. Another radical act occurred in a meeting of the department committee that was deciding which candidates for our Ph.D. program should be accepted, when I argued with the venerable chair of the department, who insisted that it was a waste of resources to award doctorates to women because they ended up just getting married and having babies.

In my third year of teaching, I finally got my first black student, who soon convinced me of the value of ethnic diversity in the classroom while we were studying *Man's Fate*, André Malraux's canonical novel about the Chinese revolution, set in 1927 Shanghai. In the middle of what seemed to me a very good class discussion, I saw his hand waving in the back row.

"Isn't the novel supposed to be about the Chinese revolution?" he asked.

"Why, yes, and about more," I answered.

"Then why is only one of the main characters Chinese?"

I tried not to show my surprise, confusion, and embarrassment. If I had had any courage and was not afraid of losing the respect of the class, I would have answered honestly, "Oh, I never noticed."

What a great lesson about ethnocentrism! I've thought about this eye-opener many times during my later decades of antiwar activism and research into the Vietnam War. It helps explain the blindness and almost incomprehensible stupidity of our political and military leaders who sponsored and then waged the thirty-year war against the Vietnamese people's quest for independence and sovereignty. How else can we explain Nixon's assertion in 1954 that the United States must send troops to Vietnam because "the Vietnamese lack the ability to conduct a war by themselves or govern themselves"? Or Lodge's argument in 1963 that we must get rid of Diem because he cannot "gain the support of the people who count, i.e., the educated class in and out of government service"? Or all the books that still argue that with a different strategy we could have won the war?

In those first few years of teaching and in my first book (*The Wake of the Gods: Melville's Mythology*, 1963), I was struggling awkwardly with some fundamental questions about literature. So when the Johns Hopkins English Department, reputed to be the Canaan for literary scholars, asked me to join its seven-man faculty, I thought I couldn't refuse. In June of 1964, Jane, Karen, Gretchen, Robert, and I set out on our pilgrimage to the Promised Land—or rather my Promised Land—in the East, pitching our two little tents as we camped across America.

We came down from the Sierras in late June, bought our first newspaper in a week, and learned that three civil rights workers—James Chaney, Andrew Goodman, and Michael Schwerner—were missing in Mississippi. Organizers for Mississippi Freedom Summer had spoken at Stanford, and Jane and I now regretted that we could not turn south and participate in what we saw as one of the most inspiring events of our time. Instead, we drove on to Jane's family farm. We arrived just in time to watch on TV the opening of the Republican convention that would nominate Barry Goldwater, which delighted Jane's parents and alarmed us. We were rooting for that great liberal hope, Nelson Rockefeller.

We got to Baltimore on July 17. We were looking forward to living in a real city, rather than the rarefied suburbia of Palo Alto. The Lawrence Lane experience had made us vow to live in an integrated neighborhood. Everyone we talked to in Baltimore said there was no such thing. We had previously written of our plan to several of my new colleagues and their wives (all the colleagues of course being male), who patiently explained that this would be impossible, since, as one put it, "Baltimore is not California." All the real estate agents we contacted either lectured us on the dangers of living among "the colored," gave us the runaround, or refused point-blank to show us any listings.

From July 18 through 21 the front pages of the newspapers we were amassing in our search for house ads told of the "Negro riots" that were sweeping Harlem, Rochester, and the Bedford-Stuyvesant section of

Brooklyn. There was no hint that this was to be the first of the "long, hot summers" that would culminate in April 1968 with simultaneous rebellions in 110 U.S. cities. The news made us even more determined to find a home that was in neither a lily-white suburb nor a black ghetto, but in a neighborhood were black and white people lived together. So we flipped from the front pages to the classified sections and pored through the houses-for-sale columns.

We almost skipped the one-line ad from the Windsor Hills Improvement Association, a name that sounded like a parody of some segregationist homeowners' outfit. But an impulsive phone query turned into a twenty-minute conversation that portrayed the Improvement Association as an organization of black and white neighbors, many of whom shared our liberal ideas.

Windsor Hills, a gently rolling area of west Baltimore, had once been an exclusive, prestigious neighborhood. When some Jews moved in after World War II, many of the wealthy WASPs flew out. When blacks began moving in from the inner city just to the east, a significant minority of the white residents decided to stay, and other whites bought some of the fine old homes at bargain prices. The white population included several couples of openly gay men who participated, some as leaders, in the social and political life of the community. The area had stabilized at about 80 percent black. It was a couple of gay officers of the Improvement Association who took us on a tour of the homes for sale and then helped us negotiate the purchase of a classic five-bedroom 1917 colonial.

Living in 2607 Talbot Road led to interesting discoveries, first inside the house and later all around us. The attic had obviously once been servants' quarters. The double-entrance staircase spoke about class or race or maybe even gender separation from whoever worked in the kitchen. The high quality of construction and materials told a tale of inflation from the pre–World War I era. When I tested a living room plaster wall to see if I could build a floor-to-ceiling bookcase on it, I found it was attached to brick and then noticed a hollow arch-shaped area at the base that I assumed must have been a fireplace. With seven-year-old Karen and five-year-old Gretchen helping to carry out the debris, Jane and I tore down the plaster, and we soon had a gorgeous brick wall with a raised-hearth fireplace. When I much later saw on the internet the fireplace featured in a 2017 sale of the house, I thought back to when past occupants sealed up dirty old fireplaces because of modern heating, and wondered whether future occupants would once again be sealing up fireplaces because of global warming. Traveling further in time and history, I thought of that brick house on the Penobscot River where one brick fireplace was our only heat source whenever the Maine winter downed the power lines and where the only evidence of black people was the Underground Railroad hideout excavated by the ship captain who had hauled all those bricks up the river.

Although most of the people living in Windsor Hills were middle-income working class and professionals, the corrupt downtown Baltimore political machine evidently thought that because the neighborhood was 80 percent black they could (and maybe should) treat it like a ghetto. So they assaulted the community by cutting back on garbage pickups and even unleashed a couple of police sweeps, with roadblocks and door-to-door house raids. The Improvement Association demanded a meeting with city administrators. The two guys they sent, who reminded me of waterfront mobsters, looked visibly shocked when they walked into the meeting room filled with almost two hundred angry Windsor Hills citizens. From then on, the community had excellent garbage service and the police raids ceased. The next confrontation with the machine wouldn't come until the November election approached, and would be more dramatic—and more educational.

Meanwhile, the news from Vietnam featured puff pieces about the sixteen thousand U.S. "advisers" who were teaching "the South Vietnamese" how to resist the "Communist terrorists" and the "invasion from the North." Occasionally, however, glimpses of the truth slipped through. An article titled "Sabotage Raids on North Confirmed by Saigon Aide" in the July 23 *New York Times* caught Jane's eye:

> The commander of South Vietnam's Air Force confirmed today that "combat teams" have been sent on sabotage missions inside Communist North Vietnam and that Vietnamese pilots were being trained for possible larger-scale attacks.
>
> Teams have entered North Vietnam by "air, sea, and land," Air Commodore Nguyen Cao Ky said at a news conference.
>
> He indicated that clandestine missions had been dispatched at intervals for at least three years.

Ky was openly boasting that U.S.-organized combat teams had been infiltrating North Vietnam before the alleged infiltration of North Vietnamese combat teams into South Vietnam. No wonder that his personal American adviser, Air Force general Joseph Moore, who stood at his elbow, nervously and hastily "tried to suggest that Commodore Ky did not have a complete command of English." Unabashed and not easily shut up, the "Commodore disclosed that he had personally piloted a plane over North Vietnam and that the raids were continuing."[16]

This would not be the last time that Ky would be an embarrassment for U.S. officialdom. Nguyen Cao Ky was a native of North Vietnam who had flown for the French against his countrymen; later, after training at Maxwell AFB in Alabama, he would become South Vietnam's ruthless ruler, infamous for proclaiming his admiration of Hitler.

If we had had a time machine, we would have recognized the raids as OPLAN 34A operations, as ordered by NSAM 273, signed by President Johnson on November 26, 1963. And we would have recognized Paragraph 7, Line B: "Plausibility of Denial," in the next day's news spin.

According to the *New York Times*, "Peking and Hanoi" are "misinterpreting as a portent of attack" on North Vietnam "the appointment of Gen. Maxwell D. Taylor, former chairman of the Joint Chiefs of Staff, as Ambassador to South Vietnam." Yet shortly after Taylor's July arrival, General Nguyen Khanh, the latest junta head of the Saigon government, led a mass rally chanting "To the North!" The *Times* assured readers that the main "concern" of the U.S. administration "is heightened by signs that Communist China still takes more seriously than Washington the likelihood of attacks upon North Vietnam in the foreseeable future." At a secret meeting, General Taylor reportedly told General Khanh that "attacks on North Vietnam" "would be contrary to the United States' policy." "Air Commodore Ky," we were assured, had been "reprimanded by both Premier Khanh and General Taylor." For what? The Saigon Defense Ministry "did not deny" his "acknowledgement that South Vietnamese 'combat teams' had been dropped inside North Vietnam on sabotage and intelligence missions," but "qualified sources" reported that at the secret meeting, Taylor had warned "that no such acknowledgement should have been given."[17]

Thanks to her service as a Strategic Air Command wife, Jane no longer trusted either our government or the *New York Times*. Worse still, she was a former stellar English major who always read closely. So the awkward spin looked to her like sand being thrown in our eyes and led her to ponder what Ky had revealed. She figured that the raids on North Vietnam had to be operations run by Washington, and it seemed obvious to her that they were supposed to be kept secret not from the North Vietnamese but from the American people.

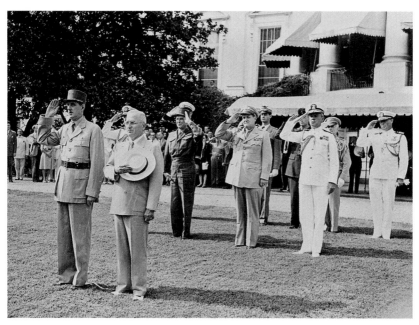

While the Vietnamese people were overthrowing Japanese rule and creating the Democratic Republic of Vietnam, French president Charles de Gaulle flew to Washington on August 22, 1945, where the Truman administration agreed to arm, finance, transport, and sponsor a French invasion of Vietnam, Laos, and Cambodia.

Credit: nsf / Alamy Stock Photo.

John Foster Dulles peering across the 38th Parallel into North Korea on June 19, 1950, six days before the start of the Korean War. Dulles was on a state visit to South Korean president Syngman Rhee, who was threatening to invade North Korea.

Credit: US Army.

The first "Crew of the Month" of the 341st Air Refueling Squadron standing under a KC-97G in 1958. Bruce is third from the left.   Credit: US Air Force.

President Kennedy meeting with Army officials during the October 1962 missile crisis.   Credit: CORBIS/Corbis via Getty Images.

The refueling of a B-47, as viewed from inside the KC-97 boom operator's pod window.

Credit: US Air Force.

A KC-97F refueling a B-47 bomber. The F model lacks the G's two underwing fuel tanks.

Credit: US Air Force.

Police dogs attacking African American youth in Birmingham on May 3, 1963.

Credit: Associated Press.

Police formations confronting massed demonstrators at the Oakland Induction Center in October 1967.　　　　　　　Credit: *Oakland Tribune, East Bay Times.*

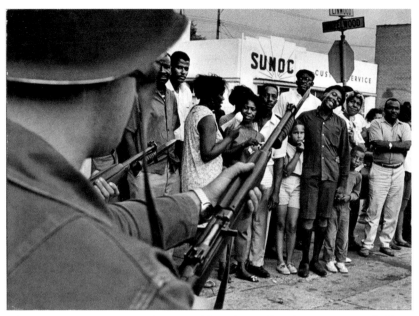

African American citizens confronting soldiers during the July 1967 Detroit rebellion.
Credit: Walter P. Reuther Library, Archives of Labor and Urban Affairs, Wayne State University.

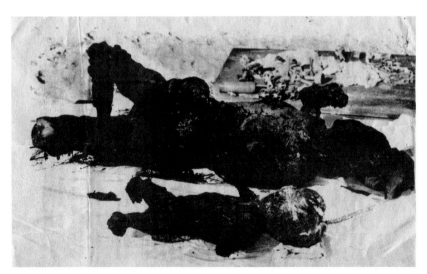

In January and February 1966, hundreds of thousands of these leaflets of a napalmed mother and child were dropped from airplanes over Disneyland, Oakland, San Francisco, troopships in San Diego Harbor, and the Long Beach Naval Station. Three of the six pilots were arrested and charged with the felony of conspiracy to litter.   Credit: Flyer by Ray Tiernan, 1966.

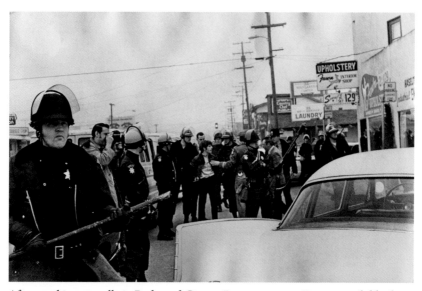

After speaking at a rally in Redwood City on January 25, 1971, Bruce was clubbed to the pavement by four San Mateo Sheriff's Office deputies and arrested for felonious assault and battery on the officers. Credit: Photo by Phil Trounstine, 1971.

Bruce arguing with Santa Clara Sheriff's Office officials on February 10, 1971, about their forcibly disbursing a large demonstration by Stanford students and faculty against the invasion of Laos and the use of Stanford's Computer Center to process Gamut-H, a secret plan for an air, sea, and land invasion of North Vietnam.

Anonymous.

Jane with an unloaded carbine at Bruce's January 5, 1972, press conference about his dismissal from Stanford. This photo appeared in "In the Matter of H. Bruce Franklin," *New York Times Magazine*, January 23, 1972.   Anonymous.

Protest against the Iraq War produced the largest nationwide and worldwide antiwar demonstration in history on February 15, 2003. But here on September 15, 2007, tens of thousands were still marching on the Capitol to protest the Iraq War, possible war against Iran, and Washington's Forever War.

"RED PT BOATS FIRE AT US DESTROYER ON VIETNAM DUTY; Maddox and Four Aircraft Shoot Back after Assault 30 Miles off Coast" blared the front page headline in the August 3 *New York Times*. The destroyer "was on a routine patrol when an unprovoked attack took place.... No effort was made to sink the PT boats, because the fleet was not at war," according to the Defense Department, which could find "no ready explanation why the PT boats would in effect attack the powerful Seventh Fleet." The same story of an "unprovoked attack" on an innocent U.S. ship was all over the media. There was no public questioning of its accuracy or veracity. Then Jane handed me the July 23 and 24 articles she had clipped and marked up. She and I (and no doubt many other Americans) were slipping—or plunging—into roles we are still playing: scrutinizing the corporate media's reportage about U.S. foreign relations for clues about any truth buried in the government propaganda, particularly clues about the next stages of our country's present and forthcoming war(s). The dishonesty of this account of what is still referred to as the "first attack" by North Vietnam on U.S. vessels in the Gulf of Tonkin was obvious to me. What I didn't know then was that almost every sentence in this article, representative of all the media coverage, was a lie. Nor did I guess what was to come in the next two days, much less the warfare waged by the United States against Vietnam in the ensuing eleven years.

The events of the next two days did set me off on a quest for years to discover, publish, and teach the truth of what happened in the Gulf of Tonkin in the first week of August 1964. My first such publications would come in the spring of 1966 and would be substantiated years later by four books by other researchers. My worst discoveries about the incompetence of one of the destroyer captains were confirmed by Captain Bill Morgan (decades before I learned about his role in the Missile Crisis). Some of the research was conducted jointly with retired Admiral Arnold True. When Admiral True later communicated with the 1968 Fulbright Committee investigation of the Gulf of Tonkin events, Navy officials tried to pooh-pooh him as just a retired officer unfamiliar with current destroyer operations, but it turned out that Admiral True, who had commanded a division of destroyers in World War II, was actually the author of the text on destroyer operations currently assigned at Annapolis.

My work with Admiral True was mainly in the fall of 1965, when I was back teaching at Stanford and back living in 982 Lawrence Lane. One day, he arranged for the two of us to meet with Leonard Laskow, flight surgeon on the USS *Ticonderoga*, the aircraft carrier involved in both of the Tonkin events. After my morning class at Stanford, I drove home, where Admiral True was to pick me up, and turned the car over to Jane, who packed the three kids into our car and drove off for a long-awaited excursion. As she turned left on Greer Road, a car parked about half a block ahead pulled out and stayed ahead as she turned right toward US 101. As she passed the 101 South exit and continued onto the overpass, the car pulled over, let her pass, and then tailed her to her final destination: the Palo Alto Duck Pond. She parked on the far end of the pond where she could be among other people and got out with the kids. The tailing car parked at the other end. Three men in dark suits emerged. They stared at Jane and the kids. They talked. They seemed puzzled. They stayed for about half an hour, furtively glancing in her direction, before finally speeding off. This was not the most ludicrous mistake involving the Gulf of Tonkin events. But it was the least tragic.

While Jane was waiting for the three suits to give up on their mission, Admiral True picked me up, took the 101 South exit, and proceeded on 101 to the Moffett Naval Air Station, where we sat down for a long lunch with Dr. Laskow in the officers' club. Because Laskow had participated in the debriefing of the pilots who had overflown the scene at low altitude, he was able to give us a very clear picture of the madness at the center of an out-standingly disgraceful event in American history.

Let's start with the true story of the first Gulf of Tonkin "incident."

In the early morning hours of July 31, eight days after Ky's boastful reve-lations, four U.S. gunboats shelled military installations on North Viet-nam's coastal islands of Hon Me and Hon Ngu.[18] This was part of ongoing OPLAN 34A operations, carried out by South Vietnamese, European, and Chinese mercenaries under U.S. command. One goal of the raids was to probe and weaken North Vietnam's coastal defenses, possibly for an even-tual invasion. U.S. warships monitored the radar and radio responses to these raids, "painting a picture" of the North Vietnamese defenses (similar to those SAC probes of Soviet defenses by bombers that we refueled).

During the two next days, the USS *Maddox*, a destroyer carrying sophis-ticated electronic equipment, prowled around in the vicinity of the two islands, coming as close as four to six miles to Hon Me (according to later U.S. admissions) while recording the location and range of radar and radio signals. On August 2, three North Vietnamese PT boats set sail from Hon Me and headed toward the *Maddox*, which turned and headed away from the coast. Each PT boat carried two torpedoes, capable of attacking a destroyer within a range of one thousand yards or less. The range of the *Maddox*'s guns was eighteen thousand yards.[19] When the three tracking boats got within 5.6 miles (9,800 yards), the *Maddox* opened fire on them. Later Raymond Connell, the *Maddox*'s gun boss, testified unequivocally that his first orders were "shoot to kill."[20]

The U.S. Navy's official account tried to spin this as "warning shots" fired "across the bows" of the approaching boats. Admiral True revealed two problems with this explanation. It is not possible to fire across the bow of a following vessel. There is no such thing as a warning shot from one vessel of war to another; such a shot signals the opening of hostile engagement. In a message to Senator Fulbright, Admiral True stated flatly that as the commander of any war vessel, "I would consider any such shot as hostile and would not only be justified but required by Navy regulations to retaliate."[21]

By opening fire, the *Maddox* thus forced the PT boats to attack. As vessels of war assigned to protect their homeland, they could hardly turn tail and scurry home. If the *Maddox* had simply continued heading out to open sea, the PT boats could have reported that they had driven it away.

When the PT boats got to within 9,000 yards (5.1 miles)—about as close as the destroyer had been to their base on Hon Me—the *Maddox* opened up with all its guns. The three boats made a futile attack, launching all their torpedoes at an ineffective range, and then turned back toward Hon Me. The destroyer pursued, firing away. Aircraft from the USS *Ticonderoga* joined the assault. One of the PT boats was damaged and several Vietnamese crewmen were killed. The only damage to the *Maddox* was one possible bullet hole.

Today, almost every reference to this first of two "Gulf of Tonkin incidents" describes it as an attack by North Vietnam on a U.S. ship. In reality the *Maddox*'s gunfire was the first admitted attack by the U.S. in its war on North Vietnam.

President Johnson ordered the resumption of OPLAN 34A attacks. Accordingly, U.S. gunboats shelled North Vietnam on the night of August 3–4.[22] The *Maddox*, joined by another destroyer, the USS *C. Turner Joy*, continued sailing along the North Vietnamese coast, but "away from area of 34-A ops," in the words of Admiral Ulysses Sharp. The only news we heard about the Gulf of Tonkin for a couple of days was that President Johnson had ordered the Navy to destroy "any other attackers."

On August 5 we awoke to this news: An unknown number of North Vietnamese PT boats had launched an unprovoked attack on two U.S. destroyers on the high seas sixty-five miles from Vietnam. The battle had lasted for three hours, with the PT boats firing many torpedoes while the destroyers fought back, aided by planes from the aircraft carriers *Ticonderoga* and *Constellation*. Some of the PT boats had been sunk. In retaliation for this unprovoked Communist attack, U.S. warplanes from the two carriers had successfully bombed and strafed several North Vietnamese naval bases. President Johnson had asked Congress for a resolution giving him authority to conduct limited military operations.

The August 5 issue of the *New York Times* had two stories so big that it ran two banner headlines, one over the other:

U.S. PLANES ATTACK NORTH VIETNAMESE BASES;
PRESIDENT ORDERS 'LIMITED' RETALIATION AFTER
COMMUNISTS' PT BOATS RENEW RAIDS

F.B.I. FINDS 3 BODIES BELIEVED TO BE RIGHTS WORKERS

And underneath the banner headlines was third major story, about the third night of violence in Jersey City. What a great class could be taught about this front page.

At first we were told few details about what had happened on August 4. Then came the big story. And what an exciting story it was. On a dark and stormy night, in the middle of the Gulf of Tonkin, sixty-five miles from land, an unknown number of North Vietnamese PT boats fired numerous torpedoes at the *Maddox* and the *C. Turner Joy*, which for three hours bravely fought back with the help of carrier-based warplanes, sinking two attackers and escaping without any damage. The story was as creative as the attack on the USS *Maine*. Or the armada of Soviet bombers poised to rain nuclear bombs on all the children hiding under their school desks. Or Saddam Hussein's vast arsenal of weapons of mass destruction ready to replace the Soviet threat against the U.S. homeland.

Here is the true story. It was indeed a dark and stormy night—in midsummer on a tropical sea, where heat concentrates patches of water vapor so densely that they appear as solid objects on radar. I have navigated planes around columns of storm clouds that looked on my radar as solid as concrete pillars. Probably everybody reading this has seen similar radar images on TV weather shows. The Gulf of Tonkin is notorious for many such phantoms as well as less understandable radar "spooks." The captains of the *Maddox* and the *Turner Joy*, already jittery from the previous encounter and the ongoing OPLAN 34A, were too quick to accept their radar reports as images of attacking vessels. Both destroyers fired away at the images, most of which vanished. Then a few crewmen, now even more excited and scared, thought they saw wakes of torpedoes. Soon the two destroyers, trying to evade the phantom torpedoes, were careening wildly back and forth from port to starboard, generating lots of erratic wakes and false sonar pings off their wakes and their own rudders. The *Maddox* alone reported dodging twenty-six enemy torpedoes. Soon planes from two aircraft carriers, the USS *Ticonderoga* and the USS *Constellation* were roaring overhead, dropping flares and futilely searching for enemy vessels, thus adding to the pandemonium.

The pilots from the *Ticonderoga* zoomed in on every enemy vessel reported to them from the destroyers. The only vessels they saw were the two U.S. destroyers. For example, the *Maddox* radioed to Jim Stockdale (later a POW in North Vietnam and after that Ross Perot's vice presidential running mate) that a hostile vessel was rapidly closing behind the destroyer. Stockdale flew back and forth as low as he could, dropping flares, searching every foot of the water, and telling the *Maddox* there was nothing there. The destroyer's commander radioed back, "He's right there. I can see his wake." Stockdale, who was convinced that the commanders of both destroyers were acting deranged, responded, "That's your own wake."[23]

The battle raged on for hours, with the night clouds lit like Fourth of July fireworks by the ships' blazing guns and the planes' dazzling flairs. This furious scene was midway between North Vietnam and the Chinese island of Hainan. The Vietnamese urgently radioed to the Chinese, and the Chinese urgently radioed to the Vietnamese, each asking the other: Are those your forces fighting with the Americans?[24]

Only once during this epic battle did any of the numerous radars find a nice solid target that didn't vanish or morph into fuzz. Patrick Park, director of the *Maddox*'s main guns, was given a target spotted by the main radar room. He directed his own radar at the target. "It was a damned big one, right on us, no doubt about this one," Park later said. "About 1,500 yards off to the side, a nice big blip." Park armed and aimed the ship's five-inch guns. Then came the order to open fire. "I shouted back 'Where's the *Turner Joy*?' There was a lot of yelling 'Goddamn,'" Park went on, "with the bridge telling me to 'fire before we lost contact.'"

"I'm not opening fire unless I know where the *Turner Joy* is." The bridge got on the phone and said, "Turn on your lights, *Turner Joy*."

Sure enough, there she was, right in the cross hairs. I had six five-inch guns right on the *Turner Joy*, 1,500 yards away. If I had fired, it would have blown it clear out of the water. All I had to do was squeeze the trigger.[25]

The *Maddox* itself was also threatened by a deadly weapon one time that night, when Jim Stockdale accidentally released a heat-seeking sidewinder missile. Fortunately he was flying so low that the sidewinder splashed in the water before it had a chance to pick up the heat from the destroyer's stack.[26]

No enemy weapon was fired at any U.S. vessel because no enemy weapon was present during this historic battle. After decades of research had proved that simple fact beyond any reasonable doubt, a clincher came from a surprising source. In 2005, the National Security Agency declassified a top-secret, exhaustive, and quite brilliant analysis of its vast trove of SIGINT (intercepted signals intelligence) from the surrounding days. This study revealed that both the NSA and the Navy had suppressed definitive evidence that no enemy vessels could have been in the vicinity of the U.S. ships, and that SIGINT proved conclusively "that *no attack* happened that night."[27]

President Johnson ordered "retaliatory" bombing of North Vietnam before any investigation and before even informing the nation of the "attack" on U.S. ships. What he now wanted was a blank check from Congress to wage any war he wished in Vietnam. So he speedily revised a resolution he had drafted months earlier and whisked this over to Congress:

> *Whereas* naval units of the Communist regime in Vietnam, in violation of the principles of the Charter of the United Nations and of international law, have deliberately and repeatedly attacked United States naval vessels lawfully present in international waters, and have thereby created a serious threat to international peace; and
>
> *Whereas* these attacks are part of a deliberate and systematic campaign of aggression that the Communist regime in North Vietnam has been waging against its neighbors and the nations joined with them in the collective defense of their freedom . . .
>
> Congress approves and supports the determination of the President, as Commander in Chief, to take all necessary measures to repel any armed attack against the forces of the United States and to prevent further aggression.

The House of Representatives debated for forty minutes before approving this resolution by a vote of 416-0. The Senate passed it with only two negative votes, Wayne Morse of Oregon and Ernest Gruening of Alaska. By allowing Lyndon Baines Johnson "to take all necessary measures . . . to prevent further aggression," Congress forked over to the president the power to make war—the power that the Constitution granted solely to Congress. By August 7, President Johnson had his blank check.

And so he could wait until after the November election to launch the overt U.S. war in Vietnam, meanwhile running as the peace candidate against Republican war hawk Barry Goldwater. On August 12, speaking before the American Bar Association, he promised never to "supply American boys to do the job that Asian boys should do," a vow he would repeat throughout the campaign. Johnson was also running as another kind of peace candidate, one who could stop the war simmering inside America.

While U.S. ships and planes were fighting phantoms in the Gulf of Tonkin, the bodies of Chaney, Goodman, and Schwerner, the murdered civil rights workers, were being dug up from a levee in Mississippi. From August 2 through August 17, black rebellions broke out in a Chicago suburb and the New Jersey cities of Paterson, Elizabeth, and Jersey City. On August 26, Johnson was nominated for president by the Democratic convention in Atlantic City. Two days later, a massive black uprising began sixty miles away in Philadelphia.

Jane and I were not so naive as to trust the president's vows not to send American troops to Vietnam, but Goldwater was openly advocating direct U.S. military intervention in Vietnam, including waging war on North Vietnam. We were both scared enough to zip to Democratic Party headquarters in downtown Baltimore to volunteer for anything we could do. Having worked in local politics and Kennedy's 1960 campaign, we were surprised that the assignments they gave to two total newcomers suggested that they had no local Baltimore resources for voter registration.

Jane was assigned to register voters by going door to door in an inner-city apartment project complex, where the office had no local contact person. Though most residents were understandably not eager to open their door to a blond stranger, Jane dutifully rang or knocked at every one in the sprawling complex and managed to register some first-time voters. The abysmal poverty she encountered in these buildings, coupled with the obvious estrangement of the Democratic Party, looked less likely to inspire enthusiastic participation in electoral politics than desperate rebellion.

I found myself delegated as the precinct captain for our neighborhood. The Windsor Hills Improvement Association, almost unanimously alarmed by Goldwater, offered to put me in touch with a couple of people with local experience. One of these was someone I'll call Raymond, an African American man maybe twenty years older than me, who showed up at our house one day, accompanied by two young African American men in army field jackets, explicitly to check me out. The two young men, who seemed to be veterans, made a point of showing that they were less interested in my opinion of them than their evaluation of me and my demeanor as I answered their many questions. They were neither friendly nor hostile, just business-like and studiously polite, maybe something like recruiting officers. Raymond seemed satisfied with the inspection and agreed to take charge of organizing half the blocks in the precinct.

Despite my repeated requests to downtown Democratic headquarters, we got no help in the precinct, not even one name of anyone in a local Democratic organization. This surprised me, for the Baltimore machine, with its Chicago-style ward bosses, was notoriously efficient. So we organized the precinct from scratch. We soon had an active block captain on each block. We took voter registration forms to every home. In the black private houses and small apartment buildings, I found an intense interest in the presidential campaign. There seemed no illusion that Johnson was less racist than Goldwater or that he would do more for black people. But if the country got any more involved in this Vietnam thing, many said, black people would be fighting and dying there. And Goldwater was going to get us in deeper while Johnson was promising not to. A few older people were so worried about a possible war that they registered for the first time in their lives.

In the last week of the campaign, the Democratic Party machine suddenly made its appearance. On street corners throughout the 7th Congressional District, which was about 90 percent black and included our precinct, groups of three men were passing out official-looking sample ballots with the heading "OFFICIAL GOOD GOVERNMENT BALLOT" filled in with the straight Democratic slate except for the U.S. Senate, where Republican J. Glenn Beall was substituted for Democrat Joseph Tydings. Raymond had me come to his house, where he explained to me that Tydings' reform activities had infuriated the Baltimore machine and that this was a crucial test of whether the bosses or "the people's own organization" would run this district.

He told me that we had to deal with this "directly," and he outlined a plan. While he was talking, his phone was constantly busy, and young men were steadily arriving. By the time we were ready to go, there were about thirty or forty of us. I was the only white. We went in two-car units, four men in each car. With one car standing by, the men in the other car would walk up to the three men handing out the bogus sample ballots, politely inform them that we were from the regular Democratic organization, that their activities were not authorized, and that they had to give us the phony ballots and leave the area. Most of the threesomes we accosted consisted of two African American men and an older white man. The white guys turned out to be part of the ward machine. The African American men had been hired at two dollars an hour to distribute what they had been told was the official Democratic Party ballot. Some seemed angry at being hoodwinked, and a few joined us in going around to the other groups.

Late in our roundup, Raymond got word on his walkie-talkie of one less cooperative group. On the scene, we encountered four burly leafleters, two white and two black, clustered close together on a street corner. Except for their race, they reminded me of typical ILA thugs I'd seen on the waterfront eight years earlier. As the four of us approached, they huddled and then turned to face us in a belligerent line. It sure looked like a goon squad sent out to stop our activities. Raymond went through our little speech. One of the white guys suggested that if we were "so interested in the handouts," we "might try taking them." Two of the young guys in our group stepped toward the speaker, and there was a little scuffling that ended abruptly when the four men in our backup car jumped out and raced over.

The machine reappeared on Election Day in the form of uniformed armed guards from a private police agency, sitting as "official Democratic Party poll watchers" at every polling place in the 7th Congressional District. But we were the official Democratic Party poll watchers, and it was illegal for private police, their weapons, and their uniforms to be in polling places. This time Raymond not only mobilized his own forces but also called his "contacts," who were having the same problem in the inner-city districts east of ours. As I went around with Raymond in our district and an adjacent one, I was amazed by the size and discipline of this organization I'd never heard of, as well its success in ejecting the private police.

The election returns in our precinct confirmed what people expressed in the campaign. A record turnout gave Johnson 1,024 and Goldwater 42, according to the official tally sheet (still a treasured possession). The machine's efforts to show its strength by mobilizing a sizable vote for Beall resulted in a switchover of merely a few dozen votes: Tydings got 940, Beall 100. Jane and I were even more delighted by the national returns, as Johnson piled up the greatest majority of the popular vote since James Monroe ran unopposed in 1820. We the people had spoken. We didn't want American boys fighting in Asia.

There was one event during the campaign that was so remote from anything I had ever experienced that it took me three years and a lot of new experience to comprehend. One day, after Raymond and I had been going door-to-door together, talking as we went, he asked me if I would like to see his private office. "Sure," I said. We went to his large turn-of-the-century house, passed the living room where he had assembled the men to halt the distribution of the fake ballots, and walked upstairs into a bedroom. He stepped into a closet, pushed aside some clothes, opened a large trap door, and pulled down a set of hinged stairs. I followed him up the stairs. All I can still recall of what I saw is a series of disjointed sharp images, perhaps exaggerated. The perimeter of this furnished attic seemed to consist of banks of radio equipment, including a large transmitter. In the center were a rack of weapons, including assault rifles. There were two or three small desks. I was introduced to four young men, who all seemed very busy. Each greeted me in the cool but polite manner of the first two men who had come with him to my house. We stayed up there perhaps a total of five minutes. As we went down, Raymond asked me what I thought. I can't remember what I said. All I know is that I was confused and that this seemed some kind of unreal game, something like the fantasies I had with other boys in our neighborhood "club" in Brooklyn. I was somewhat embarrassed, and maybe that has something to do with my lapse in memory. I didn't then comprehend that Raymond was showing an extraordinary trust in me, and I hadn't the slightest inkling of what he was evidently inviting me to join. Was this a revolutionary organization? I don't think that question even crossed my mind because "revolutionary organization" was simply not a category of my thought.

At the time I was flirting with pacifism. Perhaps Raymond saw something in me—or in the future—that I didn't know about.

I certainly didn't know about the long tradition of armed African American self-defense, and I hadn't even heard of Robert F. Williams's *Negroes with Guns*, that influential 1962 manifesto for taking the tradition to a new level of *organized* armed self-defense. Williams, an ex-Marine living in rural North Carolina, had created a large African American NRA chapter that had successfully repelled the onslaughts of armed white terrorist mobs. A short book with enormous influence, *Negroes with Guns* argued that nonviolence and armed self-defense are mutually interdependent tactics. It provided the model for the creation in 1964 Louisiana of the armed Deacons for Defense and Justice, mainly veterans of World War II and the Korean War, who protected nonviolent activists of the Congress of Racial Equality (CORE) from the rampant Ku Klux Klan violence. It helped inspire Stokely Carmichael's leadership in 1965 of the Lowndes County Freedom Organization in Alabama, whose activists openly carried arms while building a black political organization with a black panther icon (to confront the white rooster, official symbol of the Democratic Party organization). And it most famously influenced Huey Newton, Bobby Seale, and Bobby Hutton in their 1966 creation in Oakland, California, of the Black Panther Party for Self-Defense, originally formed to protect black neighborhoods from everyday police violence.

All this is now well known. But what about Raymond's well-armed, highly disciplined, semisecret black Baltimore organization? Was it just a unique outlier? In 1968, as a member of an armed, self-declared revolutionary organization, I had some working contact with a strikingly similar black organization in Oakland, also well armed, highly disciplined, and semisecret, that had obviously been in existence for quite some time. In 1968 I also worked in conjunction with a similar, but more recently formed, organization in San Mateo County. It's hard to believe that there were not many such organizations waking up in 1960s America.

What I was doing most of the year we lived in Baltimore was being an assistant professor of English and American literature at Johns Hopkins University. The professional study of literature was at the heart of the intellectual life of my colleagues at Hopkins. There were eight of us in the department, and we were all expected on days we taught to eat at the same table in the faculty club. This fraternal lunch had sounded appealing back at Stanford, where department members seldom ate together. But my picture of high-intellectual camaraderie at Hopkins had not included table service by black waitresses to white gentlemen dining on fine china on an antique table above thick carpet under the austere but approving stares from oil portraits of the illustrious white gentlemen who created the university and its traditions.

The table conversation was extraordinary, though not quite as I had imagined. Since each department member was supposed to be a superstar in his particular period, the lunchtime atmosphere was charged—not with crass competition—but with high expectations. Each of us was expected to display, without ostentation, his exceptional learning and wit. Sometimes it felt like being in a gang made up of the top gunfighters of the West, where you didn't want to make any sudden move or thoughtless remark. At other times the image came from *All-Star Comics*, where each team member has a unique power to contribute to the unbeatable unit. I wondered when I would be detected as a social and intellectual impostor.

The aptly named Tudor and Stuart Club, which met every other week, was another regularly scheduled intellectual gathering, where a learned paper was read by an English Department faculty member or graduate student. When I told my colleagues at lunch that Jane was interested in the topic of the first meeting and planned to attend, there was an uncomfortable silence. One of them finally responded, with a slight hint of embarrassment, that no females—not even our own female graduate students—were permitted to attend the Tudor and Stuart Club. Trying not to show my outrage, I just said as calmly as possible, "Well, I cannot in good conscience attend a segregated meeting," half expecting that they might say something about possibly altering the policy. They didn't. So I never did get to attend the Tudor and Stuart Club, and I guessed that my days at Hopkins would be limited.

Not gaining admittance to the inner sanctum of the Hopkins English Department turned out to be less serious for Jane than not gaining admittance to a Baltimore doctor's office. When she tried to make an appointment with a doctor about a medical problem, calling every appropriate doctor listed in the thick yellow pages of the Baltimore phone directory, one office after another told her they were not taking new patients. Of course they didn't inform her that they were not taking patients with her southern accent and a last name common among a certain category of Baltimore residents. Finally, she called the wife of Earl Wasserman, our department chair, who easily got Jane an appointment with her own physician.

I liked and respected my colleagues and found them generous, friendly, and unassuming, especially when not at the lunch ritual but just one-on-one. Yet I tried in vain to persuade any of them of the crucial relations between the history we were living—such as the escalating war in Southeast Asia or the rat-infested inner-city ghettos that might be about to blow and where our black waitresses might be living—and the literature we studied and taught. For instance, Jane and I went one night to hear Martin Luther King speak at a "freedom rally" in the Cornerstone Baptist Church of Christ in the heart of the inner city. The audience of over a thousand included about five whites. King's talk overwhelmed us all. The world of brotherhood he projected seemed to exist right there as we all sang "We Shall Overcome," our arms and hands intertwined with those of our neighbors in the pews. The next day I described King's speech, which was not mentioned in the regular media, at our lunch table. My presentation may have been a bit overenthusiastic. Most seemed embarrassed. The only comment came from the senior man in American literature (whom I had been hired to replace before his imminent retirement), who explained, almost condescendingly, that King was effective because he had mastered all the rhetorical tricks of Negro preachers. In vain I argued that sermons are taught as literary works in American literature courses, where attention is paid mainly to their content, and that those seventeenth-century Puritan, eighteenth-century revivalist, and nineteenth-century Unitarian sermons are probably less significant, as well as less eloquent, than Dr. King's sermons.

Meanwhile, the Stanford English Department and I had been discussing the possibility of my returning. They offered an associate professorship. I remember clearly a phone conversation with Tom Moser, the chairman.

"Does this carry tenure?" I asked. "I know my ideas are controversial and upset some people. I don't want to wake up one day to find I'm being fired."

"No sweat," said Tom.

On February 2, 1965, Hanoi and the National Liberation Front of South Vietnam proposed negotiations. The February 5 *New York Times* discussed "the apparent readiness" of "the Reds" to seek a "face-saving" settlement. On Sunday morning, February 7, the *Times* brought to our home the news that Soviet premier Aleksey Kosygin had been received enthusiastically when he arrived in Hanoi on a peace mission. It also told of two "Vietcong" guerrilla attacks that had killed seven American "advisers."

While Jane was washing the breakfast dishes, the radio brought an interview with Secretary of Defense Robert McNamara, who announced that American warplanes had been launched in a massive air assault on North Vietnam in "retaliation" for the previous day's guerilla raids, which were a "brazen example" of "North Vietnamese aggression." As she listened to McNamara's lies, she realized how badly we had been fooled, despite all our suspicions, by LBJ, the peace candidate. She called the Friends Meeting House and asked if they were going to do anything. She was referred to a woman from the Baltimore chapter of Women Strike for Peace, which turned out to have been disbanded. Jane got the numbers of former members and managed to pull the chapter back together to join the WSP mobilization in Washington on February 10, where she was thrilled by the busloads of demonstrators pouring into the capital. Jane had become an antiwar organizer. She didn't know she would be playing that role for more than the next five decades.

That WSP mobilization was the vanguard of larger and larger antiwar rallies and marches. On April 17, a march against the war called by an obscure little organization named Students for a Democratic Society (SDS) turned out to be the largest antiwar demonstration so far in the history of Washington—twenty-five thousand people, most neatly dressed in jackets and ties or skirts and dresses. That many people would not even be noticeable among the half million or more who converged on Washington in 1969 and again in 1971.

Meanwhile, I agonized. On Monday, I bought a newspaper after teaching a morning class and read President Johnson's reassurance that the air strikes were "a limited response," that "we seek no wider war," and that this was certainly not the beginning of regular air raids on North Vietnam. That single "retaliatory" raid turned into a continual aerial bombardment that went on, with a few pauses, for seven years.

I decided to eat lunch that day with Maurice Mandelbaum of the Philosophy Department, a likable down-to-earth guy who was also an international luminary in the field of ethics. I assumed that Maury was sharing my anguish and outrage about the bombings and that he would have thoughts about what professors and other intellectuals ought to be doing. When I mentioned the raids, he said, "Oh, that's just preliminary to negotiations," and changed the subject.

From that day on, I ate lunch in the student cafeteria, which was interpreted by my English Department colleagues as an act of treason. In the cafeteria, I met three other faculty misfits who had deserted the Faculty Club. We formed the first faculty antiwar group, which started out sedately placing ads in newspapers. Then we organized a Vietnam teach-in at Hopkins, joining the wave of teach-ins sweeping across hundreds of campuses and involving perhaps hundreds of thousands of students and faculty that spring.

President Milton Eisenhower called two of our group to his office and ordered us to cease using the name Johns Hopkins University in identifying our antiwar organization or any member. "No member of the faculty," he said, "may indicate his affiliation with Hopkins while making statements about the war or engaging in any other political activity." He was reminded that he had been introduced as president of Johns Hopkins University when he had made a nominating speech at the Republican convention. Ignoring this, he responded that neither the university nor its name could be used "to strengthen any position on Vietnam."

On April 3, McGeorge Bundy was invited to Hopkins to defend administration policy on Vietnam. On April 7, President Milton Eisenhower introduced President Lyndon Baines Johnson, who gave a major address proclaiming his determination to defend the "freedom" and "independence of South Vietnam," pledging, "We will not withdraw, either openly or under the cloak of a meaningless agreement," and asserting that continual "air attacks . . . are a necessary part of the surest road to peace."[28]

On April 9, Henry Cabot Lodge came to Johns Hopkins and declared that "the North Vietnamese seem only to understand force, and of course when they use force they must be met by force, as they were in the Gulf of Tonkin."[29]

8 ▸ BURNING ILLUSIONS

Nineteen sixty-five was the year when the Vietnam War awakened an organized national antiwar movement. Because the war seemed so blatantly irrational and immoral, at first we were optimistic. All we needed were effective tactics, such as demonstrations bigger than those organized by Women Strike for Peace and Students for a Democratic Society that spring. Or direct action. Inspired by the civil rights movement and often led by its veterans, in the summer of 1965, hundreds of people were arrested for antiwar civil disobedience in Washington, public burnings of draft cards began, and in northern California people responded literally to the "put your body on the line" motto by lying on the tracks to block munitions trains. Or moral witness. Three people took moral witness to its ultimate by immolating themselves in 1965: Alice Herz in Detroit (March 26); Norman Morrison, outside the Pentagon (November 2); and Roger La Porte in front of the United Nations (November 10).

Then there was rational discourse. Many of us opposed to the war in those early days naively believed—and this is embarrassing to confess—that the war was just a mistake, something our government had somehow blundered into, perhaps because our leaders were simply ignorant about Vietnamese history. So if we invited government representatives to teach-ins, lobbied Congress, and published well-researched articles and letters to editors and the president, Washington would respond, "Oh, my! We didn't realize that Vietnam was a single nation. Did the Geneva Agreements really say that? And we stopped the elections because we knew Ho Chi Minh would win? And he wanted to be our ally? And all our domestic priorities are going up in smoke? Golly gee, we had better put a stop to this foolish war."

The first event at Stanford in the fall of 1965 was typical. It was an October teach-in where I and others addressed a crowd of two hundred as the kickoff for a three-day camp-in on the campus, followed by a march to Palo Alto on the 15th, part of an international day of protest, including fifteen thousand marching in Berkeley and twenty thousand marching in Manhattan. Pictures of our little march display our earnestness and quest for respectability, with men and women dressed appropriately for dinner with the governor.[1]

But we also thought about direct action. The most horrifying images of the war came from napalm, and a local company—United Technology Center—was manufacturing portable napalm dispensers south of San Jose, not far from Stanford. Not long after the teach-in, some people tried leafleting the workers there, but they were met mainly by security guards.[2]

We needed some way to make the horrors of napalm visible to the American people. Stanford Law student Ray Tiernan launched a spectacular plan to use the military's own means of dispensing napalm to dispense anti-napalm: air power. Since he had no way to train pilots or manufacture airplanes, his first step was recruiting—in local bars—pilots with their own planes. He found six eager for the missions. He then arranged the mass-production of hundreds of thousands of leaflets featuring a photograph of napalm's hideous results, the charred corpses of a Vietnamese mother and small child. The first test flight almost ended in disaster, as some of the air-dropped leaflets got stuck in the plane's tail rudder, temporarily disabling controlled turns, but Ray and the pilots soon devised a safe way to release their paper weapons.

On January 1, three planes assembled in a southern California desert for their first target: the Rose Bowl. However, the truck that delivered their leaflets arrived too late for them to make the game. So they bombarded their two alternate targets: Disneyland and the Long Beach Naval Station. Before returning to the Bay Area, they struck again, hitting troopships in San Diego Harbor. On January 10, Ray's leaflets showered from the sky on downtown Oakland. The *San Francisco Chronicle* wondered whether that raid had anything to do with "the mysterious dropping of leaflets on Disneyland and the Long Beach Naval Station on New Year's night."[3] San

Francisco itself was the next target. Before the February arrest of Ray and three of his six pilots at the small Palo Alto Airport, the squadron had dispensed over a quarter million "Mother and Child" leaflets. They were charged with a felony: conspiracy to litter.

Despite Ray's efforts, most Californians, not to mention most Americans, had still not yet heard of napalm. Typical was the woman in the suburban town of Redwood City, California, who answered her doorbell in April 1966, in the first weeks of the local anti-napalm campaign. Asked to sign a petition against the production of napalm in her city, she responded: "Napalm? No thank you. I'm not interested. I always use Tide."

But by the end of that year, a national and global campaign against napalm had changed the consciousness of tens of millions. That campaign was initiated by a handful of people in and around Stanford University in January 1966. It was a turning point in the lives of many people, including my own.

Looking back, I realize that I cannot understand how I became the person I am today without mentally recapitulating the stages of my metamorphosis during that napalm campaign, a campaign that incinerated the remaining cocoon of illusions within which much of my consciousness had been formed. The campaign offers both a microcosm of how the movement against the Vietnam War changed the lives of ordinary individuals and a nation and an instructive example of spectacularly successful organizing.

How could a campaign directed against a single weapon profoundly transform minds and lives? The answer lies mostly in the process of activism and the discoveries about self and society made in this process. That is the main story I tell in this chapter. But merely learning the history of this particular weapon also has some transformative powers, as I soon learned. Because of my Air Force experience, I was assigned the job of doing this research.

It was this research that led to the story told in chapter 2 of how napalm was used to cremate almost every city in Japan, specifically targeting the civilian population, thus incorporating the Fascist theory of aerial warfare into American ideology and preparing for the atomic bombing of Hiroshima and Nagasaki. The use of napalm in the Korean War was even more genocidal. The United States rained down on Korea twice as much napalm as it had on Japan. Curtis LeMay himself wrote, "We burned down just about every city in North Korea and South Korea *both*." Eighteen major cities in North Korea were turned into charred ruins. In Pyongyang, a modern industrial city of half a million people, only two buildings were left standing.[4] Hundreds of villages and vast areas of farmland were turned into scorched wastelands. Whole forests were burned to the ground. Much of the population was forced to live underground. Decades after the war, Koreans in the northern half of the country would show visitors a lone tree that survived the holocausts, referring to it as a "prewar tree."[5]

But U.S. weapons technology never stands still. In early January 1966, a worker from United Technology Center (UTC), perhaps inspired by one of our leaflets, secretly communicated to a few of us antiwar activists the news that his company had just received a subcontract from Dow Chemical to develop a new, improved kind of napalm. The contract, we discovered, was for the development of napalm-B, a thicker gel, which would ignite more reliably, burn more intensely, and stick more tenaciously to human skin.

Napalm-B consisted of 25 percent gasoline, 25 percent benzene, and 50 percent polystyrene, the marvelous new thickener, which was to be manufactured in quantity especially for napalm by Dow Chemical at Torrance, California. If UTC could successfully complete the research and development, production was scheduled to reach mammoth proportions. The information we gathered was later verified in the March 1966 issue of *Chemical and Engineering News*, which reported that the forthcoming use of polystyrene in napalm-B would be 25 million pounds a month, so much that the normal industrial supplies would be severely overstrained. According to this figure, the production of napalm-B was to reach 500 million pounds each year, three times the total dropped on Japan during all of World War II.

The antiwar movement at Stanford was then embodied by the Stanford Committee for Peace in Vietnam, accurately described by its vague, innocuous name. About two hundred students had signed up as members of SCPV. The steering committee consisted of about two dozen students, faculty members, and people from the surrounding suburbs, each more or less fitfully active against the war. It included a few people who called themselves pacifists, two who called themselves Marxists, and most who no longer knew what to call themselves.

Jane and I were part of that last category. We didn't let our children play with toy guns, and we were in favor of something called "militant, nonviolent protest." Our opposition to "violent" protest was not philosophical but tactical (it might "alienate" people). We opposed aggressive anti-Communism, but we avoided political ideology, particularly Marxism, about which we knew virtually nothing except that it was a musty old nineteenth-century dogma of little relevance to the modern world, especially to an advanced industrial society like the United States. We were in favor of anything that would help stop the war.

SCPV as a whole expressed a similar outlook. Each weekly meeting was spent mainly debating proposals for actions to take the following week. We were looking for the one spectacular action that would quickly educate the American people, bring the government to its senses, and end the "senseless killing" in Vietnam. We felt this was urgent because we believed that the Vietnamese would soon be destroyed as a people. SCPV had no interest in any long-term programs to change American society.

When SCPV got the word about the local contract to develop napalm-B, we thought we could at last do something concrete—stop this local production. And practically everyone saw a great potential for some kind of mass campaign that would swiftly educate people about the "immoral" nature of the war and the illusions of our government. Only two members disagreed.

One of the two, a self-declared Marxist, argued something like this: "A campaign against napalm would only build false consciousness. It would suggest that the Vietnam War would be fine if it were fought with conventional weapons. Who would this kind of campaign appeal to? Only middle-class liberals. In fact, it will alienate working-class people, because they want to use whatever weapons are necessary to support our troops. We must focus all our efforts on demanding immediate withdrawal of all our troops. That's the only demand that working-class people can support."

The other naysayer took a position that seemed almost the precise opposite: "There's only one way to deal with a napalm plant, and that's to deal with it. Anyone who is interested, see me after this bullshit meeting is over."

These two seemingly opposite positions in fact had much in common, for both were based on the assumption that we could not build effective mass opposition to napalm. I do not believe either proposed course of action was wrong. It was necessary to build a mass movement calling for withdrawal of the troops, and it certainly did get built. At some point the napalm plant should have been sabotaged (and in fact one of UTC's barges loaded with napalm later was sunk, evidently by a scuba diver). But a mass movement against napalm, as it turned out, was not a diversion from either of these roads.

One person, possibly only one in our little group, understood all this back then. That was Keith Lowe, a doctoral candidate in Stanford's English Department. Evidently Keith saw both the potential and the limitations of the situation. He also had the patience to lead some of the rest of us step-by-step through a process of political and personal development that produced not only a mass anti-napalm campaign spreading from the San Francisco peninsula across the country and around the world, but also a number of people, including Jane and me, who finally came to understand that just as the use of napalm revealed the true nature of the Vietnam War, this war revealed the true nature of the political-economic-cultural system that created it.

A short and wiry Jamaican citizen of Chinese descent, with features suggesting a globalized mix of the European, Asian, and African peoples who had mingled on that island, Keith responded to other human beings as though he were a stranger to none. Soft-spoken and intense, yet often with a hint of smile, he always seemed both relaxed and under control, even when dancing. In 1969, Keith, then a revered assistant professor of English at the University of California, San Diego, lost that job and all hope of securing another when he was denied a visa to reenter the United States from Jamaica. The main evidence against him in his immigration file consisted of statements from the administration of Stanford identifying him as a "subversive."

Keith's response to the news of the napalm contract was something unheard of—at least to most of us—at that time. He proposed that we carry the issue right to the people in the napalm company. Most of the members of SCPV were excited by this proposal, but there were two contradictory views on how to apply it. Some thought this meant we should go directly to the workers and try to persuade them not to help develop and produce the new form of napalm. Others thought that only the management had the power to pull the company out of the napalm business, so we should go to them. Most groups of activists I have seen since would then have plunged into endless debate. Some would argue that it was impractical to go to the workers. Others would call them anti–working class. They in turn would be branded as dogmatists. If any action had come out of the debate it would be crippled by the divisive struggle that had brought it forth. What Keith apparently understood was that the proponents of neither position had ever verified their arguments in experience and that most of us would use the debate, if we could, as an excuse to avoid getting our hands dirty, our feelings hurt, or maybe our noses bloodied in the arena of practical struggle. Keith did not discount the importance of theory, but he pointed out that many theories seem persuasive until they are tested and modified in practice. So we soon found ourselves testing both ideas. Because we ourselves were so naive, we applied each in a somewhat ridiculous manner. We leafleted the workers, as if a leaflet could convince them to quit their "immoral" jobs, and we sat down with the top management to convince them that they should cease being war profiteers.

The main office of United Technology was in Sunnyvale, ten miles south of Stanford, in the heart of what was later to be called Silicon Valley. In 1950, Sunnyvale had been a sleepy little burg with a population of ninety-eight hundred. The aerospace and electronics complex developed by Stanford had changed all that, transforming Sunnyvale into a boomtown. By 1960, its population was almost fifty-three thousand; in 1966 it had reached one hundred thousand.

Four delegates were selected to visit the company headquarters. Our mission: to meet with the president of UTC and convince him, through rational dialogue, that the development and manufacture of napalm were immoral acts and so his company should refuse the contract. Off we went on January 25, 1966, all neatly and conservatively attired, the three men in jackets and ties, the one woman in a modest dress, and we soon arrived at the shimmering mid-century modern office complex of UTC, strung out amid similarly well-landscaped offices of other corporate, manufacturing, and banking centers.

After some last-minute dickering, we were admitted into the office of Barnet Adelman, the president. He was flanked by three other officers of UTC. Two were retired generals, one a retired admiral. We then had our rational dialogue about the Vietnam War and napalm-B.

Mr. Adelman seemed a pleasant, mild-mannered scientist. We knew that he was Jewish, had gotten his master's degree in chemical engineering from Columbia in 1948, and then had worked in rocketry for the Jet Propulsion Lab, Cal Tech, the rocket-fuels division of Phillips Petroleum, and Ramo-Wooldridge. He also co-designed the Minuteman ICBM. He belonged to the American Ordnance Association and the American Rocket Society. He assured us that he was just as interested in having the Vietnam War end quickly as we were.

"After all," he said, "our business has suffered a great deal from the war. Our main work is in long-range liquid-fueled space rockets. These have no immediate military application. The Defense Department has taken away all our funds for these rockets because of Vietnam. So we have no choice. Even if we didn't want to work on napalm, we would have to just to stay in business."

"So you would do anything just for money?" asked Cyril Sia, an Asian American Stanford student on our delegation.

"Napalm will help shorten the war," responded Mr. Adelman. "Isn't that what we all want? Besides, whatever our government asks us to do is right."

Elena Greene, who had visited China and Vietnam with her husband, filmmaker Felix Greene, brought up Nuremberg and pointed out that one of the main defenses of the war criminals there was that their government had ordered them to do it.

"But that was not a legally elected government," said Mr. Adelman.

Graduate student Steve Marx appealed to Mr. Adelman directly as a person whose own people had been the victim of war crimes. He responded, "That was Germany. This is America."

Since I had been assigned to do much of the research for our materials, I now went into some of the history of Dow Chemical itself and its connections with Nazi war crimes, professorially reading from my research notes:

"In the 1930s, Dow Chemical and the giant German chemical corporation I. G. Farben formed an international cartel. They agreed to restrain U.S. production of magnesium and allow Germany to take world leadership in this element. So, when World War II began, Germany was producing five times as much magnesium as the United States.

"During the war, it was the Farben subsidiary, Badische Anilin and Soda-Fabrik, that developed and manufactured Zyklon-B, the poison gas used at Auschwitz and Dachau. Dow maintained secret ties with Badische throughout the war. As soon as the war was over, it formally renewed its prewar connection with Farben by going directly through Badische. Right now, Dow Chemical and Badische are in partnership in a giant chemical plant in Freeport, Texas, called the Dow-Badische Company."

My little speech had no visible effect on Mr. Adelman, not to mention his three colleagues. Finally one of the other delegates asked if we could have an opportunity to discuss the issue with the employees.

"I *am* the employees of UTC," said Mr. Adelman. He then informed us he had to "take care of other business," and our discussion was "terminated."

So next a much larger group went to the workers, taking with us a leaflet asking, "*Is* Barnet Adelman the employees of UTC?"

UTC's napalm test site was located on a rambling old ranch off a dirt road several miles from the rural crossroads community of Coyote, south of San Jose. A few hundred yards back from the narrow dirt road were several mysterious-looking low buildings, a small tower, and some large chemical storage tanks. Along the road ran a barbed-wire fence, and the property stretched as far back as the eye could see into the hills.

We were nervous the first day, especially since all the workers in America, according to the media, staunchly supported the war. We stood at the gate in the fence and tried to hand leaflets to the workers as they drove through. That first day, most of them stopped to take the leaflet. Some went out of their way to be friendly. A few tried to run us down. On the second day, security guards and a photographer were at the gate. Almost every worker driving through now pretended we didn't exist, except for a few who again tried to run us down. It looked as though the workers were as reactionary as the media said. Then two people began leafleting back down the road where it met U.S. Highway 101, three miles away from the company guards and photographer. Here the response was even friendlier than the first day. Some workers got out of their cars to talk. They told us that management was very nervous and had posted plainclothes security guards inside the plant to keep an eye on the workers. Most people, they explained, were fearful of losing their jobs if they showed any sympathy for our position.

One of our leaflets asked the workers, of all things, to quit their jobs in protest. Two or three actually did and were quickly blacklisted from all employment in the area.

In the first week of February, we had an open meeting at Stanford to get people together for a caravan to Coyote, where we would hold a rally as the workers were leaving the day shift. One of the speakers was a young black man from the Student Nonviolent Coordinating Committee (SNCC), invited by his friend Keith Lowe. Tall, thin, slightly stooped, unsmiling, he seemed wound up tight enough to explode. Speaking in a soft voice, filled with barely restrained anger, he told us about a new political party he had helped organize in Alabama. It had split off from the regular state Democratic Party in order to conduct voter registration and run candidates in predominantly black Lowndes County. Since the symbol of the Alabama Democratic Party was a snowy white rooster, they had chosen the Black Panther as their symbol.

The speaker, Stokely Carmichael, then said he had just received his draft induction notice. He spoke of draft resistance. "I intend to walk right into that draft office and tell them," he said so softly you had to cock your head to hear, "I don't belong to you, so you have no power over me." I heard this then as an existentialist affirmation, as well as an act in the civil disobedience tradition of Thoreau. I realize now that I missed altogether the significance of what Carmichael was saying, because I knew nothing about revolutionary Black Nationalism. I heard Carmichael projecting himself as a representative of every individual human being. In reality he was defying the draft as a representative of the African American people. He was disputing the power of the draft board to claim ownership not so much of his own human essence, but of the lives of a people kidnapped from Africa.

At the Coyote rally, Carmichael spoke again. Standing at a microphone directly facing the gate in the barbed-wire fence across the dirt road, covered with the red dust churned up by the workers' cars, he spoke about the Vietnam War itself, his voice now loud, his words ringing out toward the napalm test site and the rolling hills beyond. Afterward, I walked up in my tweed sports jacket, white button-down shirt, and striped tie and was introduced. I enthusiastically put out my hand and said, "That was a wonderful speech." Carmichael limply put his hand in mine for a second, glanced at me, stared past my head toward the chemical storage tanks, and mumbled something like, "Yeah?"

Several weeks later, SNCC held a national conference at which Stokely Carmichael was elected chairman. It was this conference that issued the historic paper entitled "The Basis of Black Power," a modest statement demanding self-determination for blacks and asking "progressive whites" to organize in white communities. The mass media suddenly barraged the country with the name of Stokely Carmichael, depicting him as a "black racist," a "disciple of hatred and race war," a "fiery inciter of passions." These words obviously didn't describe the man who had come to help in our campaign against napalm. It never occurred to me then that Carmichael had stuck his neck out to try to ally the black movement with the antiwar movement and that we ought to be thinking about what we could do to further that alliance. I was too busy working to stop napalm.

About this time, both Jane and I began to notice cars following us and mysterious things happening on our telephone. Jane was then often on the phone successfully turning the San Francisco call-in shows into forums on the war. Once, after dialing and before the phone was picked up at the other end, she heard a man's voice say, "Oh, she's just calling one of those damned shows again."

I discovered in 1976 that the Air Force Office of Special Investigations (OSI) had forwarded to the CIA a September 14, 1966, report about me stating, "FRANKLIN has acted as spokesman for the Stanford Committee for Peace in Vietnam and appeared on a television program to invite his viewers to participate in an anti-napalm demonstration to be held at UTC." The report concluded with this revelation: "OSI source reported that SUBJECT was a signer of a 1961 letter to the late President Kennedy protesting the building of bomb shelters in the United States."[6]

One such TV program took place at 8 A.M. in San Francisco. At 5 A.M. I found under the front door the picture Keith had promised: a Vietnamese boy, hideously disfigured by napalm, with his chin fused to his chest. I concealed it under my jacket until late in the interview, when I held it directly in front of the camera.

One afternoon one of the workers who had quit UTC phoned and asked me to come to his home in Santa Clara, another aerospace and electronics boomtown. After supper, I drove to his moderately prosperous suburban community and, wary enough already to try to conceal our meeting, parked a few blocks away. He was still in contact with some of the other UTC workers, who said that many workers privately were opposed to making napalm, but the plant had been turned into a virtual police state. Their casual conversations were being spied on, and even their personal reading matter was being inspected surreptitiously.

On my way home, I thought I was being followed on the freeway. When I got to Palo Alto, I drove to a gas station and went to a telephone to call Jane to find out where SCPV was meeting that night. Suddenly a car pulled in and rolled right up to the phone booth, blocking the door and fixing me in its headlights. I could barely make out the silhouettes of two men, wearing what seemed to be felt hats and business suits, in the front seat. I told Jane what was happening. I could see the front license plate, so I made it obvious to the men in the car that I was reading its numbers into the phone. I continued facing the car and kept talking to Jane. After what seemed a very long time, probably just a few minutes, the car backed up and sped off, ostentatiously burning rubber. Was someone sending me a message?

By the middle of March, UTC had completed its contract for the development of napalm-B. They received their reward: a contract to produce huge quantities of napalm bombs. They selected as the site for this production an unused Standard Oil storage facility in the port of Redwood City, at the end of a causeway sticking two miles out into the San Francisco Bay. This site was on publicly owned tidal land. Therefore, all leases and uses of it were under the jurisdiction of the Redwood City Port Commission, and its rulings were legally subject to override by the citizens of Redwood City.

On March 21, the port commission convened in an old frame building amid the unused petroleum storage tanks Standard Oil was asking to sublease to UTC. About fifty protesters showed up. Some were members of Concerned Citizens, a Palo Alto peace organization in which Jane worked. Others came from a Unitarian congregation in Redwood City. Most of the men wore jackets and ties, the women dresses. The most casually dressed were a few Stanford students. The room where the commissioners met could hold only about a dozen of us, so we presented them with our formal written protest and asked them to move to a larger facility. After much arguing, they agreed to adjourn to an auditorium in the county office building in downtown Redwood City.

By the time the meeting reconvened, almost two hundred people had gathered. The middle-aged white gentlemen on the commission set up ground rules for public participation, specifically ruling out of order "the moral question" and "the federal policy of war in Vietnam." Speaker after speaker rose to reason with the commissioners: a local minister, several Redwood City housewives, workers, students. Olive Mayer, an engineer from Redwood City who had inspected the gas ovens of Belsen, calmly stated: "As a professional engineer I knew that other members of my profession planned and engineered these ovens as execution chambers. The manufacturer's name was proudly displayed over the door of the ovens. Engineers had to calculate the number of victims to be accommodated, means of ingress and egress, how many to be executed at one time, and so on. Local government and professional people had to be involved in providing locations for the manufacture of these ovens, just as you commissioners are now called upon to make a decision concerning a napalm factory."

I rose, intending to speak about the specific qualities of napalm, based on my Air Force experience and recent research. I got as far as my name. The chairman turned tomato red and shouted out angrily, "We know who you are and what you have to say, and we don't want to hear it. Sit down!" I asked why I wasn't allowed to speak. The chairman yelled to the police at the back of the room, "Get that man out of here! Right now!" Two cops rushed up, twisted one arm behind my back, muscled me to the aisle, and started lugging me toward the rear door. Seven-year-old Gretchen burst into tears. The audience stared in shocked disbelief at the scene in the aisle. By the time the police got me to the door, I noticed that the commissioners were packing their briefcases and starting to leave. I broke loose, ran back down the aisle, and demanded, "What are you doing?" People began calling out: "What's going on?" "Why are you leaving?" "Aren't you going to discuss it?" "Aren't you even going to bother to vote?" The chairman looked over his shoulder, laughed, bent down to a microphone, and said: "We just did vote to grant the sublease. We also voted to adjourn. You probably couldn't hear because of all the commotion you people were making."

During the next few days, we investigated the legal options open to us. We discovered that the vote of the commission could be overturned in a referendum called by an initiative petition signed by 10 percent of the registered voters of Redwood City. When our lawyer went for help in preparing the papers, the city attorney gave him false information that cheated us out of thirteen days of the thirty we were supposed to have. So we had only seventeen days to find volunteers, build an organization, and get signatures of 10 percent of the voters. And this was the period when, according to the media and their polls, everyone but a handful of "dissidents" supported the war.

Signatures could be solicited only by registered voters of Redwood City. Redwood City was a suburban bedroom community of about fifty thousand, almost 100 percent white, mostly middle-income working-class, small-business, and professional people. The city boundaries had been drawn to exclude the sizable population of Chicano, black, and poorer white working-class people, concentrated in the unincorporated area known informally as East Redwood City. Redwood City had no history of radical politics. There wasn't even a liberal political organization to be found in town. On top of all these obstacles, the local press launched a campaign to block the petition. The influential *Palo Alto Times* tacitly encouraged violence against us, and then, in two wonderfully revealing editorials, explained that if the people were allowed to vote on such matters, the country would be unable to wage war and the national government would be shattered:

> There is no question that considerable pressure is being brought by a small but vocal minority that objects to our use of napalm in the Viet Nam war. It is the same minority that objects to our involvement in the war at all. . . . The voters of Redwood City do not have the right to preempt these decisions for themselves, to make the decisions for the rest of the country. . . . [T]o place on a municipal ballot decisions on military and foreign policy is to invite chaos. If all cities in the United States were to decide for themselves whether to permit the manufacture of military aircraft, bombs, rifles, grenades, rockets, torpedoes and other war material, they would wreck our armed forces. If all of them were to arrogate to themselves decisions on foreign policy, they would wreck the national government. [April 16, 1966]

> While there may be some question about the use of napalm in warfare, it is not a question to be decided by the voters of Redwood City or any other municipality. . . . It is easy to see what would happen if every city were to be allowed to make its own decision as to what war material is acceptable to its citizens.

The people of Sunnyvale could vote on whether Polaris missiles should be manufactured by Lockheed. The people of Palo Alto could vote on whether electronics equipment for guided missiles should be built in the city. The citizens of San Francisco or Oakland could vote on whether their municipal port facilities should be permitted to load materials of war, such as napalm and atomic weapons, onto ships headed for the war.

The result would be chaos. [April 20, 1966]

But in a few days we had our volunteers and an organization. One hundred and ten citizens of Redwood City, most of them working people, were out actively soliciting signatures. The regional local of the International Longshoremen's and Warehousemen's Union sent a telegram of support, a small donation, and three volunteers. Thirty-four local clergymen signed a statement of support. Although the *Redwood City Tribune* at first called us "treasonous," it began editorializing about the people's right to vote. On April 17, the *New York Times* did a story on the campaign, and in the next three days the Huntley-Brinkley NBC television show and CBS television news had on-the-scene reporting, with both concluding that the people of Redwood City ranged from indifferent to hostile. ABC television did interviews but never aired them. On the seventeenth day we stayed up all night verifying and counting the signatures on the petitions. Fifteen percent of the registered voters of Redwood City had signed.

Anyone who has done petition work knows this figure represents overwhelming support. In a petition campaign, it's good work just to *see* 15 percent of the registered voters in *thirty* days. On April 20, as we officially filed the petitions, we were confident we were going to win the election, and we knew this would have national and even international significance.

Meanwhile, UTC had started production of napalm bombs. As you drove out along the causeway to the napalm facility, you now passed acres of stacked crates of 500-pound and 750-pound bombs. You could even stand at the high chain-link fence to watch as the empty bomb casings were swung over to a raised platform and pumped full of napalm. On May 1, a barge partly loaded with napalm bombs mysteriously developed two holes in its hull and began to sink. A vigil began across from the plant. On May 16 and 17, a Palo Alto psychiatrist, two students from Stanford, and Chicano jazz musician Aaron Manganiello were arrested for lying down in front of some trucks bringing empty bomb shells to be filled.

The signatures on the petitions still lay, uncounted, in the city clerk's office. The city attorney had been using one legal maneuver after another to block the election. On May 20, Superior Court judge Melvin Cohn ruled that the petition was invalid because it had attacked the original sublease from Standard Oil to UTC. He disclosed that on April 26, six days after we had filed the petition, Standard Oil, UTC, and the port commission had secretly scrapped the old sublease and arranged a new one. Judge Cohn informed us that, in order to be valid, a petition would have to attack this new lease. Since the new lease had gone into effect on April 26, we would have until May 26, only six days, to draw up a new petition, get signatures, and have it filed. It was now obvious that, even if we could have performed that miracle, Standard Oil, UTC, and the port commission would merely draw up still another lease. A few weeks later we discovered that Judge Cohn was a personal friend of Barnet Adelman, president of UTC, and that their children attended the same Sunday-school class. But we now knew that had little to do with his Alice-in-Wonderland decision. We had been forced to recognize that judges—like port authority commissions, city attorneys, policemen, FBI agents, newspapers, and armies—were there to do whatever corporations required of them.

The following day, Aaron Manganiello began a one-man fast and vigil across the road from the napalm plant. Aaron had just been suspended from the College of San Mateo, the local public community college where he had been studying music, for distributing literature against the Vietnam War. Each night, men from UTC would hose him down every hour. After six days, Aaron had pneumonia and had to give up the vigil. He also gave up his pacifism and became the minister of information of the Brown Berets, a militant Chicano organization. Later Aaron played an important role in my life as a friend and the chair of the revolutionary California organization Venceremos.

On May 28 we officially launched the national campaign against napalm with a rally at a stadium in downtown Redwood City and a march to the gates of the napalm plant out on San Francisco Bay. The speakers at the rally included three antiwar congressional candidates, the publisher of *Ramparts* magazine, African American publisher and California gubernatorial candidate Carlton Goodlett, Felix Greene, Admiral Arnold True, and a San Jose truck driver running as a peace candidate for the state assembly. Despite a virtual news blackout before the event, thirty-five hundred people, including many families with small children, showed up. The demonstrators were "mostly well-dressed and clean-shaven," noted the *Redwood City Tribune*.

Robert, who had just celebrated his third birthday, rode his trike on the four-mile march through downtown Redwood City and out along the causeway to the napalm plant. Karen, looking back decades later on this and many experiences that were to follow, remembered that "family outings were marches, demonstrations, sit-ins against the war." The march ended with more speeches, delivered from a flatbed truck outside the front gates of the napalm plant. The principal speaker was Oregon senator Wayne Morse, who rambled on for half an hour, telling a couple of anecdotes to show he was still good friends with Lyndon Johnson and never mentioning napalm. The rally concluded, and people began strolling to the buses we had chartered to take them back to their cars. Suddenly dozens of squad cars appeared as if from nowhere. They had been carefully concealed behind buildings surrounding the rally. We counted hundreds of police from five different agencies. Many of the squad cars displayed shotguns and contained six police officers in full riot gear, something most people there had seen only on TV. The Redwood City Police Department and the San Mateo County Sheriff's Office had prepared an elaborate ambush and were obviously disappointed that they had not found a chance to "teach you some patriotism," as one yelled out a car window.

Only local newspapers reported on the march and rally, and they intentionally underestimated the size of the crowd, claiming that citizens of Redwood City were hostile to such activities. Bruce Brugmann, the *Redwood City Tribune* reporter who had been covering the napalm campaign, became so disgusted by the blatant censorship and rewriting of his stories that he left to found the influential radical weekly newspaper, the *Bay Guardian*. Even a mere twenty miles away, the press, radio, and TV in San Francisco imposed a total news blackout. This did keep many people in ignorance. But it also educated tens of thousands about the role of the media. Almost everyone in the area knew an important event had taken place and could not help but wonder why it was not reported to others and how many events from other areas were not reported to us.

In fact, we had succeeded in breaking through the media isolation and misrepresentation. The national boycott of Dow Chemical Corporation products, announced at the rally, had already begun. That very day, fifty pickets demonstrated outside the New York offices of Dow Chemical, and over two hundred picketed Dow's big plant for production of polystyrene in Torrance, outside Los Angeles. But none of us would have predicted that in the next few years there would be hundreds of demonstrations, involving hundreds of thousands of people, against Dow Chemical, its campus recruiters, and its subcontractors. Through the campaign against napalm, tens of millions of Americans and people around the world were to learn deep lessons about the true nature of America's war against the people of Vietnam.

9 ▸ FRENCH CONNECTIONS

TOURS, 1966

In December 1920, a thirty-year-old Vietnamese man known as Nguyen Ai Quoc boarded a train in Paris and headed for the city of Tours, on the south bank of the Loire River. The previous year, he had drafted a petition asking the world leaders assembled in Versailles to grant to the Vietnamese people the universal rights proclaimed by U.S. president Woodrow Wilson. Brushed off like some annoying fly, Nguyen became more and more radicalized as he read Marx, Engels, and Lenin while plunging ever deeper into activism with the French Socialist Party. Now he was going as the Indochinese delegate to the Socialist Party's fateful Congress of Tours, which was to decide whether to stay with the reformist Second International or join the Third International, the Comintern organized by Lenin in the midst of the Russian Revolution. Making his way from the Tours train station, Nguyen found his destination—the building reserved for the congress—a huge riding academy right next to the thirteenth-century church of Saint Julien. The cavernous interior of the riding academy, festooned with red banners floating about its makeshift meeting hall, soon echoed with fierce debates. The slim, wiry Nguyen rose, eyes blazing, with a passionate call for the French working class to link to the struggles of the oppressed peoples of Indochina and the other French colonies. His call touched off an uproar of objections. When a delegate interrupted to announce, "I have spoken in favor of the natives," Nguyen demanded more than lip service for the workers and peasants of the colonies. So he joined the 70 percent of the delegates who united with the Third International. Nguyen Ai Quoc—later to be known as Ho Chi Minh—thus became a founding member of the French Communist Party.[1]

In June 1940, the Nazi army sweeping southward from Paris was halted on the north side of the Loire. Its artillery fired across the river into Tours, destroying the riding academy and many other structures along the river. Saint Julien was badly damaged then and again in 1944, this time by Allied bombs aimed at the retreating Nazi forces. After the war, modern apartments were constructed in place of the destroyed buildings. In 1960, the booming Stanford University converted one of these apartment buildings into Stanford-in-France, one of its first overseas campuses, complete with a dining hall, classrooms, administrative offices, and apartments for eighty students and one of the two Stanford professors there for a half-year stint. The building faced rue Nationale, a block from where that street crossed the Loire over the rebuilt Pont Woodrow Wilson, which the French had dynamited in 1940 to slow the Nazi advance.

Across the rue Nationale, a small but elegant apartment in another post-war building was reserved for the other Stanford professor, the one with the larger family. From September 1966 until March 1967, this was home for Jane and me and our three children. History was all around us. From our windows, we gazed across a courtyard at the thirteenth-century church of Saint Julien, its walls still pockmarked from the World War II bombardments. We didn't know that our building sat right on the site of the riding academy where Ho Chi Minh had helped found the French Communist Party. And of course we couldn't guess the swirl of events into which we were about to be swept.

Stanford-in-France was an apt name for the tiny American enclave. In contrast to later Stanford programs for overseas study, any integration of the Stanford students into French life was minimal and controlled. Stanford's conservative French administrators assigned each student to a French family—carefully selected for proper social class and political sentiments—for an occasional meal. Other than that, the students, professors, and administrators ate together, and the students' social life was almost entirely among themselves. About the only exceptions among the American students were our two girls. Jane and I plopped Karen (age nine) and Gretchen (age seven) into the local public school, sink or swim. They swam, while three-year-old

Robert preferred staying on the American island. The most memorable culture shock in the girls' immersion in French language, education, and culture came on December 16, the day when news of Walt Disney's death reached their school, leaving all the other girls sobbing and asking them why they weren't crying.

The other professor was Paul Hohenberg, a political scientist about my age but, unlike me, bilingual in French and fluent in German. Our mission in our courses and field trips to the châteaus of the Loire Valley and other sites in France, Italy, and Spain was of course to enrich the students' knowledge and understanding of European history and culture. The only leftist works I selected for my two-term Literature and Society course were Émile Zola's *Germinal* and Ivan Yefremov's *Andromeda*, and these were counterbalanced by such anti-revolutionary works as André Malraux's *Man's Fate*, Fyodor Dostoevsky's *Notes from Underground*, and Yevgeny Zamyatin's *We*. On the field trips, I was more a student than a teacher. So at first everything was going along as programmed.

We were surprised to find on the newsstands, openly displayed just like any ordinary newspaper, stacks of *L'Humanité*, the daily tabloid of the French Communist Party. We were not in Kansas, or even Brooklyn, where Murray, my Communist boss at Mayfair Photofinishing, had to get his copy of the *Daily Worker* furtively sneaked to him over the soda fountain counter. The second week we were there, Jane found in *L'Humanité* a notice of a major event to be held right in Tours. A delegation from Vietnam—representatives of both the Democratic Republic of Vietnam and the National Liberation Front of South Vietnam—were to appear at a "soirée" celebrating the forty-sixth anniversary of the founding of the French Communist Party. The article gave a brief history of that fateful 1920 conference in Tours, including Ho Chi Minh's role in forming the party.

Eager for a chance to actually see and hear the Vietnamese who were already having a profound influence on our lives, and both curious and nervous about attending a Communist Party event, Jane and I arrived with our emotional stew at the proper time and address for the big event. What we found was a large theater, quite closed. Jane, whose French was far better than mine, inquired of a small group of people chatting under the marquee. They looked at us with obvious curiosity.

"You are Americans?" We nodded. They whispered.

"Talk to that man over there."

The man over there was craggy faced, about forty-five years old, in a trench coat and a black wool watch cap pulled down at an angle across his forehead, a cigarette dangling from his unsmiling thin lips. Jane and I timidly walked over and meekly introduced ourselves as Americans who had come to attend the soirée with the Vietnamese.

"You are tourists?"

"No," I said. "I am a professor at Stanford-in-France."

"You must see Labeyrie," he said flatly.

"What is 'Labeyrie'?" I asked.

"Labeyrie," he said with the first hint of a smile, "is the man you must see." He took our telephone number and told us that the soirée was postponed one week.

"Before then," he added dramatically, "you will hear from Labeyrie."

Two days later, Labeyrie called and arranged to come to our apartment. A burly guy in a leather jacket with a weathered face, maybe in his early or mid-fifties, showed up. He was friendly, charming, disarming, and obviously there to figure out who and what we might be. Of course Jane and I were trying to figure out who and what he might be. He opened one line of communication by telling us that he was a professor of biology at the University of Orléans. But he projected something, maybe with his resolute demeanor and unwavering gaze, that did not quite fit the academic role. After he left, Jane and I decided that he looked and acted more like the kind of Résistance fighter we knew from World War II movies.

Only later did we discover that we had it backward. Labeyrie wasn't playing a movie role. He was the real thing. During the German occupation, he had been in a Résistance cell that had machine-gunned several Gestapo officers. Another member of his cell was Madeleine Riffaud, the famous Résistance fighter who was captured and fiendishly tortured by the Nazis. Labeyrie had joined the Communist Party and their underground Résistance in 1941, several months after the beginning of the Nazi occupation and their puppet Vichy regime. He was now a fairly high official in the Communist Party of the region.

Before Labeyrie left, we asked him if it would be appropriate for Stanford students to come to the soirée. He was enthusiastic about the possibility. I announced the meeting at supper, giving some background on relevant local history and assuring the students that they would be welcome. None showed any interest. The local director of Stanford-in-France, M. Paul LeMoal, rushed up to say he didn't think it "proper" for American students to be associating with "the enemy." But Alice and Steve Mick, a married couple who had both recently graduated from Stanford and who served as counselors, said they would like very much to go along.

Labeyrie was waiting for us, and the four of us sat with him and some companions. The theater quickly filled. A young Frenchwoman went to the microphone on stage and welcomed everybody to this celebration of "the unity between the peoples of France and Vietnam." She spoke about Ho Chi Minh's role in founding the Communist Party of France in this very city and of the duty of the people of France to support the Vietnamese now in the hour of their need. She omitted, I noticed, any mention of the role of the French Communist Party during the 1946–1954 French colonial war against Vietnam. She then introduced the four Vietnamese guests, noting that each had at least one close relative slain by U.S. forces.

A young peasant woman from the north, who was credited with shooting down several U.S. planes, described daily life in the countryside under continual air assaults, including how the people of her village had devised means for protecting the children and for developing cross fire against strafing attacks. A somewhat older factory worker from Hanoi told how his plant managed to fulfill its production quota, despite constant air raids on the city, including direct hits on his factory. A student from Saigon studying in Paris and a diplomatic representative to France from the Democratic Republic of Vietnam extolled the antiwar movement as inspirational for the Vietnamese. Although I believed every word about the horrors of the bombing, I was skeptical about all their claims of successful resistance. How many U.S. fighter-bombers could be shot down by the rifles of peasants? How could Hanoi's factories produce significantly under the bombing? And could demonstrations in France and America truly inspire the Vietnamese facing the mightiest military power in human history?

As the program ended, Labeyrie took me by the arm up to the Vietnamese and announced, "I would like you to meet an American who has been very active in the movement against the war, Professor Bruce Franklin." I was deeply embarrassed. Besides the guilt and shame I felt for being an American, I now felt like a fraud. What had I done to stop this genocidal war, except inconvenience myself a bit from time to time? And would these Vietnamese respond politely to a U.S. citizen? They didn't. They threw their arms around me, hugged me, kissed my cheeks. Tears streamed down the faces of all four. Tears started trickling out of my own eyes. A cynical thought flashed through my mind. Were they just putting on an act calculated to move me to greater support? But the pressure of their bodies, the passion blazing in their eyes and burning away my World War II comic book–conditioned responses to "Oriental eyes," their embarrassed attempts to express their feelings in French—a language foreign to all five of us—all this made me more ashamed of my cynicism than I had been for our national guilt and my part-time activism. Then arose another interpretation, less jaundiced but more racist: maybe this was merely a cultural expression of "the beautiful, simple Vietnamese people."

Months later I saw a Vietnamese friend show a rare burst of anger when an American liberal openly attributed the heroism of the Vietnamese national liberation struggle to the "culture" of "the beautiful Vietnamese people." "Ngo Dinh Diem is also part of the Vietnamese people," was his response, "and so are the landlords and businessmen who work with every foreign invader. And so are the pimps in Saigon, and the secret police who put your electric instruments to the testicles and breasts of our comrades. What gives us our internationalism and our certainty that we will win is our understanding of history."

That night in Tours, I managed to tell the Vietnamese a few words about the struggle against the napalm plant in Redwood City. I also said that there were certain things about the latest napalm they should know. They asked if we could meet privately in two days. I agreed.

With new misgivings, I ventured at dusk two days later to the address I had been given in an old part of the city. I found it on a narrow cobble-stoned street in a workers' district. I rang. Footsteps on a stair, and a challenging male voice: "Qui est là?"

"L'ami Américain de Labeyrie," I responded as instructed.

The heavy oak door was unbolted. I was led up a rickety staircase and was motioned to a seat on a wooden chair in a hallway. After a few minutes, I was ushered into a bare room almost filled with an old battered conference table around which were seated the craggy-faced man we met at the theater the first night, Labeyrie, another Frenchman, and eight Vietnamese men of various ages all dressed in ill-fitting dark suits and conservative ties. Evidently they thought what I had to say was a lot more important than I believed it was.

After some awkward attempts at small talk, one of the Vietnamese said, "You told our comrades you had some information you wished to give us."

Was I a traitor for what I was about to do? Or would I be a traitor for not doing it? I hesitated, and then, in my primitive French, helped by doing sketches to illustrate some technical points, I made the long statement I had been rehearsing with Jane's help. Not being native speakers, the Vietnamese and I left little gaps between our words instead of eliding them, making it easier to understand one another's French.

I briefly told of the napalm struggle. I next described the napalm bombs being made in Redwood City. Up until then, napalm had been used in Vietnam almost entirely by fighter-bombers carrying one bomb under each wing (or so I thought at the time). I explained that many of the bombs in Redwood City were designed to be racked in B-52s. I gave them the figures on the vastly expanded production of napalm and noted that the bombs were all labeled "MUST BE USED WITHIN ONE YEAR."

"What this all means," I said, "is that the U.S. is now going to use napalm as a strategic weapon. Waves of B-52s will saturate entire areas with napalm. The fire will become so hot it will generate big winds, firestorms burning all vegetation and consuming the oxygen. Nothing will live in these areas."

What I didn't know was that much of the napalm was intended for one of the more fiendish Pentagon programs, the plan to burn down the rain forests of South Vietnam by generating self-sustaining firestorms. The first attempt, Operation Sherwood Forest, had been launched in March 1965, with waves of B-52s dropping M35 incendiary cluster bombs and napalm just west of Saigon on the Boi Loi Wood, which for two months had already been drenched with Agent Orange and other deadly defoliants. The rain forest—the lungs of the world—had become America's enemy. But the Pentagon had underestimated the natural enemy as much as they had underestimated the human enemy. The forest extinguished the conflagration. The Pentagon then enlisted the U.S. Forest Service, with its extensive knowledge of forest fires, to aid in the next attempt, Operation Hot Tip, which targeted forests in two South Vietnamese provinces. Lacking sufficient quantities of the bomb designed for napalm-B, the Air Force relied mainly on the M35 for Hot Tip, which was carried out—unsuccessfully—in early 1966.

Unlike me, the Vietnamese at the old conference table were no doubt well aware of these attempts to burn their precious forests. The information I was giving them might have helped them foresee the waves of B-52s that would indeed carpet bomb with napalm the forests in Tay Ninh and Phuoc Long provinces from January through April 1967, a few months after our meeting, but the knowledge would have insignificant effect on the outcome, in which U.S. technology would kill many of the people who lived in those forests but would again be defeated by nature.[2]

After the Vietnamese men huddled for a brief conference, the man who seemed the eldest then addressed me as "camarade," a label that filled me with very mixed feelings, and promised to forward my information to the "camarades" in Vietnam. Then he made a little speech that went something like this: "No weapon can frighten us into submission. What you have told us is very grave. But we have always known that your government has many terrible weapons, including atomic bombs. But not even atomic bombs can turn back history. The people of Vietnam are more powerful than any weapon. Eventually we will free our entire homeland. And every weapon used against us will bring more of the people of the world to our side."

As the meeting ended, another Vietnamese man bowed slightly and ceremoniously presented me with a small box. Inside was an aluminum comb, inscribed in Vietnamese and artfully crafted in the shape of an F-4 jet fighter.

"This comb," he said, "is a small symbol of our friendship. It was made from the metal of another terrible weapon, a plane that could fly even faster than sound. That plane was brought down by a peasant woman armed with a rifle from the First World War."

The next morning, I started combing my hair with this symbol. I recoiled in shock. Wasn't the pilot of that downed plane a young man like me when I was in the Air Force? Shouldn't my loyalties be with him, rather than with these people whose life was alien from my own? How could I make light of his death, or captivity, by combing my hair with a piece of his plane's wreckage? But I was glad that his plane was no longer dropping napalm or cluster bombs on the Vietnamese or strafing their villages.

I kept thinking about the comb. Where did the aluminum come from? Maybe a bauxite mine in Jamaica. What corporation made the jet fighter-bomber? Likely it came from Lockheed or McDonnell-Douglas or some other California factory. Who worked in that factory, and were they proud of their product? Was the plane really downed by a peasant woman pulling the trigger of a World War I rifle? Not improbable, since many World War I rifles, such as the British Lee-Enfield, the German Mauser, the French Fusil Automatique, and the Springfield M1903 (the original .30-06) were high-velocity, long-range weapons quite capable of downing a jet. Whose rifle had it once been? Had it once killed Americans almost half a century ago, or had an American doughboy used it to kill Germans? Who brought it to Vietnam? Maybe a French or even a Nazi soldier on one of the U.S. troopships that brought the French invasion army to Saigon in the fall of 1945. Who made the comb and etched its Vietnamese message? Was it the painstaking work of another villager, or was it mass-produced on an assembly line in Hanoi? My mind filled with a vision of people whose lives might be connected in the possible history of this comb, this product of the tortured history of the twentieth century. I went back to combing my hair with that symbolic piece of aluminum. But in all the decades since that morning, I have used it as a comb no more than three or four times. I showed it to my

Vietnam class a few times, but then stopped doing that. It lies unused amid miscellaneous objects in a dresser drawer. It weighs exactly half an ounce, but it is too heavy to wield.

A few nights after the meeting with the Vietnamese, Labeyrie took Jane and me on a wild ride, careering at scary speeds through dense fog along the banks of the Loire. We were on our way to attend a workers' antiwar meeting in Blois, a small industrial city thirty-five miles up the river from Tours. The meeting was held in a large classroom with Labeyrie chairing from the teacher's desk. There were about eighty factory workers, members of the CGT (Confédération générale du travail), the huge union then led largely by Communists, including many veterans of the Résistance. About a dozen speakers rose to discuss Vietnam and to give detailed reports on the antiwar organizing in each factory in Blois and the surrounding area. My French was not only poor but bookish, so I could barely get the gist of this living, working-class French.

Toward the end of the meeting, I did hear Labeyrie announce, "We are most fortunate to have with us tonight a comrade from the United States. He is going to tell us all about the movement against the war in the United States." Loud applause. My blood froze. I have never been more terrified. If I could have pushed a button to eject through the roof or maybe even vaporize myself, I believe I would have pushed it. How could I give a speech in French to French workers? I had heard horror tales of how the French loathe foreigners, most especially Americans, who mutilate their language. Why hadn't Labeyrie called on Jane, whose French was obviously better than mine?

I couldn't speak in English because there was nobody there to translate. There was no way out. I took my time getting to the front of the room, trying to organize a few sentences, getting more embarrassed by the continuing applause. But when I got to the front and looked directly into the faces of these French workers, a surprising thing happened. I saw friendly faces and found myself strengthened by warm feedback, a sense of mutuality erasing national boundaries and dissolving alienation. I felt I had something very precious in common with these workers of another nation. I can't remember anything of what I said, except for criticism of the lagging role of the U.S. Communist Party. But my words were not our main communication. For days after, my ribs were sore from their embraces.

For anyone with anxiety about public speaking, I recommend an experience like this as a sure cure. I have never again had any fear about speaking in public, as long as it's in my own language. (Maybe that's how my public speaking later got me in so much trouble.)

Labeyrie would no doubt have continued to single out me, a fellow male and a fellow professor, as the visiting representative of the U.S. antiwar movement. Fortunately, I was sick the day of our next antiwar event, so Jane for once got to go as a separate individual rather than the Professor's Wife. The occasion was a massive demonstration organized by the two giant labor confederations, the CGT and the big Catholic union.

Jane left around 5 A.M. to board a chartered train, already almost filled with workers. Into Paris, the hub of France's rail network, came similar trains from all regions of the country. Delegations were selected to meet with the embassies of each country still supporting the U.S. war in Vietnam. Jane was chosen to visit the embassy of South Korea, whose hundreds of thousands of soldiers in Vietnam had been accused of numerous massacres. The main spokesperson for her group of four was a tough-looking twenty-five-year-old factory worker in a black leather jacket. He made the South Korean diplomat who met them begin to visibly shake. He introduced Jane as a representative of the American people opposed to the war. When she began to condemn the brutal activities of the South Korean troops in Vietnam, the diplomat missed his ashtray by a couple of inches as he snuffed out his cigarette on his desk and hastily fled the room.

The demonstration ended under a steady downpour with huge jubilant marches converging from all quarters of Paris into the Place de la Bastille. Jane, who had been suffering for weeks from a respiratory syndrome common in the Loire valley, returned that night exuberant and miraculously cured.

One of the Vietnamese we had met the night of the soirée was Nguyen Ngoc Giao, secretary of the Union of Vietnamese Students in France. Giao had enthusiastically accepted my invitation to come talk to the Stanford students. After a couple of months, during which, we later learned, Giao and another Vietnamese student gave themselves a crash course in English, they came. By this time, Alice, Steve, Jane, and I had convinced most of the Stanford students to attend.

Although the hundreds of students from South Vietnam sent to study in France had been handpicked as loyal to the government in Saigon, almost all of them—as well as their organization—were in fact on the side of the National Liberation Front of South Vietnam, a.k.a. the Viet Cong. So the visitors were no doubt going to be what Stanford-in-France's director M. LeMoal had labeled "the enemy."

Giao and his companion brought two films, one made in each half of their divided homeland. The one from the north showed bombing raids on cities, villages, farms, schools, and hospitals. It also showed the air defense that we had heard described by the Vietnamese villager at the soirée from which, as I had been told, came my aluminum comb. One sequence showed a group of Vietnamese village women, armed with—sure enough—bolt-action Springfield rifles, blazing away at a flight of four McDonnell Douglas F-4 Phantom jets strafing the fields at low level. One of the jets suddenly started trailing dense black smoke, spun wildly out of control, then crashed and exploded in a wooded area. Several people clapped. Some angry hisses responded from the darkened room.

The other film, made by the National Liberation Front (NLF), showed the development of hospitals, schools, child-care centers, and small-weapons manufacture in areas of the south controlled by the Front. Villagers told of torture, rape, looting, the burning of villages, and massacres carried out by U.S. forces. One film segment, shot astonishingly from hand-held hidden cameras, showed a U.S. patrol entering a village. We saw torture, houses being torched, bags of rice being slit open and scattered around, medical supplies stomped into the ground under GI boots. Most of the villagers conformed to the media image of the South Vietnamese peasantry: stooped over in their age-old peasant garb, looking blank, numb, merely enduring, timelessly indifferent to all sides, just wanting to be left alone. The GIs marched out of the village. Suddenly, everything was transformed. An impromptu guerrilla theater broke out, with the villagers doing exaggerated imitations of both the U.S. soldiers and themselves, now stooped over even lower, looking even blanker and more obsequious. The camera followed several to a carefully concealed trap door. They took out a variety of weapons: bolt-action rifles, M1 carbines, two AK47s, assorted pistols, one mortar, and one tripod-mounted machine gun. The weapons were distributed to a group of men and women sitting in a circle sketching plans in the dirt. This group then set off on the trail the troops had taken to leave. The last shot, taken from a concealed ambush site in the forest, showed the U.S. patrol entering a clearing.

After the films, the two visitors gave a brief outline of Vietnamese history and the present military and political situation. They said they would answer all the questions they could. The discussion lasted three hours.

Some of the questions asked by the Stanford students were representative of the consciousness and ignorance of history of most Americans, at least in the 1950s and through the mid-1960s. "Why should we let a democratic nation like South Vietnam be destroyed by a Communist dictatorship?" "Do you think we Americans enjoy having to go around the world policing people who can't take care of their own affairs?" "Isn't it true that the Catholics in North Vietnam were tortured to death or put in slave-labor camps?" "Why won't North Vietnam allow free elections?"

These questions were actually more logical and less oblivious to Vietnamese reality than the thinking of our leaders. Consider the two examples I previously cited of such thinking during Washington's two most important decisions. As the Vietnamese in the spring of 1954 were completing their defeat of France after eight years of war, Vice President Richard Nixon argued in these words for sending American troops to replace the French forces: "[T]he Vietnamese lack the ability to conduct a war by themselves or govern themselves. If the French withdrew, Indochina would become Communist-dominated within a month. The United States as a leader of the free world cannot afford further retreat in Asia."[3] When John F. Kennedy's administration in 1963 was planning the overthrow of Ngo Dinh Diem, the puppet installed by President Eisenhower during the 1954 Geneva Conference, U.S. ambassador to Vietnam Henry Cabot Lodge wrote these words in that top-secret telegram to Secretary of State Dean Rusk: "We are launched on a course from which there is no respectable turning back: the overthrow of the Diem government.... [T]here is no turning back because there is no possibility, in my view, that the war can be won under a Diem administration, still less that Diem or any member of the family can govern the nation in a way to gain the support of the people who count, i.e., the educated class in and out of government service, civil and military—not to mention the American people."[4]

Of course most of these Stanford students probably had little knowledge of the history of the war in Vietnam and lacked perspective on their own consciousness. But students entering Stanford as freshmen while we were all preparing to leave for France in September might have had a far more sophisticated understanding, because in orientation week they were assigned the book that incarnated quintessential American consciousness in CIA agent Alden Pyle, the novel's title character: Graham Greene's *The Quiet American*.

With what seemed saintly patience, the Vietnamese answered each question, never—with one exception—even showing irritation. Were Asians, as we had been taught, less emotional and more cunning than other peoples? Months later, Giao, who had become a close friend, revealed to Jane and me that he could eat few foods because of his severe ulcer. The one question to provoke anger came late.

"Isn't it a fact," said a six-foot, blond, amiable Stanford sophomore, the son of an executive of a big bank, "that we are only in Vietnam to protect you from the Chinese?"

"Are you really saying to us," shouted Giao's companion, who looked maybe a couple of years older than the American, "that you invade our land and butcher our people to protect us from foreign invasion? Don't you Americans understand by now that we can defend ourselves and nobody can invade Vietnam? Even your forces, with all your great weapons, will not conquer us. We do not need America to protect us from anybody!"

Then, in a softer voice and with his face once more composed, he said, "I am sorry to have spoken in anger. But you do not know what it is to have your homeland invaded and destroyed."

One day Labeyrie invited me to attend a *déjeuner-débat*, a luncheon discussion meeting for Communist Party cadres. The subject was to be "Marxism and Art." Though I was beginning to think of myself as a Marxist, I was apprehensive about participating in an ideological Communist meeting. Back came the old images of sinister, manipulative, dogmatic Communist fanatics. And would they figure out that I was just a liberal American academic?

Steve Mick was happy to go along and drive. To our surprise, the directions to the meeting led to one of the most elegant restaurants in the region, built into a cave in the countryside. After introducing ourselves at the door, we were admitted into a large dining room, where several dozen leading Communist Party cadres from the surrounding region were gradually arriving. We were introduced to the guest of honor and main speaker, none other than Roger Garaudy, chief theoretician of the party. We assembled at the splendidly set banquet tables, where we were served a magnificent lunch.

The time came for the main speech. Garaudy's presentation was witty and urbane. Then followed a general discussion of his main theme, posed like this: "Do we want to raise the level of the workers up to the level of the culture, or lower the level of the culture down to the level of the workers?"

The answer, needless to say, was that we should try to raise the level of the workers up to the level of the culture. I was terribly confused. All during Garaudy's talk, I kept thinking I must be misunderstanding because of my poor French. After all, this was a meeting of the Communist Party of France, not some wealthy do-gooders in Westchester or Beverly Hills. Steve, whose French was excellent, assured me the problem didn't lie in my understanding.

He and I put our heads together and framed a question, which Steve asked: "Couldn't there be a culture that came from the workers themselves, that spoke to their needs, that they could understand and appreciate without lessons?"

"No," said Garaudy, smiling patiently, "there is only one culture. That is the culture of Tchaikovsky and Beethoven, of Goethe and Shakespeare, of Michelangelo and Rodin." Garaudy's list of cultural incarnations from five European countries didn't strike me as "Eurocentric," a word that was not yet part of my critical vocabulary. After all, in four years acquiring a bachelor's degree as an English major at Amherst College and three years acquiring a Ph.D. in English and American Literature at Stanford University, I had never been asked to read a single work by any author of color. But I was taken aback by his apparent lack of any class consciousness. After all, for years I had been teaching and writing about a contemporary of Marx who proclaimed that "a whale-ship was my Yale College and my Harvard" and who brazenly wrote from a lowly worker's point of view from the first paragraph of his first book to the last lines of his last book, composed with the "tarry hand" of a sailor with an "artless *poetic* temperament." In fact, the elite critics of Herman Melville's era sought to "freeze him into silence" because his writing was "ungrammatical" and struck "at the very foundations of society."[5]

I tried to think of an artist, known to both us and them, who at least drew his art from the culture and needs of the common people, who spoke directly to them and was therefore widely popular. The most obvious at the time was Bob Dylan. I offered him as an example, not necessarily of a "great" artist, but of an important artist, popular among millions of working- and middle-class youth. The response was scattered polite laughter. Had I made a mistake in French? But they would not be so impolite as to laugh out loud, and the laughter was too friendly to be aimed at me. The truth sank in. They thought I was making a sophisticated joke. To them, the popularity of Dylan was just more evidence of the backwardness of the masses.

The discussion got back to business. A young woman described her experience in Saint-Pierre-des-Corps, a nearby town, home to many railroad workers, that had been a Communist stronghold, with a Communist mayor, since the end of World War II. "Well, out in Saint-Pierre-des-Corps we have no difficulty getting the workers to go to the cinema. Our trouble comes in getting them to discuss it afterward." The subject now became: How do you get workers to discuss culture?

While this was going on, we were being served cheeses, wines, sherbet, coffee, mints, and cordials by a precision corps of waiters, waitresses, and busboys, all clad in starched, ironed, spotlessly white uniforms. It would have been unthinkable to turn around and ask any of these workers what they thought of the discussion. The people serving our food and removing our dirty dishes were as tactfully unobtrusive as well-programmed robots. And I never saw on the faces of these people doing the work a flicker of a sign that they heard any of the words being spoken at the tables. What *were* they thinking?

Since then, I have thought a lot about this scene. More than any other single event, it changed my beliefs about art, its study and teaching, and its relationships with the rest of human activities. My stream of thought flowed directly into the book published twelve years later, originally titled *The Victim as Criminal and Artist: Prison Literature in America.* The scene also made me later understand why the French Communist Party, despite its wide base in the working class, would soon be doomed to almost as little historical relevance as the American Communist Party.

Then my thinking about the politics of these cultural questions abruptly got shunted onto a different track by one of the most influential artists of the twentieth century. Labeyrie told us that he would like us to meet "a friend I think you will like." So he soon showed up at our apartment with Jean Davidson. Jean was an American expat, a journalist who had spent years in Washington covering the United States for Agence France-Presse. He now lived on a country place outside Saché, a village about twenty miles from Tours, and was a passionate foe of the Vietnam War. His wife, Sandra, was the daughter of Alexander Calder, and for many years Jean had been a close associate of that fabulous innovator of modern art. Jean had convinced Calder to move into the pastoral beauty surrounding Saché, helped him design and build his immense studio there, and had just completed a series of interviews with the sculptor published later in 1966 as *Calder: An Autobiography in Pictures.*

As a high schooler, my favorite work of art was always Calder's huge mobile that swirled and danced over the palatial staircase leading up to the second floor of New York's Museum of Modern Art. So when Jean invited us to spend a day with the Calders and Davidsons, we soon packed the kids into a rented car and drove on winding roads past small, neatly tilled farms on gently rolling land to their homestead, a bucolic arcadia that fit right into the surrounding countryside—except for the gigantic Calder stabile sitting outside what looked like a barn big enough to comfortably house a dozen elephants. The jumbo windows running from end to end of the building revealed that it was the studio of the artist now working in elephantine proportions.

Sandy, as everyone called him, was every bit as playful and mischievous as his early miniature circus, his later mobiles, and his latest phase: his colossal steel stabiles. Rather than worrying, like the Communists at the *déjeuner-débat*, about whether to "raise the level of the workers up to the level of the culture, or lower the level of the culture down to the level of the workers," he had enlisted workers as his partners in the creation of great art. Calder, originally an engineer, designed his stabiles in his Saché studio and then produced them in collaboration with the engineers, boilermakers, and other iron and steel workers in Etablissements Biémont, a factory complex in Tours. Sandy glowed as he told us of the enthusiasm and pride the factory workers expressed about their creations.[6]

Sandy shared our outrage and frustration about the Vietnam War, as well as our shame as Americans. He, his wife Louisa, Jean, Sandra, Jane, and I concocted and signed various public antiwar messages, including a telegram to Pope Paul VI, also printed as a letter in the December 27 *International Herald Tribune*: "Who speaks in the name of the Church, Cardinal Spellman for the war or Your Holiness for Peace? It is urgent to state what the church stands for: Pax Americana or universal conciliation." Such futile gestures of course had little effect on anything, but Sandy had a major effect on my life and Jane's by putting us in contact with an antiwar organization he had cofounded in the city where we were about to spend six of the most formative months of our lives.

PARIS, 1967

Holding his sword straight up and looking straight ahead along the Avenue du Président Wilson, George Washington still sits astride a powerful battle horse, a front leg raised, with rider and steed perpetually ready to charge on their towering pedestal in Place d'Iéna in Paris's elegant 16th arrondissement. If Washington could have looked down at midday on April 7, 1967, he might have noticed Jane with her long blond hair, clutching four-year-old Robert's hand, amid a cordon of women bearing a long pole with a large furled American flag. He could not have seen what was concealed under the American flag: a bright red banner with a yellow star, the flag of the Democratic Republic of Vietnam, waiting to be brandished.

Waves of people were pouring from the Iéna metro stop into the plaza, where swarms of police clad in their dramatic swirling dark-blue capes—weighted with lead to be swung at demonstrators—were hastily fencing off the crowd with metal stanchions ordinarily used as bicycle racks. Between the police and the equestrian statue were French and American military officers, a brightly uniformed band, a color guard carrying the French tricolor and the American star-spangled banner, local dignitaries, and several American officials in dark suits. Jane couldn't see her husband, who was just beyond the fringe of the crowd, handing out leaflets to passersby and new arrivals. The leaflets were addressed to Vice President Hubert H. Humphrey, who was due to arrive any minute. Neither side knew what the other side was about to do.

We had just arrived in Paris in March. Finding an apartment in or near Paris prior to Airbnb all by myself with my primitive French had been a harrowing but educational epic. Newspaper ads took me to a revoltingly posh apartment in the 16th arrondissement, to a tiny row house like the Flatbush home where I grew up, on a long train ride past miles of blocky apartment buildings almost as alienating for a Brooklyn boy as similar neighborhoods in the Bronx, and to a cramped apartment in the workers' banlieues. The epic's happy ending was a vacationing dentist's spacious apartment on Rue de Grenelle overlooking the Rue du Dragon in the 6th arrondissement. We enrolled Karen and Gretchen into a working-class school on the other side of the Boulevard Saint-Germain, giving them every school day a tourist's walk past the Café Deux Magots and the church of Saint Germain des Prés.

As soon as we got more or less settled, we followed Sandy's instructions and contacted Maria Jolas, president of the Paris American Committee to Stop War, an organization Sandy had cofounded with Jolas and June Van Ingen in 1965. PACS at the time had several hundred members, mostly American expatriates. We were just in time to join in the final planning for Humphrey's state visit. The plans included a surprise for our vice president: that red flag with the yellow star that the PACS women would unfurl in the midst of the welcoming festivities.

The day before Humphrey's arrival, the Communist daily L'Humanité had printed a map of his itinerary, along with the hope that "the citizens of Paris would give M. Humphrey an appropriate welcome." The paper urged workers and students not to be outdone by their comrades in Italy, hundreds of thousands of whom were shown in photographs fighting through police lines surrounding Humphrey. Although his first official duty in Paris was to lay a wreath before that equestrian statue of Washington in the Place d'Iéna, fighting had already broken out at the airport even before he deplaned.

The police knew this, but I didn't as I handed out my bundle of PACS leaflets, with its rather innocuous declaration in French and English:

> Vice-President Humphrey!
>
> This statue of George Washington is: "Given by the women of the United States of America in memory of the Friendship and Fraternal Aid given by France to their fathers during their fight for Independence."
>
> Is napalm burning "Freedom and Fraternal Aid"?
>
> Today Americans are fighting the Vietnamese who want:
>
> their FREEDOM
>
> their INDEPENDENCE
>
> their OWN COUNTRY!
>
> What are we doing in Vietnam?
>
> Washington and Lafayette would be ashamed of us.
>
> VIETNAM FOR THE VIETNAMESE!
>
> (signed) Americans in Paris

For about ten minutes, I politely handed out my leaflets to some of the thousands streaming into the plaza. Suddenly a thickset man in a trench coat rushed up and snatched all the leaflets out of my hands. Two men behind me each grabbed one of my arms and twisted it up behind my back. The guy with my leaflets crumpled a handful and waved them in my face.

"What are these, eh?" he snarled in French.

I desperately tried to recall the French word for "leaflet" but came up blank.

"Des papiers," I said lamely.

"Des papiers? Des papiers? Des papiers, eh?" he roared, his furious red face a few inches from mine. "What kind of fool do you think I am?" Then, to the two twisting my arms, "Away with him!"

They threw me into an oversized windowless black van with no markings, heaved me in, and locked me up. A few minutes later, the back opened again and a young man was thrown in, blood streaming from his nose and mouth. Within another few minutes, two more were prodded in with clubs.

Then we heard motorcycles and the band playing "The Star-Spangled Banner." We figured Humphrey must be arriving. The band struck up with "La Marseillaise." Then I heard police whistles, shouting, sirens, tires screeching, thuds, people running, screams. In the background we could still hear a singer:

> ... Contre nous de la tryannie,
> L'étendard sanglant est levé ...

Where were Jane and Robert? I had terrible visions.

Our van was rapidly packed with prisoners, some battered and bloody. As we attended to their injuries, they told us the latest news from the street. The police had trapped hundreds, who were being beaten and arrested. No one remembered seeing a blonde woman with a little boy. Men in the back peeking through a slit were able to see vans and buses behind us being loaded with prisoners. Soon we went in a caravan to a massive old church whose cavernous basement had been turned into a prison.

We were unloaded in small groups, booked, and shoved into our spacious dungeon. As the hours went by, load after load of prisoners were brought in. We cheered each group as they arrived. Steve was brought in. He said Alice had also been arrested. The last time he saw Jane and Robert they were still safe and maybe outside the police trap. Each vanload and busload brought the latest news. At Place d'Iéna, several groups had broken through the police lines. For a while Humphrey had been cut off from his motorcycle escort. The police had managed to extricate him and take him straight to his hotel, around which they had thrown ring upon ring of riot police. In the early hours, the heaviest fighting had been between police and students in the Latin Quarter of the 5th arrondissement, with the police getting the better of it. But then quitting time came at many factories. Soon two hundred thousand workers joined the battle. During the first hour after the workers got into it, sixty police were hospitalized, according to a police statement on the radio. The American Cultural Centers in Paris, notorious fronts for the CIA, had all been sacked. The main American Express office was under siege. Two major train depots were now controlled by the people. Several hundred thousand people were in the streets, most of which had been conceded to them by the police.

I have never met anyone living in the United States at that time who was aware through the media of any protest against Humphrey. Most people I've described it to thought I must be thinking of May of 1968, not April of 1967. It could be considered a dress rehearsal for the failed revolution of 1968.

Weeks later, I finally got to see the demonstration I missed. I was doing the English translation of the French narrative of the Vietnamese sequences and the English narrative of the U.S. sequence for *Loin du Vietnam*, the 1967 film made by Chris Marker, Jean-Luc Godard, Alain Resnais, William Klein, Claude Lelouch, and Joris Ivens. The cineastes had reels and reels of the fighting from all over Paris. In the final version of the film, Chris Marker spliced together wild scenes of Humphrey's actual reception with this U.S. news coverage: "Vice-President Humphrey arrived today in Paris and received a warm welcome. The expected antiwar protest failed to materialize." In the scene of the melee at Place d'Iéna, one can see Jane with Robert in her arms barely escaping as the police sweep in, their clubs and lead-weighted capes flying.

Except for being arrested as a "juvenile delinquent" in Greenwich Village and as a right-wing delinquent for tearing down in 1952 an Adlai Stevenson banner strung across a street in Northampton, Massachusetts, this was my first arrest. Later ones would be on more serious charges. But this was by far the most educational.

Our dungeon, one of many makeshift prisons filling up in Paris that day, eventually held about seven hundred men. Two or three hundred women were on the other side of an ancient stone wall. The women started a chant, and we joined in. Dozens of guards ran in. We stopped. As they left, we started again. After we tired of this cat-and-mouse game, someone began singing "The Communist Internationale," a song I'd never heard. I joined the thousand voices as soon as I picked up the refrain:

C'est la lutte finale,
Groupons-nous, et demain
L'Internationale
Sera le genre humain.

After the singing in French, some people sang in Italian, with most of the prisoners joining in the chorus. Some guys then shouted "En anglais! En anglais!" looking to us dozen or so Americans. We gathered in a little ring while two older men, expatriate American journalist Schofield Coryell and someone I would soon know as "Tomi" and later as "Max," wrote out the words for the rest of us. A short, fat, balding man with beady eyes and a square black mustache, who had been following me around at a distance, slithered up and stood on tiptoe, trying to peer over someone's shoulder at the conspiratorial plan we were drafting. As we caught on to his identity, he hastily scurried to the iron door and whistled to the guards, who let him out.

After our clumsy but hearty English rendition of the "Internationale," a voice called out, "Time for a meeting." The meeting turned into a prolonged—and increasingly heated—discussion of how to organize the antiwar movement in Paris in coming months. Even with Steve explaining some of the ideological differences beyond the level of my French, I was puzzled by why they were generating so much passion and anger. But it was for me a wonderfully educational hours-long seminar and introduction to the simmering political cauldron of 1967 Paris, which was to boil over in 1968, the year when our own country would also erupt. Late that night, we were released.

Over the next couple of weeks, French police agencies ordered me in twice for questioning. Each interrogation lasted a full day. Two-man teams of interrogators took each other's place and went over the same ground again and again. I pretended that my French was even worse than it was. Each team consisted of the usual good-cop/bad-cop act. One questioner was always harsh, angry, threatening. The other would say little, except an occasional word on my behalf. Then the bad cop would leave, to take a phone call, gather more "evidence," or search for a pack of cigarettes. When he was gone, the good cop would disclose, in a hushed voice and friendly tone, that he thought I was a decent fellow, the other guy was a mean bastard, I would be out of there in ten minutes if I just told them what they needed to know, his partner wanted to torture me, and he couldn't restrain him much longer. The only thing I believed was that both of them regretted that they had no authorization to torture me.

Operatives of the CIA and less notorious U.S. agencies were swarming all over Europe, especially Paris, which was a nest of intrigue. Two interesting documents turned up in my 1976 Freedom of Information Act (FOIA) suit: an apparently routine query from the CIA to the FBI asking whether I could be enlisted as a source of intelligence while abroad, and an emphatic "no" from the FBI. No wonder American professors abroad are often regarded as intelligence agents.

Jane and I learned lessons that proved valuable later when we became prime targets of Operation COINTELPRO and the subjects of numerous FBI attempts at entrapment and frame-ups, well documented in our FOIA files. One lesson was that some of the most insidious informers were people whose hearts and heads were on the side of the people they betrayed.

For example, we had a delightful visit in our apartment from a likable and respected progressive journalist, who wrote insightful columns for a leading U.S. leftist publication. After he left, we discovered that he had sto-

len 500 francs (about $100). When confronted on the telephone, he con-
fessed, apologized profusely, promised to pay back the money as soon as
possible, and said he wanted to take us and the kids out on Saturday for ice
cream at a nearby café, where he would explain all. At the café, he explained
that he had a lifelong psychological problem and couldn't control his stealing. He begged us not to report him. By the time the conversation was over
and the ice cream all eaten, we were feeling so sorry for him that we paid the
check. When we returned to our apartment, we discovered that it had
been thoroughly and expertly searched, especially our papers. Nothing
was missing.

Ambiguous characters flitted through our new world. Especially inscru-
table, brilliant, and intriguing was an African American, maybe in his fifties
or sixties, who called himself Van Elliott and claimed to be teaching us how
to be effective revolutionaries. The first time he visited our apartment, he
showed up unannounced in the kitchen, having taken a back staircase.
Every time he visited, he carried something—a tool box, a case for a musical
instrument, even an artist's easel. He advised us to always carry something,
"So when you need to carry something, no one will think it's suspicious." I
was then working on my annotated edition of Melville's *The Confidence-
Man: His Masquerade*, and like a passenger on Melville's Mississippi steam-
boat, I couldn't resist trying to fathom this mysterious stranger. One day,
Van asked me to bring my small portable typewriter in its case while he
took me someplace. I felt like Alice racing to keep up with the Red Queen as
we darted from train to train in the Paris metro, ostensibly to lose anyone
tailing us. We ended up sitting at a small table surrounded by U.S. military
men in a United Service Organizations center, where Van had me take out
the typewriter and then began dictating a revolutionary manifesto. "Why
here?" I asked, incredulous. "Because," he said, "this is the last place they
would be expecting us to be doing this." I just laughed and cased the typewriter, possibly failing his ultimate gullibility test.

Whoever he was and whatever his intentions, Van had a major influence
on my subsequent life. Once as we were discussing the relations between
culture and material history, Van made some reference to Christopher
Caudwell, a name I had never heard. Van acted shocked at my ignorance
and gave me a quick rundown on *Studies in a Dying Culture* by the British
Communist who gave his life at age twenty-nine while manning a machine
gun to hold off the Fascist troops in the fateful 1937 Battle of Jarama in
the Spanish Civil War. "You must read that book," Van ordered. "It will
change your life." He was right. Published a year after Caudwell's tragic

death and four years after I was born, *Studies in a Dying Culture* is the book that pushed me onto the path that led to doing the kind of cultural history found in most of my subsequent writings.

Beside my conversations with Van, other encounters in Paris also helped me realize that my four years of college and three years of graduate school in the elite American institutions of late 1950s and early 1960s America had succeeded in producing, at least in my case, a pretentious impostor. Even my doctorate in English and American Literature was somewhat fraudulent, with my seven years of "higher learning" devoted exclusively, without exception, to the work of white writers.

So imagine my case of impostor syndrome when I was asked to be on a July 8 panel with Aimé Césaire and Alioune Diop, sponsored by La Société Africaine de Culture and Présence Africaine, to speak on "Afro-American Liberation." Knowing next to nothing about my hosts and co-panelists, I had to plunge into a nonstop reading binge to learn about their leading roles in the anti-colonial struggles sweeping the globe and to understand the conflicts in theory swirling through these struggles. Césaire's 1955 *Discourse on Colonialism* forced me to look on modern history from a painfully disorienting point of view. Fundamentally acculturated in World War II America, I naturally thought of France, Britain, Holland, and Belgium as enlightened democracies, not just as the wartime enemies of Nazism and Fascism but also as their exemplary antitheses. Of course I was aware of colonialism's gruesome history; I shared Mark Twain's outrage at the horrors inflicted by Belgium on the Congo and by America on the Philippines, and I concurred with Melville's judgment that "the civilized white man" is "the most ferocious animal on the face of the earth."[7] Yet I was stunned by how Césaire connected the dots, arguing that before other Europeans became the victims of Nazism "they were its accomplices, that they tolerated Nazism before it was inflicted on them, that they absolved it, shut their eyes to it, legitimized it, because, until then, it had been applied only to non-European peoples." Hitler's crime was simply "that he applied to Europe colonialist procedures which until then had been reserved exclusively" for Arabs, Asians, Africans, and other non-European peoples.[8]

Another absurd and disgraceful deficiency in my education was never having read a word of Marx or Engels in my nineteen years of formal education, including that dubious "doctorate," in a society whose main goal seemed to be combating Marxism. According to Stanford's University Relations Office in 1964, "The overwhelming majority of professors at this university are actively engaged in the explanation and repudiation of Communism and Marxist ideologies."⁹ How could anyone join the crucial cru-sade against Marxism—a body of theory or belief—without knowing what it is? Evidently no teacher in my high school, college, or graduate school had dared to assign even excerpts of writing by Marx or Engels. Even more revealing, I had been so deeply acculturated—dare I say brainwashed—that when I first picked up a copy of *The Communist Manifesto* I felt like I had as a kid when I had to sit on an unpapered public toilet seat expecting to contract syphilis (as I had often been warned). Of course there are few if any documented cases of anyone getting syphilis or any other STD from a toilet seat, but it is difficult to contract Marxism without reading Marx.

So Jane and I helped organize a Marxist study group that met weekly at George Whitman's historic Shakespeare and Company bookstore. The results are obvious in my subsequent political life, teaching, and writings. Our meetings were open to all. One regular participant, an American per-haps in his thirties, spoke with a slow Tennessee drawl and studiously took lots of notes. One day his ballpoint pen dropped to the floor between his feet and those of an attractive young woman sitting next to him. She picked it up and held it out to him. "That's not mine," he said, looking straight ahead. The gold letters on the side of the pen read "U.S. GOVERNMENT." When I next met this shy gentleman, he would be playing a different role, but no more adroitly.

Of course when Jane and I began spending time with our friend Nguyen Ngoc Giao and others in the Union of Vietnamese Students in France, intelligence operatives began buzzing around us like yellow jackets at a bar-beque. Because practically all these students, so carefully chosen as loyal to the Saigon government, openly supported the NLF as soon as they arrived in France, Saigon stopped sending more because, as one official put it, "the Viet Cong were too strong in Paris." Four of the hundreds of students, however, were open supporters of the government. When we formed a Vietnamese-American Friendship organization that sponsored film and lecture events, the CIA asked these four students to help form a rival Vietnamese-American organization to put on programs to show how the United States was supporting democracy in Vietnam and protecting South Vietnam from invasion from the north.

The first meeting of this rival organization was publicly announced for a room in the Cité Universitaire at 8 P.M. But the CIA operatives had no intention of holding a public meeting, because an open event would of course be flooded with antiwar people. So at 7:45 a notice was suddenly posted at the Cité Universitaire room explaining that the meeting had been changed to 7 P.M. in a building on the opposite side of Paris. Unfortunately for this ingenious plan, two of the four "loyal" Vietnamese were secretly reporting every CIA move to Giao. So when three casually dressed male CIA operatives—including one I recognized—showed up at 6:30 P.M. with their Vietnamese friends in tow at the new meeting room, they were met by twelve members of the Union of Vietnamese Students and two of us from PACS.

They were not Oscar-quality actors. Their faces fell. One blurted out, "But how did you—" He was quickly interrupted by a man whose body and facial language proclaimed "leader." He politely asked us to wait a few minutes while they "conferred." Amused and curious, we were happy to give them space and as much time as they wanted for their conference, which included a five-minute pay phone call by Mr. Leader. Finally, he announced, "We think after all a meeting among us might be useful." Now it was our turn to have a conference. We agreed to meet.

At the meeting, the CIA guys dropped their inept covers, including the slow Tennessee drawl affected by the guy who had dropped his pen in the Marxist study group. Mr. Leader proposed that a new way to "solve" the "problem" in Vietnam was to create a "third force," "neither Communist nor under orders from Washington, but honestly patriotic." He might have been a reincarnation of Alden Pyle, the CIA agent in Graham Greene's 1955 novel The Quiet American, who gets killed trying to bomb his Vietnamese "third force" into existence. A couple of Vietnamese calmly debunked this brilliant scheme. Neither I nor the other American from PACS said anything as the CIA contingent continued trying to get the Vietnamese to listen to American reason. Finally, the only member of the trio who also had not spoken said to the Vietnamese, "Look, we're the only thing standing between you and China. If it wasn't for us, China would be devouring Vietnam." Just like the response to the Stanford student who had expressed the same idea came the only words of anger that evening.

"Don't you people know anything at all about our history? For two thousand years we fought for our independence from China. When we won it, France took it away. We defeated France. We will defeat America."

As two other Vietnamese went on with their history lesson for their American opponents, I began to sense that the conflict, not just in this room, but also in Vietnam was not an even match. After seeing the Vietnamese in action that day, I no longer doubted that they would win.

No matter how much U.S. military leaders studied the theory of Vo Nguyen Giap, which guided the Vietnamese wars of independence against

France and the United States, they could not possibly develop a strategy to defeat it. Why? Because Giap's military theory was based on a *moral* premise: the Vietnamese wars for independence were "just" wars waged against "unjust" wars of foreign domination. Giap of course was not naive enough to believe that wars are always won by the good guys. Central to Giap's analysis was the belief that the people of the invading nation, and hence their soldiers, would—given enough time and faced with a strategy that neutralized their material advantages—come to recognize the unjust nature of their war and therefore refuse to support and wage it. Hence the three stages of Giap's protracted war strategy: guerrilla war evolving into mobile war evolving into traditional positional war. Just like their French predecessors, the White House and the Pentagon fatally misunderstand the moral dimensions of their war.

Although our leaders claimed that our strategy was "winning the hearts and minds" of the Vietnamese people, in the field "winning the hearts and minds" of the "gooks," "dinks," and "slopes" was cynically known by its acronym: WHAM.[10] How many hearts and minds of a people can be won by incinerating their villages, crops, and forests? The massive use of napalm exposed the true nature of the U.S. war. So did the chemical warfare campaign named Operation Ranch Hand, the saturation bombing of *South* Vietnam by fleets of B-52s, the "free fire zones," the "strategic hamlets," and the systematic murder of civilians named Operation Phoenix. It was moral outrage that drove millions of Americans—including tens of thousands of active-duty servicepeople—to move from protest to organized and active resistance. What besides moral outrage would drive Jane and me, two American citizens leading a comfortable and privileged life, to commit serious crimes to help defeat our government by supporting that resistance inside the military?

We did have an experienced guide to help us across the boundary into the land of treason. In 1938 at age ten, Tomi Schwaetzer fled with his family from his native Austria to escape the Nazis. Orphaned in England at age eleven, he lived in foster homes during World War II, plane-spotting for the war effort and gathering spent shells and other scrap metal for pocket money. At twelve he became an organizer for the Young Communist League and at sixteen worked his ship passage to the United States. Then came multiple careers as a factory worker, union and radical organizer, geophysicist, and journalist in America, Israel, Cuba, and France. When Tomi entered our lives, he still had a slight Austrian accent, an unruly mop of dark hair, a muscular body with an encroaching paunch, and the nom de guerre of Max Cook. He has become better known as Max Watts, a name he took after his expulsion from France. Tomi/Max was domineering, devious, witty, boundlessly energetic, hopelessly individualistic, full of surprises, and somehow lovable, and a phenomenal organizer who combined ingenious clandestine work with publicity extravaganzas. He would soon lead deserters and active-duty servicepeople in forming RITA (Resistance inside the Army), which would play a significant role in the collapse of the U.S. Army. After Germany kicked him out for that activity, he went on to anti-corporate work in Australia, where he died in 2010 at the age of eighty-two.[11]

Tomi showed up in our apartment one evening with an audacious proposal: that we harbor an American GI who had just deserted his unit in Germany. He delivered his take-it-or-leave-it proposal in Edward G. Robinson tough-guy style, but with his Austrian accent and deep voice that made him sound like Henry Kissinger. We took it.

So that night, "Baby B," as Tomi code-named him, came to live with us for a while. He was part of the first wave, but more accurately trickle, of deserters arriving in France from the U.S. bases in Germany. Baby B had followed the most common route for the deserters' "underground railroad," which ran from Germany through the Netherlands, where they were welcomed by Quakers, assorted leftists, and the politicized hippies known as "Provos." As the deserter network spread in Europe, about the only leftists who refused to participate were the traditional Communist parties, including the French party, which was adamant in its refusal.

No Communist nation in Europe was ever willing to offer sanctuary to any of the deserters, though eventually the underground railroad developed a long branch that ran from Japan across the Soviet Union to Sweden.[12] At first, no European government was ready to face the wrath of Washington by giving political asylum to deserters. So wherever they went, these men had to be hidden, fed, clothed, and kept out of trouble. Thanks to overwhelming popular opposition to the war and to President Charles de Gaulle having pulled the country out of its NATO obligations, France in May became the first nation to give political asylum to a deserter, when it granted residency and work permits to a penniless deserter arrested for vagrancy.[13] Months later, Sweden and then Canada opened their gates.

Baby B, a stocky young man in his early twenties whose sandy hair was just recovering from its military crew cut, at first seemed uncomfortable amid our professorial family in our lavish rental apartment, but he soon warmed up and told us something of his life. The son of a Detroit beer-truck driver, he had finished high school, where the main thing he seemed to have been taught was that he wasn't smart enough for college. Like most of the deserters, he knew enough about the Vietnam War to know that it was not something to die or kill for. He seemed far more intelligent than our leaders, especially when he committed himself to doing what he could do stop the war.

When Baby B received his French residency and work permits, he got himself established in an independent Parisian life. While Jane and I were working on leaflets to be distributed to the GIs stationed at the German bases, he volunteered to pen and design one. The result was this wonderfully effective masterpiece (a copy of which I still treasure):

TO THOSE GUYS STILL IN THE ARMY
I used to be in there too. Now you guys listen cause I am going to tell you some good things:

First—There have been more than 10 guys that I know of that have gotten papers and I am one of them. **Listen.** Second—I have a job—I go dancing and my pay is more than P.F.C. gets and I'm getting a raise shortly. Third—life is a great deal better than being in Vietnam. Fighting for a cause that isn't what it's built up to be.

What this thing means is this: DESSERT.

Notice the spelling in **DESSERT**—It's not a bitter thing to Desert. It's the sweetest thing in the world.

Each new arrival claiming to be a deserter had to submit to interrogations on two different days, designed by Tomi to weed out possible infiltrators and opportunists. The questions randomly moved from the GI's motivation to details about his life—the schools he attended, street addresses, model and year of any car he had, names of various relatives, his service record, and so on. We had little interest in his answers about motivation because those could be so easily faked. The purpose of the second interrogation was to scan for inconsistencies about the details of his life, because only someone with a prodigious memory could pass this test. Of course this was hardly infallible since an infiltrator could provide true details. But the dual interrogations also gave good opportunities to assess reactions.

When a BBC film crew, eager to find a contact in the deserter network for a possible documentary, arrived in Paris, Tomi first made sure that it would not find one—so that he could orchestrate a media coup that would nullify all the government and media efforts to conceal the deserter movement. Tomi's plan was to use impenetrable security partly as bait to generate maximum publicity. So he dropped clues around the city, luring the BBC team into a tantalizing mystery thriller that led to a rendezvous with a man reading an upside-down *Le Monde* at a Café Deux Magots sidewalk table. The man with no name in turn arranged a clandestine rendezvous with Tomi, who knew that the BBC people were now so excited and in so deep that they would accept his outrageous, unprecedented, and nonnegotiable terms, including a sizable cash payment and two copies of the finished documentary for our own use.

Tomi somehow arranged the use of a magnificent country chateau several miles outside Paris, temporarily vacant because its usual resident, Maurice Couve de Murville, was presently serving as France's minister of foreign affairs.[14] Late on the appointed night, we loaded the BBC crew and their equipment into a large van. When we produced blindfolds for our British passengers, they refused to wear them. "Fine," said Tomi, "we'll just call off the operation." Of course they capitulated. Our driver—a woman who had driven an ambulance in the World War II French Résistance—used all her skills to give us an appropriately terrifying ride on unlit narrow rural roads.

We carefully ushered the still-blindfolded crew with their cameras and lights into the setting for the shoot, the enormous grand ballroom of the chateau. Hanging from the lofty ceiling were several bedsheets, cutting off a third of the length of the room.

"What's with the sheets?" asked the young woman in charge of the crew as she got her first look.

"The deserters vill be behind them," Tomi said in his Kissinger voice, slightly exaggerating his Austrian accent.

"You're telling me that the viewers will not be able to see them?"

"Vee have placed lights behind them. Viewers vill see their profiles as silhouettes."

"That's ridiculous! We're not going to shoot a bunch of shadows."

"Vee have to protect thees men's identity. Thees are not actors. Vee vill not put their faces on TV. They are taking a big risk just being here."

"That's just not acceptable," she insisted.

"Okay. Vee vill just call off the show," Tomi said with a shrug. "Load up your equipment. Vee vill drive you back."

Of course they were now far too deep in our cloak-and-drama conspiracy to want to crawl out. The resulting BBC documentary demolished the official dike of secrecy, and soon the media were clamoring for interviews. Tomi's bedsheet screen with anonymity for the deserters remained standard operating procedure for media interviews until December 1967, when deserter Rick Perrin, accompanied by Stokely Carmichael, stepped through the sheets to speak on camera with CBS.[15] The trickle of deserters from the U.S. bases in Germany turned into a flood on three continents.[16]

In our historical memory of the Vietnam War, there is still keen awareness, indeed smoldering controversy, about the many Americans who evaded or refused the draft. But there is almost no awareness of the role of desertion (a serious military crime defined by being away without leave more than thirty days and intending never to return), which was far more common and effective in ending the war. The historic antiwar movement by tens of millions of American civilians, including the great sacrifices of those who resisted the draft, made it difficult for Washington to turn its war in Southeast Asia into a Forever War, as it has been doing in Southwest Asia and the Middle East. The resistance inside the military, including the great sacrifices of the deserters, made it impossible.

The number of deserters from the active-duty armed forces dwarfed the number of draft evaders and resisters. During fiscal year 1971 alone, 98,324 servicemen deserted, bringing the rate to an astonishing 142.2 for every 1,000 men on duty.[17] Revealing statistics briefly flashed by as President Gerald Ford was pondering the amnesty for draft evaders he declared in September 1974 (at the same time he also issued his illegal pardon of ex-president Nixon for any and all federal crimes he may have committed while in office). According to the Department of Defense, there were 503,926 "incidents of desertion" between July 1, 1966, and December 31, 1973. From 1963 through 1973 (a period 150 percent longer), only 13,518 men were prosecuted for draft evasion or resistance. The admitted total of deserters still officially "at large" at the time was 28,661—six and a half times the 4,400 draft evaders or resisters still "at large."[18] These numbers only begin to tell the story.

Deserters—many of whom called themselves "resisters"—became politically active in other countries, including Germany, Sweden, Canada, the Soviet Union, Japan, England, Switzerland, the Netherlands, and France. An underground railroad, or rather sea-road, was created from Asia to Europe. The network of deserters and civilian supporters built an underground organization in Western Europe that vastly expanded RITA's infrastructure inside the army and helped publish and distribute about four hundred GI antiwar newspapers.[19] The deserter infrastructure played a significant role in the near revolution that shook France in May 1968.[20] In England, organized deserters helped arrange a 1971 antiwar demonstration by more than a thousand active-duty servicepeople.[21]

The resistance inside the military helped doom Washington's wars in Southeast Asia—and the draft. Events in America in 1968 and the ensuing years would force the leaders of our Forever War to rely on armed forces separated as much as possible from other American citizens, who would be trained to recite, "Thank you for your service."

10 ▸ COMING HOME

PERHAPS THE MOST important thing Jane and I learned from our year in France was that we were both Americans, through and through, for better or for worse. Although much had changed while we were away, when we came home everything seemed amazingly familiar. Yes, we were home, and home was still being torn asunder in ways we could not have imagined before the early 1960s. But that's because we didn't know, much less understand, the real history we had been living through in the 1930s, 1940s, and 1950s.

Even our gloriously united World War II America was a bit of an illusion. Back on August 14, 1945, while I was yelling my heart out in that jubilant Brooklyn motorcade celebrating V-J Day, eleven-year-old Jane was bouncing down the steps of her family's North Carolina tobacco farm to announce the great news she had just heard on the radio. The first people she met were African American men with whom she hung tobacco, tenant farmers standing behind the house waiting to be paid by her father. She raced to share the joyous news with them. They just smiled indulgently at the excited girl they called "Carrot Top" and continued their patient wait. For many years, she was puzzled by their response. It would be decades before Jane and I heard about the African American rebellions during World War II, much less the 1944 Port Chicago Mutiny.

We were home during the "long, hot summers" of rebellions in America's urban areas that began in 1964 and mushroomed in 1965 and 1966. We missed the summer of 1967, when there were 150 uprisings in eighty-two cities. Both the 82nd and 101st Airborne Divisions were deployed to suppress the Detroit uprising, which lasted five days and left forty-three dead, seventy-two hundred arrested, and more than two thousand buildings burned. The media had speculated extensively about what caused the "riots," as if it were some byzantine mystery. Back in 1943, when Jane and I were nine years old, six thousand federal troops had been deployed to suppress Detroit "riots," which left thirty-four dead. That same year there were also black "riots" in Harlem, Los Angeles, and Mobile.

Newark erupted a week before Detroit in July of 1967, lasted five days, and left twenty-six dead. When I started teaching at the Newark campus of Rutgers University in 1975, many of the surrounding buildings were still pockmarked from rifle and machine-gun fire, and some of the most profound discussions in my classes were based on papers that narrated the memories of African American students, who had hidden on the floor of their homes from the gunfire and National Guard tanks, and suburban white students, whose fathers had been trapped in their Newark offices.

Those long, hot summers had revealed a simmering state of warfare between African American communities and the police forces that were accurately perceived as an army occupying their neighborhoods. Machine guns, tanks, and military helicopters were becoming commonplace features of urban life. Meanwhile, the draft was snatching young black men out of the same desperate areas, exacerbating the causes of the urban rebellions while intensifying the military rebellions that helped lead to the collapse of the U.S. armed forces in Vietnam.[1]

Martin Luther King's brilliant April 4, 1967, sermon had given a great history of the Vietnam War, related the war to basic questions about violence and nonviolence in America, and suggested that the nation's main problem was that it was fighting "on the wrong side of a world revolution." He had been profoundly shaken by his experience during "the last three summers": "As I have walked among the desperate, rejected, and angry young men, I have told them that Molotov cocktails and rifles would not solve their problems. . . . But, they asked, what about Vietnam? . . . Their questions hit home, and I knew that I could never again raise my voice against the violence of the oppressed in the ghettoes without having first spoken clearly to the greatest purveyor of violence in the world today—my own government."[2]

Many of the urban conflagrations were ignited by a police killing of a black person (a pattern familiar in later decades, as seen in Ferguson, Charlotte, Milwaukee, and Baltimore just between 2014 and 2016). In 1966, the Black Panther Party for Self-Defense had formed in Oakland to prevent both the ongoing violence of the police and the violent response of the black populace, which the Panthers saw as devastating for the community. Armed with firearms and books of California laws, they patrolled the most oppressed neighborhoods, observing the police and advising people of their rights and their need to be armed. There was nothing revolutionary about this part of their program. For decades, the African American movement had combined the tactics of nonviolence with armed self-defense, as I learned after working with Raymond in Baltimore in 1964. Martin Luther King himself had formerly kept what has been called an "arsenal" in his home, and after the 1956 bombing of his home had applied (unsuccessfully) for a permit to carry a concealed pistol.[3] The Panthers' actions were also perfectly legal. In California, as in most states, "open carry" had long been assumed to be a right guaranteed by the Second Amendment.

But the lawmakers of California had no intention of allowing black people to bear arms in civil society. They followed a venerable American tradition. In the atrocious 1857 *Dred Scott* decision, Supreme Court chief justice Roger Taney wrote that Negroes, whether slave or free, should not be allowed to become citizens for that would grant them the constitutional right "to keep and carry arms wherever they went." From the Civil War on, various jurisdictions in the North and well as the South enacted laws designed to prevent blacks from owning and bearing arms.

In direct response to the Panthers' legal use of arms to deter police violence, right-wing Republican assemblyman Donald Mulford of Oakland drafted a 1967 bill specifically designed to criminalize their actions. On May 2, while the bill was being debated, two dozen openly armed Black Panthers entered the Assembly chamber to protest. Their action gave the organization spectacular national publicity, inspiring fervent support in some quarters and a powerful backlash in others. The Mulford Act, which made it illegal to openly carry a loaded firearm except in unincorporated areas, was vigorously supported by the National Rifle Association and enthusiastically signed by Governor Ronald Reagan.[4] So much for color-blind support of the right to bear arms.

Like other militant black organizations throughout the nation, including one in Oakland very similar to Raymond's in Baltimore, the Panthers—despite the violence inflicted on them by local, state, and federal authorities and the violence they inflicted on themselves—consistently and successfully worked to deter spontaneous mass uprisings. In 1969, I was meeting with some of the Panther leaders in their headquarters at 3106 Shattuck Avenue on the Berkeley-Oakland border. It was early afternoon. A young man burst into the office, gasping for breath and shouting, "The pigs just shot a kid!" He led us to the scene, a neighborhood of small row houses a few blocks west and south. The apparent victim, who looked to be in his mid- or late teens, was in the back seat of a police car, blood streaming from the right side of his head. Nobody else was in the car. About a dozen police with drawn weapons were milling around the car and the sidewalk. More police cars were arriving. Angry people were pouring from the houses and down the steps from their front doors. The Panthers fanned out and rushed to these neighbors, urging them to stay calm. The police were aiming their guns at the Panthers. Except for almost all the cops, I was the only white person on the scene. A skinny cop who looked like a teenager was standing about six feet from me, his shotgun pointed at my chest, his finger on the trigger, his hand trembling. Sweat was streaming down his face, ashen white from fear. The scene ended with the Panthers convincing the neighbors to stay on their steps and convincing the police to drive the wounded boy to a hospital.

The antiwar movement was largely unaware of the crucial role armed self-defense had played in supporting nonviolence in the African American civil rights movement.[5] So there was a tendency to try to graft nonviolence as an ideology as well as a tactic onto the movement against the war. This led to divisions within the movement, with nonviolence being challenged not by armed self-defense but by "direct action." The lines were often more complex than that since some of the most dedicated pacifists, such as Philip and Daniel Berrigan as well as other religious men and women, advocated and committed audacious violence against property—seizing draft board files and burning them with homemade napalm, hammering missile launchers and nuclear nose cones, wrecking equipment in Dow Chemical Company offices, and stealing many reams of devastating COINTELPRO files in a daring burglary of the FBI field office in Media, Pennsylvania.

Although I had deep respect for the committed practitioners of nonviolence, my own feelings were formed by being continually bullied at P.S. 99 until I decided to defend myself. Not being willing to fight back always seemed to be an incitement to being bullied. How did that apply to the philosophical and tactical debates about nonviolence boiling in the antiwar movement in 1967 and 1968?

One spin-off from the Redwood City anti-napalm movement of 1966 was the Port Chicago Vigil, which began in August 1966 at the entrance to the Concord Naval Weapons Station, through which flowed the napalm bombs and 90 percent of the other munitions being shipped to Vietnam. There was another reason why Port Chicago had been chosen for the vigil.

It was also the main port of shipping munitions to the Pacific during World War II. The extremely dangerous work of loading munitions onto the ships was forced upon fourteen hundred untrained black sailors, chosen for this round-the-clock virtual slave labor because the Navy deemed them unfit for other assignments, and was supervised by white officers who systematically dragooned them into speedups. On the night of July 17, 1944, a colossal explosion instantly destroyed one partially loaded ship, vaporized another, killed hundreds of the black sailors, and wounded hundreds more. Ordered back to work a few weeks later, over 250 of the men refused. All but fifty capitulated when threatened with court-martial for mutiny, which could bring a death sentence. The fifty holdouts were tried together, not allowed to testify in their own defense, convicted of mutiny, and sentenced to eight to fifteen years of hard labor in federal prison.[6]

So the 1966 vigil was a memorial to the victims of the 1944 tragedy as well as a protest against napalm and the Vietnam War. From its first day on, stalwart practitioners of nonviolence maintained their round-the-clock vigil every day, week after week, month after month, with frequent acts of civil disobedience. And from its inception, they were subjected to almost continual harassment, with frequent beatings and other physical attacks from the Marine guards and gangs of local youth. Support came from concerts by Pete Seeger and Country Joe and the Fish, as well as supporters who acted as observers to minimize the abuse.

In September, a couple of weeks after returning from France, I went one night with five other men to offer our support. As we arrived, we found a gang of six or seven young guys knocking men and women off their chairs and kicking them on the ground. We yelled for them to stop. They didn't. Morgan Parker, who had organized our little group, grabbed one of the vigil's flimsy wooden folding chairs and broke it over the head of the guy who seemed to be leading the assault. He whirled around and said, "I thought you people don't believe in violence." I laughed and said, pointing to their victims, "They're nonviolent. We aren't."

His buddies started glowering at us and muttering assorted threats. There was a little scuffling, but Morgan had picked out the right guy, so that soon changed into mere verbal back and forth. Then that changed into arguments, and the arguments then metamorphosed into conversations, joined by a couple of the vigil folks. We spent the next two hours talking with these guys about the draft, the war, war profits, jobs, and the local economy, about which they had interesting things to say. By the time we were ready to go home, there was fairly broad agreement about most of these topics. We shook hands and left, confident about the safety of the vigil people, at least for the rest of that night.

I was already involved, as a member of the Bay Area steering committee, in the complex and divisive struggle swirling around the issue of nonviolence in some of the plans for our national Stop the Draft Week in late October. Everybody supported the proposal by the newly formed Resistance organization for a national turn-in of draft cards beginning on October 16, and the event was a bonanza, with thousands of draft cards collected or ignited. But what should be the role, as well as the limits, of nonviolence in the two major physical events of the week: the blockade of the Oakland Induction Center and the siege of the Pentagon?

Draftees from northern California, as well as parts of Oregon and Nevada, were inducted through the Oakland Induction Center, located downtown a block from City Hall. Almost all came in buses. Our aim was to prevent them from reaching the entrances for as long as possible. The advocates of pure nonviolence wanted the participants to lie or sit in front of the entrances, forming an unyielding but passive blockade of human bodies. Many of us, including me, believed this would limit the activist participants to those willing to be arrested and able to afford the consequences, including fines, possible jail time, and an arrest record. We wanted the event to have a much broader class and race appeal. We argued that nonviolence tends to alienate working-class people, who often regard it as a kind of holier-than-thou performance. Those members of the steering committee who were veterans of the civil rights struggle split on the issue, with some arguing from their own experience that nonviolence actually incites the blood lust of the police and other potential assailants. Nobody advocated violence, but many of us were unwilling to surrender our right to self-defense or to forgo other tactics that could be more effective in preventing the inductees from reaching and entering the Induction Center. The meetings deadlocked. Most, but not all, of the nonviolence proponents split from the steering committee. We did all agree, however, that Monday, October 16, would be restricted to the people willing to practice or support nonviolence and to passive observers.

On Monday, only about six or seven hundred people showed up at the Induction Center. I was not one of them. One hundred nineteen were arrested, including Joan Baez, to whom the *New York Times* devoted both pictures and two of its seven brief paragraphs. Here's one of them: "Miss Baez appeared at 6 A.M., wearing a white shirt with long sleeves and French cuffs, a leather vest, pants with black and white stripes and a red wool shawl over her shoulders."[7]

On Tuesday, I was one of the three thousand demonstrators who came before dawn to try to actually shut down the Induction Center. We were a bit surprised to find no police at the scene. There were police informers in all our meetings, so they were well aware of our plans. They could easily have cordoned off the entrances to the center as well as a route for the buses, as they were used to doing for parades. But that was obviously not what they wanted. Unmolested, many of us packed the entrances and the adjacent side street. We easily detected a large police presence in the parking garage directly across Clay Street from the center, and we were more or less aware of an impending ambush. At 7 A.M., several hundred officers from the Oakland Police Department, California Highway Patrol, and Alameda County Sheriff's Office emerged from the parking garage and marched in formation into the crowd, swinging three-foot riot batons at people's heads. Most of us retreated out of their way. But about a hundred people intent on practicing nonviolence either sat down or lay down. Then came a sickening horror show. I can still hear the sounds, like baseball bats hitting watermelons, of the batons smashing skulls. Those of us who had moved aside kept yelling, "Don't sit down! Get up! Run!" Some of these nonviolent targets of the police blood lust did get up and escape. Several people in later years told me that these few minutes made them lifelong converts from nonviolence.

The police then unleashed their violence on the thousands of people at some distance from the center, most of whom had come just to demonstrate their passive support of those trying to block the entrances physically. Alternatively wielding clubs and spraying people in the eyes with Mace, the police attacked anyone they could. Especially vulnerable were news reporters and photographers, evoking angry accusations later from the Northern California Radio-Television News Directors Association. Steven Lindstedt, who had resigned from the Berkeley police force a month earlier, came with a female companion just as spectators. She was hit across the forehead by a nightstick. He was knocked down, beaten by six highway patrolmen, and arrested on felony charges. He published an account of his experience, including this prophetic statement, which sounds almost quaint more than half a century later: "It was a radicalizing day and an enlightening day. Old illusions give way to new perspectives: the image of the police as community servants has been replaced by an image of armed mercenaries. The police across the nation are rapidly becoming militarized; they are preparing for battle. Urban police forces have increasingly employed military tactics and military equipment."[8]

"Bloody Tuesday," as it came to be called, was indeed a radicalizing day and an enlightening day for the thousands of us attacked by the police. The main lessons we learned were the very opposite of the one that police and their overseers were trying to teach us. Because as we retreated from the police, we found ourselves in possession of the intersections through which the inductees' buses would have to pass. We also discovered that as the area of their assault expanded, the ranks of the police were getting so thin that we were able to temporarily hold intersections in a wide perimeter around the center, briefly paralyzing downtown Oakland.

We decided to use Wednesday and Thursday for large peaceful demonstrations that would give the police no pretext for renewed assaults while we prepared for Friday. In fact, our monitors kept the thousands of demonstrators orderly and even worked with the police to prevent any incidents, angering some picketers who wanted to take the streets.

At 6 A.M. on Friday, ten thousand people moved out of our staging area, broke into small groups, and followed monitors to specific intersections. People wore helmets, protective clothing, and equipment to deal with Mace and tear gas. Our Stanford contingent was equipped with shields we had made—three-by-four-foot plywood, decorated with pictures and slogans, with a canvas strap for holding on one arm. Once in their assigned intersection, each group constructed barricades out of parking meters, potted plants, cars, trucks, and two buses. The police had to come to us. They soon discovered that the six hundred men they had used on the three previous days could not handle this situation. Fourteen hundred additional police were rushed in. When they assembled enough force to clear an intersection, we just moved, according to plan, out further to another intersection, thus widening the perimeter. This thinned the police ranks enough to allow us to retake some of the intersections, creating an almost stalemated ebb and flow.

The Stanford contingent with our shields often found ourselves protecting other people, including bystanders—who were the most vulnerable— from the police fury. My most memorable moment, one that I found extraordinarily educational, came as I stepped between an Oakland cop and a woman he was about to club. The tall, burly cop, his face contorted and red with savage anger, aimed his riot stick at my head with a powerful overhead swing. I raised my shield to block it. I heard and felt the force of his fury as his stick bounced off the plywood. I lowered the shield, figuring that he would next thrust the stick at my balls. I expected his rage to explode. But to my amazement, his face crumbled—and aged. He almost looked like an old man as he shuffled off to join some other cops, shoulders hunched, never looking back. I came close to feeling a twinge of pity.[9]

We held and paralyzed downtown Oakland for five hours. As the buses finally inched toward the Induction Center, the draftees passed the wreckage cleared from their path and read the antiwar and pro-GI messages painted all over every intersection. Some flashed V signs at us. Those who later got shipped to Vietnam had already experienced a militant antiwar movement—on their side.

By this date, thirteen thousand Americans had been killed in Vietnam. I sometimes wonder how many of those scared young faces I saw peering out from the windows of the buses would be among the next forty-five thousand.

The following day, Saturday, October 21, one hundred thousand people assembled in Washington for the March on the Pentagon. A small library has been written about this historic event, including Norman Mailer's *The Armies of the Night: History as a Novel, the Novel as History*, which won a Pulitzer Prize and a National Book Award. In the two years since sixteen thousand people, most neatly and respectfully attired in suits or dresses, had staged the first demonstration in Washington against the Vietnam War, the war had rudely shoved the antiwar movement and American society out of the culture of the 1950s and into a cultural maelstrom. The October 21 assemblage embodied that cultural storm of the 1960s, ranging from a revival of 1930s leftism through middle Americans earnestly seeking to restore traditional American ideals all the way to the far-out fringes of the counterculture. After all, the Long, Hot Summer of Detroit, Newark, and those 150 uprisings in eighty-two cities had also been the Summer of Love, when as many as one hundred thousand hippies descended on San Francisco's seedy Haight-Ashbury district to make love and music, do drugs, set new dress styles, and declare independence from the government, the taboos of their parents, and the politics of post–World War II America. But most of those who had come to march on America's palace of war were college students.

After listening to speeches and singing songs, the throng marched across the Potomac to begin the siege of the Pentagon. Both sides of the war, at home and in Vietnam, flew their flags over the opening rally and march, with the Stars and Stripes contesting with the single gold star on the blue and red banners of the National Liberation Front of South Vietnam.

The Pentagon was defended by five thousand National Guard soldiers, federal and DC police, MPs, and U.S. marshals, and six thousand paratroopers from the 82nd Airborne Division, fresh from their deployment to put down the Detroit insurrection. Massed demonstrators faced lines of soldiers, eye to eye, often inches apart. The confrontation between the two forces lasted through the day and night and resumed on a much smaller scale the next day, ending in the wee hours of Monday morning.

Some people, including a number of celebrities, engaged in civil disobedience and were arrested on the steps of the Pentagon. Others tore down a wire fence, allowing a mass occupation of forbidden turf. One contingent led by NLF flags stormed the Pentagon, with about a dozen members breaking into the building, where they were promptly roughed up and tossed out, with one badly beaten and arrested, leaving a trail of blood on one of the corridors of war. Jerry Rubin and Abbie Hoffman led an evidently unsuccessful incantation to levitate the Pentagon and expel its evil spirits. The iconic photo of the siege showed a young woman with a flower confronting a line of soldiers with fixed bayonets on leveled rifles. Other soldiers' rifle butts smashed faces, especially of women. A mass burning of draft cards twinkled like little stars on Saturday night. Later that night, long after the buses and most people were long gone and when there were no longer photographers clicking away, U.S. marshals and soldiers savagely tore into the lingerers peacefully and legally camped on the plaza, inflicting brutal injuries, again particularly on young women, some of whom were beaten in what appeared to be an orgiastic frenzy.[10] During the siege, tear gas was fired, 683 people were arrested, and there were countless injuries, many serious. When the antiwar movement returned to Washington in November 1969, it would not be with only one hundred thousand people but with a force of over half a million.

President Johnson believed that the Pentagon demonstration had been masterminded by Vietnamese Communists.[11] This was delusional. He also believed that it strengthened Washington's enemy in Vietnam. This is undeniable. What could he do? The president immediately called General William Westmoreland home to tell the nation that America was on the verge of winning the Vietnam War.

So in November 1967, the month after Stop the Draft Week, General Westmoreland, commander of half a million U.S. troops and three-quarters of a million foreign and Vietnamese troops on the U.S. payroll, came home— to do public relations. Addressing the National Press Club, he informed the nation's leading opinion makers that "the enemy's hopes are bankrupt," his forces are "declining at a steady rate," "he can fight his large forces only at the edges of his sanctuaries" in other countries, and we have entered the phase "when the end begins to come into view," when the South Vietnamese army will "take charge of the final mopping up of the Vietcong."[12] The *New York Times* promptly echoed his assertions that "the Vietcong now control only 2,500,000 people," little more than half what they had controlled in 1965, and "it is now merely a matter of time until this trend forces the enemy not to negotiate but to fade away into the jungle."[13] The *Times* followed up with a late December series of front-page analyses of the war by Hanson Baldwin, ace military correspondent of the corporate press. Baldwin told us that "the enemy is weaker than he appears to be" and is gripped by "desperation," that his recent offensive is just a public-relations ploy keyed "to strengthening opposition to the war in the United States and influencing American and world public opinion during a Presidential election year," that the morale of U.S. troops is "excellent" whereas there is "irrefutable evidence of a decline in enemy morale," that "the enemy can no longer find security in his South Vietnamese sanctuaries," that "the allies are winning" and "there seems little reason to doubt that Hanoi has abandoned the hope of conquest of South Vietnam by military force."[14]

Who knew that back in June, Secretary of Defense Robert McNamara had commissioned the Pentagon Papers, that super-top-secret forty-seven-volume documentary history that proved the government's version of the war and its purpose was a putrid river of lies and that every U.S. military strategy had already failed? McNamara kept the existence of the Pentagon Papers secret even from President Johnson, Secretary of State Dean Rusk, and National Security Adviser Walt Rostow. Only the men who compiled the papers knew of the study and what it revealed. Fortunately, one of them was Daniel Ellsberg.

Jane and I didn't believe any of this Pollyanna PR for the war. The Paris confrontation I had attended between the Vietnamese and the CIA had revealed the illusions, deceptions, and ignorance central to the U.S. war, the daily war reports in the same *New York Times* contradicted the wishful thinking of its own analysts and editors, and we were reading in the underground press the reporting and analysis of Wilfred Burchett, the only western correspondent on the ground with the National Liberation Front.

As early as 1964, Burchett had actually accompanied insurgent fighters all the way to the outskirts of Saigon.[15] Writing in the *National Guardian* on December 23, 1967, Burchett claimed that the National Liberation Front had taken the initiative in the war, had begun a major offensive, and was "now able to mount simultaneous attacks on widely separated objectives in divisional strength." On January 6, 1968, Burchett argued in the *National Guardian* that "the true facts about the war have been denied the U.S. public by the extraordinary antics of Gen. William Westmoreland and his public relations team in Saigon": "Unable to present any successes in terms of terrain reoccupied or population won back from areas controlled by the NLF, the U.S.-Saigon command has resorted to an old trick the French used until the fall of Dien Bien Phu—the claim to be wiping out tens of thousands of enemy troops for the loss of a handful of their own." Burchett boldly declared: "As the new year begins, the National Liberation Front of South Vietnam (NLF) is on the offensive at all points. . . . This indigenous peasant army is clearly winning the war."

We would have to wait only one month to find out who was telling us the truth about the war in Vietnam. We already knew who was not telling us the truth about the war in America because we were combatants on the other side.

Baldwin began his three-part series with the assertion that "the main battleground in 1968 will be in the United States." He meant a figurative battleground, where the struggle would be waged with words and images. With the old goal of "winning the hearts and minds" of the Vietnamese becoming ever more illusory, the goal would have to shift to the more realistic mission of winning the hearts and minds of the Americans. The Vietnam War was coming home to its birthplace.

11 ▸ THE WAR COMES HOME

Earthquakes rocked the nation in 1968, destroying America's faith in the stability of its currency, the invincibility of its military, the fairness of its elections, the righteousness of its causes, and a brighter future. These seismic events also left deep cracks in the nation's foundation, cracks that have become increasingly ominous fault lines.

The first thirty days of the new year were deceptively quiet. The major news reported about Vietnam concerned possible peace negotiations. The sparse battlefield reports did not seem to corroborate the government and media line that the "Viet Cong" and "North Vietnamese" were desperately trying to pull themselves together in remote jungles and foreign sanctuaries. Just between January 2 and 10, the *New York Times* reported: "enemy attacks U.S. air base at Danang"; "smashes at two American artillery bases in Queson Valley"; "almost wipes out allied platoon defending hamlet near Hoian"; "strikes district headquarters town of Phuloc 25 miles SE of Hue" while attacking five U.S. Marine Corps positions in the area; attacks government forces 24 miles northeast of Saigon; "fights way to center of Khiemcuong 21 miles west of Saigon"; and "overruns U.S. airfield at Kontum, blowing up several planes." Reading the news reports as trained 1950s English majors, Jane and I discovered much more than the *Times* intended. Here's one we found especially revealing: "Vietcong guerrillas, attacking in regimental force, killed 26 American infantrymen and wounded 111 early today in rubber plantation country near Tayninh, 50 miles northwest of Saigon."[1] Since there are thousands of combatants in a regiment, how do guerrillas attack "in regimental force"? And so close to Saigon? It looked to us like Wilfred Burchett might not be exaggerating when he wrote on January 6 that the National Liberation Front (NLF) "is on the offensive at all points." Still, she and I were taken completely by surprise—like the American military and the rest of America—by the Tet Offensive.

On January 31, during the Vietnamese New Year's Tet holiday, the NLF and the People's Army of Viet Nam exposed the official U.S. version of reality as a flimflam of illusions and lies. Simultaneously they attacked in every part of South Vietnam, hitting U.S. and puppet forces in five of the six major cities, thirty-six provincial capitals, sixty-four district capitals, and almost every military base. U.S. airfields, ammunition dumps, and supply centers were devastated, and some were overrun, providing the insurgent forces with vast quantities of modern arms. Possibly as many as two hundred thousand prisoners were freed, more than making up in numbers for battlefield losses. Vietnam's old capital city of Hue was overwhelmed in hours and held for weeks against all-out U.S. air, sea, and ground attacks. Sections of Saigon itself were seized, forcing the United States to bomb and strafe the capital with fighter-bombers and helicopter gunships.[2]

Those aircraft had to take off from Saigon's Tan Son Nhut air base, which was itself under assault, and as they launched they were immediately under fire from aircraft artillery on the edge of the base. When the American Embassy in downtown Saigon had to request air support from Tan Son Nhut to repel commandos storming the compound, the response was neatly dramatized in a poem by Horace Coleman, the Air Force officer in charge of directing the flights:

But there's nothing like trying to get a chopper load of guns and ammo
to the American Embassy during Tet when the VC are downstairs
    blowing doors
and grunts are throwing hand guns through the windows
to staff racing to the roof and I'm giving directions
to a chopper from the boonies with an old street map
. . . and I can't even see the bird on radar
he's so close and so low but he finally finds the place—and gets
    shot down
and I wonder "Who's got the guns now?"[3]

In disbelief we watched General Westmoreland on television, standing in front of the embassy compound with dead bodies, the battle-scarred building, and sounds of explosions in the background, declaring to America and the world that this whole offensive was merely "diversionary" from an imminent invasion "across the Demilitarized Zone."[4] Perhaps he could hardly do otherwise without acknowledging that he had just committed one of the most colossal blunders in military history, moving his most effective combat units to counter the feint at the remote and insignificant outpost at Khe Sanh, thus stripping the defenses from the urban and densely populated regions that were the real targets of the offensive.[5] The forces that were still supposedly besieging Khe Sanh had crossed the country from the western frontier to capture Hue, the old capital city on the eastern coast.

We saw General Nguyen Ngoc Loan, chief of the Saigon national police, put a snub-nosed revolver to the temple of a prisoner wearing shorts and a plaid shirt, his hands manacled behind his back; the man's head jolts, he collapses to the pavement, and a fountain of blood gushes from his temple. The next day, we saw Eddie Adams's iconic photo of the murder in the *New York Times*. We heard American officials proclaiming a major U.S. victory in Saigon because we had recaptured the embassy compound, repulsed an assault on the Presidential Palace, and driven NLF forces back to the perimeter of Tan Son Nhut. Sporadic fighting was to go on in Saigon for months, while sections of the capital and its suburbs would remain covert rebel strongholds for the rest of the war. War aims were now expressed most trenchantly in the infamous words of an officer who explained why our warplanes and artillery had devastated the Mekong Delta city of Ben Tre, capital of Ben Tre province: "It became necessary to destroy the town to save it."[6]

The front-page headline of Wilfred Burchett's article in the February 10 *National Guardian* read: "Vietnam: The Lies Crumble." On February 23, the *Wall Street Journal* editorialized: "We think the American people should be getting ready to accept, if they haven't already, the prospect that the whole Vietnam effort may be doomed; it may be falling apart beneath our feet. The actual military situation may be making academic the philosophical arguments for the intervention in the first place."

The Tet Offensive and its immediate aftermath ended any prospect that Washington had of "winning" the war. From then on, it was almost inevitable that the NLF and Hanoi would eventually achieve their goal: a unified and independent sovereign nation of Vietnam.

Nevertheless, debate still rages about whether the Tet Offensive was actually a "military defeat" for the Vietnamese revolutionaries, which was turned into a decisive "psychological victory" by a craven U.S. administration and a complicit American press. Indeed, the dominant history of the war we have heard ever since the early 1980s adopts this view, regurgitating General Westmoreland's argument that the Tet Offensive was a desperation move that exhausted the strategic potential of the "VC," producing a "colossal military defeat" for them and a decisive military victory for the United States, which had "never been in a better position in South Vietnam."[7]

By drawing a distinction between "military" and "psychological," our leaders merely proved that they remained incapable of understanding either the war they were fighting or the people on the other side, which by late 1967 included Jane, me, and countless other Americans. For example, while napalm no doubt killed many "enemy" combatants in Vietnam, it also created far more enemies in Vietnam, in America, and around the world. The U.S. war depended on support from the American people, and that support depended partly on the belief that we were fighting in Vietnam to help the people of South Vietnam. Since the Tet Offensive counted on almost total surprise, it would not have been possible without overwhelming support from the people of South Vietnam.

To believe the Tet Offensive was a U.S. military victory, one must also ignore some inconvenient facts. If Westmoreland had achieved a decisive military victory with the forces on hand, why did he submit an emergency request for an additional 206,000 soldiers, an increase of 40 percent? And if the White House was sincere in echoing his claims of victory, why did it sack him in March? And if the insurgents were crippled by their losses in the Tet Offensive, how were they able to mount subsequent attacks on bases and cities throughout South Vietnam? The NLF and Hanoi would launch an equally devastating offensive in May, another coordinated attack in August, a repeat of Tet on its 1969 anniversary, and an even larger offensive in May 1969, when U.S. troop strength (which had steadily increased while the United States was supposedly de-escalating) was at its maximum of over 542,000.[8]

Three years later, when we got to read the Pentagon Papers, we discovered that our leaders' claims of "victory" were out-and-out lies:

The Johnson Administration began 1968 in a mood of cautious hope about the course of the war. Within a month those hopes had been completely dashed. In late January and early February, the Viet Cong and their North Vietnamese supporters launched the massive Tet assault on the cities and towns of South Vietnam and put the Johnson Administration and the American public through a profound political catharsis on the wisdom and purpose of the U.S. involvement in Vietnam.... One of the inescapable conclusions of the Tet experience ... [was that] the bombing had been a near total failure.[9]

The enemy's TET offensive ... although it had been predicted, took the U.S. command and the U.S. public by surprise, and its strength, length, and intensity prolonged the shock.[10]

The primary focus of the U.S. reaction to the Tet offensive was ... avoiding defeat or disaster in the South.[11]

The enemy is operating with relative freedom in the countryside, probably recruiting heavily and no doubt infiltrating NVA units and personnel.... To a large extent the VC now control the countryside.[12]

Both the administration and the Pentagon were forced to recognize in secret that the Tet Offensive proved that all their previous beliefs in "progress in many ways had been illusory" and that a U.S. "military victory was probably not possible."[13] They worried about their ability "to convince critics that we are not simply destroying South Viet Nam in order to 'save' it" and to maintain the economic and military "resources for the ghetto fight." The Pentagon strategists foresaw "increased defiance of the draft and growing unrest in the cities" combining to provoke "a domestic crisis of unprecedented proportions."[14]

This direct damage from the Tet Offensive and its aftershocks was obvious. The earthquake also triggered a psychological tsunami that swept across the nation and the planet.

When it hit international markets, the entire system of international capitalist finance looked like it might collapse. Immediately there were predictions that financing the Vietnam War and bearing the other burdens of empire would lead to ever-increasing deficits in the U.S. budget and balance of payments, endemic inflation, and the demise of the gold standard.[15] Unable to raise taxes to finance an unpopular war, the government had been forced to budget for 1968 the largest deficit since World War II, greater than the deficits of the previous five years combined. As the Tet Offensive washed away the myth of U.S. invincibility, U.S. dollars were dumped on a grand scale, thus shattering by early March the $35 per ounce fixed price of gold, which had held since 1934 despite World War II and the Korean War. The gold standard itself was put on life support and officially buried three years later. Today all currencies are fiat money, and virtual money seems as real as gold.

The psychological tsunami from the Tet Offensive had wildly different effects on the antiwar movement. Many of us suddenly found ourselves surfing on its crest, a thrilling and exceedingly precarious position.

For two years, more and more people had been finding themselves identifying with "the enemy." There was I—a World War II superpatriot and an ardent postwar Cold Warrior—in Tours in 1966, giving the Vietnamese technical information about the napalm bombs being manufactured in Redwood City. There was Jane in April 1967 amid that cordon of women planning to ambush Vice President Hubert Humphrey with their flag of the Democratic Republic of Vietnam lurking inside their furled Star-Spangled Banner. The thousands of demonstrators who broke from the peaceful March on the Pentagon to storm the building were led by a phalanx of NLF flags. "Ho, Ho, Ho Chi Minh, the NLF is going to win" was becoming a familiar chant. The Tet Offensive turned this gradual evolution into a dramatic transformation. Historian David Hunt described the psychological effect when Tet proved to the antiwar movement that the Pentagon's Harvard-trained experts "had been wrong, and we had been right, more right even than we had dared to imagine":

> As the insurgents burst into view, "shouting their slogans and fighting with nerve-shattering fury," we realized that they were not just noble victims, but that they were going to win the war. Trying to make sense of the details of the Offensive, we were bowled over by the sheer ingenuity of it, the thrilling spectacle of people performing miraculous feats. Tet brought into focus with blinding clarity just how much human beings are capable of accomplishing. Carried along by the momentum of their endeavor, we wanted to be associated with the Vietnamese revolutionaries . . . and to figure out how our newly discovered vision of "power to the people" might be realized here in the United States.[16]

A record of this metamorphosis can be viewed in the movement press. From February 1968 on, the dominant image of the Vietnamese would no longer be decapitated or napalm-mutilated bodies but triumphant fighters, not victims but heroes. The photo of a female guerrilla with a bayonetted rifle slung over her shoulder, which ran alongside Burchett's first article on Tet in the February 10 *Guardian*, would soon become iconic, often appearing on posters next to Jane's poem, "To the Women of Vietnam."

Throughout 1967 the Stanford-based *Midpeninsula Observer* portrayed the Vietnamese as victims, emphasized the need for humanitarian aid, and

consistently referred to "the peace movement." Its first issue after the Tet
Offensive openly identified with the NLF for the first time, in a revealing
way. The front page featured an article about women's contrasting roles in
American society, in the movement, and in Vietnam. It displayed three
recent pictures from recent periodicals: a model in scanty lace lingerie, captioned "Women Power, Playboy Style"; a torso sporting a political button
next to deeply cleaved breasts, captioned "Women Power, Ramparts Style";
and that heroic guerrilla, captioned "Women Power, Guardian Style." The
vocabulary of the opening sentence suggests how thoroughly the military
victories of the NLF were influencing the movement's conceptualizations,
even of domestic concerns: "Somewhere between playmate-of-the-month
and liberation soldier, today's U.S. radical woman is fighting on several
fronts."[17]

Militant African American organizations were already identifying their
struggle as part of the revolution in the Third World, with Vietnam in the
vanguard. The March 16, 1968, issue of *The Black Panther* featured a long
article on the Tet Offensive titled "Ocean of People's War Engulfs South
Viet Nam Cities and Villages Alike" and Huey Newton's call for "20,000,000
black people armed to the gills."

In December, the *Observer* would bring the war into the American home
with a jolly Santa Claus on the cover, about to slide down the chimney, his
finger on the trigger of his grenade launcher, chanting "Ho! Ho! Ho Chi
Minh!"[18] The same month, *New Left Notes*, the official weekly newspaper of
Students for a Democratic Society (SDS), made the message explicit in a
cover picture of NLF guerrillas brandishing assault rifles with this caption:
"December 20 marks the 8th anniversary of the founding of the NLF. The
NO [National Office] is planning on issuing this picture as a poster. Revo-
lutionaries are invited to show solidarity through appropriate actions."[19]
Liberation News Service (LNS), the AP and UPI of the movement, spelled
out its role as a revolutionary alternative to the media of the "corporate
rich" in a midyear article equating the underground press with the deadly
sorceress of Greek myth: "1968: Year of the Heroic Guerilla MEDEA."
All subsequent 1968 LNS news bulletins would bear on the address page the
Cuban version of that slogan: "Año de guerrilla heroica."[20]

The Tet Offensive transformed the rest of the American political scene as
dramatically as it transformed the antiwar movement. Running as the
peace candidate in 1964, Lyndon Johnson had been elected president by
the highest percentage of the popular vote in modern history, a record that
still stands. The Tet Offensive put Johnson's long political career on life

support; in less than a year that career would die in disgrace. When Senator Eugene McCarthy announced in November 1967 that he was running for president as an antiwar candidate, it seemed a mere symbolic protest. But on March 12, less than six weeks after the Tet Offensive began, McCarthy came within a few hundred votes of defeating the incumbent president from his own Democratic Party in the New Hampshire primary and walked away with twenty of its twenty-four delegates. Four days later Senator Robert Kennedy entered the race for the Democratic presidential nomination as a second explicitly antiwar candidate. The day we heard that news, Jane said, "Now we know who our next president will be. Nobody can stop him."

On March 31, Jane and I wondered all day why President Johnson had chosen to address the nation. As we listened that evening, his speech at first seemed laughably predictable. He claimed that the offensive by "the Communists" had achieved none of their goals, that during his administrative there had been "substantial progress" in building a "durable government" in South Vietnam, and that our strength is "invincible." Then he presented his magnanimous proposal: we would stop bombing most of North Vietnam if Hanoi would agree to negotiations to secure a peace "based on the Geneva Accords of 1954."

Obviously the president calculated—no doubt accurately—that precious few Americans knew that restoring the Geneva Accords was precisely what Hanoi and the National Liberation Front had been demanding and then fighting to achieve ever since Washington had torpedoed the accords in the summer of 1954. Johnson knew that most Americans did not realize that the U.S. attempt to make South Vietnam a separate nation flagrantly violated the most basic principle of the Geneva Accords, which declared that all of Vietnam was a single nation, with "full independence and sovereignty." For fourteen years, the Eisenhower, Kennedy, and Johnson administrations and their subservient media had done their best to keep the American people ignorant of the fact that the 17th parallel was established merely as a temporary demarcation between the French army and the army of the Democratic Republic of Vietnam and that the Geneva Conference declared unequivocally that this "military demarcation line is provisional and should not in any way be interpreted as constituting a political or territorial boundary."

The antiwar movement's main weapon against the American people's ignorance of the Geneva Accords and the rest of Vietnamese history was *Viet Nam: History, Documents, and Opinions on a Major World Crisis*, a mass-market paperback edited by Marvin Gettleman, first published in 1965, and selling more than six hundred thousand copies in multiple printings and editions. Anyone familiar with the documents in this volume knew that the president's speech, like the Vietnam War itself, depended on an elaborate fraud and a brazen rewriting of history. It would take almost four years of U.S. genocide and ecocide in Vietnam, the deaths of over a million more Vietnamese and well over half the deaths memorialized on the Wall in Washington, before our government would capitulate and finally agree that Vietnam was one country, not two. Here is the complete text of Article 1 of the "Agreement on Ending the War and Restoring Peace in Viet-Nam," the U.S. surrender document signed in Paris in 1973: "The United States and all other countries respect the independence, sovereignty, unity, and territorial integrity of Viet-Nam as recognized by the 1954 Geneva Agreements on Viet-Nam."[21]

It was no surprise to Jane and me that Hanoi immediately accepted the president's proposal, and peace negotiations soon began. If Johnson had been willing to accept the terms Nixon finally agreed upon in 1973, he could have ended the war in December 1963. Do we dare think about a more plausible alternative reality? Imagine Johnson, elected in that 1964 landslide as the peace candidate, agreeing to the terms of the 1973 Paris Accords in 1965, shortly after being inaugurated as the elected president. Now hugely popular, in the next eight years he would enact all the visionary promises of his Great Society, using the enormous resources that would have been squandered if he had continued the war. More than 95 percent of the war's American and Vietnamese casualties would never occur. And then a peaceful and prosperous future would not become an unimaginable fantasy, as it has in our actual twenty-first century.

Like most everyone, we were stunned by the president's concluding thunderbolt: "I shall not seek, and I will not accept, the nomination of my party for another term as your President." Now I had to agree with Jane that Bobby Kennedy was destined to be America's next president.

Four days after Johnson's speech, Martin Luther King was murdered in Atlanta, supposedly by a lone assassin. And war came home to America. African American smoldering anger erupted in volcanic fury in 125 U.S. cities and towns. It took fifty-five thousand troops and many tens of thousands of police just to contain the rebellions. In the eleven days after King's murder, the killed and wounded on the home front approached the casualty rate in Vietnam. One month after television had shown U.S. Marines fighting street by street to retake the Vietnamese city of Hue, we saw nine thousand federal troops struggling to regain control of Washington itself, while in the background massive columns of black smoke from numerous torched buildings towered above the Capitol.

The Democratic primaries proved one thing: the people who in 1964 had overwhelmingly elected the candidate who had pledged not to widen the Vietnam War now wanted a president who would end the full-scale Vietnam War that he had created. Robert Kennedy and Eugene McCarthy swept these primaries with overwhelming majorities (winning between them 83 percent in Pennsylvania, 63 percent in Wisconsin, 78 percent in Massachusetts, 63 percent in the District of Columbia, 69 percent in Indiana, 83 percent in Nebraska, 82 percent in Oregon, 67 percent in New Jersey, 70 percent in South Dakota, 72 percent in Illinois, and 88 percent in California). The two antiwar candidates polled 69 percent of the total popular vote, while slates of electors representing Hubert Humphrey, Johnson's loyal vice president, squeaked out 2.2 percent.

Going into the decisive June 4 primary in California, McCarthy was running ahead of Kennedy in the popular vote and had won more states. But when Kennedy was declared the victor in California, it was once again possible to imagine a brighter future for America. Late that night, at the joyous party celebrating the victory of the man destined to be our next president, Robert Kennedy was assassinated, purportedly by a lone assassin. From then on, anyone who doubted that Malcolm X, John F. Kennedy, Lee Harvey Oswald, Martin Luther King, and Robert F. Kennedy had each been murdered by a lone unassisted gunman would be labeled a "conspiracy theorist."

If the Democratic Party were then to follow the will of its voters, expressed overwhelmingly in its primaries, Eugene McCarthy would have been chosen as its candidate and it would have been able to break from Johnson's disastrous war. Instead, the party would soon destroy itself. Before the grotesque Democratic Convention opened in Chicago on August 26, the Republican Convention had chosen a peace candidate in Miami Beach on August 7.

A line of tanks had to seal Miami Beach off from Miami, where a black rebellion raged for two days, leaving soldiers holding one hundred blocks of the city amid what a police official described as "fire-fights like in Vietnam" that got within a mile of the convention.[22] In his acceptance speech, Richard Nixon noted that "as we look at America, we see cities enveloped in smoke and flame," and he vowed that "if the war is not ended when the people choose in November," "I pledge to you tonight that the first priority foreign policy objective of our next Administration will be to bring an honorable end to the war in Vietnam."[23]

In the weeks between Robert Kennedy's assassination and the opening of the Democratic Convention, its southern and big-city bosses, led by Chicago mayor Richard J. Daley, and its rabid anti-Communist union bosses, who had purged virtually every progressive union official in the 1950s, had somehow secured more than enough delegates to steal the nomination for Humphrey. The final vote was 1,759 for Humphrey, 601 for McCarthy. Just to be sure that nobody could possibly think that the Democratic Party wished to end the Vietnam War, the convention voted 1,567 to 1,041 to reject a moderate "Peace Plank" proposed for the platform. Inside the amphitheater, Mayor Daley's goons roughed up McCarthy delegates and newsmen, including Mike Wallace and Dan Rather. Outside, twelve thousand of Daley's Chicago police and six thousand National Guardsmen, backed up by six thousand federal troops and one thousand Secret Service agents, spent several days teargassing and viciously beating antiwar demonstrators, McCarthy supporters, newspeople, and any Chicago residents or visitors unlucky enough to be in their vicinity. A sadistic orgy of cops and soldiers inflicting vicious atrocities was filmed for posterity under the klieg lights and TV cameras massed in front of the Hilton Hotel.

While the antiwar demonstrators were being clubbed and gassed in Chicago, another antiwar front was being opened by soldiers who were missing from the Chicago action. When the 1st Armored Cavalry Division at Fort Hood outside Killeen, Texas, received orders for pending action at the Democratic Convention, 160 black soldiers held an all-night protest meeting on August 22–23. Even a visit by the commanding general failed to stop their defiance, resulting in the arrest and court-martial of forty-three GIs for refusal to obey orders. As of sunrise on August 23, the base was reported to be "still in a state of near rebellion." White soldiers at the base, who were using the Oleo Strut coffeehouse as their center of antiwar activities, provided legal defense for their black brothers. The Oleo Strut was also the home of the *Fatigue Press*, an influential GI newspaper whose editor, PFC Bruce Peterson, was immediately arrested and sentenced to eight years of hard labor on a blatantly phony marijuana charge.[24] The antiwar movement within the military at home and abroad was a stark reminder of the entanglement of the American war in Vietnam and the war within America. In Vietnam, antiwar organizing, mutinies, and fragging were becoming commonplace, while in America soldiers and veterans were emerging as leaders of an increasingly radical antiwar movement.

In February, soldiers at Fort Gordon in Georgia issued a public declaration of resistance, and at Fort Jackson in South Carolina twenty-five soldiers in uniform held a militant antiwar demonstration, leafleted the other soldiers, and got support from students at the nearby University of South Carolina.[25] *Vietnam GI*, a newspaper published by Vietnam veterans, jumped its printing from ten thousand copies in January to thirty thousand in October, including thousands read by soldiers in Vietnam; it headlined its April issue: "War in the States?"[26] In October, 120 active-duty soldiers from Texas bases participated at an antiwar rally organized by University of Texas students.[27] There was also a role reversal, as active-duty GIs and veterans now led teach-ins to educate students, professors, and other civilians. Vietnam veterans conducted teach-ins on about two dozen college campuses where they showed "army training films and talked about military life . . . to get students to resist the draft."[28] One year after the Oakland Induction Center confrontation, I worked in GIs and Vets for Peace to help organize a local march. Although the bases in the area scheduled special inspections and drills for the Saturday of the march, on October 12 over five hundred active-duty servicepeople, many risking court-martial by participating in uniform, led fourteen thousand antiwar marchers through the streets of San Francisco to the Presidio military base.

Three years later, a much larger contingent of active-duty servicemen would lead two hundred thousand antiwar demonstrators on a seven-mile march through San Francisco to Golden Gate Park. The same day, April 24, 1971, half a million antiwar protesters assembled in Washington to besiege our government.[29] They were led by a thousand Vietnam veterans who for a week had been conducting Operation Dewey Canyon III, lobbying and testifying to Congress while camping on the Mall in defiance of a Justice Department injunction. The Nixon administration had hastily constructed a wall around the Capitol building to protect it from the vets. On April 23, almost one thousand Vietnam veterans lined up, and one by one hurled their medals—thousands of medals—over the fence. There were many Purple Hearts, Silver Stars, and Bronze Stars and a few Distinguished Service Crosses. Most men made brief statements including "Power to the People!" and "If we have to fight again, it will be to take these steps." One badly wounded career sergeant angrily shouted, "This is for my brothers," as he threw away nine Purple Hearts, a Bronze Star, a Silver Star, and a Distinguished Service Cross.[30]

Two months later, the *Armed Forces Journal* published "The Collapse of the Armed Forces," which concluded: "By every conceivable indicator, our army that now remains in Vietnam is in a state approaching collapse, with individual units avoiding or having refused combat, murdering their officers and noncommissioned officers, drug-ridden, and dispirited where not near mutinous."[31] What could President Nixon do?

His invasion of Cambodia in 1970 had ignited massive protests, including a nationwide strike during which National Guard soldiers killed four and wounded nine Kent State University students, further convulsing the nation and its armed forces. He had started withdrawing ground troops in mid-1969 and was relying increasingly on the Vietnamese to do the fighting.

The first big test of the "Vietnamization" policy came with Operation Dewey Canyon II in early 1971 when tens of thousands of Vietnamese troops, with U.S. assistance, invaded Laos. The result was a military catastrophe, with the Vietnamese soldiers fleeing in panic, and another giant antiwar wave at home, including such droplets as my speeches at Stanford for which I was fired. The U.S. poured even more massive amounts of money and arms into South Vietnam, giving the Saigon government overwhelming superiority in numbers, firepower, and modern weapons, including the world's fourth largest air force. But in the spring of 1972, any remaining belief that the people of the south wanted to defend "South Vietnam" from their compatriots in the north evaporated when the Democratic Republic of Vietnam (DRV) launched a major offensive that routed Saigon's army, despite all its numerical and technological advantages, and captured large sections of the south. All that saved Saigon's forces from total collapse was U.S. airpower.

"Vietnamization" did accomplish one thing. Richard Nixon fulfilled Lyndon Johnson's electoral promise of not using "American boys to do the job Asian boys should do"—because now the American "boys" were unwilling to do the job. So by mid-1972, U.S. combat forces in Vietnam had been reduced to almost the same number as when Johnson had made that promise in 1964.

To retain some kind of military credibility in this critical period of the negotiations that had been going on since early 1968, Washington would have to rely almost entirely on aerial bombing. Round-the-clock bombing was supposed to come from a flotilla of Seventh Fleet aircraft carriers massed in the Gulf of Tonkin, bringing warplanes closer than the fighter-bombers based in Thailand and the B-52s on Guam to targets all along the narrow land of Vietnam. This strategy was torpedoed by a massive antiwar movement among the sailors, who combined escalating protests and rebellions with a widespread campaign of sabotage.

Unlike the fraggings, sabotage, and mutinies by the ground troops, these sailors' actions cannot be written off as attempts to avoid being killed or wounded. Their ships were never in any danger of enemy attack. The movement against the Vietnam War, begun by hundreds of American sailors in the fall of 1945, was now being spearheaded by tens of thousands of American sailors. Back in 1945 the sailors were dismayed by American participation in imperialism and believed that their petition to Congress and the president might prompt the nation to return to its ideals. The sailors in the 1970s, far beyond such illusions, resorted to direct action. Their movement was led by black sailors, many of whom identified with the Vietnamese as fellow victims of American imperialism.

In late 1971, the sailors' antiwar activities coalesced into a coherent movement called SOS (Stop Our Ships / Support Our Sailors) that emerged on three of the gigantic aircraft carriers crucial to the Tonkin Gulf strategy: the *Constellation*, the *Coral Sea*, and the *Kitty Hawk*. On these three ships alone that fall, thousands of crewmembers signed antiwar petitions, published onboard antiwar newspapers, and supported the dozens of crew members who refused to board for Vietnam duty.[32]

In March 1972, when the aircraft carrier *Midway* received orders to leave San Francisco Bay for Vietnam, its sailing was delayed by a wave of protests and sabotage that swept the ship.[33] In June, the attack carrier *Ranger* was ordered to sail from San Diego to Vietnam. The Naval Investigative Service reported a large-scale clandestine movement among the crew and at least twenty acts of sabotage, culminating in engine destruction that delayed the ship's sailing until mid-November. In December, the *Ranger*, all repaired now, finally made it to the Gulf of Tonkin, where it was immediately disabled by a deliberately set fire.[34] The Navy admitted this was the sixth major disaster on a Seventh Fleet carrier since October 1. In July, the aircraft carrier *Forrestal* was prevented from sailing by a major fire deliberately set by crewmen.[35] In September and October, the crew of the *Coral Sea*, which had been publishing the antiwar newspaper *We Are Everywhere* for a year, staged renewed protests, with over a thousand crewmen signing a petition to "Stop Our Ship." The *Coral Sea* was forced to return to San Francisco Bay, where crew members held a national press conference and helped organize support rallies and other demonstrations. Almost a hundred crew members, including several officers, refused Vietnam service and jumped ship.[36] In September, crew members of the aircraft carrier *Ticonderoga* organized their own "Stop It Now" movement, and Navy intelligence tried unsuccessfully to break up the large SOS movement on the showpiece carrier *Enterprise*.[37]

When the *Kitty Hawk*, fresh from an eight-month tour off Vietnam (during which the crew published the antiwar newspaper *Kitty Litter*), was ordered back to Vietnam in October, African American members of the crew led a major rebellion, fought hand-to-hand battles with the Marines sent to break up their meeting, and reduced the ship to a chaos of internal fighting for hours. Four days later, fighting spread to the *Kitty Hawk*'s oiler, the *Hassayampa*. The *Kitty Hawk* was forced to retire to San Diego, from whence it sailed to San Francisco in early January, where it underwent a "six-month refitting job."[38] The sailors' movement had thus removed this major aircraft carrier from the war.

The House Armed Services Committee, investigating hundreds of reports of "successful acts of sabotage," concluded that the rebellion on the *Kitty Hawk* had been precipitated by the orders to return to Vietnam, orders mandated because two other aircraft carriers had been disabled: "This rescheduling apparently was due to the incidents of sabotage aboard her sister ships *Ranger* and *Forrestal*."[39]

Rebellion had been brewing on the *Constellation* since April 1971, when a petition by fifteen hundred of its crew members demanded that Jane Fonda's antiwar show *FTA* be allowed to perform on its flight deck. Turned down by the ship's commander, thousands of the sailors attended her show on May 15 in San Diego.[40]

In October and early November of 1972, incidents of sabotage and an open revolt on the *Constellation* made it return to San Diego, where 130 sailors prevented the ship's departure for two months by refusing to reboard and staging a militant demonstration on shore, thus forcing their discharge from the crew. The media called this a "racial outbreak," but the picture in the *San Francisco Chronicle* captioned "The dissident sailors raised their fists in the black power salute" shows mainly white sailors with upraised arms and clenched fists.[41]

The *Constellation* arrived in San Diego on November 9. I got there on the morning of November 10. I was there in public until late that night, a fact that would save me from spending fifteen or more years in federal prison. In the afternoon and evening, I gave scheduled talks at the University of California, San Diego, and San Diego State University. I ate a potluck supper at Liberty House, where I gave another talk. That night I was taken around to bars and movement centers to meet sailors from the three aircraft carriers—the supercarriers *Kitty Hawk* and *Constellation* plus the *Ranger*—that had been forced out of the war by their crews. I learned about the antiwar—and increasingly revolutionary—newspaper published on board each vessel. I briefly addressed hundreds of men from the carriers and their attendant vessels. What they were now doing in San Diego was getting together to build a fleet-wide organization.

The *Constellation*—one of the two carriers that had launched the August 5, 1964, attacks on North Vietnam—was now not even able to sail from San Diego for Vietnam until January 5, 1973, three weeks before the Paris Peace Accords were signed. The rebellious crewmen had in effect permanently removed another major aircraft carrier from the war.[42] Not since Pearl Harbor had the U.S. Navy been so crippled, and then it was by an enemy that could be defeated in combat.

Nixon was left with only one military option: using B-52s to rain massive amounts of bombs indiscriminately on the cities and countryside of North Vietnam. This was the theory of "strategic" bombing (developed by Italian Fascist admiral Giulio Douhet, Billy Mitchell, and British general Arthur "Bomber" Harris) to make a nation capitulate by terror bombing its whole population. The giant eight-engine B-52s had previously been used mainly for carpet bombing the countryside and attempting to burn down the rain forests of South Vietnam, the country we were supposedly trying to save from invasion. Now they would be turned loose on the people of North Vietnam.

On December 18, Nixon launched Linebacker II, better known as the Christmas bombing, a twelve-day all-out bombardment of North Vietnam, with concentration on the cities of Hanoi and Haiphong. Accompanied by fighter-bombers, the B-52s flew 729 sorties, unloading their bombs in strings two miles long. There was massive damage to structures, but civilian casualties, though serious, were limited by the prior evacuation of Hanoi, ingenious concrete bomb shelters, and effective air defense.

According to the Nixon administration and mythmakers ever since, Linebacker II forced the North Vietnamese to sign the Paris Accords. But that treaty signed by Richard Nixon in January 1973 was in fact a total capitulation to terms Washington had been offered throughout the war, with the addition of a secret pledge of several billion dollars to help undo all the devastation the United States had inflicted. In this treaty the United States finally recognized precisely what it had been attempting to deny by every possible means since 1954: Vietnam was and is one country, not two. Furthermore, the agreement incorporated *word for word* practically every demand of the "Ten-Point Program" put forward by the National Liberation Front as its initial negotiating position in May 1969.[43]

The Vietnamese call the Christmas bombing "America's Dien Bien Phu in the air," comparing it to France's defeat in its last desperate strategic move in 1954. In each case, their imperial enemy threw its best forces against Vietnam—and lost. The Pentagon admitted losing twenty-one B-52s and thirteen fighter-bombers, while Hanoi's claims of thirty-four B-52s and forty-seven fighter-bombers were possibly closer to the truth. At least 121 airmen were lost, including 44 captured, ironically increasing by 8 percent the number of U.S. POWs held in North Vietnam.[44]

Jane got up early on December 19. Just after dawn she was reading the *San Francisco Chronicle*'s front-page story about the bombing of North Vietnam while eating breakfast, when our dog started barking and the doorbell rang. She saw through the front-door peephole a group of men in suits clustered at the door. She ran down the hall to our bedroom shouting, "Bruce, I think the FBI is here." We had been expecting this ever since I had been fired in January. "Let them in," I said as I jumped out of bed. She got back to the front door just as it was being kicked open.

More than a dozen men poured through the door with leveled handguns and shotguns, yelling "FBI! Don't make a move! Put your hands up." As Jane stepped back, one of the suits shoved her down onto the couch. Another pointed a shotgun at her chest and snarled, "Where's your father?" Jane was then, like me, thirty-eight.

"It's her husband, Jim," whispered a guy behind him, looking embarrassed at this breach in movie-style G-man prowess.

A bunch of them charged down the hall to the bedrooms. Robert, then nine years old, was asleep inside the first room they reached. One agent threw open his door, pointed a shotgun at his head, and shouted, "Stay in bed! Go back to sleep!" Sixteen-year-old Karen was in the shower and at first didn't hear the FBI banging on the bathroom door and bellowing, "FBI! FBI! Open up!" She finally stepped out, still wet, her shower cap on, a towel hastily wrapped around her, and faced a leveled shotgun. The commotion awakened Gretchen, then fourteen. She grabbed a pair of jeans and pulled them on, but was still bare from the waist up. As she picked up a shirt, one of them pointed a shotgun at her chest and shouted, "Put that down!" Two of them forced her to stand topless against the wall.

Other agents ran down the hall yelling, "Franklin, don't move! You're under arrest! Put your hands up! Come out of that room!" I had pulled on a pair of slacks. Through my mind flashed the images of Fred Hampton and Mark Clark murdered in just such a raid in Chicago—Fred riddled with bullets and shotgun slugs while still in bed—and Bobby Hutton, gunned down in Oakland while surrendering with his hands over his head. If I walked out of the room toward them, they could claim I was making an "aggressive" move. If I stepped away, they could say I was trying to escape through the window. So I raised my hands and stood still.

They grabbed my arms, pulled me into the hall, shoved me face first up against the wall, handcuffed my arms behind my back, and searched me. I had been arrested a few times before and have been since. This one was scary, right out of that nightmare world of the arbitrary secret police raid.

"What's the charge?" I asked, in a voice as calm as I could manage.

"Harboring a federal fugitive," said a voice behind my head.

I felt a mixture of relief and apprehension. This was one crime I knew I hadn't committed. I almost asked "Who?" but checked myself, figuring that this might sound as if I had harbored so many federal fugitives that I didn't know which one they meant.

A three-car FBI motorcade drove me in handcuffs to San Francisco, where I was booked, jailed, arraigned, and released on bail. When I got to read the indictment, I learned that my crime had been committed in Palo Alto, at 7 P.M. on November 10, where and when I had given false ID papers and a thousand dollars to an escaped convict, who had been busted out of prison in a raid during which a prison guard had been murdered. The sole witness was the convict. How could I possibly disprove such an allegation? I couldn't even recall where I had been on November 10, much less at 7 P.M. But knowing that the FBI had made several other attempts to frame or entrap me, we kept documentary evidence of my daily whereabouts in a bank's safe-deposit box. Opening the box with trepidation, I was elated to discover that I had been 476 miles from Palo Alto, no doubt committing more serious crimes by conspiring in San Diego with those sailors to support their revolutionary activities. On January 3, 1973, the charge against me was dismissed for lack of evidence. The Justice Department then failed to win an indictment of me from a San Francisco grand jury, and then later tried and failed again before a Las Vegas grand jury. Eventually the convict was forced to admit under oath that he had lied as part of the attempt to frame me.[45]

When I started catching up on the Christmas bombing, I was amazed to learn that antiwar resistance in the Air Force had actually spread to my alma mater, the Strategic Air Command. Individual pilots—one with more than two hundred previous combat missions—refused on moral grounds to participate in the bombing.[46] After the first nights of heavy losses, many of the B-52 crews voiced their opposition to the kinds of risks they were being asked to take in a war that had obviously been decided. The B-52s were also menaced by antiwar actions within the supersecret 6990th Air Force Security Service based on Okinawa, whose mission was eavesdropping on North Vietnamese air defense communications in order to give timely warnings to the B-52s. They staged a work stoppage verging on open mutiny, during which there were cheers whenever a B-52 was shot down. Some of the men were later court-martialed under stringent security.[47]

The movement of tens of millions of ordinary American citizens spearheaded by soldiers, sailors, fliers, and veterans finally helped to end the thirty-year war with a recognition that Vietnam could be neither divided nor conquered by the United States. No, it was not Vietnam but the United States that ended up divided by America's war. And the division cut even deeper than the armed forces, biting down into the core of the secret government itself.

When members of the intelligence establishment joined the antiwar movement, they inflicted damage that has outlasted the war. The perfidy of the Central Intelligence Agency in Vietnam was revealed by one of its highest agents in South Vietnam, Ralph McGehee, author of *Deadly Deceits: My Twenty-Five Years in the C.I.A.*[48] Philip Agee decided in 1971 to publish what eventually became *Inside the Company: CIA Diary* because "[n]ow more than ever exposure of CIA methods could help American people understand how we got into Vietnam and how our other Vietnams are germinating wherever the CIA is at work."[49] Daniel Ellsberg's 1971 leak of the top-secret Pentagon Papers exposed all the official narratives as a putrid swamp of lies.

Interviewed in the Oscar-winning 1974 documentary *Hearts and Minds*, Ellsberg outlined the history of the Vietnam War by tracing the "lies" told by Presidents Truman, Eisenhower, Kennedy, Johnson, and Nixon. "The American public was lied to month by month by each of these five administrations," he explained. "It's a tribute to the American public that their leaders perceived they had to be lied to." Then he paused and added, "It's no tribute to us that it was so easy to fool the public."

The end of the war did not end the lies, but it did bring the longest period since 1941 when America was not directly fighting or overtly sponsoring at least one war: 1975–1978, that time when everybody was agreeing on "no more Vietnams." Then in 1979 Washington began secretly supporting the war being waged in Afghanistan by the jihadist "mujahedeen," President Jimmy Carter's "freedom fighters," thus engendering and empowering a potent enemy of America in a Forever War that would soon replace the Cold War.

The internal American war over the Vietnam War did not end in 1973, or 1975 when the U.S. client government was swept away by the Vietnamese people. By 1980, the history of the war was being systematically rewritten and reimaged as a "noble cause," the term first used by Ronald Reagan in the August presidential campaign speech that also first gave us the term "Vietnam syndrome":

> For too long, we have lived with the "Vietnam Syndrome." Much of that syndrome has been created by the North Vietnamese aggressors. . . . Over and over they told us for nearly 10 years that we were the aggressors bent on imperialistic conquests. . . . It is time we recognized that ours was, in truth, a noble cause. A small country newly free from colonial rule sought our help in establishing self-rule and the means of self-defense against a totalitarian neighbor bent on conquest.[50]

The Noble Cause story, this tall tale of how America had generously and heroically tried to rescue the democratic nation of the south from the invasion by the evil Communist nation of North Vietnam, was designed as a necessary cultural foundation for new imperialist wars.

As soon as Reagan was inaugurated in 1981, he presided over a frenzied rewriting and reimaging of history, a cultural brain-wipe to induce national amnesia.

I was alarmed and angered by this attack on all the painful truths and lessons the war had taught us at such great cost to its millions of victims in Vietnam, Laos, and Cambodia, as well as to us. No one, as far as I could determine, was teaching a college course on the war. I decided to inaugurate one, which I listed as a "special topics" course (thus not requiring faculty approval) in the Rutgers Newark Schedule of Courses for the upcoming fall 1980 semester. I was hoping that at least twelve students would enroll, the minimum needed for an undergraduate course. Instead, so many students signed up that I had to ask the registrar for a lecture hall and two smaller section rooms for discussion.

While feverishly working at home to change the syllabus from a seminar to a lecture course and trying to find appropriate books, since of course there were no appropriate texts back then, I heard the phone ringing. It was David Hosford, the Dean of the School of Arts and Humanities, i.e., my boss. After a couple of pleasantries, he said, "I see you are giving a course on the Vietnam War."

"Yes," I said, thinking, oh no, here we go again.

"And I see that the course is quite overenrolled."

"Yes," I said, wondering whether Rutgers would somehow follow the lead of Stanford in dealing with me.

"So," Dean Hosford went on, "I was wondering whether you would like some extra funds to bring in speakers or show films or whatever you wish."

Wow! How did I get so fortunate as to end up at the Newark campus of Rutgers, the State University of New Jersey?

Thus from 1980 until my retirement in 2016, I taught Vietnam and America as an undergraduate course every year and as a graduate seminar every three years.[51] I sometimes found myself saying in public, "The State of New Jersey pays me to teach what I was firing for saying at Stanford." Over these three and a half decades, these courses became magnets, first for military reservists and others in programs where tuition was paid by the military, and later for an increasing flow of veterans of our various wars. The 9/11 attacks brought a dramatic change in the composition of the classroom when four reservists, who were dutifully performing their weekend training sessions, were suddenly called to active duty in the middle of the semester, forcing them to complete the course from Afghanistan. Many of the veterans were severely traumatized by combat. Most of these vets were quite reluctant to speak in class, but some were eager to talk privately with me, and many wrote powerful essays.

One African American Marine reservist remained imperturbably gung-ho throughout every class, test, and writing assignment. Several years later, he inexplicably turned up at my office and asked if he could speak with me. He was so visibly angry that I was a bit concerned about my safety. Then he told his story. His unit had been one of the first to engage in combat in Operation Desert Storm, our 1991 invasion of Iraq. "There we were," he said, "dying from the heat in our full chemical warfare outfits. It was over 110 degrees. Our officers kept lecturing us about Saddam's WMDs and telling us that we could be hit any minute by his poison gas. Then one day a British unit marched by wearing shorts. We knew right then that we were being lied to. So we stripped off those suits and left them lying there out in the desert."

But that wasn't the only cause of his fury. The only combat opposition they met came from occasional sniper fire. The rules of engagement didn't allow them to fire back unless they had a verifiable enemy as a target. "So," he fumed, "we could get killed for nothing, just for a bunch of lies, without ever fighting back." I was just listening. Finally he got to the decision, which he evidently thought would please me. "I've had it with the Marines," he said. "As soon as I can get out, I'm going to join the Air Force."

In 1985, Rambo asked, "Do we get to win this time?" as he headed back to Vietnam to free all those abandoned American POWs. His next heroic mission, in 1988, was in Afghanistan, where he helped lead the glorious battles of the triumphant jihadists. On March 1, 1991, at the conclusion of Operation Desert Storm, President George H. W. Bush would boast, "By God, we've kicked the Vietnam syndrome once and for all."[52] On May 1, 2003, his son President George W. Bush would dramatically arrive in a jet on an aircraft carrier and, posing in the flight suit he had worn as the jet's passenger, proclaim under a huge "MISSION ACCOMPLISHED" banner: "Major combat operations in Iraq have ended. In the Battle of Iraq, the United States and our allies have prevailed. . . . In this battle, we have fought for the cause of liberty, and for the peace of the world."[53] But America's last real victory celebration was on August 14, 1945, the very same day when Vietnam launched the August Revolution.

We cannot understand what America is becoming today without comprehending how our nation could have simultaneously produced both as shameful an abomination as the Vietnam War and as admirable an achievement as the decades-long movement that helped defeat it. When we figure that out, maybe, just maybe, we will find our way out of the Forever War.

ACKNOWLEDGMENTS

Because this is a book I've been trying to write for decades, pieces of it have appeared in earlier forms over the years: Some of the autobiographical accounts appeared in a more primitive form in *Back Where You Came From* (New York: Harper's Magazine Press, 1975). Parts of chapter 1 appeared in an earlier form in "American Memory of the Vietnam War in the Epoch of the Forever War," *Los Angeles Review of Books*, July 16, 2014. Parts of chapter 2 appeared in an earlier form in *War Stars: The Superweapon and the American Imagination*, expanded ed. (Amherst: University of Massachusetts Press, 2008) and "Hiroshima, Nagasaki, and American Militarism; or, How We Lost World War II," review essay on Paul Ham's *Hiroshima Nagasaki: The Real Story of the Atomic Bombings and Their Aftermath*, *Los Angeles Review of Books*, August 3, 2014. Earlier versions of chapter 8 appeared in Mary Susannah Robbins, ed., *Against the Vietnam War: Writings by Activists* (Syracuse, NY: Syracuse University Press, 1999), and *Vietnam and Other American Fantasies* (Amherst: University of Massachusetts Press, 2000).

Gretchen Franklin used her enviable writing skills and brilliant logic to vastly improve the draft manuscript. Carolyn Karcher and Martin Karcher read the entire manuscript and gave many valuable suggestions. Karen Franklin's prodigious memory helped keep me from wandering off course. Robert Franklin was an invaluable consultant, thanks in part to his vast and insightful knowledge of military history. Leslie Mitchner, who in her illustrious editorial career has helped create so many invaluable books, was the perfect dream editor of this book. Whatever success this book may have will owe much to the outstanding work of Lisa Banning, Jennifer Blanc-Tal, Courtney Brach, Jeremy Grainger, Micah Kleit, Elisabeth Maselli, and Victoria Verhowsky of Rutgers University Press, and Melody Negron and Judith Riotto of Westchester Publishing Services.

I am profoundly grateful to Rutgers University, the only college or university in the United States willing to hire me and thus end my years of being blacklisted, and to my colleagues, friends, and students at the Rutgers Newark campus for four thrilling decades of truly collegial and fulfilling life. As always, my greatest debt is to Jane Morgan Franklin, the love of my life, who contributed to this book in more ways than can ever be acknowledged and who has always led the way in trying to make this a better world.

NOTES

CHAPTER 1   THE LAST VICTORY?

1. Robert J. Samuelson, "Syria and the Myth That Americans Are 'War Weary,'" *Washington Post*, September 4, 2013; William Kristol, "War-Weariness as an Excuse," *Weekly Standard*, March 24, 2014; Condoleezza Rice, "Will America Heed the Wake-Up Call of Ukraine?," *Washington Post*, March 7, 2014; Daniel Henninger, "American Fatigue Syndrome," *Wall Street Journal*, March 20, 2014; Bill Brockman, "Our Warriors Earned Weariness; Most of You Haven't," letter, *Wall Street Journal*, March 25, 2014.

2. "Poll: Most Say U.S. Doesn't Have a Responsibility in Ukraine," CBS News, March 25, 2014, 7:00 A.M.; "Syria Poll Finds Airstrike Opposition Rising Dramatically," *Huffington Post*, September 10, 2013; "Syria Strike Poll Finds Support for Military Action Keeps Falling," *Huffington Post*, September 11, 2013.

3. "Troops Oppose Strikes on Syria by 3-1 Margin," *Military Times*, September 12, 2013, http://www.militarytimes.com/interactive/article/20130911/NEWS/309110009/Troops-oppose-strikes-Syria-by-3-1-margin, accessed March 28, 2014.

4. "America as Science Fiction: 1939," *Science-Fiction Studies* 9 (March 1982): 38–50. Also in *Coordinates: Placing Science Fiction and Fantasy*, ed. George Slusser, Eric Rabkin, and Robert Scholes (Carbondale: Southern Illinois University Press, 1983), 70–80.

5. Numerous books and articles have been written about this "forgotten war." Especially well researched and provocative is Stuart D. Goldman, *NOMONHAN, 1939: The Red Army's Victory That Shaped World War II* (Annapolis, MD: U.S. Naval Institute Press, 2012). Goldman has a valuable summary of the book's argument at http://thediplomat.com/2012/08/the-forgotten-soviet-japanese-war-of-1939, accessed December 8, 2016.

6. Michael S. Sherry, *The Rise of American Air Power: The Creation of Armageddon* (New Haven, CT: Yale University Press, 1987), 102.

7. Franklin D. Roosevelt, "The President Appeals to Great Britain, France, Italy, Germany, and Poland to Refrain from Air Bombing of Civilians," *The Public Papers and Addresses of Franklin D. Roosevelt: 1939 Volume* (New York: Macmillan, 1941).

8. For the early history of nuclear weapons in science fiction, see chap. 2 of H. Bruce Franklin, *War Stars: The Superweapon and the American Imagination*, rev. and exp. ed. (Amherst: University of Massachusetts Press, 2008).

9. "Drop That Post!" *Saturday Evening Post*, September 8, 1945, 8.

10. "Writer Charges U.S. with Curb on Science," *New York Times*, August 14, 1941. For a discussion of nuclear weapons in American culture from 1939 to August 1945, see chap. 8, "Don't Worry, It's Only Science Fiction," in Franklin, *War Stars*.

11. "Statement by the President Announcing the Use of the A-Bomb at Hiroshima," August 6, 1945, http://www.presidency.ucsb.edu/ws/?pid=12169, accessed January 3, 2018.

12. Ho Chi Minh, *Selected Works*, 4 vols. (Hanoi: Foreign Languages Publishing House, 1960–1962), 3:17–21.

13. Michael Gillen, "Roots of Opposition: The Critical Response to U.S. Indochina Policy, 1945–1954" (unpublished dissertation, New York University, 1991), 106–107.

14. Archimedes L. A. Patti, *Why Viet Nam? Prelude to America's Albatross* (Berkeley: University of California Press, 1980), 325.

15. Gillen, "Roots of Opposition," 117–122.

16. "Transcript of the Proceedings at the Meeting in Celebration of the Second Anniversary of the Independence of the Republic of Viet-Nam, 1947," typescript, Cornell University Library. Tara McAuliff unearthed this document and provided me with a copy.

17. Martin Luther King Jr., sermon delivered at Riverside Church in Manhattan, April 4, 1967, authorized version, slightly condensed for publication by Dr. King, in *Vietnam and America: A Documented History*, rev. and enl. ed., ed. Marvin Gettleman, Jane Franklin, Marilyn Young, and H. Bruce Franklin (New York: Grove Press, 1995), 317.

18. Gettleman et al., *Vietnam and America*, 52.

19. Senator Ernest Gruening and Herbert Wilton Beaser, *Vietnam Folly* (Washington, DC: National Press, 1968), 100–105.

20. Gruening and Beaser, *Vietnam Folly*, 105.

21. Gillen, "Roots of Opposition," 379–383, 402. As Gillen notes, some sources incorrectly attribute this speech to Lyndon Johnson.

22. Gillen, "Roots of Opposition," 402.

23. The documentary record of this history is contained in Gettleman et al., *Vietnam and America*.

24. Ronald Reagan, "Restoring the Margin of Safety," speech to the Veterans of Foreign Wars convention, Chicago, August 18, 1980, https://www.reaganlibrary.gov/sites/default/files/archives/reference/8.18.80.html, accessed January 3, 2018.

25. For my extended exploration of the gender issue in the POW/MIA movies, see *M.I.A., or Mythmaking in America* (New Brunswick, NJ: Rutgers University Press, 1993), 140–156.

26. John Stauber and Sheldon Rampton, *Toxic Sludge Is Good for You: Lies, Damn Lies and the Public Relations Industry* (Monroe, ME: Common Courage Press, 2002), chap. 10.

27. George H. W. Bush, "Remarks to the American Legislative Exchange Council," March 1, 1991, http://www.presidency.ucsb.edu/ws/?pid=19351, accessed January 3, 2018.

28. Survivors' stories, including that of Miyagawa, are now available on the internet. His is at http://www.youtube.com/watch?v=uyIoLJWrZog, viewed April 20, 2014.

29. "Remarks by the President at the Commemoration Ceremony of the 50th Anniversary of the Vietnam War," news release, May 28, 2012, http://www.whitehouse.gov/the-press-office/2012/05/28/remarks-president-commemoration-ceremony-50th-anniversary-vietnam-war, accessed June 8, 2014. The official proclamation can be found at http://www.whitehouse.gov/the-press-office/2012/05/25/presidential-proclamation-commemoration-50th-anniversary-vietnam-war, accessed June 8, 2014.

CHAPTER 2   THE BOMBS BURSTING IN AIR, OR HOW WE LOST WORLD WAR II

1. "Statement by the President Announcing the Use of the A-Bomb at Hiroshima," August 6, 1945, Public Papers Harry S. Truman, 1945–1953, Harry S. Truman Presidential Library, https://www.trumanlibrary.org/publicpapers/index.php?pid=100, accessed January 24, 2018.

2. For an extended analysis of racist propaganda and the thirst for vengeance in the bombing of Japan, see John Dower, *War without Mercy: Race and Power in the Pacific War* (New York: Pantheon, 1986), chaps. 4–7, and Michael S. Sherry, *Rise of American Air Power: The Creation of Armageddon* (New Haven, CT: Yale University Press, 1987), 245–251.

3. See my in-depth discussion of responses in chap. 10 of *War Stars: The Superweapon and the American Imagination*, rev. and exp. ed. (Amherst: University of Massachusetts Press, 2008).

4. Leo Szilard, *Leo Szilard: His Version of the Facts*, ed. Spencer R. Weart and Gertrud Weiss Szilard (Cambridge, MA: MIT Press, 1978), 211. Leslie Groves, head of the Manhattan Project, never forwarded the petition.

5. Robert H. Ferrell, ed., *Off the Record: The Private Papers of Harry S. Truman* (New York: Harper & Row, 1980), 53; Robert L. Messer, "New Evidence on Truman's Decision," *Bulletin of the Atomic Scientists* 41 (August 1985): 50–56.

6. Historian Tsuyoshi Hasegawa, whose fluency in Japanese, Russian, and English enabled him to study all the relevant archival records, conclusively proves and effectively dramatizes this race in *Racing the Enemy: Stalin, Truman, and the Surrender of Japan* (Cambridge, MA: Harvard University Press, 2005).

7. Hasegawa, *Racing the Enemy*, 146–147, details the changes in the texts.

8. Hasegawa, *Racing the Enemy*, 152.

9. Paul Ham, *Hiroshima Nagasaki: The Real Story of the Atomic Bombings and Their Aftermath* (New York: St. Martin's Press, 2011), 258. Using Tokyo time, Ham dates the broadcast as July 26, which was July 25 in the United States.

10. Truman's repeated claims that Japan had promptly rejected the Potsdam Proclamation are false. There was no official response because the proclamation was never submitted to the government. The prime minister's response to a radio reporter was "No comment," misinterpreted in English. See Kazuo Kawai, "Mokusatsu, Japan's Response to the Potsdam Declaration," *Pacific Historical Review* 19, no. 4 (November 1950): 409–414.

11. Ham, *Hiroshima Nagasaki*, 199–201.

12. Ham, *Hiroshima Nagasaki*, 474–477.

13. Hasegawa, *Racing the Enemy*, 198.

14. Hasegawa, *Racing the Enemy*, 204; Ham, *Hiroshima Nagasaki*, 380–381.

15. Hasegawa, *Racing the Enemy*, 234.

16. Hasegawa, *Racing the Enemy*, 237.

17. P. M. S. Blackett, *Fear, War, and the Bomb: Military and Political Consequences of Atomic Energy* (New York: Whittlesey House, 1948), 139.

18. Examples of earlier fine research and well-documented scholarship that definitely make this case include Gar Alperovitz, *Atomic Diplomacy: Hiroshima and Potsdam*, exp. and updated ed. (New York: Penguin, 1985); Ronald W. Clark, *The Greatest Power on*

Earth: The International Race for Nuclear Supremacy (New York: Harper and Row, 1980); Gregg Herken, *The Winning Weapon: The Atomic Bomb in the Cold War 1945–1950* (New York: Vintage Books, 1982); Robert Messer, *The End of an Alliance: James F. Byrnes, Roosevelt, Truman and the Origins of the Cold War* (Chapel Hill: University of North Carolina Press, 1982); Peter Wyden, *Day One: Before Hiroshima and After* (New York: Simon and Schuster, 1984); Richard Rhodes, *The Making of the Atomic Bomb* (New York: Simon and Schuster, 1986). In this chapter I have relied on twenty-first-century works that probe even deeper into the Japanese, Soviet, and American archives.

19. Leo Szilard, "A Personal History of the Atomic Bomb," *University of Chicago Roundtable*, No. 601, September 25, 1949, 14–15.

20. Herken, *The Winning Weapon*, 17–18.

21. Ham, *Hiroshima Nagasaki*, 472–473.

22. This cultural history is the main subject of *War Stars*, where I document Truman's reading of science fiction that featured American presidents who use the ultimate superweapon to bring about perpetual peace.

23. Roaul Drapeau, "The Norden Bombsight: Accurate Beyond Belief?," Warfare History Network, July 21, 2016, http://warfarehistorynetwork.com/daily/wwii/the-norden -bombsight-accurate-beyond-belief, accessed December 19, 2016.

24. Chapter 5 in Robert M. Neer's *Napalm: An American Biography* (Cambridge, MA: Belknap Press of Harvard University Press, 2013), offers a bone-chilling narrative of the firebombing of Japan, including pictures of the model Japanese homes.

25. Wesley Frank Craven and James Lea Cate, eds., *The Army Air Forces in World War 11*, 7 vols. (Chicago: University of Chicago Press, 1948–1958), 5:620.

26. Ronald Reagan, with Richard G. Hubler, *Where's the Rest of Me?* (New York: Elsevier-Dutton, 1965), 118–119.

27. "Barcelona Horrors," *Time*, March 28, 1938, 13; quoted in George E. Hopkins's superb "Bombing and the American Conscience during World War II," *Historian* 28 (May 1966): 451–473, which shows almost universal American condemnation of bombing cities prior to 1938.

28. Kathy Sawyer, "Venus Spacecraft Finds Signs of Active Volcano, 2nd Probe Has Photo Session with Asteroid," *Washington Post*, October 30, 1991.

29. The resolution can be found in Edward T. Linenthal and Tom Engelhardt, eds., *History Wars: The Enola Gay and Other Battles for the American Past* (New York: Metropolitan Books, 1996), 260, a volume containing the history of the Smithsonian battle and incisive essays by eight leading scholars.

30. "Dole Aims a Barrage at 'Intellectual Elites,'" *New York Times*, September 5, 1995.

31. The 1951 civil defense film starring Bert the Turtle is available on YouTube. American culture's response to the atomic threat is projected brilliantly in the 1982 documentary masterpiece *The Atomic Cafe*.

CHAPTER 3   NEW CONNECTIONS

1. Anyone working in this area owes a big debt to Amiri Baraka's seminal book, *Blues People: Negro Music in White America* (New York: William Morrow), published in 1963 when his name was LeRoi Jones.

2. I discuss the history of this front in the culture wars in *Prison Literature in America: The Victim as Criminal and Artist*, exp. ed. (New York: Oxford University Press, 1989), xxvi–xxxi, 73–98.

CHAPTER 4   WORKING FOR COMMUNISTS DURING THE KOREAN WAR

1. James F. Schnabel, *United States Army in the Korean War: Policy and Direction; The First Year* (Washington, DC: Office of the Chief of Military History, United States Army, 1972), 8–11; Dean Rusk as told to Richard Rusk, *As I Saw It* (New York: W. W. Norton, 1990), 124. Rusk remembers the date of the line drawing as August 14, but here, as in many places in this book, his memory is faulty.

2. Rusk, *As I Saw It*.

3. Schnabel, *United States Army in the Korean War*.

4. Bruce Cumings, *The Korean War: A History* (New York: Modern Library, 2011), 104–107. This widely available paperback is essential reading and a fine updated introduction to Cumings's prodigious scholarship and cogent analysis, which have fundamentally changed our (and certainly my) knowledge and understanding of the history of Korea and the Korean War.

5. Central Intelligence Agency, "The Current Situation in Korea," ORE 15-48, March 18, 1948. The nine-page report can be downloaded from the CIA's online library at https://www.cia.gov/library/readingroom/docs/DOC_0000258335.pdf.

6. See the excellent and well-documented account in Cumings, *The Korean War*, 110–146.

7. I. F. Stone, *The Hidden History of the Korean War* (New York: Monthly Review Press, Second Modern Reader Paper Edition, 1971), 18. Originally published in 1952 after being rejected by twenty-eight publishers at the height of the Red Scare, Stone's volume, with its priceless information and piercing analysis, remains an essential read for anyone interested in the political history of the Korean War even though subsequent scholarship has of course contradicted some of his surmises.

8. MacArthur's statement, carried by an Associated Press dispatch of February 23, 1942, appeared in hundreds of U.S. newspapers. His words were later emblazoned on various posters for Russian War Relief.

9. Ellen Schrecker, *Many Are the Crimes: McCarthyism in America* (Princeton, NJ: Princeton University Press, 1998), 88–94.

10. Churchill's speech can be read at https://www.winstonchurchill.org/resources/speeches/1946-1963-elder-statesman/the-sinews-of-peace/ and can be heard at http://www.winstonchurchill.org/wp-content/uploads/1946/03/1946-03-05_BBC_Winston_Churchill_The_Sinews_Of_Peace.mp3; both accessed January 24, 2018.

11. In Greece, the British had been fighting since 1944 against the Communist-led partisans who had been waging successful war against the Italian Fascist and German Nazi armies that had invaded their homeland. But the British had to withdraw military resources needed for their struggle to retain their global empire. So they called on Washington to take over the fight. Although we were told that the Soviet Union was trying to conquer Greece, Stalin in fact had conceded Greece to the British sphere of

influence and was opposing Yugoslavia's military assistance to the partisans, thus leading to the split between Stalin and Tito, Yugoslavia's leader. U.S. intervention would lead to the victory of neo-Fascist forces that included many former collaborators with the Nazi occupiers. For a brief, incisive account of the tragic history of U.S. intervention in Greece, see William Blum, *Killing Hope: U.S. Military and CIA Interventions since World War II* (Monroe, ME: Common Courage Press, 1995), 34–38. As for Turkey, the only conflict was a diplomatic dispute over the right of Soviet warships to pass from the Black Sea through the Turkish Straits (the Bosporus and the Dardanelles) on the way to the Aegean Sea and the Mediterranean. The dispute was settled with minor changes to a 1936 treaty curtailing free passage of Black Sea nations' warships through the Turkish Straits.

12. David Caute, *The Great Fear: The Anti-Communist Purges under Truman and Eisenhower* (New York: Simon and Schuster, 1978) is the classic overview and a fine reference volume. Ellen Schrecker's *Many Are the Crimes* (Princeton: Princeton University Press, 1998) explores a variety of individual cases and gives an insightful analysis of how the anti-Communist repression crippled the labor movement and devastated American cultural and political life. Schrecker's *No Ivory Tower: McCarthyism and the Universities* (New York: Oxford University Press, 1986) is a definitive exploration of the repression's effects on higher education. In both of her volumes, Schrecker makes clear that McCarthy himself was a latecomer to McCarthyism.

13. "Remarks of Honorable J. Howard McGrath, Attorney General of the United States," to the Advertising Club of America of New York, April 19, 1950, https://www.justice.gov/sites/default/files/ag/legacy/2011/09/12/04-19-1950.pdf, accessed January 24, 2018.

14. Schrecker, *Many Are the Crimes*, 144.

15. Steven Casey, *Selling the Korean War: Propaganda, Politics, and Public Opinion 1950–1953* (New York: Oxford University Press, 2008), 35–36. This book is a fine political and cultural history of the various conflicting lines and tactics the Truman administration used to gain and maintain support for the war.

16. "Drive to End Korean War Is Begun by UN Troops in Northwestern Sector," *New York Times*, November 24, 1950.

17. "UN Forces Launch General Assault in West Korea to Close Vise on Reds; M'Arthur at Front, Aims to End War," *New York Times*, November 24, 1950.

18. "15-Mile Gain Made; Resistance Met at Only One Point on First Day of UN Offensive; M'Arthur Flies to Border," *New York Times*, November 25, 1950.

19. "China's Reds Stall U.N. Push in Korea; Aim to Split Front," *New York Times*, November 27, 1950.

20. General William Westmoreland, commander of U.S. and allied forces in Vietnam from 1964 to 1968, apparently held and applied such comic-book visions to the Vietnamese people as he expressed in that great 1974 documentary *Hearts and Minds*: "The Oriental doesn't put the same high price on life as does a Westerner. Life is plentiful. Life is cheap in the Orient."

21. Casey, *Selling the Korean War*, 205.

22. Casey, *Selling the Korean War*, 240.

23. See Charles S. Young's splendid book, *Name, Rank, and Serial Number: Exploiting Korean War POWs at Home and Abroad* (New York: Oxford University Press, 2014).

24. Schrecker, *Many Are the Crimes*, 191–192. Schrecker's account of the case is meticulously documented, and her analysis of its consequences is extremely insightful.

25. Schrecker, *Many Are the Crimes*, 194.

26. Schrecker, *Many Are the Crimes*, 198.

27. "Remarks of Honorable J. Howard McGrath, Attorney General of the United States," to the Advertising Club of America of New York, April 19, 1950.

28. For 1964–2012 results, ANES, http://www.electionstudies.org/nesguide/toptable /tab5a_2.htm; for 1958, University of Michigan, Center for Political Studies, http:// inside.sfuhs.org/dept/history/US_History_reader/Chapter14/polldata.pdf;for "Trust the Federal Government," 1958–2012, ANES, http://www.electionstudies.org /nesguide/toptable/tab5a_1.htm; all accessed January 23, 2017.

29. *New York Times*: "Far East Superfort Down in Japan Sea," June 15, 1952; "Oceanside Flier Missing," June 18, 1952; "Latvians Describe U.S. 1950 Loss," June 20, 1952; "Plane Incidents Listed: Three U. S. Aircraft Lost in Alleged Border Violations," August 2, 1952. Larry Tart and Robert Keefe, *The Price of Vigilance: Attacks on American Surveillance Flights* (New York: Ballantine, 2001), 15, 22–23.

30. Hanson Baldwin's article appeared in the Sunday Magazine section of the December 9, 1951, edition.

31. Stone, *Hidden History of the Korean War*, 338–343.

32. Martin Bauml Duberman, *Paul Robeson* (New York: Knopf, 1988), 338–342. The most authoritative known transcription of Robeson's remarks is the official French transcript of the proceedings; I use my very literal translation of the French as printed by Duberman, 686–687.

33. Jordan Goodman, *Paul Robeson: A Watched Man* (London: Verso, 2013), Kindle ed., Kindle locations 786–788. What Robeson actually said is still not entirely certain. Goodman has the widest range of reports.

34. Duberman, *Paul Robeson*, 389–403. Curiously, Duberman has no mention of the August 20 concert on Randall's Island.

35. Decades later, empowered by the wonders of twenty-first-century technology, I did locate the *New York Times* coverage, a tiny article titled "10,000 Attend Rally Opposed by V.F.W." buried on page 13 of the August 21, 1952, issue. The only mention of Robeson was a three-word sentence: "Paul Robeson sang."

36. Dwight D. Eisenhower, "I Shall Go to Korea" speech, Detroit, October 25, 1952, https://www.eisenhower.archives.gov/education/bsa/citizenship_merit_badge /speeches_national_historical_importance/i_shall_go_to_korea.pdf, accessed January 25, 2018.

CHAPTER 5   ON THE WATER FRONT

1. Fifty years later I discovered that *spuyten duyvil* also meant—at least according to Washington Irving's *A Knickerbocker's History of New York*—"in spite of the devil," because there the devil took the avatar of a giant menhaden, the title character of my

book *The Most Important Fish in the Sea: Menhaden and America* (Washington, DC: Island Press, 2007).

2. "One Dead, 24 Hurt as Flyer Jumps Rails at Bridgeport; One Dead, 24 Injured in Wreck at Bridgeport; 7 Cars of New Haven Flyer Plunge Thirty Feet," *New York Times*, July 15, 1955.

3. "Port Operations Leave Pennsy Head Gloomy," *New York Times*, October 2, 1970.

4. H. Bruce Franklin, "Plantation to Penitentiary," *Prison Literature in America: The Victim as Criminal and Artist*, exp. ed. (New York: Oxford University Press, 1989), 73–123; David Oshinsky, *Worse Than Slavery* (New York: Free Press Paperbacks, 1996), 57–60.

5. For the story of this conspiracy between the Navy and organized crime, the Navy's long cover-up, and the eventual exposé, see Rodney Campbell, *The Luciano Project* (New York: McGraw-Hill, 1977).

6. Marc Levinson, *The Box: How the Shipping Container Made the World Smaller and the World Economy Bigger*, 2nd ed. (Princeton, NJ: Princeton University Press, 2016), 102.

7. "Reputed Mobster Acquitted by Jury," *New York Times*, April 17, 1988; "Body of a Reputed Mobster Is Found in a Bag in a River," *New York Times*, May 27, 1988; "La Cosa Nostra—State of New Jersey Commission of Investigation 1989 Report—The Genovese/Gigante Family: DiGilio," http://mafianj.com/sci89/genovesegigantedigilio .shtml, accessed February 20, 2017; "Defendant in Mob Trial Is Found Dead in His Car," *New York Times*, July 6, 1998.

8. Vernon Jensen, *Strife on the Waterfront: The Port of New York since 1945* (Ithaca, NY: Cornell University Press, 1974), 36–53; Tom Robbins, "Joseph Ryan Quiet Curses," *New York Daily News*, June 3, 1999; Malcolm Johnson, *Crime on the Waterfront* (New York: McGraw-Hill, 1950), 155; Howard Kimeldorf, *Reds or Rackets? The Making of Radical and Conservative Unions on the Waterfront* (Berkeley: University of California Press, 1992), 154. Kimeldorf's book is an insightful exploration of how the ILA and ILWU could develop into such polar opposites.

9. Ellen Schrecker, *Many Are the Crimes: McCarthyism in America* (Princeton, NJ: Princeton University Press, 1998), 339–340, 379–380; David Caute, *The Great Fear: The Anti-Communist Purge under Truman and Eisenhower* (New York: Simon and Schuster, 1978), 354–359; Kimeldorf, *Reds or Rackets?*, 5–6. The Electrical, Radio and Machine Workers Union (UE) managed to survive, but only as a fragment of its former important self.

10. Harry Bridges, "On the Beam," *The Dispatcher* (the official newspaper of the ILWU), January 2, 1953.

11. Jensen, *Strife on the Waterfront*, 65–94; Robbins, "Joseph Ryan Quiet Curses."

12. Jensen, *Strife on the Waterfront*, 119.

13. Jensen, *Strife on the Waterfront*, 114.

14. Jensen, *Strife on the Waterfront*, 128–135.

15. "Union Urges End of Dock Agency," *New York Times*, November 22, 1955.

16. "Discharge of Ex-Convict Stirs New Wildcat Strike at Pier 57," *New York Times*, August 23, 1955.

17. "Docker Walkout Ties Up Port Here," *New York Times*, August 24, 1955.

18. "Port Shut Down by Pier Walkout," *New York Times*, September 8, 1955.

19. "Other Ports Hit in Pier Walkout; Court Is Defied," *New York Times*, September 9, 1955.

20. "Dock Union Calls a Coastal Tie-Up" and "Walkout Causing Loss in Millions," *New York Times*, September 13, 1955.

21. Orville Prescott, "Books of the Times," *New York Times*, September 9, 1955; James Kelley, "In a Harbor of Greed and Violence," review of *Waterfront* by Budd Schulberg, *New York Times*, September 11, 1955.

22. Jensen, *Strife on the Waterfront*, 117.

23. "It's Our Battle, Too," *The Dispatcher*, October 28, 1955.

24. Richard Sasuly, "Why They Stick to the ILA," *Monthly Review* 7, no. 9 (January 1956): 366–370.

25. "I.L.A. Calls Waterfront Unit Lax in Investigating Reds on the Piers," *New York Times*, November 1, 1955.

26. Levinson, *The Box*, 1–2.

27. Levinson, *The Box*, 7.

CHAPTER 6   THIRTEEN CONFESSIONS OF A COLD WARRIOR

1. For a wonderful vintage look at this plane as the ultimate in air luxury, check out Pan American's 1950 promo film, *The Double-Decked Strato Clipper*, on YouTube: https://www.youtube.com/watch?v=v92U2F9gbU0.

2. Marcelle Size Knaack, *Post-World War II Bombers* (Washington, DC: Office of Air Force History, 1988), 121.

3. I've simplified both our celestial navigation and that of your cell phone, which gets some calculations prepackaged in the signals it receives from the nearest cell tower via A-GPS (assisted GPS). Although I have a cerebral comprehension of how GPS works, to me it still looks like magic. Besides celestial, we sometimes could cross a sun or moon line of position with a line of position from LORAN, a radio broadcast system, but LORAN was unreliable in the far north. Over water we could use pressure pattern, which gave a PLOP (pressure line of position) based on our computation of wind direction and velocity derived from a series of measurements of the difference between pressure altitude and radar altitude.

4. Discussions of U.S. aerial espionage intrusions into the USSR generally justify the flights as necessary for national security. A cluster of three books, all glorifying the aerial spy campaigns and having access to U.S. military records, appeared between 2000 and 2002: Curtis Peoples, *Shadow Flights: America's Secret Air War against the Soviet Union* (Novato, CA: Presidio Press, 2000, 2002); William E. Burroughs, *By Any Means Necessary: America's Secret Air War in the Cold War* (New York: Farrar, Straus and Giroux, 2001); and Larry Tart and Robert Keefe, *The Price of Vigilance: Attacks on American Surveillance Flights* (New York: Ballantine Books, 2001).

5. As a by-product of the Vietnam War's POW/MIA obsession, a U.S.-Russian Joint Commission on POW/MIAs, established in 1992, produced a wealth of material on ten Soviet shootdowns. This is well presented in Tart and Keefe, *Price of Vigilance*, 15–35.

6. "Capital Explains; Reports Unarmed U-2 Vanished at Border after Difficulty," *New York Times*, May 6, 1960. For a fine early account of the story, see David Wise and Thomas B. Ross, *The U-2 Affair* (New York: Random House, 1962).

7. "Text of the U.S. Statement on Plane," *New York Times*, May 6, 1960.

8. Tart and Keefe, *Price of Vigilance*, 111.

9. Tart and Keefe, *Price of Vigilance*, 137.

10. Tart and Keefe, *Price of Vigilance*, 136; Burroughs, *By Any Means Necessary*, 209.

11. John M. Carroll, *Secrets of Electronic Espionage* (New York: E. P. Dutton, 1966), 134–135.

12. The United Press dispatched is reprinted as "This Is Article Cited by Soviet in Its Criticism of U.S. Flights," *New York Times*, April 19, 1958.

13. Allen W. Dulles, *The Craft of Intelligence* (New York: Harper and Row, 1963), 149; (New York: Signet, 1965), 139.

14. See chapter 17 of my *War Stars: The Superweapon and the American Imagination*, rev. and exp. ed. (Amherst: University of Massachusetts Press, 2008).

15. *Recent False Alerts from the Nation's Missile Attack Warning System: Report of Senator Gary Hart and Senator Barry Goldwater to the Committee on Armed Services, United States Senate* (Washington, DC: U.S. Government Printing Office, 1980).

16. Knaack, *Post-World War II Bombers*, 138.

17. Knaack, *Post-World War II Bombers*, 139, describes pop-up bombing.

18. "B-47 Crashes Investigated," *New York Times*, April 17, 1958. Datelined April 16.

19. "Defect Is Found in B-47 Bombers: Modification Set," *New York Times*, May 3, 1958.

20. An invaluable listing of the B-47 losses is maintained by the B-47 Stratojet Association and is available at http://b-47.com/wp-content/uploads/2014/03/Boeing-B-47-Losses-and-Ejections.pdf.

21. *The History of the Aircraft Structural Integrity Program* (Aerospace Structures Information and Analysis Center, June 1980), 1, 7, 13, 14. A pdf of the full report can be downloaded at http://oai.dtic.mil/oai/oai?verb=getRecord&metadataPrefix=html&identifier=ADA361289.

22. Events of March 10, July 27, and November 30, 1956; October 11, 1957; January 31, February 5, March 11, and November 27, 1958. Boeing B-47 Stratojet: All Losses and Ejections, b-47.com, http://b-47.com/wp-content/uploads/2014/03/Boeing-B-47-Losses-and-Ejections.pdf, accessed January 27, 2018.

23. Eric Schlosser's terrifying *Command and Control: Nuclear Weapons, the Damascus Accident, and the Illusion of Safety* (New York: Penguin Books, 2014) describes several blood-curdling accidents involving B-52s and thermonuclear weapons.

24. David Wise and Thomas B. Ross, *The Invisible Government* (New York: Bantam, 1965), 125.

25. President Eisenhower's speech to the nation, October 31, 1956, http://www.presidency.ucsb.edu/ws/?pid=10685, accessed October 10, 2016.

26. Richard J. Barnet, *Intervention and Revolution: America's Confrontation with Insurgent Movements around the World* (New York: New American Library, 1968), 147–151.

27. "Statement of the President following the Landing of United States Marines at Beirut, July 15, 1958," American Presidency Project, http://www.presidency.ucsb.edu /ws/?pid=11133, accessed January 27, 2018.

28. Jerry Lembcke, *The Spitting Image: Myth, Memory, and the Legacy of Vietnam* (New York: New York University Press, 1998), 20; Lembcke argues persuasively that the myth of the spat-upon vet was what won widespread emotional support for the war.

29. "President Bush Outlines Iraqi Threat," White House news release, October 7, 2002, https://georgewbush-whitehouse.archives.gov/news/releases/2002/10/20021007 -8.html, accessed January 27, 2018.

30. Wise and Ross, *U-2 Affair*, 337; Irene Gendzier, *Notes from the Minefield: United States Intervention in Lebanon and the Middle East, 1945–1958* (New York: Columbia University Press, 2006), passim. Deeply researched in previously classified documents, this updated edition shows the central role of U.S. oil interests; it is indispensable for any understanding of the history and chronology of events.

31. Gendzier, *Notes from the Minefield*, 310–311.

32. Gendzier, *Notes from the Minefield*, 13, 245–249, 253.

33. Hanna Batatu, *The Old Social Classes and the Revolutionary Movements of Iraq* (Princeton, NJ: Princeton University Press, 1978), chap. 41, which is the primary source for all other accounts of the 1958 revolution. Widely recognized as the indispensable history of modern Iraq, this 1,300-page masterpiece of scholarship and analysis is difficult to obtain. Therefore, references are to the Kindle edition (London: Saqi Books, 2012), Kindle locations 16904–16918, 16936–16942, 16987–16994.

34. Tim Weiner, *Legacy of Ashes: The History of the CIA* (New York: Anchor Books, 2008), 258, 262.

35. While writing this, I wondered if my memory might be wrong and the B-52 launch was really on the night of July 15. But my Air Force Form 5A, the official log of my flights, records my night flight from Dow to Loring on July 14 and my day flight from Loring to Dow on July 15.

CHAPTER 7   WAKE-UP TIME

1. For my earlier thoughts about my undergraduate and graduate education in the 1950s and the early 1960s, see "English as an Institution: The Role of Class" in *English Literature: Opening up the Canon*, ed. Leslie A. Fiedler and Houston Baker Jr. (Baltimore: Johns Hopkins University Press, 1981), 92–106.

2. "Housing Discrimination: A Closed Door in Palo Alto," http://www.paloaltohistory .org/discrimination-in-palo-alto.php, accessed March 15, 2017.

3. "Housing Discrimination."

4. Conversations with Gerda Isenberg, 1962; Loretta Green, "Lawrence Tract: A Bold Experiment in Integrated Living," *Peninsula Times-Tribune*, March 31, 1980; "California Native Plants Nurserywoman, Civil Rights Activist, and Humanitarian: Oral History Transcript," interviews with Gerda Isenberg conducted by Suzanne B. Riess in 1990, 1991, https://archive.org/stream/nativeplantsnurseooisenrich/native plantsnurseooisenrich_djvu.txt, accessed March 20, 2017.

5. Martin Luther King Jr., "Beyond Vietnam—A Time to Break Silence," sermon, April 4, 1967, Riverside Church, New York; *Vietnam and America: A Documented History,* rev. and enl. ed., ed. Marvin Gettleman, Jane Franklin, Marilyn B. Young, and H. Bruce Franklin (New York: Grove Press, 1995), 308–318, 312. This is the authorized, published version.

6. Jane Franklin, *Cuba and the U.S. Empire: A Chronological History* (New York: Monthly Review Press, 2016), 25–45.

7. "Track and Field's Greatest Dual Meet Is Turning 50," reprinted from the *Peninsula Times Tribune* of 1992, *Palo Alto Online,* https://www.paloaltoonline.com/news/2012/07/19/track-and-fields-greatest-dual-meet-is-turning-50, accessed April 21, 2017.

8. H. R. McMaster, *Dereliction of Duty* (New York: HarperPerennial, 1998), 28–29, documents Kennedy calling LeMay "mad." McMaster, appointed national security adviser in 2017 by Donald Trump, argues that Kennedy and Johnson should have paid more attention to the advice offered by the Joint Chiefs.

9. David G. Marr, "The Rise and Fall of 'Counterinsurgency': 1961–1964," in Gettleman et al., *Vietnam and America,* 207–208. Marr, the squadron's intelligence officer and the only Vietnamese speaker, later became a preeminent scholar of Vietnamese history.

10. "Mrs. Nhu Charges U.S. Incited Coup," *New York Times,* November 2, 1963; Cablegram from Ambassador Henry Cabot Lodge to Secretary of State Dean Rusk, August 29, 1963, *The Pentagon Papers,* Gravel ed., 4 vols. (Boston: Beacon Press, 1971), 2:738, reprinted in Gettleman et al., *Vietnam and America,* 227.

11. John R. Tunheim and Thomas E. Samoluk, "Assassination Questions Remain: With Much Revealed, CIA Still Holds Back," *Boston Globe,* November 21, 2013. Tunheim and Samoluk were the chairman and deputy director of the board. The withheld evidence concerns George Joannides, a high-ranking CIA operative who in 1963 was evidently using an anti-Castro group he supervised to help make Oswald appear as a prominent Castro supporter, very possibly to implicate Castro in the forthcoming assassination. In 1978, the CIA brought Joannides out of retirement to be the agency's link to the House of Representatives Select Committee on Assassinations, where he played a major role in misdirecting the committee's investigation.

12. The facts that I cite about the assassination are documented in these and other books.

13. *Vietnam and America,* 205–215, 424–470.

14. *Foreign Relations of the United States, 1961–1963,* vol. 4, *Vietnam, August–December 1963,* Document 331; Gettleman et al., *Vietnam and America,* 242.

15. See Gettleman et al., *Vietnam and America,* 242–244, for passages from the Pentagon Papers authorizing some of the secret OPLAN 34A operations.

16. "Sabotage Raids on North Confirmed by Saigon Aide," *New York Times,* July 23, 1964.

17. "Demands Puzzle U.S.," *New York Times,* July 24, 1964; "Raids on North at Issue," *New York Times,* July 24, 1964.

18. Documentation of the following account can be found in my "How We Started Our War against North Vietnam," *Sequoia Stanford Literary Magazine* 11, no. 2 (Spring 1966): 4–12, and Gettleman et al., *Vietnam and America,* 248–255. Details not docu-

mented in these sources are documented in Edwin Moise's *Tonkin Gulf and the Escalation of the Vietnam War* (Chapel Hill: University of North Carolina Press, 1996), which adds some details not found in the three earlier books on the Gulf of Tonkin events: Joseph C. Goulden, *Truth Is the First Casualty: The Gulf of Tonkin Affair—Illusion and Reality* (Chicago: Rand McNally, 1969); Anthony Austin, *The President's War: The Story of the Gulf of Tonkin Resolution and How the Nation Was Trapped in Vietnam* (Philadelphia: J. B. Lippincott, 1971); Eugene Windchy, *A Documentary of the Incidents in the Tonkin Gulf* (Garden City, NY: Doubleday, 1971).

19. Moise, *Tonkin Gulf*, 70–71.

20. Austin, *President's War*, 155.

21. Congressional Record—Senate, March 27, 1968, S3442.

22. Captain Herrick on board the *Maddox* sent a cable expressing his belief that the North Vietnamese believed that the destroyer was involved in these attacks. "The Gulf of Tonkin, the 1964 Incidents," *Hearing before the Committee of Foreign Relations United States Senate*, February 20, 1968 (Washington, DC: U.S. Government Printing Office, 1968), 53.

23. Interview with Leonard Laskow. Laskow's account was precisely verified by Stockdale's own published version, which describes the irrational conduct on both destroyers, the total absence of any enemy vessels, and the irresponsible and unjustifiable behavior of President Johnson. Jim Stockdale and Sybil Stockdale, *In Love and War*, rev. and updated ed. (Annapolis: Naval Institute Press, 1990), 17–25.

24. Moise, *Tonkin Gulf*, 106.

25. Interview with Patrick Park, in Goulden, *Truth Is the First Casualty*, 146–147.

26. Stockdale and Stockdale, *In Love and War*, 20.

27. Robert J. Hanyok, "Skunks, Bogies, Silent Hounds, and the Flying Fish: The Gulf of Tonkin Mystery, 2–4 August 1954," *Cryptologic Quarterly* (Spring 2001): 1–55, http://nsarchive.gwu.edu/NSAEBB/NSAEBB132/relea00012.pdf, accessed May 8, 2017.

28. Lyndon B. Johnson, "This Painful Road" (the text of his April 7 address), *Johns Hopkins Magazine*, April 1965, 4.

29. Henry Cabot Lodge, excerpts from his April 9 speech, *Johns Hopkins Magazine*, April 1965, 15.

CHAPTER 8   BURNING ILLUSIONS

1. "Peace Speakers Launch Vietnam Protest," *Stanford Daily*, October 14, 1965, http://www.a3mreunion.org/archive/photos/1965-1966_photos/stanford_committee/scpv/index.html, accessed January 29, 2018.

2. Eric Prokosch, *The Technology of Killing: A Military and Political History of Antipersonnel Weapons* (Atlantic Highlands, NJ: Zed Books, 1995), 127.

3. "Anti-War Air Drop in Oakland," *San Francisco Chronicle*, January 11, 1966.

4. Robert M. Neer, *Napalm: An American Biography* (Cambridge, MA: Harvard University Press, 2013), 99–100.

5. Bruce Cumings, *The Origins of the Korean War*, vol. 2, *The Roaring of the Cataract, 1947–1950* (Princeton, NJ: Princeton University Press, 1990), 705–707, 753–755;

Cullum A. MacDonald, *Korea: The War before Vietnam* (New York: Free Press, 1986), 234–236.

6. "FRANKLIN, Howard Bruce, #E446 863," September 14, 1966. Part of several thousand pages received from the CIA and FBI in response to a Freedom of Information Act (FOIA) request submitted in 1976 after the Colorado Board of Regents vetoed my appointment to the faculty of the University of Colorado, Boulder.

CHAPTER 9   FRENCH CONNECTIONS

1. William J. Duiker, *Ho Chi Minh* (New York: Hyperion, 2000), 72–73; David Halberstam, *Ho* (New York: Knopf, 1987), 33–34.

2. Edwin A. Martini, "Forest Fire as a Military Weapon: The American War on Nature in Vietnam," paper presented at the annual meeting of the American Studies Association, Washington, DC, November 7, 2009 (personal copy). See also Joseph Trevithick, "Firestorm: Forest Fires as a Weapon in Vietnam," *Armchair General*, June 13, 2012, http://www.armchairgeneral.com/firestorm-forest-fires-as-a-weapon-in-vietnam.htm, accessed May 31, 2015.

3. Nixon's speech, as printed in the *New York Times,* April 17, 1954, is available in *Vietnam and America: A Documented History*, ed. Marvin Gettleman, Jane Franklin, Marilyn Young, and H. Bruce Franklin (New York: Grove Press, 1995), 53.

4. Cablegram from Lodge to Rusk, August 29, 1963, *The Pentagon Papers as Published in the New York Times* (New York: Quadrangle Books, 1971), 203, reprinted in Gettleman et al., *Vietnam and America*, 227.

5. George Washington Peck, *American Whig Review*, November 1852, quoted in my "The Worker and Criminal and Artist: Herman Melville," in *Prison Literature in America: The Victim as Criminal and Artist*, exp. ed. (New York: Oxford University Press, 1989), 36–37.

6. A few days before writing this paragraph, I was fishing for salmon on a party boat several miles out in the Pacific west of San Francisco. I asked the guy fishing next to me the meaning of "FIREARTSCOLLECTIVE.COM," emblazoned on his T-shirt. It turned out that he was a union iron worker whose hobby was creating large metal artworks for the annual Burning Man festival. His latest creation was a long reptile that slithered and seemed to breathe as it burned.

7. Herman Melville, *Typee* (New York: Penguin Books, 1996), chap. 17, p. 125 in this edition.

8. Aimé Césaire, *Discourse on Colonialism* (New York: Monthly Review Press, 1972), 14–15.

9. Robert E. Miller Jr., University Relations Officer, Stanford University, 1964, quoted in the *Stanford Daily,* December 2, 1971.

10. David Marr, "The Rise and Fall of 'Counterinsurgency,'" in Gettleman et al., *Vietnam and America*, 209. President Johnson spoke frequently about winning hearts and minds, most famously in 1965: "The ultimate victory will depend upon the hearts and the minds of the people who actually live out there." "Lyndon B. Johnson: Remarks at a Dinner Meeting of the Texas Electric Cooperatives, Inc.," May 4, 1965, American

Presidency Project, http://www.presidency.ucsb.edu/ws/index.php?pid=26942, accessed June 2, 2017.

11. "Activist Scribe Struck from the Left: Max Watts, 1928–2010," *Sidney Morning Herald*, December 29, 2010, http://www.smh.com.au/comment/obituaries/activist-scribe -struck-from-the-left-20101228-1997z.html, accessed June 15, 2017.

12. See Terry Whitmore, *Memphis-Nam-Sweden: The Story of a Black Deserter* (Jackson: University Press of Mississippi, 1997; originally published by Doubleday in 1971), the fascinating memoir of a wounded soldier who deserted in Japan, traveled in a Russian fishing boat to the Soviet Union, and eventually made his way to Sweden, where he was still living in the late 1990s; he died in Memphis in 2007. Also Richard DeCamp, "The GI Movement in Asia," *Bulletin of Concerned Asian Scholars* 4 (Winter 1972): 110; Richard Moser, *The New Winter Soldiers: GI and Veteran Dissent during the Vietnam Era* (New Brunswick, NJ: Rutgers University Press, 1996), 77. Many more deserters, of course, simply walked or drove across the border to Canada; see "The Flow of GI Deserters to Canada," *San Francisco Chronicle*, October 10, 1969.

13. "De nombreux jeunes Américains fuient la guerre du Vietnam," *Le Monde*, May 5, 1967; "Louis Armsfield, le jeune Noir américain interpellé a Paris," *Le Monde*, May 11, 1967; "NATO Accord Not Applicable to U.S. Deserter," *International Herald Tribune*, May 12, 1967; "L'affaire Armsfield: Le Jeune Déserteur Américain a Obtenu un Permis de Séjour Temporaire en France," *L'Humanité*, May 21, 1967.

14. Max Watts, e-mail, June 2, 2008. Tomi, a.k.a. Max, didn't tell us at the time whose château it was.

15. John Hess, "GI Deserter Tells Why He Opposes the War: Recounts 'Resistance inside Army' in U.S., Vietnam, Western Europe," *International Herald-Tribune*, December 11, 1967.

16. "How Anti-Vietnam Deserters Go Underground," *The Times* (London), August 17, 1967; "1,000 GIs in Europe Said Planning Protest Desertion," *International Herald-Tribune*, August 18, 1967; "A Travers L'Europe, Un Mystérieux Réseau, Celui des Déserteurs Américains," *Paris Match*, September 2, 1967, 5–6.

17. "Army Deserters Nobody Looks For," *San Francisco Chronicle*, January 17, 1972.

18. "Issue of Granting Amnesty Echoes Division over War," *New York Times*, August 20, 1974.

19. "Déserteurs américains en France," *L'événement* (Paris), March 1967, 13–14; "De nombreux jeunes Américains fuient la guerre du Vietnam," *Le Monde*, May 5, 1967; "Leaflets Urge GIs to Desert," *International Herald-Tribune*, May 29, 1967; "The Resister/Deserter Underground," *The Nation*, November 1967, 487–491; Hess, "GI Deserter"; "American Deserters Explain Their Motives," *The Times* (London), February 12, 1968; "U.S. Deserters Plan to Step Up Their Campaign in Europe," *International Herald Tribune*, February 12, 1968; "The New Men without a Country: Why GIs Defect—Report on a Strange Stockholm Colony," *San Francisco Sunday Examiner & Chronicle*, March 31, 1968; "Tomi Schwaetzer" (Max Watts), 61-page mimeographed pamphlet on history of deserter underground, Heidelberg, [ca. 1969]; Max Watts, *US-Army—Europe: Von der Desertion zum Widerstand in der Kaserne oder wie die U-Bahn zur RITA fuhr* (West Berlin: Harald Kater Verlag, 1989); David Cortright and Max

Watts, *Left Face* (Westport, CT: Greenwood Press, 1991); David Cortright, *Soldiers in Revolt: GI Resistance during the Vietnam War* (Chicago: Haymarket Books, 2005).

20. Watts, *U.S.-Army—Europe*, 54–60; e-mails from Watts, April 7, 1999, and May 1, 2008.

21. "1000 GIs in Britain Stage Vietnam Protest," *San Francisco Chronicle*, June 1, 1971.

CHAPTER 10   COMING HOME

1. Commander George L. Jackson, "Constraints of the Negro Civil Rights Movement on American Military Effectiveness," *Naval War College Review*, January 1970, 100–107; Colonel Robert D. Heinl Jr., "The Collapse of the Armed Forces," *Armed Forces Journal*, June 7, 1971, 30–37. Both essays are reprinted in Marvin Gettleman, Jane Franklin, Marilyn Young, and H. Bruce Franklin, eds., *Vietnam and America: A Documented History*, rev. and enl. ed. (New York: Grove Press, 1995).

2. Gettleman et al., *Vietnam and America*, 310–318.

3. Charles E. Cobb Jr., *This Nonviolent Stuff'll Get You Killed: How Guns Made the Civil Rights Movement Possible* (Durham, NC: Duke University Press, 2016), 7. Nicholas Johnson, *Negroes and the Gun: The Black Tradition of Arms* (Amherst, NY: Prometheus Books, 2014), 262–268, gives a history of King's relation to armed self-defense.

4. Jacob Sullum, "When the NRA Opposed Open Carry," Reason.com, June 17, 2014, https://reason.com/blog/2014/06/17/when-the-nra-opposed-open-carry, accessed August 8, 2017.

5. See Robert Williams's *Negroes with Guns* (New York: Marzani & Munsell, 1962), Cobb, *This Nonviolent Stuff'll Get You Killed*, and Johnson, *Negroes and the Gun*, for valuable histories.

6. Robert L Allen, "The Port Chicago Disaster and Its Aftermath," *Black Scholar* 13, nos. 2–3 (Spring 1982): 2–29; Erika Doss, "Commemorating the Port Chicago Naval Magazine Disaster of 1944: Remembering the Racial Injustices of the 'Good War' in Contemporary America," *American Studies Journal*, no. 59 (2015), http://www.asjournal.org/59-2015/commemorating-port-chicago-naval-magazine-disaster-1944, accessed August 10, 2017.

7. "Antiwar Demonstrations Held Outside Draft Boards across U.S.: 119 Persons Arrested on Coast," *New York Times*, October 17, 1967.

8. "Cops 'Armed Mercenaries,' Says Ex-Cop," *The Movement* 3, no. 11 (November 1967): 1, https://libraries.ucsd.edu/farmworkermovement/ufwarchives/sncc/27-November%201967.pdf. Most of the sixteen pages of this issue of *The Movement* (the monthly newspaper of SNCC and SDS) were devoted to accurate narratives and judicious analyses of Stop the Draft Week in Oakland.

9. Two years later, when I stepped without a shield in front of three San Mateo sheriffs about to arrest a young woman on probation, one did swing his baton at my balls. I barely blocked it, was beaten in the middle of the street with riot sticks by a gang of sheriffs, and ended up being charged with felonious assault on a police officer.

10. Tom Wells, *The War Within: America's Battle over Vietnam* (New York: Henry Holt, 1994), 202. Nancy Zaroulis and Gerald Sullivan, *Who Spoke Up? American Protest against the War in Vietnam, 1963–1975* (Garden City, NY: Doubleday, 1984), 139, and

other sources also document the especially brutal attacks on women. Wells, *The War Within*, 195–205, is a well-documented account of the demonstration. See also David Caute, *The Year of the Barricades: A Journey through 1968* (New York: Perennial Library, 1988), 3–7, and Robert G. Sherrill, "Bastille Day on the Potomac," *The Nation*, November 6, 1967, 454–455. Some striking footage appears in the film *Loin du Vietnam* [Far from Vietnam].

11. Wells, *The War Within*, 204–205.

12. "Westmoreland Says Ranks of Vietcong Thin Steadily," *New York Times*, November 22, 1967.

13. James Reston, "Washington: Why Westmoreland and Bunker Are Optimistic," *New York Times*, November 22, 1967.

14. Hanson W. Baldwin, "Vietnam Report: Foe Seeks to Sway U.S. Public," *New York Times*, December 26, 1967; Hanson W. Baldwin, "Vietnam Report: The Foe Is Hurt," *New York Times*, December 27, 1967; Hanson W. Baldwin, "Report on Vietnam: Sanctuaries Viewed as a Major War Factor," *New York Times*, December 28, 1967.

15. Burchett narrates his six-month epic journey through the liberated areas of South Vietnam in *Vietnam: Inside Story of the Guerilla War* (New York: International Publishers, 1965).

CHAPTER 11   THE WAR COMES HOME

1. "Americans Die in Vietcong Attack before Truce Ends," *New York Times*, January 2, 1968. Jane has several filing cabinets full of her clippings from the war.

2. *The Pentagon Papers: The Defense Department History of United States Decisionmaking in Vietnam*, Gravel ed., 4 vols. (Boston: Beacon Press, 1972), 4:232, 234–235, 539, 548, 604; David Hunt, "Remembering the Tet Offensive," in *Vietnam and America: A Documented History*, rev. and enl. ed., ed. Marvin Gettleman, Jane Franklin, Marilyn Young, and H. Bruce Franklin (New York: Grove Press, 1995), 366.

3. Horace Coleman, "The Adrenaline Junkie and 'The Daily Emergency,'" in *The Vietnam War in American Stories, Songs, and Poems*, ed. H. Bruce Franklin (Boston: Bedford Books, 1996), 246.

4. "Saigon under Fire," CBS News Special Report, January 31, 1968.

5. Robert Pisor, *The End of the Line: The Siege of Khe Sanh* (New York: Ballantine, 1983), is a perceptive and readable account.

6. "Survivors Hunt Dead of Ben Tre, Turned to Rubble in Allied Raids," *New York Times*, February 8, 1968, based on AP story, February 7, 1968.

7. "Allied Gains Seen by Westmoreland; Position in War Best Ever, General Says on Ending Talks at White House," *New York Times*, April 8, 1968. Westmoreland gave his analysis of the Tet Offensive, riddled with bogus statistics and glaring contradictions, in his *Report on the War in Vietnam (as of 30 June 1968), Section 2: Report on Operations in South Vietnam, January 1964–June 1968* (Washington, DC: U.S. Government Printing Office, 1968); an annotated version is available in Gettleman et al., *Vietnam and America*, 342–359.

8. None of the foregoing is meant to imply that the NLF did not suffer very heavy casualties. For a helpful overview, see Marilyn Young, *The Vietnam Wars: 1945–1990*

(New York: Harper Collins, 1991), 216–225. For a detailed military and political history, see Gabriel Kolko, *Anatomy of a War: Vietnam, the United States, and the Modern Historical Experience* (New York: Pantheon, 1985), 303–337. An important corrective to most U.S. scholarship comes from Ngo Vinh Long's on-the-scene interviews with NLF participants, who reported that their severe casualties came in the May and August offensives: "The Tet Offensive and Its Aftermath," *Indochina Newsletter* 49 (January–February 1988), 1–5; 50 (March–April 1988), 2–10; 60 (November–December 1989), 1–10. To compare contradictory arguments and evidence on the Tet Offensive, see Don Oberdorfer, *Tet!* (New York: Da Capo, 1984); *Vietnam and America*, 339–400; and *The Tet Offensive*, ed. Marc Jason Gilbert and William Head (Westport, CT: Praeger, 1996), which includes a version of Ngo Vinh Long's analysis.

9. *Pentagon Papers*, 4:232. Some relevant sections of the *Pentagon Papers* are reprinted in Gettleman et al., *Vietnam and America*, 378–397.

10. *Pentagon Papers*, 4:539.

11. *Pentagon Papers*, 4:238.

12. *Pentagon Papers*, 4:547. This is from General Earle Wheeler, Chairman of the Joint Chiefs of Staff and one of the most optimistic voices among the decision makers.

13. *Pentagon Papers*, 4:604.

14. *Pentagon Papers*, 4:564, 583.

15. See, for example, the remarkably prescient "Gold, Dollars, and Empire," *Monthly Review* 19 (February 1968): 1–9.

16. David Hunt, "Remembering the Tet Offensive," *Radical America* 12 (February 1978): 95–96, reprinted in Gettleman et al., *Vietnam and America*, 371–372.

17. Mary Lou Greenberg, "Does Double Standard Exist in the Movement?," *Midpeninsula Observer*, February 19–March 4, 1968, 1, 9. See also Bernardine Dohrn, "The Liberation of Vietnamese Women," *LNS*, November 1, 1968.

18. *Midpeninsula Observer*, December 9, 1968.

19. *New Left Notes*, 3 (December 4, 1968).

20. Harvey Wasserman, "1968: Year of the Heroic Guerilla MEDEA," *LNS*, July 10, 1968, 2–3. The slogan appears in issues from July 17 on.

21. The full texts of the Geneva Accords and the Final Declarations of all the conferees, the Johnson speech, and the 1973 Paris Peace Accords are available in Gettleman et al., *Vietnam and America*, 66–81, 401–409, 472–486.

22. "Racial Violence Erupts in Miami," *New York Times*, August 7, 1968; "3 Negroes Killed in New Miami Riot; Policemen Battle Snipers—Troops Hold 100 Blocks amid Looting and Fires," *New York Times*, August 9, 1968.

23. *Nixon Speaks Out: Major Speeches and Statements by Richard Nixon in the Presidential Campaign of 1968* (New York: Nixon-Agnew Campaign Committee, 1968), 235.

24. Thorne Dreyer, "Know Your Enemy," *LNS*, August 30, 1968; *Great Speckled Bird*, August 30–September 12, 1968; Tom Cleaver, "Texas GIs Join Antiwar Rally," *Guardian*, October 26, 1968; David Cortright, *Soldiers in Revolt: GI Resistance during the Vietnam War* (Chicago: Haymarket Books, 2005), 56–57.

25. *LNS*, February 5, 14, 15, 1968.

26. *Vietnam GI*'s publication history is discussed in an interview with the paper's editors, "The New Left and the Army: Let's Bridge the Gap!," *The Movement* 4 (October

1968): 10–11. Its Vietnam circulation figures appeared in ads in the movement press; see, for example, the back page of *New Left Notes*, May 13, 1968.

27. Cleaver, "Texas GIs Join Antiwar Rally."

28. Mary Hamilton, "U.S. Military Is Target for GI Week," *Guardian*, October 19, 1968; "GIs Hold Teach-In," *The Ally* (newspaper produced by GIs), September 1968.

29. Carrie Iverson, "GIs' 'Bout Face," *Peninsula Observer*, October 7–13, 1968, 7; *LNS*, October 21, 1968; Nancy Zaroulis and Gerard Sullivan, *Who Spoke Up? American Protest against the War in Vietnam, 1963–1975* (Garden City, NY: Doubleday, 1984), 360.

30. *The Veteran* (journal of Vietnam Veterans against the War) 7, no. 2 (April 1977): 16. The footage of the men throwing away their medals frames the powerful eighteen-minute documentary *Only the Beginning*, produced by the revolutionary media collective Newsreel in 1971 and now available on CD from its successor, Third World Newsreel.

31. Colonel Robert D. Heinl Jr., "The Collapse of the Armed Forces," *Armed Forces Journal*, June 1971, 30–37, reprinted in Gettleman et al., *Vietnam and America*, 326–335. See also Commander George L. Jackson, "Constraints of the Negro Civil Rights Movement on American Military Effectiveness," *Naval War College Review*, January 1970, 100–107; reprinted in Gettleman et al., *Vietnam and America*, 321–326. For fuller treatments of the insurrection in the armed forces and its effect on the military history of the war, see Larry G. Waterhouse and Mariann G. Wizard, *Turning the Guns Around: Notes on the GI Movement* (New York: Delta Books, 1961); Richard Boyle, *Flower of the Dragon: The Breakdown of the U.S. Army in Vietnam* (San Francisco: Ramparts Press, 1972); Cortright, *Soldiers in Revolt*; Richard R. Moser, *The New Winter Soldiers: GI and Veteran Dissent during the Vietnam Era* (New Brunswick, NJ: Rutgers University Press, 1996); and H. Bruce Franklin, "The Antiwar Movement We Are Supposed to Forget," in *Vietnam and Other American Fantasies* (Amherst: University of Massachusetts Press, 2000).

32. See Cortright, *Soldiers in Revolt*, 110–113, for an excellent history of this movement and its ties to the civilian antiwar movement.

33. "Midway's Bay Spill Called 'Deliberate,'" *San Francisco Chronicle*, May 24, 1972.

34. "Ship Engine Damaged," *Palo Alto Times*, July 15, 1972; "Suspect in Navy Sabotage," *San Francisco Chronicle*, August 6, 1972; "Sailor Accused of Carrier Sabotage," *San Francisco Chronicle*, November 7, 1972; "Sailor Charged with Sabotage Asks Out on Bail," *Palo Alto Times*, November 11, 1972; "Carrier Ranger Hit by Fire," *Palo Alto Times*, December 13, 1972; "Fire Aboard the Ranger," *San Francisco Chronicle*, December 14, 1972; "Incidents on the Ranger: Naval Investigative Service List," unsigned pamphlet [San Francisco, November 1972]; "Sabotage Immobilizes USS Ranger," pamphlet issued by Eric Seitz [attorney for sailor accused of deliberately damaging the engine], [San Francisco], November 6, 1972, showing that incidents of sabotage continued after his client was jailed.

35. "Suspect in Carrier Fire," *San Francisco Chronicle*, July 18, 1972; "Sailor Accused of Carrier Sabotage," *San Francisco Chronicle*, November 7, 1972.

36. "Stop Our Ship," leaflet, San Francisco, October 1972 (in author's possession); Moser, *The New Winter Soldiers*, 86–87.

37. Cortright, *Soldiers in Revolt*, 114–115.

38. "Sailor Accused of Carrier Sabotage," *San Francisco Chronicle*, November 7, 1972; "10 Marines Charged in Racial Fight," *San Francisco Chronicle*, January 10, 1973; Cortright, *Soldiers in Revolt*, 120–121; "Kitty Hawk Arrives Here for Refitting," *San Francisco Chronicle*, January 10, 1973.

39. Quoted by Cortright, *Soldiers in Revolt*, 125.

40. Cortright, *Soldiers in Revolt*, 112.

41. "Sailors' Shipside 'Strike,'" *San Francisco Chronicle*, November 10, 1972; "Strife-Torn Constellation Resumes Duties," *San Francisco Chronicle*, January 6, 1973; Cortright, *Soldiers in Revolt*, 121–122, 124. Henry P. Leifermann's article in the *New York Times Magazine* (February 18, 1973), 17–32, never mentions the antiwar movement on board and presents this "first mass mutiny in the history of the U.S. Navy" as a purely racial event.

42. "Strife-Torn Constellation Resumes Duties," *San Francisco Chronicle*, January 6, 1973.

43. The text of the Paris Accords, along with the text of Nixon's secret promise of reparations, can be found in Gettleman et al., *Vietnam and America*, 472–478; compare to the text of the Ten-Point Program on 430–433. As a key Kissinger aide put it, "We bombed the North Vietnamese into accepting our concessions." See Marilyn Young, *The Vietnam Wars: 1945–1990* (New York: HarperCollins, 1991), 269–279.

44. Gareth Porter, *A Peace Denied: The United States, Vietnam, and the Paris Agreement* (Bloomington: Indiana University Press, 1975), 161–162; Gabriel Kolko, *Anatomy of a War* (New York: Pantheon Books, 1985), 440; James William Gibson, *The Perfect War: Technowar in Vietnam* (Boston: Atlantic Monthly Press, 1986), 416–417; Young, *The Vietnam Wars*, 278–279; Jeffrey Kimball, *Nixon's Vietnam War* (Lawrence: University Press of Kansas, 1998), 365.

45. "Franklin Lie Admitted: Garry Opens Attack on Beaty Testimony," *Palo Alto Times*, May 10, 1973; "Beaty Admits Lying to Shield 3," *San Jose Mercury*, May 10, 1973; "Convict in Escape-Slaying Admits Lying; Tried to 'Frame' Franklin," *Palo Alto Times*, February 14, 1974. On November 11, I went from San Diego to Los Angeles; on the 13th I went from Los Angeles to Ontario, California. Evidence of the FBI's attempt to "neutralize" me, to use their term, is in the FOIA files I donated to Berkeley's Bancroft Library.

46. Cortright, *Soldiers in Revolt*, 135.

47. Seymour M. Hersh, *The Price of Power: Kissinger in the Nixon White House* (New York: Summit Books, 1983), 628–629.

48. Ralph McGehee, *Deadly Deceits: My Twenty-Five Years in the C.I.A.* (New York: Sheridan Square Publications, 1983). In 1991, McGehee began to publish CIABASE, a very useful electronic database on the CIA that is available at http://www/webcom/com/~pinknoiz/covert/ciabase.html.

49. Philip Agee, *Inside the Company: CIA Diary* (Harmondsworth, Middlesex, England: Penguin Books, 1975), 563.

50. Ronald Reagan, speech to the Veterans of Foreign Wars Convention, Chicago, August 18, 1980, http://www.presidency.ucsb.edu/ws/?pid=85202, accessed December 1, 2017.

51. The first avatar of the course was the subject of my article "Teaching the Vietnam War in the 1980s," *Chronicle of Higher Education*, November 4, 1981. The lack of texts for courses about the war led Marvin Gettleman, Jane Franklin, Marilyn Young, and me to create *Vietnam and America: A Documented History* (1985, rev. ed. 1995), which is frequently cited in this book.

52. George Bush, "Remarks to the American Legislative Exchange Council," March 1, 1991, http://www.presidency.ucsb.edu/ws/?pid=19351, accessed January 30, 2018.

53. George W. Bush, "Text of Bush Speech," May 1, 2003, https://www.cbsnews.com/news/text-of-bush-speech-01-05-2003, accessed December 1, 2017.

INDEX

ABOUT THE AUTHOR

Former Air Force navigator and intelligence officer H. BRUCE FRANKLIN is a progressive activist and the author or editor of nineteen books and hundreds of articles that have won him the highest awards for lifetime achievement from the American Studies Association and several other major academic organizations. He is the John Cotton Dana Professor of English and American Studies, emeritus, of Rutgers University, Newark. See his home page: hbrucefranklin.com.